D0926704

UNIVERSITY OF WINNIPEG
LIBRARY
515 Portage Avenue
Winnipeg, Manitoba R3B 2E9

DISCARDED

AMERICAN HIEROGLYPHICS

PS
217
· H54 -
I 7
1980

AMERICAN HIEROGLYPHICS

The Symbol of the Egyptian Hieroglyphics
in the American Renaissance

JOHN T. IRWIN

New Haven and London
Yale University Press

Copyright © 1980 by Yale University.
All rights reserved. This book may not be
reproduced, in whole or in part, in any form
(beyond that copying permitted by Sections 107
and 108 of the U.S. Copyright Law and except by
reviewers for the public press), without written
permission from the publishers.

Designed by Sally Harris
and set in VIP Baskerville type.
Printed in the United States of America by
Vail-Ballou Press, Binghamton, N.Y.

Library of Congress Cataloging in Publication Data

Irwin, John T
  American hieroglyphics.

  Includes index.
    1. American literature—19th century—History and
criticism. 2. Hieroglyphics in literature.
3. Egypt in literature. 4. American literature—
Egyptian influences. 5. Egyptian language—Writing,
Hieroglyphic. I. Title.
PS217.H54I7   810'.9'15   80-130
ISBN 0-300-02471-1

10   9   8   7   6   5   4   3   2   1

For Laura,
the face in the misty light,

and for
the outrageous Harold

Regard the capture here, O Janus-faced,
As double as the hands that twist this glass.
Such eyes at search or rest you cannot see;
Reciting pain or glee, how can you bear!

Twin shadowed halves: the breaking second holds
In each the skin alone, and so it is
I crust a plate of vibrant mercury
Borne cleft to you, and brother in the half. . . .

Look steadily—how the wind feasts and spins
The brain's disk shivered against lust. Then watch
While darkness, like an ape's face, falls away,
And gradually white buildings answer day.

Let the same nameless gulf beleaguer us—
Alike suspend us from atrocious sums
Built floor by floor on shafts of steel that grant
The plummet heart, like Absalom, no stream.

Hart Crane, "Recitative"

"But you are trying to reconcile the book and the author. A book is
the writer's secret life, the dark twin of a man: you can't reconcile
them. And with you, when the inevitable clash comes, the author's
actual self is the one that goes down, for you are of those for whom
fact and fallacy gain verisimilitude by being in cold print."

Julius Kauffman in Faulkner's Mosquitoes

CONTENTS

PREFACE

American Hieroglyphics is the third part of a triangular work whose first two parts are John Bricuth's *The Heisenberg Variations* (1976) and my *Doubling and Incest / Repetition and Revenge* (1975). In its own way, each of these books deals with the notion of the writer's corpus as an inscribed shadow self, a hieroglyphic double. The present book begins by examining the impact of the decipherment of the Egyptian hieroglyphics on nineteenth-century American literature, and then, ranging back and forth over literary history, practical criticism of individual works, and speculative criticism, it relates the image of the hieroglyphics to the larger reciprocal questions of the origin and limits of symbolization and the symbolization of origins and ends. The only part of the book that may pose some difficulty for the reader is the series of speculative digressions in the section on Poe. In the process of providing background material for Poe's work, these digressions sometimes elaborate their specialized lines of inquiry at such length that Poe seems to fade into the background and vanish—an enactment of the kind of figure/ground reversal that is one of the themes of the Poe section. Yet this reversal inevitably reverses itself in turn, and the figure of Poe reemerges against a more complex background with, one hopes, even greater definition.

I began work on *American Hieroglyphics* in 1971, and during the early stages of my research I was guided by the generous advice of four of my colleagues at Johns Hopkins—Don Cameron Allen, Earl Wasserman, Larry Holland, and Hans Goedicke. During the lengthy period of the book's composition, its scope and methodology altered substantially, due in part to the suggestions of friends with whom I discussed the manuscript. I want to thank Hillis Miller, Ron Paulson, Harold Bloom, Geoffrey Hartman, Dick Brodhead, Stanley Cavell, Bill Irwin, Hugh Kenner, Guy Davenport, Del Hillers, George Krotkoff, and Bill McClain for their help. I also want to express my deep appreciation to two friends—Harry and Claudia Sieber—whose kindness and encouragement sustained me during the years that I worked on the book. Kathleen Tavel of the University of Georgia Library and Martha Hubbard of the Milton S. Eisenhower Library helped me in my research; and Mary Camerer and

Dorothy DeWitt assisted me in the final preparation of the manuscript. Laura Irwin helped revise and proofread the manuscript and shook her head when the sentences got too long. Finally, I want to thank the editors of *American Quarterly* and *New Literary History* for permission to reprint material that had previously appeared in their magazines.

Baltimore, August 1979

PART ONE
Emerson, Thoreau, and Whitman

No, I think that if you examine our rewriting of the equation once again you will be struck as I was by how much it reminds me of Emerson's remark that man's "victorious thought comes up with and reduces all things, until the world becomes at last only a realized will,—the double of the man." That is a remark of Emerson's that has never been properly appreciated because Emerson never said it, and in fact isn't that the way of the world? for my equation is at once a reduction and a mirroring, it simultaneously occupies a border point and is self-generative.

John Bricuth, "A New Model of the Universe,"
from *The Heisenberg Variations*

The name Champollion appears in some of the most important literary works of the American Renaissance—Emerson's "History," Poe's *Eureka*, Thoreau's *Walden*, and Melville's *Mardi* and *Moby-Dick*, to name a few. Yet for most modern readers, it is a name that requires an identifying footnote. Jean-François Champollion was the Frenchman who, in the 1820s, deciphered Egyptian hieroglyphic writing with the aid of the bilingual text of the Rosetta stone—a discovery that marked the beginning of modern Egyptology. Yet surely that piece of information provokes another question. Why would Champollion be mentioned in works as seemingly remote from his achievements as Thoreau's account of a stay at Walden Pond or Melville's story of the hunt for a white whale? That Europe and America, during the period 1800–50, were swept by a wave of interest in the antiquities of Egypt is nowadays one of the less well remembered facets of nineteenth-century history.[1] When Napoleon invaded Egypt in 1798, he was accompanied by a group of 150 scientists and artists (mostly from the Académie des Inscriptions) whose task was the investigation of the conquered territory. With the surrender of the French army in Egypt (1801), the British claimed as spoils of war all the antiquities gathered by the French scientists. Among these antiquities was the Rosetta stone, which arrived in England in February 1802.

By 1806 a soldier of fortune named Mohammed Ali had forced the Turks to recognize him as pasha of Egypt, and during his long reign he encouraged the competition between the French and English *agents d'art* operating in his country, a competition that resulted in the flooding of Europe and then America with every shape and form of Egyptian artifact. In a tone at once Olympian and Yankee, Edward Everett remarked in *The North American Review* (1823), "Since the days of the Romans, who plundered Egypt of obelisks and transported whole colonnades of marble pillars from Italy to Constantinople, this magnificent kind of robbery never flourished more than at the present moment."[2]

At the time Everett wrote, the Egyptian revival in America was just beginning. In 1823 an Egyptian sarcophagus was presented to the city of Boston by a Smyrna merchant named van Lennep.[3] In 1826 two mummies were displayed at Peale's Museum and Gallery of Fine Arts in New York. These curios later came into the possession of the showman P. T.

Barnum.[4] In 1832 Colonel Mendes Cohen of Baltimore returned from Egypt with 680 antiquities to establish the first private collection of ancient Egyptian artifacts in America.[5] This collection, donated to the Johns Hopkins University in 1884, is still in existence. In the summer of 1835 an Englishman named Chandler who was touring the United States with an exhibit of mummies and their burial paraphernalia stopped in Kirtland, Ohio—at that time the headquarters of Joseph Smith and the Latter-Day Saints. The Mormons bought from Chandler a group of artifacts that included a papyrus (containing a late version of the Book of the Dead) and a hypocephalus (a disk placed under the head of a mummy). The writing on these two objects was "translated" by Joseph Smith and was published in a small book entitled *The Pearl of Great Price*. The papyrus and the inscribed disk represented, according to the Prophet, a record begun by Abraham and finished by Joseph in Egypt.[6]

At the same time that Egyptian antiquities were arriving in America, the Egyptian style in architecture was changing the appearance of American towns. The style left its mark on structures as various as the Washington Monument (1845–85), the entrance to the Grove Street Cemetery in New Haven, and the New York Halls of Justice (1836–38)[7]—the famous "Tombs" where Melville's Bartleby dies and of which the narrator remarks, "The Egyptian character of the masonry weighed upon me with its gloom."[8] As one writer has noted, the most important moderating influence on the Greek revival in American architecture was the Egyptian revival.

In 1842 George Gliddon, who had been American vice-consul in Cairo, came to Boston to give a series of lectures on Egyptian antiquities. The talks, illustrated with artifacts loaned by Colonel Mendes Cohen, were so successful that Gliddon toured the country for the next two years. His audiences often ran as high as 2,000 persons at a single performance, and the small book that he published in 1843 sold 24,000 copies.[9]

Besides the popular interest in Egyptian antiquities, there was also an academic interest, as indicated by the numerous articles on Egypt in American scholarly magazines of the period. Of these magazines, *The North American Review* was at once the most typical and the most influential. In 1823 it carried an article by Edward Everett on the Zodiac of Denderah (see note 2), the same zodiac that Melville described some years later in *Moby-Dick*. In 1829 Henry Wheaton, the noted legal historian and diplomat, published in the *North American* a twenty-five-page review of one of Champollion's works.[10] In 1831 Everett again returned to an Egyptian subject with a thirty-page article on hieroglyphics. For these men the issue of real importance in the Egyptian revival was not styles in architecture or mummies or obelisks, but rather Champollion's decipherment of the hieroglyphic writing, which he had announced in the famous letter to Monsieur Dacier in 1822. Everett contends, "The discoveries of M. Champollion are perhaps the most extraordinary of a merely literary kind, which the history of modern learning contains."[11] Discussing the controversy between Champollion and the Englishman Thomas Young over priority of decipherment, Everett decides in favor of Champollion but notes, "If the mathematical discoveries of Leibnitz and Newton are the most brilliant which the modern world has produced in exact science, those of Young and Champollion are entitled to the same rank in critical learning, and are destined to throw, we doubt not, a flood light on a chapter of the history of mankind, hitherto almost a blank" (32:113). Everett's article was in part a response to a fifty-page essay in the December 1826 issue of the British *Edinburgh Review,* in which the controversy between Champollion and Young had appeared as simply a continuation of the struggle between France and England for the treasures of Egypt. Naturally, the writer for the *Edinburgh Review* had decided in favor of Young, though he made Champollion's books the basis for his discussion of the hieroglyphics.

It is significant that most of the early reviews of Champollion's work combine praise for his achievement with a summary dismissal of the nearly four centuries of symbolic interpretations of the hieroglyphs that had preceded his discovery. In his article for the *North American* in 1831, Everett characterized the work of Father Athanasius Kircher, the most prolific of the seventeenth-century metaphysical interpreters, as "utterly baseless" and "laboriously absurd," adding that "absurdities like these continued to be broached on this subject, down to the present day." Thus "the astrological symbols, composing what was called the zodiac of Denderah, have been pronounced within the present day, a Psalm of David" (32:101). The writer for the *Edinburgh Review* was no less vigorous: he accused Kircher of finding in the hieroglyphics "the cabalistic science and monstrous fancies of a refined system of Daemonism."[12]

The modern tradition of interpreting the hieroglyphics as metaphysical emblems, of which Kircher's work is perhaps the high point, had begun in 1419 with the discovery of Hor Apollo's *Hieroglyphica,* and its continuance through four centuries had made the words "hieroglyphic" and "emblem" synonymous.[13] Yet for hardheaded nineteenth-century gentlemen such as Everett, the relationship of Kircher's style of exegesis to Champollion's translations was simply that of a fanciful art to a logical science. Champollion's discoveries did not, however, topple the metaphysical school of interpretation. It continued, often using misreadings of Champollion's work as justification for its efforts; and the tension between these two kinds of interpretation was to have a significant influence on the literature of the American Renaissance.

In the process of deciphering the hieroglyphics, Champollion had to examine the various ways in which a sign can be linked to its referent. He found that the hieroglyphics were a composite writing, that is, that three different types of signs were used at the same time in any given inscription. In the words of the writer for the *Edinburgh Review,* these types were "1. *figurative characters,* which literally represented the object meant to be expressed; 2. *symbolic, tropic,* or *aenigmatic characters,* which expressed an idea by the image of a physical object having an analogy true or false, direct or indirect, near or remote, with the idea to be expressed; and 3. *phonetic characters,* which, by the images of physical objects, represented sounds merely" (45:144–45). Concerning this last type, J.G.H. Greppo in his *Essay on the Hieroglyphic System of M. Champollion* (Paris, 1829) noted that "phonetic signs form the most considerable part of all kinds of Egyptian texts," and he added:

> The adoption of *phonetic* signs, (which must be posterior to the use of the two other kinds of signs—the only element of primitive writing, as there is reason to believe), would not destroy the homogeneousness of the writing where they were employed. The three kinds of hieroglyphic signs, differing only in their *mode of expression,* were alike in regard to their *material forms;* and they all presented images of physical objects that were designed either to represent those objects *properly,* or to recall *symbolically* ideas related to the objects, or lastly, to express *phonetically* articulations which were the elements of the words in the spoken language. The *figurative* signs were employed for the notation of the most simple ideas, those of sensible objects; the *symbolical* signs denoted very simple abstract ideas; and the *phonetic* characters served to express the most complicated ideas,

such as could not be represented by the other two orders of signs, and could not be rendered intelligibly, except by means of words written down by the hand in a manner correspondent to their pronunciation.[14]

Greppo makes explicit two important assumptions: first, that the figurative and symbolic signs represent an earlier, more primitive state of hieroglyphic writing than the phonetic signs; and second, that the development from the figurative to the phonetic is the movement from writing able to present simple, concrete ideas to writing that can convey complex, abstract ideas. This development of the phonetic from the figurative involved in its most basic form the use of a sign to stand, not for the object that it depicted, but simply for the initial sound of the name for that object. Thus in Egyptian the word for "hawk" was *ahé*, and the sign for "hawk" could be used phonetically to represent the sound of the letter *a*. According to this view, Egyptian writing moved from a state in which there was a necessary, emblematic connection between a sign and its referent to a state in which for the most part that connection had become arbitrary and conventional.

Interestingly enough, such a view of the development of Egyptian writing was capable of satisfying both the metaphysical and the scientific schools of interpretation. What mattered was whether one valued simplicity or complexity. The metaphysical interpreters worked in a Christian tradition that considered man's present state to be the result of a fall from original simplicity. In his unfallen state man did not need a complex, abstract language. He was in such harmony with his environment that he used the language of nature, of natural signs—that world of objects created by God to stand as emblems of spiritual facts. But since the fall was from simplicity to complexity, the farther man moved from his original state, the more complex and involved his language became, and the more obscure became the old emblematic relationship between a sign and its referent. For the scientific school, on the other hand, the development of hieroglyphic writing could support an exactly opposite interpretation. The movement from a writing made up entirely of figurative signs capable of presenting only simple, concrete ideas to a writing composed largely of phonetic signs capable of presenting the most complex, abstract ideas demonstrated both evolution and progress. The metaphysical and scientific interpreters would not have disagreed, then, about the direction of the development of hieroglyphic writing. What they would have disputed was the meaning and value of that direction. Part of the importance of Greppo's treatise on Champollion's system is that its author tries to operate in both the metaphysical and scientific modes at once. The complete title of his work is *Essay on the Hieroglyphic System of M. Champollion, Jun., and on the Advantages which it offers to Sacred Criticism.* Greppo, a French priest and vicar general of Belley, spends the first quarter of his book discussing Champollion's decipherment and the remaining three-quarters trying to show that the resultant discoveries in Egyptian history and chronology are not at odds with the historical accuracy of the Old Testament. (The decipherment of the hieroglyphics and Darwin's theory of evolution were probably the two severest blows delivered by nineteenth-century science to the credibility of Genesis and to Bishop Ussher's widely accepted Biblical chronology, which placed the date of creation at 4004 B.C.)

Greppo's book is important for our purposes because an English translation of it, done by the American Isaac Stuart, was published in Boston in 1830; this translation was used by Sampson Reed as a source for his article on hieroglyphics in the October 1830 issue of the *New Jerusalem Magazine,* and it was reviewed by Edward Everett in the January 1831 issue of the *North American.* Both Everett and Reed were important formative influences on Emerson: Everett was Emerson's favorite teacher at Harvard, while Reed, the foremost American member of the Swedenborgian New Church, was the man whom Emerson called his "early oracle."[15] During the 1820s and 1830s Emerson was so taken with Reed's philosophy that he kept up with everything that the New Church spokesman published. Reed's essay on the hieroglyphics is a good example of metaphysical interpretation applied to scientific data. He begins, "Many of our readers may already know, that a key has been found to the meaning of the hieroglyphics of Egypt . . . , and it is certainly among the signs of the times, among the proofs of the coming of a new era, that enquiries, so long urged in vain, are at last answered."[16] Most of Reed's New Church brethren would have recognized the phrase "a key . . . to the meaning of the hieroglyphics" as an allusion to Swedenborg's book *The Hieroglyphical Key to Natural and Spiritual Mysteries by way of representations or Correspondences* (1784).[17] At least it was so understood by a Mr. J. D. of New York City who, in a letter to the editor published in the February 1831 issue of the *New Jerusalem Magazine,* praised Reed's article and remarked of the hieroglyphics, "Such is their intimate connexion with the doctrine of correspondences, as revealed to us in the New Jerusalem, that none but a New Churchman will ever be able thoroughly to decipher them."[18]

No doubt Mr. J. D. was referring to that portion of Reed's article in which he discussed the class of signs called "anaglyphs" by Champollion. Champollion thought that the anaglyphs, though connected with hieroglyphic writing, were not true hieroglyphics themselves, but rather symbolic pictures employing hieroglyphiclike figures. He backed up this contention by pointing out that most of the "figures which compose the anaglyphs, are accompanied by small legends in true hieroglyphic writing, which explain them."[19] But Reed, borrowing Champollion's phrases and reversing their meaning, says that the anaglyphs are the true hieroglyphic writing, as shown by the fact that they have "legends" written in phonetic signs near them, "containing their signification." Reed adds that in spite of Champollion's discoveries, these true hieroglyphics "still remain obscure, and probably will be so until an examination is made of them in a different spirit and manner, and on a different ground, from the present" (4:71).

If one of the points that the metaphysical and scientific schools of interpretation disputed was the relative value of simplicity and complexity, it is clear from Reed's article that another point at issue was the relative value of mystery. Implicit in Reed's doubt that Champollion's phonetic signs were the true hieroglyphics was the traditional belief that the hieroglyphics must contain the mysterious "wisdom of the Egyptians." Since the phonetic writing that Champollion had translated contained no such occult lore, it could not be the real hieroglyphic writing. The anaglyphs, on the other hand, were difficult, if not impossible, to construe; their purpose was obscure; therefore they must be the true hieroglyphics in which the Egyptian priests had encrypted their mysterious wisdom to keep it from the eyes of the profane. Such writing could only be deciphered by an initiate, by one of the select few who knew "the doctrine of correspondences, as revealed to us in the New Jerusalem." The metaphysical interpreter's interest in the simple and the necessary was perforce an interest in the hidden and the mysterious, for to his way of thinking the old emblematic relationship between words, objects, and spiritual facts had become progressively more obscure to man's fallen intellect. In contrast, the scientific interpreter's interest in the complex and the conventional represented an impulse to greater openness and to the demystification of the world.

In the course of his article, Reed makes numerous mistakes in interpreting Champollion's work—at one moment confusing phonetic signs and demotic writing, at the next moment mixing ideographic signs and anaglyphs—yet these alterations cannot all be accidental. They are due at least in part to Reed's assumption that Champollion as a scientist, as an observer of the surfaces of physical nature, missed the metaphysical significance of the facts that he observed. Champollion's discoveries are not to be belittled, but as Reed implies, they do need to be corrected and qualified by someone with a broader perspective and a deeper insight.

A similar attitude marks Emerson's reference to Champollion in his essay "History." In the essay Emerson expounds one of his central themes: the correspondence of the little and the large, exhibited in this case by the recapitulation, within the individual life, of the entire course of human history. Emerson deplores those students who stop at the surface of historical fact, and he urges, "We must in ourselves see the necessary reason of every fact—see how it could and must be."[20] For him, there are two kinds of students: "Some men classify objects by color and size and other accidents of appearance; others by intrinsic likeness, or by the relation of cause and effect. The progress of the intellect is to the clearer vision of causes, which neglects surface differences" (2:12). He continues: "The identity of history is equally intrinsic, the diversity equally obvious. There is, at the surface, infinite variety of things; at the centre there is simplicity of cause" (2:14). As a metaphysical interpreter, Emerson identifies the simple and the necessary with the hidden, with that which is beneath the obvious surface of things. If in studying history one understands that "it is the spirit and not the fact that is identical" (2:17), then everyday experience will always be "verifying some old prediction to us and converting into things the words and signs which we had heard and seen without heed" (2:18). That is, under the impulse of metaphysical insight, the arbitrary language of convention ("words and signs") will be penetrated to reveal once more the necessary, emblematic language of nature ("things") from which it sprang. Illustrating his doctrine of emblematic correspondences, Emerson says that the child who has suffered under the tyranny of an adult, who is himself at the mercy of the "names and words and forms" of a repressive dogma, understands from the core of his own being "the priestcraft of the East and West":

"The fact teaches him how Belus was worshipped and how the pyramids were built, better than the discovery by Champollion of the names of all the workmen and the cost of every tile" (2:28–29). Certainly, Emerson did not mean by this remark to scorn Champollion's achievement but simply to put it in its proper place: to point out that science remains ancillary to metaphysics, that the physical fact serves the spiritual fact. Indeed, one can judge from the following entry in Emerson's journal how important he considered Champollion to be: "In the year 1832 died Cuvier, Scott, Mackintosh, Goethe, Champollion, Leslie."[21] It is impressive company, and in the late essay "Behavior," from *The Conduct of Life* (1860), Emerson again included Champollion in a distinguished list, this time ranking him with Aristotle, Leibnitz, and Junius as one of the most important grammarians in history (6:190).

It is not surprising that Emerson was interested in Champollion's work, for the symbol of the hieroglyphics, through the influence of the Neoplatonists and the American Swedenborgians, was already central to Emerson's thought. In his first book, *Nature* (1836), Emerson asserts, "Every man's condition is a solution in hieroglyphic to those inquiries he would put" (1:4). In the essay "Self-Reliance" he notes that for people in times past, the king "was the hieroglyphic by which they obscurely signified their consciousness of their own right and comeliness, the right of every man" (2:63). In *Representative Men* (1850) Emanuel Swedenborg is characterized as one of those for whom the world is "a grammar of hieroglyphs" (4:142). In the essay "Poetry and Imagination," Emerson says that the poet "shall use Nature as his hieroglyphic" (8:65), recalling Shelley's remark in "A Defence of Poetry" that poets are "those who have employed language as the hieroglyphic of their thoughts,"[22] being themselves "the hierophants of an unapprehended inspiration; the mirrors of the gigantic shadows which futurity casts upon the present" (p. 297). And in "The Poet" Emerson observes that Nature "offers all her creatures to him as a picture-language" (3:13). The concept of the hieroglyphical emblem pervades *Nature:* "1. Words are signs of natural facts. 2. Particular natural facts are symbols of particular spiritual facts. 3. Nature is the symbol of spirit" (1:25). For anyone who has missed the point, he adds, "The world is emblematic" (1:32).

During the period in which he was writing *Nature,* Emerson was reading an English translation of the introduction of G. Oegger's *Le Vrai Messie* (Paris, 1829), and he quotes a sentence from this introduction in

his own work: "'Material objects,' said a French philosopher, 'are necessarily kinds of *scoriae* of the substantial thoughts of the Creator, which
must always preserve an exact relation to their first origin; in other
words, visible nature must have a spiritual and a moral side'" (1:35).
Oegger was a Swedenborgian, and the translation that Emerson used in
manuscript during July and August 1835 was probably made by the
American Transcendentalist Elizabeth Peabody.[23] Miss Peabody published this translation in 1842 as *The True Messiah; or The Old and New
Testaments, examined according to the Principles of the Language of Nature.*
Oegger says that in his interpretation of the Bible, he is attempting to
penetrate "to that language of Nature, which, as every one will easily
conceive, must have preceded all languages of convention."[24] He continues:

> The passage from the language of nature to the languages of con-
> vention, was made by such insensible degrees that they who made it
> never thought of tracing the latter back to their source.... Primi-
> tively, men could not name objects, they must show them.... When
> that primitive faculty of seeing and showing the immediate object of
> thought, and the natural emblem of sentiment was weakened, then,
> only, exterior signs came to join it. Thence the language of gestures,
> spoken at first more particularly by the eyes, the mouth, and the
> particular composition of the face, which at length introduced con-
> ventional sounds, and all exterior signs, such as are still found
> among the deaf and dumb; and, finally, those offered by hiero-
> glyphics and writing the Scripture.[25]

In *Nature* Emerson gives a similar account of this original language and
its subsequent decline: "As we go back in history, language becomes
more picturesque, until its infancy, when it is all poetry; or all spiritual
facts are represented by natural symbols. The same symbols are found to
make the original elements of all languages.... A man's power to connect his thought with its proper symbol, and so to utter it, depends on
the simplicity of his character, that is, upon his love of truth and his
desire to communicate it without loss. The corruption of man is followed
by the corruption of language" (1:29).

Oegger maintains that traces of the language of nature can still be
found in the languages of convention, and Emerson gives us an example
of this principle in *Nature* when he works back through the meanings of

conventional language to the roots of the original picture language: "Every word which is used to express a moral or intellectual fact, if traced to its root, is found to be borrowed from some material appearance. *Right* means *straight; wrong* means *twisted. Spirit* primarily means *wind; transgression,* the crossing of a *line; supercilious,* the *raising of the eyebrow*" (1:25). Emerson's method, as well as one of his examples, recalls the passage on the origin of abstract words in Locke's *An Essay Concerning Human Understanding* (1690). Locke observes "how great a dependence our words have on common sensible ideas; . . . v. g. *to imagine, apprehend, comprehend, adhere, conceive, instil, disgust, disturbance, tranquillity,* &c., are all words taken from the operations of sensible things, and applied to certain modes of thinking. *Spirit,* in its primary signification, is breath; *angel,* a messenger: and I doubt not but, if we could trace them to their sources, we should find in all languages, the names which stand for things that fall not under our senses to have had their first rise from sensible ideas."[26] In his use of etymology to analyze the origins of human culture, Emerson is operating in a tradition whose most learned eighteenth-century locus in English is the opening chapter, on radicals, of Jacob Bryant's *An Analysis of Antient Mythology* (1774–76).[27] In an attempt to systematize ancient mythology, Bryant begins by establishing the earliest forms of mythological names and showing their derivation from an emblematic language of objects. Oegger remarks of his own attempt to interpret the language of the Bible by means of the language of natural objects: "He who has the least idea of the emblems of nature and their signification, reads the Bible as if with a microscope. . . . It is like Egyptian hieroglyphics read by means of Champollion's system."[28]

As the hieroglyphical emblem represents for a writer like Emerson a basic understanding of the nature of the universe, so it dictates the form that his writing must take in treating that universe. In a sense, an Emersonian essay is simply the decipherment of a hieroglyph. The strategy is always the same: he presents the emblem in all its outer complexity and then, through the doctrine of correspondences, he penetrates the emblem to reveal its inner simplicity, to show the hidden relationship between outer shape and inner meaning. Indeed, most of his essays begin with a verse epigraph that is an encryption of the theme that the prose essay deciphers. The emblem can be a human concept like history, an emotion like love, a virtue like prudence, a geometric shape like the circle, or a power of the spirit like the intellect. It can be a type of man, as

in "The Poet," or a series of great individuals, as in *Representative Men.*
Yet even when Emerson deals with a great individual, it is always to treat
him as a type, to present his life as emblematic. The titles of the essays in
Representative Men make this clear: "Plato; or The Philosopher,"
"Swedenborg; or The Mystic," "Napoleon; or The Man of the World."
Though they may be meant to illustrate an inner simplicity, the subjects
of Emerson's essays are never themselves simple illustrations. The sense
of the people and things that Emerson writes about is that their real
meanings are hidden, that to confront them is necessarily to involve
oneself in a process of interpretation whereby the surface is penetrated
and inner necessity revealed.

Section 2
Thoreau: The Single, Basic
Form—Patenting a Leaf

If the hieroglyphical emblem is central to Emerson's thought and style, it
is no less important to the work of his
friend and protégé Thoreau. Thoreau's *Walden* (1854) is basically a
series of explicated emblems. In his account of a symbolic year spent in
the microcosmic world of Walden Pond, Thoreau presents the reader
with detailed descriptions of his house, his economy, his farming, his
diet, his reading, his walks, the surrounding countryside, the animals,
birds, fish, and flowers, the seasons, the weather, and so on. He depicts
all of these things as hieroglyphic emblems whose meanings are hidden
from the majority of men because the petty concerns and busyness of life
have degraded their powers of intellect and observation. Thoreau's descriptions of the external shape of his world are at the same time explica-
tions of the world's inner significance.

One of the best known examples of this emblematic technique in *Walden*, and certainly one that is most germane to a discussion of the hieroglyphics, is Thoreau's description of the thawing of a sandbank in spring.
The streams of sand, he says, are a kind of "hybrid product, which obeys
half way the law of currents, and half way that of vegetation. As it flows it
takes the forms of sappy leaves or vines, making heaps of pulpy sprays a
foot or more in depth, and resembling, as you look down on them, the
laciniated, lobed and imbricated thalluses of some lichens; or you are
reminded of coral, of leopards' paws or birds' feet, of brains or lungs or
bowels, and excrements of all kinds. It is truly *grotesque* vegetation,
whose forms and color we see imitated in bronze, a sort of architectural

foliage."[29] Thoreau adds that seeing this sand foliage produced on a single spring day, "I am affected as if in a peculiar sense I stood in the laboratory of the Artist who made the world and me,—had come to where he was still at work, sporting on this bank, and with excess of energy strewing his fresh designs about. I feel as if I were nearer to the vitals of the globe, for this sandy overflow is something such a foliaceous mass as the vitals of the animal body. You find thus in the very sands an anticipation of the vegetable leaf. No wonder that the earth expresses itself outwardly in leaves, it so labors with the idea inwardly" (p. 306).

Thoreau, in his attempt to find a single form underlying the variety of natural forms, shows the influence on his work of three of Emerson's representative men—Goethe, Swedenborg, and Plato. Thoreau's image of the vegetable leaf as a basic, all-pervading natural form derives from the central idea in Goethe's *Die Metamorphose der Pflanzen* (1790). Summarizing Goethe's contributions to natural science, Emerson says, "Goethe suggested the leading idea for modern botany, that a leaf or the eye of a leaf is the unit of botany, and that every part of a plant is only a transformed leaf to meet a new condition; and, by varying the conditions, a leaf may be converted into any other organ, and any other organ into a leaf. In like manner, in osteology, he assumed that one vertebra of the spine might be considered the unit of the skeleton: the head was only the uppermost vertebra transformed" (4:275). Goethe's attempt to find a single basic form beneath the multiplicity of forms in external nature and to show that the multiple forms derive from that basic form is an analogue of Emerson's effort to penetrate the outer complexity of nature's hieroglyphical emblems and discover the inner simplicity that unites them—an effort that is itself emblematic, as Emerson points out in *Nature* when he remarks that it is "not so pertinent to man to know all the individuals of the animal kingdom, as it is to know whence and whereto is this tyrannizing unity in his constitution, which evermore separates and classifies things, endeavoring to reduce the most diverse to one form" (1:67).

Emerson says that Goethe in his scientific investigations "has contributed a key to many parts of nature, through the rare turn for unity and simplicity of his mind" (4:274–75). The phrase "a key to many parts of nature" recalls the work of another of Emerson's representative men—Swedenborg's *The Hieroglyphical Key to Natural and Spiritual Mysteries by way of representations or Correspondences.* In his essay on Swedenborg,

Emerson discusses the Swedish mystic's own version of the theory that a basic form underlies the multiplicity of natural forms: "The ancient doctrine of Hippocrates, that the brain is a gland; and of Leucippus, that the atom may be known by the mass; or, in Plato, the macrocosm by the microcosm; and, in the verses of Lucretius . . .

> The principle of all things entrails made
> Of smallest entrails; bone, of smallest bone;
> Blood, of small sanguine drops reduced to one;
> Gold, of small grains; earth, of small sands contracted;
> Small drops to water, sparks to fire contracted

and which Malpighi had summed in his maxim, that 'nature exists entire in leasts,'—is a favorite thought of Swedenborg. . . . The unities of each organ are so many little organs, homogeneous with their compound. . . . This fruitful idea furnishes a key to every secret" (4:113–14). In his essay "The Method of Nature," Emerson sounds a Goethean note when he speaks of that "catholic character" of physical nature "which makes every leaf an exponent of the world" (1:201).

Goethe saw the leaf and the vertebra not only as the basic units of plant and animal life but also as two related forms of a still more basic form. Thoreau, in his description of the thawing sandbank, makes this same connection between the vegetable leaf and the animal body in imagery that recalls Emerson's quotation from Lucretius. Pointing out that the sandy foliage of the bank is "an anticipation of the vegetable leaf," Thoreau remarks that in this phenomenon one can also "see perchance how blood-vessels are formed. . . . In the silicious matter which the water deposits is perhaps the bony system, and in the still finer soil and organic matter the fleshy fibre or cellular tissue. What is man but a mass of thawing clay? The ball of the human finger is but a drop congealed. The fingers and toes flow to their extent from the thawing mass of the body. . . . Is not the hand a spreading *palm* leaf with its lobes and veins? The ear may be regarded, fancifully, as a lichen, *umbilicaria*, on the side of the head, with its lobe or drop. . . . Each rounded lobe of the vegetable leaf, too, is a thick and now loitering drop, larger or smaller; the lobes are the fingers of the leaf" (pp. 307–08). The basic form that unites the animal body and the vegetable leaf is, for Thoreau, the lobe or drop. Considering how great the influence of Plato was on both Emerson and Thoreau, we can see behind this image of the lobe or drop another image—the Platonic sphere, that original, perfect form that, Plato says in the *Timaeus* (62d), God gave to the universe. Emerson begins "Circles," one of his most Platonic essays, with the epigraph:

> Nature centres into balls,
> And her proud ephemerals,
> Fast to surface and outside,
> Scan the profile of the sphere;
> Knew they what that signified,
> A new genesis were here.
>
> (2:299)

In the same essay he says that the circle or sphere is "the highest emblem in the cipher of the world" and that "throughout nature this primary figure is repeated without end" (2:301).

What is most significant for our purposes in Thoreau's description of the thawing sandbank is that he connects the attempt to find a basic unifying form beneath the multiplicity of natural forms with the attempt to penetrate the language of convention and discover within it the original language of nature, that basic verbal form with its emblematic relationship between words and things. Remarking that "the world expresses itself outwardly in leaves, it so labors with the idea inwardly," Thoreau continues, "The atoms have already learned this law, and are pregnant by it. The overhanging leaf sees here its prototype. *Internally,* whether in the globe or animal body, it is a moist thick *lobe,* a word especially applicable to the liver and lungs and *leaves* of fat (λείβω, *labor, lapsus,* to flow or slip downward, a lapsing; λοβός, *globus,* lobe, globe; also lap, flap, and many other words), *externally,* a dry thin *leaf,* even as the *f* and *v* are a pressed and dried *b.* The radicals of lobe are *lb,* the soft mass of the *b* (single lobed, or *B,* double lobed,) with the liquid *l* behind it pressing forward" (p. 306). Earlier, Thoreau had remarked that the thawing sandbank made him feel "nearer to the vitals of the globe, for this sandy overflow is something such a foliaceous mass as the vitals of the animal body," and in his philological speculation on "the radicals of lobe," he observes, "In globe, *glb,* the guttural *g* adds to the meaning the capacity of the throat" (p. 306). Alluding to the Latin root of the word "guttural" (*guttur,* "throat"), Thoreau evokes, in hieroglyphic fashion, the image of the throat as a passage or channel for fluid movement between the inner, globular vitals of the body and the outer world of leaves and the significant shapes inscribed upon them. In this image of the guttural channel, he may also be suggesting the word "gutter" and its Latin root *gutta* ("a drop"), and the word "gut" derived from the Anglo-Saxon verb *geotan,* "to pour or gush." He continues: "The feathers and wings of birds are still drier and thinner leaves. Thus, also, you pass from the lumpish grub in the earth to the airy and fluttering butterfly. The very globe continually transcends and translates itself, and becomes winged in its orbit. Even ice begins with delicate crystal leaves, as if it had flowed into moulds which the fronds of water plants have impressed on the watery mirror" (pp. 306–07).

Thoreau's essay in creative etymology reminds us of Emerson's similar efforts in *Nature* and in particular of his remark: "A leaf, a drop, a crystal, a moment of time, is related to the whole, and partakes of the perfection of the whole. Each particle is a microcosm, and faithfully renders the likeness of the world" (1:43). The general method recalls as well the passage in Plato's *Cratylus* (426c–427d) in which Socrates discusses the correspondence between sound and sense exhibited by "original names."[30] Socrates points out that "the imposer of names"

> observed the liquid movement of λ, in the pronunciation of which the tongue slips, and in this he found the expression of smoothness, as in λεῖος (level), and in the word ὀλισθάνειν (to slip) itself, λιπαρόν (sleek), in the word κολλῶδες (gluey), and the like; the heavier sound of γ detained the slipping tongue, and the union of the two gave the notion of a glutinous clammy nature, as in γλίσχρος, γλυκύς, γλοιῶδες. The ν he observed to be sounded from within, and therefore to have a notion of inwardness; hence he introduced the sound in ἔνδον and ἐντός; α he assigned to the expression of size, and η of length, because they are great letters; ο was the sign of roundness and therefore there is plenty of ο mixed up in the word γογγύλον (round). Thus did the legislator, reducing all things into letters and syllables, and impressing on them names and signs, and out of them by imitation compounding other signs. (P. 461)

It is worth noting that the last example that Socrates gives is less a case of the correspondence of sound and sense than the correspondence of visual shape and sense. The letter *o* is described as "the sign of roundness" rather than its sound, and one suspects that Socrates' final example is a Platonic ideograph of the original form—the circle.

In his own speculation on phonetic roots, Thoreau wants to demonstrate that the relationship of the lobe to the leaf is that of inner form to outer form, that the lobe is the moist, thick internal unit whose external equivalent is the dry, thin leaf. A proof of this relationship, says Thoreau, is to be seen in the very shape of the words "lobe" and "leaf." The radicals of the word "lobe" are *lb,* "the soft mass of the *b* (single lobed, or *B*, double lobed,) with the liquid *l* behind it pressing it forward." This description suggests, of course, the image of the sandbank, where "first there pushes forward from the thawing mass a stream of softened sand with a drop-like point" (p. 307). If the basic creative process in terms of natural forms is the accretion of fluid matter into globes or lobes, then the word "lobe" is an emblem of that process and of the form that it creates; for we can see that in the word the liquid *l* like the moisture in the sandbank presses forward against the soft mass of the *b,* and that the shape of the letter *b* is nothing more than that same liquid *l* with a circular drop or lobe appended to it like the sandy lobes of the bank. In a similar manner the shape of the word "leaf" is emblematic: that a leaf is simply the thin, dry, outer equivalent of the thick, moist, inner lobe is reflected by the fact that the *f* in "leaf" and the *v* in "leaves" are a "pressed and dried *b.*" That is, if the lobe on the letter *b* were broken off during some fanciful process of pressing and drying such as natural science collectors of the nineteenth century used in preserving once-living objects, then we would be left with two shapes that resemble the letters *f* and *v*. In this imaginative exercise Thoreau shows us that what he had considered to be phonetic signs bearing only an arbitrary, conventional relationship to their referent are, to the initiated eye, hieroglyphic signs whose shape is an obscure picture of the object they stand for.

Having penetrated the emblematic world of natural forms to discover the inner, unifying form, and then having presented as an analogue of this process the penetration of the language of convention to discover the original language of nature in which words are emblems of things, Thoreau concludes: "Thus it seemed that this one hillside illustrated the principle of all the operations of Nature. The Maker of this earth but patented a leaf. What Champollion will decipher this hieroglyphic for us, that we may turn over a new leaf at last?" (p. 308). The answer to that question is, obviously, Thoreau himself. He says later on, "The earth is not a mere fragment of dead history, stratum upon stratum like the leaves of a book, to be studied by geologist and antiquaries chiefly, but living poetry like the leaves of a tree, which precede flowers and fruit—not a fossil earth, but a living earth" (p. 309). Though he invokes the name of a scientific translator like Champollion, Thoreau, in the leaves of his own book, gives a metaphysical interpretation of what is written in the leaves of the book of nature.

Section 3
Whitman: Hieroglyphic Bibles and Phallic Songs

It is a short step from Thoreau's image of the leaves of a tree as "living poetry" to Walt Whitman's *Leaves of Grass* (1855) and its poetic reading of the hieroglyphical book of nature. In "Song of Myself" Whitman says that the grass

> ... is a uniform hieroglyphic
> And it means, Sprouting alike in broad zones
>   and narrow zones,
> Growing among black folks as among white,
> Kanuck, Tuckahoe, Congressman, Cuff, I give them the
>   same, I receive them the same.[31]

Later in the poem, Whitman cites Champollion's decipherment as an example of the progress of science:

> Hurrah for positive science! long live exact demonstration!
> Fetch stonecrop mixt with cedar and branches of lilac,
> This is the lexicographer, this the chemist, this made a
>   grammar of the old cartouches. . . .
>
> (7:51)

A cartouche is an oval ring used in hieroglyphic writing to set off the characters of a royal or divine name. The earliest examiners of the Rosetta stone had noticed that a group of characters enclosed in an oval appeared at a point in the hieroglyphic inscription corresponding to the place where the name of the pharaoh Ptolemy Epiphanes occurred in the Greek inscription. The general surmise had been that these characters comprised the pharaoh's name and that the oval ring was an unvarying marker of royal names. Since the name Ptolemy was Greek in origin, the investigators reasoned that it must have been written phonetically in Egyptian, and they proceeded to isolate the name's phonetic elements in the demotic text of the Rosetta stone. Champollion, following the lead of earlier researchers like de Sacy, Akerblad, and Young, concentrated his efforts at decipherment on proper names and on establishing the relationship between demotic writing and the hieroglyphics. Having at first rejected Young's contention that demotic writing was a cursive script ultimately derived from the hieroglyphics, Champollion finally accepted it; and in September 1822, working with copies of inscriptions from the temple at Abu Simbel, he deciphered the names of the pharaohs Rameses and Thothmes. Champollion suddenly realized that phonetic signs were used for writing not only foreign names but Egyptian names as well, indeed that they were "original and integral elements of the hieroglyphical system as such."[32] It was this discovery that he announced in the letter to Monsieur Dacier, though "the actual demonstration and proof of this revolutionary assertion was reserved for a subsequent publication."[33]

Whitman's interest in Egyptian antiquities seems to date from the years 1853 or 1854.[34] At about that time he began to visit the Egyptian museum of Dr. Henry Abbott in New York. In *Good-Bye My Fancy* he says, "The great 'Egyptian Collection' was well up in Broadway, and I got quite acquainted with Dr. Abbott, the proprietor—paid many visits there, and had long talks with him, in connection with my readings of many books and reports on Egypt—its antiquities, history, and how things and the scenes really look, and what the old relics stand for, as near as we can now get" (9:696). Whitman's visionary description of Egypt in "Salut au Monde!" may well be based on some of the things that he had seen and discussed at Dr. Abbott's museum:

> I see Egypt and the Egyptians, I see the pyramids
>   and obelisks,
> I look on chisell'd histories, records of conquering kings,
>   dynasties, cut in slabs of sand-stone, or on
>   granite-blocks,
> I see at Memphis mummy-pits containing mummies embalm'd,
>   swathed in linen cloth, lying there many centuries,
> I look on the fall'n Theban, the large-ball'd eyes, the
>   side-drooping neck, the hands folded across the breast.
>
> (7:145)

Floyd Stovall notes that an article "on 'The Egyptian Museum' published in *Life Illustrated* for December 8, 1855, was almost certainly written by Whitman. This article shows that Whitman had absorbed a good deal of information about ancient Egypt, some of it from Abbott, no doubt, some of it from lectures by Gliddon and others, but probably a good deal more from his reading of the many books, reviews, and magazine and newspaper articles on Egypt published during the 1840's and 1850's."[35] In the article Whitman discusses the "satisfactory conclusion" to the "perplexing subject" of decipherment and remarks that Champollion "probably contributed more to that conclusion than any other man. When he returned from Egypt he knew his death was rapidly approaching. With feverish haste he completed his great work, a 'grammar of Egyptian Hieroglyphics'—he corrected the proofs on his death-bed. 'Preserve these,' said he, handing them to his friends, 'they are my visiting-cards to posterity.'"[36] Three decades later, in *A Backward Glance O'er Travel'd Roads* (1888), Whitman used this story again, as an image of his own achievement: "Result of seven or eight stages and struggles extending through nearly thirty years, (as I nigh my three-score-and-ten I live largely on memory,) I look upon 'Leaves of Grass,' now finish'd to the end of its opportunities and powers, as my definitive *carte visite* to the coming generations of the New World, if I may assume to say so" (7:562). And in a footnote he repeats the story of Champollion's death-bed reference to his "Egyptian Grammar" as his "*carte de visite* to posterity'" (7:562–63n). Whitman's source for this anecdote was probably "George Gliddon's *Ancient Egypt,* which Park Benjamin's *New World* issued in April, 1843, as a 25-cent double extra number."[37]

Like Emerson's admiring references to Champollion, Whitman's praise of positive science and the man who "made a grammar of the old cartouches" carries a qualification. In "Song of Myself," he says:

> Gentlemen, to you the first honors always!
> Your facts are useful, and yet they are not my dwelling.
> I but enter by them to an area of my dwelling.
>
> (7:51)

The physical fact is not the dwelling place because for Whitman the physical is the path to the metaphysical ("path" not in the sense that the metaphysical is located elsewhere, but in the sense that the metaphysical is a radically different way of experiencing the physical). In the preface to the 1855 edition of *Leaves of Grass,* Whitman says: "Exact science and its practical movements are no checks on the greatest poet but always his encouragement and support. . . . The anatomist, chemist, astronomer, geologist, phrenologist, spiritualist, mathematician, historian, and lexicographer are not poets, but they are the lawgivers of poets and their construction underlies the structure of every perfect poem.... In the beauty of poems are the tuft and final applause of science" (7:718-19). And in "A Passage to India" (1871), he expresses once more the notion that the poet completes the work of the scientist:

> After the seas are all cross'd, (as they seem already cross'd,)
> After the great captains and engineers have accomplish'd
>   their work,
> After the noble inventors, after the scientists, the chemist,
>   the geologist, ethnologist,
> Finally shall come the poet worthy that name
> The true son of God shall come singing his songs.
>
> Then not your deeds only O voyagers, O scientists and
>   inventors, shall be justified, ...
> All affection shall be fully responded to, the secret
>   shall be told,
> All these separations and gaps shall be taken up and hook'd
>   and link'd together,
> The whole earth, this cold, impassive, voiceless earth, shall
>   be completely justified,
> Trinitas divine shall be gloriously accomplish'd and compacted
>   by the true son of God, the poet....
>
>   (7:415)

When Whitman says that with the coming of the true poet "the secret shall be told," he echoes Emerson's belief that the significance of nature is concealed beneath the surface complexity of the physical objects examined by empirical science. In *Democratic Vistas* Whitman says, "As the purport of objective Nature is doubtless folded, hidden, somewhere here—as somewhere here is what this globe and its manifold forms, and the light of day, and night's darkness, and life itself, with all its experiences, are for—it is here the great literature, especially verse, must get its inspiration and throbbing blood" (9:419). Whitman maintains that the test of the "great literatus" who shall pierce that complexity and tell the secret of nature will be "his cheerful simplicity, his adherence to natural standards" (9:414). One is reminded of Emerson's remark that Goethe had penetrated the multiplicity of physical nature "through the rare turn for unity and simplicity of his mind." The doctrine of correspondence is clear: one penetrates the obscure hieroglyphic "characters" of the language of nature to reach the inner simplicity of their meaning by means of the inner simplicity of the human "character." Like reveals like.

One of the major image patterns associated with the hieroglyph of nature in the works of the American Renaissance is that of the cipher and the key. As Emerson speaks of "the cipher of the world," so Whitman in a poem from *Good-Bye My Fancy* called "Shakspere-Bacon's Cipher" says:

> In each old song bequeath'd—in every noble page or text,
> (Different—something unreck'd before—some
>   unsuspected author,)
> In every object, mountain, tree, and star—in every
>   birth and life,
> As part of each—evolv'd from each—meaning,
>   behind the ostent,
> A mystic cipher waits infolded.
>
> (7:544)

And as Emerson says that the poet-scientist Goethe "contributed a key to many parts of nature," so Whitman in the preface to the 1855 *Leaves of Grass* says that the poet who draws "his encouragement and support" from science is "the arbiter of the diverse and he is the key" (7:712).

Closely related to the figure of the cipher and key is the image of natural signatures. Commenting on the Renaissance belief that "buried similitudes must be indicated on the surface of things," Michel Foucault notes that in this tradition

> there are no resemblances without signatures. The world of similarity can only be a world of signs. Paracelsus says:
>
> > It is not God's will that what he creates for man's benefit and what he has given us should remain hidden. . . . And even though he has hidden certain things, he has allowed nothing to remain without exterior and visible signs in the form of special marks—just as a man who has buried a hoard of treasure marks the spot that he may find it again.

A knowledge of similitudes is founded upon the unearthing and deciphering of these signatures. . . . the face of the world is covered with blazons, with characters, with ciphers and obscure words—with "hieroglyphics," as Turner called them. And the space inhabited by immediate resemblances becomes like a vast open book; it bristles with written signs; every page is seen to be filled with strange figures that intertwine and in some places repeat themselves. All that remains is to decipher them.[38]

In this same vein Emerson, in his essay on Goethe, depicts the operations of nature as a continuous act of writing:

Nature will be reported. All things are engaged in writing their history. The planet, the pebble, goes attended by its shadow. The rolling rock leaves its scratches on the mountain; the river its channel in the soil; the animal its bones in the stratum; the fern and leaf their modest epitaph in the coal. The falling drop makes its sculpture in the sand or the stone. Not a foot steps into the snow or along the ground, but prints, in characters more or less lasting, a map of its march. Every act of the man inscribes itself in the memories of his fellows and in his own manners and face. The air is full of sounds; the sky, of tokens; the ground is all memoranda and signatures, and every object covered over with hints which speak to the intelligent. (4:261)

According to the tradition that Foucault cites, God has written two books—the book of nature and the Bible. Both are written in hieroglyphics that require interpretation, yet this continuity in the form of their writing means that they can be used to interpret one another, each book somehow being the hidden key to the other's meaning. Oegger's *The True Messiah,* which employs this mode of reciprocal interpretation, is dominated by the image of the hieroglyph. Oegger says:

Man is the true hieroglyphic of the Divinity; a hieroglyphic, infinite in its details, even when man is considered only as a material form, since his material form itself, is but the emblem of his moral being. . . . All animals, by their corporeal forms, as well as by their instincts, are hieroglyphics of the different degradations of human nature, or of detached parts of the collection of organs of life, called man.[39]

Since there are "millions of hieroglyphics which any one may easily find," Oegger proposes to provide "simple keys, by means of which the reader can, by himself, penetrate farther into the immense domains of nature" (2:95). In general, Oegger follows the method employed by Swedenborg in *Arcana Coelestia* (1749–56), though with greater flexibility. (The *Arcana Coelestia* is a decipherment of Genesis and Exodus by means of the hieroglyphical key to the language of nature.) Of Swedenborg's method, Emerson remarks: "He fastens each natural object to a theologic notion;—a horse signifies carnal understanding; a tree, perception; the moon, faith; a cat means this; an ostrich that; an artichoke this other;—and poorly tethers every symbol to a several ecclesiastic sense.... His theological bias thus fatally narrowed his interpretation of nature, and the dictionary of symbols is yet to be written. But the interpreter whom mankind must still expect, will find no predecessor who has approached so near to the true problem" (4:121).

Swedenborg's and Oegger's readings of the hieroglyphs of Scripture are closely related to the tradition of hieroglyphic Bibles, which began in the seventeenth century and continued well into the nineteenth. According to W. A. Clouston's *Hieroglyphic Bibles, Their Origin and History,* the first hieroglyphic Bible was published in Augsburg in 1687 by Melchior Mattsperger.[40] Its title was *The Spiritual Heart-Fancies, in Two Hundred and Fifty Biblical Picture-Texts* (Clouston, p. 126). The book contains eighty-four copperplate engravings in which the 250 Biblical quotations are reproduced. In each quotation, key words are replaced by pictures of the objects that the words signify. In his preface Mattsperger says that he has provided these "Biblical Figure-Sayings" so that "simple people may learn ... many a text which all their life long they might never have considered" (pp. 130–31). And he adds, "I have had printed the accompanying table of all the texts comprised in it, word by word in themselves, in which the figure is always indicated by larger type, which those who are unable to name the right word may use instead of a key" (p. 131).

Mattsperger's work was so popular that in 1692 he issued a second part with 250 more Biblical picture-texts. The first part of Mattsperger's work was reprinted in Hamburg in 1704. A selection of 150 texts from the Hamburg version was issued in Amsterdam in 1720; in 1743 the Hamburg version was reprinted in Copenhagen in German, and in 1745 in French. The unsigned prefatory verses to the Hamburg version are a learned discussion of the language of nature. Pointing out that the sun "is accustomed to express itself in figures by its rays," the poet says:

> . . . the under-world absorbs the force of those rays,
> The water shows its image, metal, and beast their nature;
> One can even read its beautiful image in stones,
> So that heaven itself carries those images in its forehead. . . .

> Yea, Dame Nature even stamps the figures on the beast:
> From the Stork will arise the beginning of the alphabet. . . .
>
> (P. 162)

The poet explains that Athanasius Kircher "*tells us, in his* Oedip. Aegypt, *how the first characters can be seen in the different positions of Ibicus or the Egyptian stork*" (p. 162). He continues:

> Intelligence is the mirror, wherein art wisely joins
> The splendour of heaven and of the sun together;
> It adorns the firmament with constellations of different names,
> And writes the doings of the ancients high up in the skies. . . .

> In this way writing in pictures descended from on high,
> In this way Nature took it to her bosom. . . .
>
> (P. 163)

"As above so below," runs this doctrine of correspondence in which earth mirrors heaven, and the human intellect in turn mirrors both. The preface notes that as Nature "began with images, so have images later on given rise to letters. This is the mother, and these are, so to speak, her daughters, which, moreover, are not so entirely degenerate but that one may recognize her in her progeny. For the Hebrew letters being, without doubt, the oldest of all, what else are they but rough sketches of what they signify, since the letters ב, ד, and ל are not only called, but represent a house, a door, and a hollow hand?" (pp. 63–64).

The first English version to derive from Mattsperger's work was published in London by T. Hodgson in 1780. Entitled *A Curious Hieroglyphick Bible*, it was meant "for the Amusement of Youth: designed chiefly to familiarize tender Age, in a pleasing and diverting Manner, with early Ideas of the Holy Scriptures" through "Select Passages in the Old and New Testaments, represented with Emblematical Figures" (p.

9). Some, if not all, of the woodcuts were done by the well-known English engraver Thomas Bewick. The work was so well received that it "went through no fewer than twenty large editions—besides four reprints published at Dublin—down to the year 1812" (p. 8), and it was reprinted in America by Isaiah Thomas. In 1794 a rival work to Hodgson's entitled *A New Hieroglyphical Bible* was published in London by G. Thompson. Thompson's work was the progenitor of numerous English hieroglyphic Bibles and at least three Continental versions, one of which (a German edition printed in Leipzig in 1842) contains a preface with an explicit statement of the relationship between the hieroglyphic book of nature and Sacred Scripture:

1. The book of Nature, which God wrote himself, of old alone announced to man the truths needed by the heart to enable it to face every fortune.

2. But, alas, finite natures did not comprehend the glorious book. The divine word, in which it was written, remained unintelligible for many a century in every land.

3. The book was too great for finite spirits, the characters themselves prevented the characters from being read, and when they were seen, men, though endowed with the keenest intelligence, failed to interpret them for want of the necessary light.

4. The wisest men looked on the sun and moon, the glittering stars in the bright night, as only floating spheres in boundless space, not as revealers of the divine power....

7. They read and read, but for all they read, they read not aright, but only confused themselves, and all their wisdom and prudence was a prolific field for all kinds of error:

8. Then God, by men, taught from within by the illuminating power of His spirit, caused the Book to arise, which destroys the darkness in the minds of men in human fashion....

10. Since he gave this Book to men, creation is intelligible and clear to them, and what they now read from earth and heaven is no longer error, but perfectly clear.... (P. 103)

In both Hodgson's edition and Thompson's, a key to the cipher accompanies each hieroglyphic passage: "The whole Sentences, which give an Explanation of the Figures, are placed at the Bottom of each Page; and the Words, which are represented by Figures, are particularly distinguished in *Italic*" (p. 11), says the author of the preface to Hodgson's second edition. In other editions the key is often placed at the back of the book and is preceded by a picture of a key. The image of the cipher and key is basic to the format of the hieroglyphic Bible, and that image is invariably connected with the motif of learning to call things by their right names. In Mattsperger's original work a table gave the names of all the flowers, trees, fruits, and so forth, whose pictures decorated the borders of each page. According to the title page of the Hamburg version, one of the purposes of the book is to teach children "how to draw everything very neatly, and to name it with its proper name" (p. 161). And the title page of the Dutch version says that the Biblical pictures are explained "for the delight of Youth, and in order to teach to accurately estimate everything, and to name [it] by its right name" (p. 172).

To call objects by their right names means to call them by their original names. It is an Adamic task that reminds us of Whitman's effort to recapture the language of physical objects in his role as poet of the Edenic New World:

> A song of the rolling earth, and of words according,
> Were you thinking that those were the words, those upright
>   lines? those curves, angles, dots?
> No, those are not the words, the substantial words are in
>   the ground and sea,
> They are in the air, they are in you. . . .
>
> Human bodies are words, myriads of words. . . .
>
> Air, soil, water, fire—those are words. . . .
>
> The masters know the earth's words and use them more than
>   audible words. . . .
>
> I swear I begin to see little or nothing in audible words,
> All merges toward the presentation of the unspoken meanings
>   of the earth,
> Toward him who sings the songs of the body and of the truths
>   of the earth,
> Toward him who makes the dictionaries of words that
>   print cannot touch.
>
> (7:219-20, 224)

One thinks of Emerson's remark about Swedenborg: "The dictionary of symbols is yet to be written," but "the interpreter, whom mankind must still expect, will find no predecessor who has approached so near to the true problem." We know that Whitman was much interested in Swedenborg's thought. Stovall notes that the poet preserved a lengthy newspaper clipping on the Swedish mystic "with the title 'The New Jerusalem' (Bucke's No. 278); and in *Notes and Fragments,* in a brief note on him, he [Whitman] says 'He is a precursor, in some sort, of great differences between past thousands of years and future thousands.'"[41] Whitman also mentions Swedenborg "in *Democratic Vistas* and in notes on Elias Hicks in *November Boughs.* Helen Price wrote Bucke that Whitman and John Arnold, a Swedenborgian who lived in the same house with her and her mother, discussed Swedenborg a great deal in her presence in the late 1850's."[42]

From his knowledge of Swedenborg's work, either directly or through Emerson, Whitman would have been familiar with the reciprocal hieroglyphic readings of the book of nature and the Bible. And since hieroglyphic Bibles were one of the most popular types of children's books during the first half of the nineteenth century, it is more than likely that Whitman would have been familiar with them as well, particularly in light of his interest in Egyptian hieroglyphics. Indeed, hieroglyphic Bibles were so popular in America that they gave rise to other hieroglyphic children's books, most notably the *Mother Goose in Hieroglyphics* "published in 1849 by Appleton of Philadelphia" and "kept in print at least until the late 1860's by a succession of Boston firms."[43] A brief comparison of this book with an American hieroglyphic Bible of the period, such as the one published by J. C. Riker in New York in 1852, shows that in the religious and secular uses of pictographs in nineteenth-century America, there existed the same distinction between an ideographic and a phonetic approach that characterized the opposing metaphysical and scientific interpretations of the Egyptian hieroglyphs. In Riker's *A New Hieroglyphical Bible,*[44] the words that are replaced by pictographs are always nouns, either concrete or abstract; and the referents are always depicted either *literally* (the picture of an object stands for the object itself) or *symbolically* (the picture of an object stands for an abstract idea associated with the object, for example, a picture of a woman blindfolded and holding a scales stands for *righteousness*). In *A New Hieroglyphical Bible,* pictures are never used to represent sounds exclusively; whereas in *Mother Goose in Hieroglyphics,* the use of pictographs as phonetic signs takes a variety of forms. Thus, for example, on a homonymic principle, the picture of an awl is made to stand for the sound of the word "all," and the picture of an eye for the sound of the pronoun "I." On a principle of phonetic resemblance, the picture of a hand evokes the sound of the conjunction "and," the picture of a toe the preposition "to." And in rebus fashion, the picture of a can plus the letter *D* evokes the sound of the word "candy." Clearly, the intention of *Mother Goose in Hieroglyphics* is not, as in the case of a hieroglyphic Bible, to teach children to call "things" by their right "names." The preface to *Mother Goose in Hieroglyphics* announces a more domestic purpose: "There is nothing like books with pictures, to keep children quiet; and this is the best that ever was written, as everybody knows" (p. 4). Riker's *A New Hieroglyphical Bible,* by using pictures to represent objects or ideas and never to stand simply for discrete sounds, follows an ideographic tradition common to the hieroglyphic Bible long before Champollion's decipherment of the Egyptian hieroglyphics—that tradition of an original language of physical objects that preceded a language of spoken words. In contrast, *Mother Goose in Hieroglyphics,* compiled in the 1840s and with no apparent metaphysical bias, may well exhibit, in its use of pictures to stand for sounds, the influence of Champollion's discovery that the hieroglyphics were a phonetic script.

I have discussed at some length hieroglyphic Bibles and the tradition of the hieroglyphical interpretation of the Bible represented by Swedenborg and Oegger because there is reason to believe that at one point Whitman conceived of *Leaves of Grass* as a kind of hieroglyphic Bible. The evidence is circumstantial but ample. To begin with, there is Whitman's interest in the hieroglyphics and Egyptology, the fact that he called his major symbol "a uniform hieroglyphic," and that in *A Backward Glance* he implicitly compared *Leaves of Grass,* "his *carte visite* to the coming generations," to Champollion's hieroglyphic grammar. Indeed, Whitman may have had in mind Emerson's remark that for Swedenborg the world was a "grammar of hieroglyphs." Next, we know that as late as June 1857 Whitman considered his ongoing work on *Leaves of Grass* as "the Great Construction of the New Bible."[45] The Bible was, of course, the major influence on Whitman's prosody, shaping his cadenced verse with its repetitions and parallelisms. Further, many of the elements found in the format of the hieroglyphic Bible are to be found in *Leaves of*

Grass as well. In addition to the figure of the cipher and the key, there is
the Adamic motif of calling things by their right names, that is, by their
original names. In characterizing Champollion's achievement as the construction of "a grammar" from "the old cartouches," Whitman emphasizes the central role of proper names in the decipherment of the
hieroglyphics; for in the metaphysical tradition the authentic "proper
names" are right, original names, and thus Champollion's decipherment
of the Egyptian hieroglyphics by means of proper names is itself a kind
of hieroglyphical representation, a veiled prefiguration, of the correct
method for deciphering the hieroglyphs of nature. According to this
tradition, when the language of words derived from the original language of objects, the words that derived first and that are still closest to
that original language were concrete nouns—the proper names of physical objects. Emerson refers to this notion in *Nature* when he remarks,
"Every word which is used to express a moral or intellectual fact, if
traced to its root, is found to be borrowed from some material appearance." And this concept of the noun also underlies Thoreau's choice of
the nouns "lobe" and "leaf" to analyze into their hieroglyphic radicals.

But Thoreau's choice of images probably contains another allusion as
well, for in selecting the word "leaf" to trace back to its radicals (*radix*,
"root"), Thoreau subtly evokes the cosmic tree that—with its roots in the
underworld, its trunk in this world, and its leafy branches extending up
into the heavens—is an image of language as mediating link between the
human and the divine. Foucault points out that the seventeenth-century
writer Christophe de Savigny in his *Tableau de tous les arts liberaux* "con-
trives to spatialize acquired knowledge both in accordance with the cosmic, unchanging, and perfect form of the circle and in accordance with
the sublunary, perishable, multiple and divided form of the tree" (p. 38).
But the cosmic tree combines the images of both the circle and the tree:
it is the fixed, unchanging point that binds together the horizontal and
the vertical. As both the center of the horizon(tal) circle of this world and
the vertical link that connects this world to the world below and the
world above, the cosmic tree is the immutable pole of the continuous
language of natural objects.[46] There is, of course, a traditional connection between language and the image of the tree. One of the most interesting traces of this connection in English is the derivation of the word
"book" from the Anglo-Saxon name for the beech tree (*bec*), perhaps
because runes were first carved on trees or because writing was done on

beech bark. And certainly behind Thoreau's reference to the leaves of a tree that are to be read like the leaves of a book and his tracing of the word "leaf" back to its "roots," as well as behind Whitman's *Leaves of Grass* and the motif of Adamic naming, there lies a network of images connecting language, the tree, and the Garden of Eden, a network of images that sheds light on *Leaves of Grass* as a kind of hieroglyphic Bible.

The Biblical account of Adam's naming of the animals would seem to be fairly straightforward: "The Lord God formed every beast of the field, and every fowl of the air; and brought them unto Adam to see what he would call them: and whatsoever Adam called every living creature, that was the name thereof. And Adam gave names to all cattle, and to the fowl of the air, and to every beast of the field" (Genesis 2:19-20). Yet there are two different traditions concerning this original naming. According to the orthodox tradition, God gave Adam the power to impose phonetic names on the animals as a mark of the dominion over the earth and its creatures that God had granted to man (Genesis 1:28). But according to the heterodox tradition that lies behind writers like Swedenborg and Oegger, God gave Adam the power to read the ideographic "names" of the animals in their physical shapes, that is, to recognize the significance of each creature from the form that God had given it. Herder alludes to the latter tradition in his *Essay on the Origin of Language* (1770), remarking that "amongst the Orientals" it is "a common turn of expression to call the recognition of a thing the naming of it."[47] In both traditions, the language of physical objects, that original "script" in which God wrote the forms of the natural world, is prior to human language. But in the former tradition, as regards human language, speech is prior to writing, that is, a language of spoken words precedes a language of written phonetic signs; while in the latter tradition a language of signs employing the natural forms of physical objects precedes a language of spoken words. In this tradition Adam's naming is not the archetypal imposition of a spoken word for each object but rather the appropriation of God-given natural forms into a language of signs, gestures, and pictures—a human language that is continuous with the language of nature because its elements are borrowed from that language. According to this tradition, a language of spoken words (representing the movement from the concrete, necessary shapes of physical objects to the arbitrary abstractions of phonetic signs) is synonymous with man's fall, with Adam's eating the fruit of the tree of the knowledge

of good and evil. The knowledge of good and evil would be interpreted
in this tradition as a poetic image of differential self-consciousness, its
opposite being that prelapsarian unitive state which Whitman might well
have described as "cosmic consciousness," to use his friend Dr. Bucke's
phrase. Certainly, the Bible depicts the fall as a break in man's unselfconscious continuity with the natural world: "And the eyes of them both
were opened, and they knew that they *were* naked; and they sewed fig
leaves together and made themselves aprons" (Genesis 3:7). Although
Adam and Eve were naked before the fall, they "were not ashamed"
(Genesis 2:25). After the fall their sense of their own nakedness, their
self-consciousness, amounts to a sense of the self's separateness, its discontinuity with the natural world, a discontinuity whose linguistic equivalent is the substitution of the arbitrary language of spoken words for
the prior and necessary language of natural signs.

The sexual overtone of this fall from innocence to experience—this
tasting of the tree of knowledge that reveals the difference between male
and female as a nakedness to be veiled—suggests that the fixed, unchanging mediatory role of the old cosmic tree ("the tree of life," Genesis
2:9) has been replaced, in the Biblical parable of man's separation from
his origins, by the phallus (the linking third term, the partial object, the
detachable signifier). (The image of the phallus pervades Whitman's
poetry; and the associative chain *tree-phallus-speech-radical* can be
glimpsed behind Whitman's reference to his poems as "Adamic songs"
[7:107], his image of the "voice resonant, singing the phallus" [7:91], and
his description of the phallus as the "love-root" [7:29] and as "the poem
drooping shy and unseen that I always carry, and that all men carry, . . .
our lusty lurking masculine poems" [7:103].) Unlike the cosmic tree, the
phallic tree of knowledge is not inseparably connected with the entities
and realms that it links. Rather, through an act of differential self-
consciousness that breaks the continuity of man and nature, of meaning
and object, and renders signification free-floating, the phallic tree of
knowledge links entities by an arbitrary imposition, by the interpolation
of the discontinuous, fecundating spoken word between mind and object. When Adam, ashamed of his nakedness, covers himself with a fig
leaf, the implicit image of the phallic stylus and the veiling sheet (sheath,
sheaf, leaf) suggests that phonetic language is a garment that can be
changed at will, an arbitrary covering for the nakedness of the self cut
off from its origins (the Indo-European root of the word "shame,"

*(s)kam-, means "to cover") as well as a covering for the nakedness of the natural world, a world suddenly become strange and hostile.

In this interpretive tradition, the Biblical account of the tower of Babel can be read as a parable of the unsuccessful attempt of the phallic linking power of human speech to supplant the cosmic tree as the center of the world:

> 1 And the whole earth was of one language, and of one speech. 2 And it came to pass, as they journeyed from the east, that they found a plain in the land of Shinar; and they dwelt there. 3 And they said to one another, Go to, let us make brick, and burn them thoroughly. And they had brick for stone, and slime had they for mortar. 4 And they said, Go to, let us build us a city and a tower, whose top may reach unto heaven; and let us make us a name, lest we be scattered abroad upon the face of the whole earth. 5 And the Lord came down to see the city and the tower, which the children of men builded. 6 And the Lord said, Behold, the people is one, and they have all one language; and this they begin to do: and now nothing will be restrained from them, which they have imagined to do. 7 Go to, let us go down, and there confound their language, that they may not understand one another's speech. 8 So the Lord scattered them abroad from thence upon the face of all the earth: and they left off to build the city. 9 Therefore is the name of it called Babel; because the Lord did there confound the language of all the earth.... (Genesis 11:1-9)

Symbolically equated with the unifying power of the single human speech, the phallic tower suggests, in the displacement of stone by brick, of nature by artifice, the displacement of the language of natural signs by the arbitrary spoken word. Indeed, the parallelism of the three tasks that the people set themselves—to build a city, to build a tower, to make a name—implies that speech is as much a product of human art as are the city and the tower, and that the pride in art, which is the apparent meaning of the people's desire to make a name for themselves, applies to the artifact of speech (the literal making of names) as much as to the making of the city and the tower.

As opposed to the cosmic tree of life that stood in the center of the natural world of the garden, the tower is the center of an urban world, an artificial world descended from the handiwork of the first city-builder

(Genesis 4:17) and first murderer, Cain. As the center of this urban world in which artificial construction is the destruction of nature, the tower shows its descent from the phallic tree of knowledge whose fruit brought death into the world. Clearly, the tower, whose avowed purpose is to link earth to heaven, is intended to take over the mediating role of the cosmic tree—but with a difference. For the tower, built in the pride of human art, is an attempt to displace heaven and earth, just as the spoken word in its power of arbitrary imposition becomes more important than the things it links, until in its ultimate abstraction it "kills" the physical object that it stands for. God thwarts this attempt by confounding man's speech. The confusion of tongues not only stops the construction of the tower and the city, it also disperses the builders—a dispersion which indicates that human speech cannot become a new center, cannot take the old central place of the cosmic tree of life. For God intends in time to restore that center in the cosmic tree of the cross, the tree bearing the embodied Logos and symbolizing by its physical shape the intersection of the vertical and horizontal worlds.

The confounding of the single speech and the dispersion of the speakers inaugurates a world of translation in which the spoken word can never wholly displace the physical object precisely because there are multiple names for the same object (at least as many as there are languages); and these names, each with its own claim to priority, neutralize one another, thus preventing any word from gaining ascendancy. Moreover, God in His providence has seen to it that the original language of natural signs has not been totally lost to man. Although the arbitrary language of spoken words has displaced the language of pictographic ideograms, God has ordained that the signs used for the phonetic transcription of spoken words should be taken from the old language of natural signs. Thus though the signs of phonetic script bear an arbitrary relationship to the sounds they represent, and though the sounds of spoken words bear in turn an arbitrary relationship to the objects they stand for, God has contrived that the physical shape of the written signs for phonetic roots should still bear, in a hidden manner, the old emblematic character of the language of natural signs. Just as phonetic script is, in this tradition, a kind of veiled hieroglyphic, so the Bible is a hieroglyphic book, not only in its written form, but in its content as well. For the Bible tells, in veiled images, the story of the loss of that original language of natural signs, while at the same time it preserves the natural emblems of that language, concealed within its own text. The world and the Bible are thus related as mutually reversible cipher and key.

It is just such a relationship that Whitman designs between *Leaves of Grass* and the world in his attempt to recapture the original language of natural objects, an attempt to journey back to the Edenic world of man's childhood prior to the fall into spoken language. As he says in "A Song of the Rolling Earth":

> I swear I begin to see little or nothing in audible words,
> All merges toward the presentation of the unspoken meanings
>   of the earth,
> Toward him who sings the songs of the body and of the truths
>   of the earth,
> Toward him who makes the dictionaries of words that print
>   cannot touch.

Since hieroglyphic Bibles were, in Whitman's day, specifically children's books, the form presented a particularly appropriate vehicle for Whitman's association of childhood with the language of natural signs. In *Leaves of Grass,* Whitman evokes mankind's ability to return to its Edenic childhood and to the language of nature as each individual's imaginative ability (symbolized by that of the poet) to return to the innocence and simplicity of "character" that one possessed as a child, to that state in which the self seemed to enjoy a direct relationship with nature without the mediation of spoken language. This image of childhood is clearly at work in a poem like "Out of the Cradle Endlessly Rocking," and the motif of the unmediated relationship between the child and nature is explicitly stated in "There Was a Child":

> There was a child went forth every day,
> And the first object he looked upon and received with wonder
>   or pity or love or dread, that object he became,
> And that object became part of him for the day or a certain
>   part of the day ... or for many years or stretching
>   cycles of years. . . .
> The horizon's edge, the flying seacrow, the fragrance of
>   saltmarsh and shoremud;
> These became part of that child who went forth every day,
>   and who now goes and will always go forth every day,
> And these become of him or her that peruses them now.[48]

In characterizing *Leaves of Grass* as a kind of hieroglyphic Bible, we should keep in mind that its model is not the Bible of orthodox Christianity. Whitman's is not a religion of the triune God but rather a religion of the human body and the body of nature conjoined in a cosmic unity. In Whitman's poetry, the physical is the pathway to the metaphysical precisely because in his poetic vision the physical is transformed into the metaphysical—man's body becomes his soul. In one of the poems from *Children of Adam,* he says:

> The thin red jellies within you or within me, the bones and
>   the marrow in the bones,
> The exquisite realization of health;
> O I say these are not the parts and poems of the body only,
>   but of the soul,
> O I say now these are the soul!

>   (7:101)

The poetic transformation of the physical into the metaphysical is synonymous with the attempt to recapture the original language of objects, for in that language physical objects were, to use Emerson's term, "transparent," their significances shone through their material shapes. Physical objects were transparently metaphysical objects, signs in which no separation or discontinuity between form and content existed because as pictographic ideograms their form was their content. Whitman's attempt to regain the original language of natural signs, his effort to replace "audible words" with "the presentation of the unspoken meanings of the earth," involves the paradoxical use of phonetic signs to restore the unspoken (nonphonetic) language of pictographic ideograms, the paradox involved in *singing* "the songs of the *body*." And it is in light of the Romantic concept of song as the transcending of the mediation of spoken language *through* the mediation of spoken language that Whitman's effort to transform the physical into the metaphysical must be understood.

For Whitman, "song" is a rhetorical figure, a trope that depicts the discontinuity between self and world, between spoken word and physical object, as a form/content dichotomy capable of being overcome by music. (In this context, of course, "music" is itself a trope—one that I shall discuss later in relation to the concepts of self-evidence and immediate conviction). "Song" is Whitman's name for that Paterian "condition of

UNIVERSITY OF WINNIPEG
LIBRARY
515 Portage Avenue
Winnipeg, Manitoba R3B 2E9

music" where "in its consummate moments, the end is not distinct from
the means, the form from the matter, the subject from the expression;
they inhere in and completely saturate each other."[49] In the Whitmanian
trope, "song" signifies an ideal interpenetration in which form fuses with
content, the spoken word with the object, the poet's self (the poem's
subject) with the song, and the song with the world. And it signifies all of
this precisely because, in Whitman's aesthetic, song is understood to be at
once a literal and figurative *expiration,* the singer's breathing out of the
self (pneuma) into the world and a filling of the self by the world, a
prefigurative *Liebestod* in which the self expires into, and becomes one
with, the world, so that self-consciousness becomes "cosmic consciousness." In "Out of the Cradle Endlessly Rocking," the poet travels by
means of his song back to his own childhood (and thus toward man's
ultimate origin, "the cosmic float," symbolized by the sea) in order to
hear once again the song of the bird calling to its lost mate. And he
realizes that the singing of the bird has a double meaning: it is at once an
image of the world calling to the separated self of the poet and an image
of the poet singing in order to "expire," to breath himself into the world:

> Demon or bird! (said the boy's soul,)
> Is it indeed toward your mate you sing? or is it really to me?
> For I, that was a child, my tongue's use sleeping, now I
>   have heard you,
> Now in a moment I know what I am for, I awake
> And already a thousand singers, a thousand songs, clearer,
>   louder and more sorrowful than yours,
> A thousand warbling echoes have started to life within me,
>   never to die.
>
> O you singer solitary, singing by yourself, projecting me,
> O solitary me listening, never more shall I cease
>   perpetuating you. . . .
>
> (7:251–52)

In Whitman's idealized conception of song, the musical component of
poetry, by raising spoken language to that condition in which its sonic
form is its content (in which vocal expiration is a return to origin, to that
original interpenetration of sign and meaning), transforms spoken language into the audible equivalent of that original language of natural

signs in which the form of the pictographic physical object was transparently its meaning. Thus in Whitman's poetry, song is presented as the mode of the poet's return to a childlike simplicity of character, to those radically simple, written characters of the original language of natural signs through which the poet's character is expressed. Whitman aims, through the fusing power of song, to turn the phallic tree of spoken language back into the cosmic tree of the language of natural signs within his own cosmic written self, the Walt Whitman whose song (*Leaves of Grass*) *is* his poetic self. In one of the poems in *Children of Adam* he says,

> Ages and ages returning at intervals,
> Undestroy'd, wandering immortal,
> Lusty, phallic, with potent original loins, perfectly sweet,
> I, chanter of Adamic songs,
> Through the new garden the West, the great cities calling,
> Deliriate, thus prelude what is generated, offering these,
>   offering myself. . . .

(7:107)

In the ideal transparency of embodiment, the singer becomes his song, the object its meaning. For Whitman song is an audible hieroglyph, a musical emblem.

PART TWO
Poe

The greatest mystery of religion is expressed by adumbration. . . . Life itself is but the shadow of death, and souls departed but the shadows of the living. All things fall under this name; the sun itself is but the dark simulachrum, and light but the shadow of God.

Sir Thomas Browne, *The Garden of Cyrus*

Who has found the boundaries of human intelligence? Who has made a chart of its channel, or approached the fountain of this wonderful Nile?

Emerson, "Natural History of Intellect"

Through words and concepts we shall never reach beyond the wall of relations, to some sort of fabulous primal ground of things. Even in the pure forms of sense and understanding, in space, time and causality, we gain nothing that resembles an eternal verity. It is absolutely impossible for a subject to see or have insight into something while leaving itself out of the picture, so impossible that knowing and being are the most opposite of all spheres.

Nietzsche, *Philosophy in the Tragic Age of the Greeks*

The beginning of Western thought is not the same as its origin. The beginning is, rather, the veil that conceals the origin—indeed an unavoidable veil. If that is the situation, then oblivion shows itself in a different light. The origin keeps itself concealed in the beginning.

Heidegger, *What Is Called Thinking?*

Section 4
*The Hieroglyphics and the Quest for
Origins: The Myth of Hieroglyphic
Doubling*

"The supposition that the book of an author is a thing apart from the author's self, is, I think, ill-founded. The soul is a cipher, in the sense of a cryptograph; and the shorter a cryptograph is, the more difficulty there is in its comprehension—at a certain point of brevity it would bid defiance to an army of Champollions."[1] So writes Poe in "The Literati of New York City" (1846). Of the major writers of the American Renaissance, Poe was the one for whom Champollion, in his role as a decipherer of cryptic writing, had the greatest personal significance. He became for Poe a kind of model of scientific intuition as opposed to the drudgeries of inductive and deductive reasoning. In *Eureka* (1848), that "survey of the Universe" (16:186) based on the first two volumes of Alexander von Humboldt's great work of natural science *Cosmos* (1845–47), Poe uses the device of a letter from the future in order to characterize retrospectively the contemporary deductive and inductive methods of reasoning as the modes of the Rams and the Hogs, the former method having derived from "a Turkish philosopher called Aries and surnamed Tottle" (16:188) and the latter from "one Hog" whose method was appropriately called "Baconian" (16:189). The anonymous correspondent, writing in the year A.D. 2848, ridicules the claim that these two methods are the only roads to truth and notes that in the past such a claim has retarded "the progress of true Science, which makes its most important advances—as all History will show—by seemingly intuitive *leaps*" (16:189): "I have often thought, my friend, that it must have puzzled these dogmaticians of a thousand years ago to determine, even, by which of their two boasted roads it is that the cryptographist attains the solution of the more complicated cyphers—or by which of them Champollion guided mankind to those important and innumerable truths which, for so many centuries, have lain entombed amid the phonetical hieroglyphics of Egypt" (16:196). The letter writer then associates Champollion's intuitive deciphering of the hieroglyphics with Kepler's intuitive grasp of the laws of gravity, and he ends his letter with a quotation from Kepler: *"I care not whether my work be read now or by posterity. I can afford to wait a century for readers when God himself has waited six thousand years for an observer. I triumph. I have stolen the golden secret of the Egyptians. I will indulge my sacred fury"* (16:198). This comparison of Champollion and Kepler as intuitive scientists suggests that Poe's own

43

"scientific reading" of the physical shape of the universe in *Eureka* is to be understood as an imaginative decipherment of the cosmic hieroglyph.

It is this same scientific intuition, the ability to make a sudden imaginative leap based on an analytic method, that Poe presents as the essential trait of the detective C. Auguste Dupin. At the beginning of "The Murders in the Rue Morgue" (1841), the narrator observes:

> The mental features discoursed of as the analytical, are, in themselves, but little susceptible of analysis. We appreciate them only in their effects.... As the strong man exults in his physical ability, delighting in such exercises as call his muscles into action, so glories the analyst in that moral activity which *disentangles*.... He is fond of enigmas, of conundrums, of hieroglyphics; exhibiting in his solutions of each a degree of *acumen* which appears to the ordinary apprehension preternatural. His results, brought about by the very soul and essence of method, have, in truth, the whole air of intuition. (4:146)

The narrator concludes that while "the ingenious are always fanciful . . . , the *truly* imaginative [are] never otherwise than analytic" (4:150). What is involved, then, is a single power with a double aspect—at once imaginative and analytic. Observing Dupin in one of his moods, the narrator says, "I often dwelt meditatively upon the old philosophy of the Bi-Part Soul and amused myself with the fancy of a double Dupin—the creative and the resolvent" (4:152). In Poe's opinion this double power is the essence of men like Dupin, Champollion, Kepler, Humboldt and, of course, Poe himself. Considering Poe's frequent admiring references to Champollion, it is tempting to speculate that one of the models for the character of Dupin—that intuitive decipherer of clues, with his fondness for enigmas, conundrums, and hieroglyphics—was Champollion.

Earlier we treated Everett and Emerson as representatives of the opposing scientific and metaphysical modes of hieroglyphic interpretation. In "A Chapter on Autography" (1841), Poe locates himself for us within that opposition when he includes Everett and Emerson in a group of 100 American literary figures whose signatures he analyzes. In the introduction to the article he says, "That a strong analogy *does* generally and naturally exist between every man's chirography and character will be denied by none but the unreflecting" (15:178). And he adds that while one of his purposes is to "illustrate our position that the mental features are indicated (with certain exceptions) by the handwriting," another is to satisfy our natural curiosity to see the signature of a famous author, because in his signature "there is something which seems to bring him before us in his true idiosyncrasy—in his character of *scribe*" (15:186). In his analysis of Emerson's signature, Poe comes right to the point:

> Mr. Ralph Waldo Emerson belongs to a class of gentlemen with whom we have no patience whatever—the mystics for mysticism's sale. Quintilian mentions a pedant who taught obscurity, and who once said to a pupil "this is excellent, for I do not understand it myself." How the good man would have chuckled over Mr. E.! His present *role* seems to be the out-Carlyling Carlyle. *Lycophron Tenebrosus* is a fool to him. The best answer to his twaddle is *cui bono?* . . .
>
> His love of the obscure does not prevent him, nevertheless, from the composition of occasional poems in which beauty is apparent *by flashes.* . . . His MS. is bad, sprawling, illegible, and irregular—although sufficiently bold. This latter trait may be, and no doubt is, only a portion of his general affectation. (15:260)

Poe's reading of Everett's penmanship is more respectful: "Mr. Everett's MS. is a noble one. It has about it an air of deliberate precision emblematic of the statesman, and a mingled grace and solidity betokening the scholar. Nothing can be more legible, and nothing need be more uniform. The man who writes thus will never grossly err in judgment or otherwise; but we may also venture to say that he will never attain the loftiest pinnacle of renown" (15:203). To Poe's way of thinking, Everett's analytic powers are not imaginative enough, while Emerson's imagination is not analytic enough. Somewhere between these two are situated Poe and his alter ego Dupin, along with their mentors Humboldt and Champollion.

The network of connections between Poe, Champollion, and Humboldt regarding the hieroglyphics is illuminating. One begins with Poe's admiration for the work of both men: on the one hand, the numerous laudatory references to Champollion in Poe's work, on the other, the fact that *Eureka* is based on *Cosmos,* that it is dedicated to Humboldt, and that a copy of *Eureka* was in Humboldt's personal library at the time of his death in 1859.[2] Alexander von Humboldt, geographer, natural scientist, explorer—not to be confused with his brother Wilhelm, the linguist and cofounder of the University of Berlin—was himself greatly interested in the hieroglyphics. He knew Champollion, attended his lectures in Paris,

and corresponded with him. He was also a friend of the Englishman
Thomas Young, whose book, *An Account of Some Recent Discoveries in
Hieroglyphical Literature, and Egyptian Antiquities* (1823), was dedicated to
Humboldt "as a mark of the highest respect, for the extent of his knowledge and the accuracy of his research, as well as for his ardent zeal in the
promotion of science, and for his candour and vigilance in the distribu-
tion of literary justice."[3] Humboldt was as well the mentor of the great
German Egyptologist Richard Lepsius. But Humboldt's interest in the
hieroglyphics preceded Champollion's decipherment of the Rosetta
stone by many years and was by no means confined to Egyptian writing.
From 1799 to 1804, Humboldt and the French botanist Aimé Bonpland
explored regions of South and Central America in what is now Ven-
ezuela, Cuba, Colombia, Peru, Ecuador, and Mexico: "Humboldt made
maps and amassed exhaustive data in countless fields—magnetism,
meteorology, climatology, geology, mineralogy, oceanography, zoology,
ethnography. In addition to observations on plant geography and
physiognomy, he made historical and linguistic investigations. . . . This
trip has justly been called 'the scientific discovery of America.'"[4]

Of the many books that resulted from Humboldt's explorations, the
most important for our purposes was his *Researches, Concerning the Institutions and Monuments of the Ancient Inhabitants of America, with Descriptions and Views of Some of the Most Striking Scenes in the Cordilleras.* The
English translation, by Helen Maria Williams, was published in London
in 1814. A large part of the book is devoted to a discussion of Aztec
hieroglyphics. Humboldt's remarks, along with William Warburton's
analysis of the hieroglyphics in *The Divine Legation of Moses Demonstrated*
(1737–41), constitute some of the most sophisticated speculations on the
subject prior to the publications of Young and Champollion. Humboldt
begins his discussion by warning that it would

> . . . be absurd to suppose the migration of Egyptian colonies
> wherever pyramidical monuments and symbolical paintings are
> found; but how can we avoid being struck with the traces of resem-
> blance offered by the vast pictures of manners, of arts, of language,
> and traditions, which exist at present among nations at the most
> remote distance from each other? . . .

We perceive that the use of hieroglyphical paintings was common
to the Toltecks, the Tlascaltecks, the Aztecks, and several other

tribes, which, since the seventh century of our era, appear successively on the elevated plain of Anahuac; but we nowhere find alphabetic characters. . . .[5]

Focusing on the Aztec hieroglyphics, Humboldt notes that although there are "great numbers of paintings, which may be interpreted or explained like the sculptures on the Trajan column," we find "only a very small number of characters susceptible of being read. The Azteck people had real simple hieroglyphics for water, earth, air, wind, day, night, the middle of the night, speech, motion: they had also for numbers, for the days and months of the solar year. These signs, added to the painting of an event, marked in a very ingenious manner, whether the action passed during the day or the night; the age of the persons they wished to represent; whether they had been conversing and who among them had spoken most" (1:158–59). Humboldt concludes that the Aztec hieroglyphics bear a greater resemblance to those Egyptian "paintings of a mixed kind" that "unite symbolical and isolated characters with the representation of an action" (1:160) than they do to hieroglyphic script, and that thus "the nations of America were very distant from that perfection which the Egyptians had obtained" (1:161) in the art of writing.

In Humboldt's work the study of the Aztec hieroglyphics is an integral part of his description of the physical nature of Latin America, and in both his linguistic and geographic inquiries one of the implicit purposes is the search for origins. Describing certain "granitic rocks, which rise on the savannahs of Guiana" and are "covered with figures of tigers, crocodiles, and other characters, which may be regarded as symbolical," he says:

The natives of these regions are unacquainted with the use of metallic tools; and all concur in asserting, that these characters already existed when their ancestors arrived in those countries. Is it to a single nation, trained to industry, and skilled in sculpture, such as the Toltecks, the Aztecks, and the tribes that emigrated from Aztlan, that these marks of remote civilization are owing? In what region must we place the seat of this culture? Is it to the north of the river Gila, on the elevated plain of Mexico? or in the southern hemisphere, in those lofty plains of Tiahuanacu, which the Incas themselves found covered with the ruins of majestic greatness, and which may be considered as the Himala and the Thibet of South America? These problems are not to be solved in the present state of our knowledge. (1:177–78)

Humboldt employs a similar method in *Cosmos* when, as part of his scientific description of physical nature, he includes a brief history of "the physical contemplation of the universe" that pays special attention to the evolution of writing, an evolution that must be understood in light of "Champollion's great discovery" of the way in which "alphabetical writing... has originated from pictorial writing" as men disregarded "the ideal signification of the symbols" in order to consider "the characters... as mere signs of sounds."[6] Yet on the subject of the search for origins, Humboldt's position has become much more conservative since the work on South America some thirty years earlier. Instead of being simply a problem that baffles "the present state of our knowledge," the question of origins now appears by its very nature to be insoluble. He says, "Geographical investigations regarding the ancient *seat*, the so-called *cradle of the human race*, are not devoid of a mythical character" (1:354–55). And he quotes from "an unpublished work *On the Varieties of Languages and Nations*" by his brother Wilhelm:

> It is in vain that we direct our thoughts to the solution of the great problem of the first origin, since man is too intimately associated with his own race and with the relations of time to conceive of the existence of an individual independently of a preceding generation and age. A solution of those difficult questions, which can not be determined by inductive reasoning or by experience—whether the belief in this presumed traditional condition be actually based on historical evidence, or whether mankind inhabited the earth in gregarious associations from the origin of the race—can not, therefore, be determined from philological data, and yet its elucidation ought not to be sought from other sources. (1:355).

It is an interesting statement: the question of the geographical point of human origin cannot be determined from philological data, and yet its solution ought not to be sought from other sources; consequently, the problem is insoluble. It seems that as scientists, both the Humboldts wanted to put the question of man's origin and the origin of language behind them and address themselves to those questions that they be-

lieved the newly evolving sciences of linguistics and comparative philology actually had some hope of solving.

During the seventeenth and eighteenth centuries the origin of lan-
guage had been a topic of continuing philosophical discussion, treated in
works like Locke's *An Essay Concerning Human Understanding* (1690),
James Harris's *Hermes, or A Philosophical Inquiry Concerning Universal
Grammar* (1745), Condillac's *L'Origine des connaissances* (1746), Rousseau's
Essai sur l'origine des langues (1749), Adam Smith's "Considerations
Concerning the First Formation of Language" in the second edition of
Theory of Moral Sentiments (1759), Herder's *Essay on the Origin of Language*
(1772), Lord Monboddo's *Of the Origin and Progress of Language* (1773–
92), and Thomas Astle's *The Origin and Progress of Writing* (1803), to
name only a few. The question had become so much a matter of
philosophical speculation that serious nineteenth-century linguists
looked on it with suspicion. Thus, for example, the Linguistic Society of
Paris, founded in 1866, "had in its bylaws the provision that it would not,
under any circumstances, accept any kind of communication on the
subject of the origin of language."[7] And half a century later, Saussure, in
the *Course in General Linguistics,* says: "No society, in fact, knows or has
ever known language other than as a product inherited from preceding
generations, and one to be accepted as such. That is why the question of
the origin of speech is not so important as it is generally assumed to be.
The question is not even worth asking; the only real object of linguistics
is the normal, regular life of an existing idiom."[8] Thus Alexander von
Humboldt, in discussing the geographical aspect of the question, describes it as "mythical." Yet when his brother Wilhelm says that the
solution to the "great problem of the first origin" ought not to be sought
from other than philological sources, Wilhelm implies that the origin of
language *is* the origin of man, that man *as* man only begins with the
acquisition or invention of language, of symbolization. And when he says
that the problem cannot be solved because "man is too intimately associated with his own race and with the relations of time to conceive of
the existence of an individual independently of a preceding generation
and age," he points out that due to the temporal nature of thought, man
cannot really conceive of a prior nontemporal state in opposition to
which the first origin, the absolute beginning of time, could be distinguished. To think the absence of time would literally be to think the
absence of thought, to be conscious of the loss of consciousness, to con-

ceive of one's own death. Similarly, to discover the ultimate origin of language in and through language, that is, in a linguistic discourse about philological evidence, would be to present in words the limit of language, the boundary line where language begins and the nonexistence of language ends. But how can one present *in* language the nonexistence of language? Impossible as these tasks are, it nevertheless seems to be inherent in the very self-conscious (self-defining) nature of thought to push itself to an absolute limit where thought dissolves, inherent in thought to seek its origin.

Clearly, the origin of man and language cannot be approached as if it were simply a question of ultimate priority in time. Regarding the myth of mankind's origin from the union of a single pair, Wilhelm von Humboldt remarks:

> The general prevalence of this myth has caused it to be regarded as a traditionary record transmitted from primitive man to his descendants. But this very circumstance seems rather to prove that it has no historical foundation, but has simply arisen from an identity in the mode of intellectual conception, which has every where led man to adopt the same conclusion regarding identical phenomena; in the same manner as many myths have doubtlessly arisen, not from any historical connection existing between them, but rather from an identity in human thought and imagination. Another evidence in favor of the purely mythical nature of this belief is afforded by the fact that the first origin of mankind—a phenomenon which is wholly beyond the sphere of experience—is explained in perfect conformity with existing views, being considered on the principle of the colonization of some desert island or remote mountainous valley at a period when mankind had already existed for thousands of years.[9]

According to Humboldt's "structuralist" point of view, what the myth of origin actually reveals is the origin of myths, reveals it as "an identity in the mode of intellectual conception, . . . an identity in human thought and imagination." And what Humboldt draws our attention to is that the origin of man, "a phenomenon which is wholly beyond the sphere of experience," has always been conceived in light of experience, conceived as if *coming first* were simply the ultimate form of *coming before,* as if origination were merely "the colonization of some desert island or remote mountainous valley." But origination cannot be understood in terms of temporal priority precisely because it has to do with simultaneity—not a priority in time, but a priority to time. As Humboldt suggests in referring to "an identity in human thought," man and language (thought) come into existence simultaneously through a continuous network of mutually constitutive, differential oppositions; yet the ground of this network by which man and language exist in time is itself, insofar as it is *simultaneous,* above the flow of time. Whether we call it the synchronic aspect of language as opposed to the diachronic or the atemporal as opposed to the temporal, it involves, as the origin and ground of human consciousness, the simultaneous, mutual constitution of sameness and difference. In the originating act, the knowing subject and the known object are simultaneously held apart as different and held together as the same. This atemporal act of origination is a continuing act: it brings man and language into existence, and it holds them in existence. The originating ground reveals itself, then, as that really absent but virtually present totality of language that by its absence allows, and by its virtual presence underpins, the real presence of the individual, partial act of language (symbolization) in time.

The continuous network of differential oppositions establishes man in an essentially mediate, relational condition between the poles of primal dualities (left/right, up/down, light/dark, and so on), poles that, because they are mutually constitutive, are always conceptually implicit in their opposites. Yet in his quest for self-definition, for the absolute limits of self-consciousness, man attempts to transcend his relational condition, to leave his position between the polar opposites and, by journeying to one extreme or the other, to establish an absolute upper or lower limit through an ascent into the sublime or a descent into the abyss. Both poles are, however, simultaneously the sublime and the abyss, for what one seeks in moving toward one polar opposite or the other, is to transcend the mediate and reach that unmediated ground where the bipolar oppositions of language are fused, to reach that totality of undifferentiated Being that, because it is without differentiation, can only be experienced as a kind of nothingness—a sublime that is an abyss.

In dealing with the question of the origin of language, as he inherited it from the English Romantics and the German Idealists, Poe makes his most perceptive and original use of the symbol of the hieroglyphs. And certainly anyone familiar with Poe's work will already have recognized one of his recurring scenarios in the image of a polar journey that becomes a descent into the abyss.

To understand the way that Poe uses the hieroglyphics in treating the question of the origin of language, we must begin by considering three related "hieroglyphical" methods of interpreting physical shapes—signature analysis, physiognomy, and phrenology. Each represents a means of reading "character"—by the shape of a man's handwriting, by the shape of his body and the features of his face, and by the configuration of his skull. Each of these methods of "reading" assumes that outer shape reflects inner meaning, that the reflection or correspondence, once transparent, is now hidden, and that consequently the reading in which each method engages is really the deciphering of a cryptographic script. Thus Poe's interest in ciphers, apparent in works like "The Gold Bug" and "Cryptography," merges with his interest in the analysis of signatures, facial features, and shapes of skulls.

Believing that "the soul is a cipher, in the sense of a cryptograph," Poe attempts in "Autography" to interpret the cryptographic characters of contemporary literary figures through an analysis of their signatures, while in "The Literati of New York City," he reads human character by using phrenology and physiognomy to decipher significant bodily features. He notes of the editor Evert A. Duyckinck that his "forehead, phrenologically, is a good one" (15:60), and of Professor George Bush that "his countenance expresses rather benevolence and profound earnestness than high intelligence. The eyes are piercing; the other features, in general, massive. The forehead, phrenologically, indicates causality and comparison, with deficient ideality—the organization which induces strict logicality from insufficient premises" (15:7). In the essay on Freeman Hunt, he describes Hunt's chin as "massive and projecting, indicative (according to Lavater and general experience) of that energy which is, in fact, the chief point of his character" (15:43). Lavater is, of course, Johann Kaspar Lavater (1741–1801), the author of *Physiognomische Fragmente, zur Beförderung der Menschenkenntniss und Menschenliebe* (1775).

As methods of reading "hieroglyphic" writing, physiognomy, phrenology, and the analysis of signatures all have a double application: though they originally pertained to the analysis of human forms, they can by analogy be applied to physical nature as well. In *Cosmos*, Alexander von Humboldt remarks, "Notwithstanding a certain freedom of development of the several parts, the primitive force of organization binds all animal and vegetable forms to fixed and constantly-recurring types, determining, in every zone, the character that peculiarly appertains to it, or *the physiognomy of nature*" (2:105). Humboldt notes that there is also a "physiognomy" of languages:

> Languages, as intellectual creations of man, and as closely interwoven with the development of his mind, are, independently of the *natural* form which they exhibit, of the greatest importance in the recognition of similarities or differences in races. This importance is especially owing to the clew which a community of descent affords in treading that mysterious labyrinth in which the connection of physical powers and intellectual forces manifests itself in a thousand different forms. The brilliant progress made within the last half century, in Germany, in philosophical philology, has greatly facilitated our investigations into the *national* character of languages and the influence exercised by descent. (1:357)

Just as Poe analyzes the characters of famous authors through their signatures, so there is also a long-standing tradition of reading the signatures in nature to grasp the character of its Author. Poe operates in an interesting variant of this tradition in *Eureka* when he discusses the physical shape of our galaxy. He points out that although the galaxy's shape is generally described in astronomical treatises as resembling "that of a capital Y," this is simply an effect of perspective. "In reality," he says, "the cluster in question has ... a certain general—*very* general resemblance to the planet Saturn, with its encompassing triple ring. Instead of the solid orb of that planet, however, we must picture to ourselves a lenticular star-island, or collection of stars; our Sun lying eccentrically— near the shore of the island—on that side of it which is nearest the constellation of the Cross and farthest from that of Cassiopeia. The surrounding ring, where it approaches our position, has in it a longitudinal *gash*, which does, in fact, cause *the ring, in our vicinity*, to assume, loosely, the appearance of a capital Y" (16:271).

The distinction between the shape of the galaxy as it is "in reality" (that is, for an omniscient observer without the limitations of a partial perspective) and the shape as it appears to man with his limited perspective on earth is a subtle expression of the epistemological dilemma that results when man tries to be simultaneously inside and outside the circle of his own knowledge, when he tries to use a subjective knowing process to test the objective accuracy of that knowledge. For what man has ever observed our galaxy, or anything else, from any but an individual, limited perspective? One is reminded of the famous passage in *Nature* where, looking at the starry heavens, Emerson confronts the "noble doubt" as to "whether nature outwardly exists":

> It is a sufficient account of that Appearance we call the World, that God will teach a human mind, and so makes it the receiver of a certain number of congruent sensations, which we call sun and moon, man and woman, house and trade. In my utter impotence to test the authenticity of the report of my senses, to know whether the impressions they make on me correspond with outlying objects, what difference does it make, whether Orion is up there in heaven, or some god paints the image in the firmament of my soul? The relations of parts and the end of the whole remaining the same, what is the difference, whether land and sea interact, and worlds revolve and intermingle without number or end,—deep yawning under deep, and galaxy balancing galaxy, throughout absolute space,—or whether, without relations of time and space, the same appearances are inscribed in the constant faith of man? Whether nature enjoy a substantial existence without, or is only in the apocalypse of the mind, it is alike useful and alike venerable to me. Be it what it may, it is ideal to me so long as I cannot try the accuracy of my senses. (1:47-48)

Since the whole point of the appearance of the world, according to Emerson, is to convey meaning (that is, morality) through physical shape, and since that meaningful shape is the same whether embodied in a real, external world from which we abstract it or imprinted directly on our minds by God, what difference does it make whether or not we can test the reliability of our senses and establish the objective existence of external nature? The point of nature is its use and design, not its substantial existence. One could, of course, reply that the question of whether or not the world really exists makes, literally, a world of difference. For if the design is directly imprinted on our minds, then the appearance that we call "the world" is an illusion and not that objective measure and common meeting ground of thought and language wherein men mediate their subjective, partial perspectives. Each man is locked in his own mind, unable to test the accuracy of his knowledge of the world. And if man's inquiries must all end in an act of faith, then those inquiries are pointless exercises. The "noble doubt" about "whether nature outwardly exists" haunted Emerson all his life, receiving its most complex statement in the late essay "Illusions," where Emerson's leap of faith becomes a somersault. This post-Kantian doubt of the certainty of knowledge inevitably raises questions about how one reads inner meaning from outer shape, questions that are "hieroglyphical" in nature, whether they pertain to pictographic writing or to the shapes of physical nature or to the form and features of the human body. And these basic questions of meaning inevitably turn out to be questions of origins and ends. From the time of the Romantic poets on, the investigation of man's linguistic relationship to the world frequently takes the form of literary works whose inquiry into the origin of their own written presence on the page is a synecdoche for the inquiry into the simultaneous origin of man and the world in the act of symbolization. It is this tradition of which Poe, in his most sophisticated use of the hieroglyphics, is very much the heir.

Poe's interests in the hieroglyphics, in physiognomy and phrenology, and in the question of origins all come together in a fairly simplified form in the humorous tale "Some Words with a Mummy" (1845). The narrator of the tale, having fallen asleep after an enormous dinner, is suddenly awakened by a message from his friend Doctor Ponnonner inviting him to be present at the unswathing of an Egyptian mummy belonging to the City Museum. The implication is that the awakening, invitation, and subsequent events at Ponnonner's are all part of the narrator's after-dinner dream. Like so many of Poe's tales, "Some Words with a Mummy" is purposely set in an epistemologically uncertain state between waking consciousness and the world of dreams and illusions. When the narrator arrives at his friend's home, he finds the mummy laid out on the dining room table. The mummy "was one of a pair brought, several years previously, by Captain Arthur Sabretash, a cousin of Ponnonner's, from a tomb near Eleithias, in the Lybian Mountains, a considerable distance above Thebes on the Nile" (6:117). Examining the mummy case, the narrator observes:

> It was thickly ornamented with paintings, representing funeral scenes, and other mournful subjects, interspersed among which in every variety of position, were certain series of hieroglyphical

characters intended, no doubt, for the name of the departed. By good luck, Mr. Gliddon formed one of our party; and he had no difficulty in translating the letters, which were simply phonetic, and represented the word, *Allamistakeo*. (6:118)

Undoubtedly, the narrator's "Mr. Gliddon" is George Gliddon, former American vice-consul at Cairo and popular lecturer on Egyptian antiquities. We know that Poe was familiar with Gliddon's work in Egypt. In his review of John Lloyd Stephens's *Incidents of Travel in Egypt, Arabia Petraea, and the Holy Land* (1837), published in the *New York Review* (October 1837), Poe mentions Gliddon's efforts as American consul to assist Stephens in his journey to Idumaea (10:19).

In having the fictionalized Gliddon translate the figures on the mummy case as the phonetic hieroglyphs of a proper name, Poe may well be alluding to Champollion's discovery of the key to the phonetic character of the hieroglyphics through the translation of Egyptian proper names. In this connection one thinks immediately of Poe's most famous tale of decipherment, "The Gold Bug" (1843), in which the key to the cipher is a phonetic hieroglyph of a proper name. In that tale Legrand, the decipherer of the code, notices that the scrap of parchment that his servant has found on the beach shows, when held to the fire, the figure of a death's-head in one corner and the figure of a goat in the other. Legrand interprets the death's-head as a pure pictograph, an ideogram for "pirate." He suddenly realizes, however, that the figure of the animal is not an ideogram but a phonetic sign, for the animal is not a goat but a kid. As he explains to his friend, "You may have heard of one *Captain* Kidd. I at once looked on the animal as a kind of punning or hieroglyphical signature. I say signature; because its position on the vellum suggested this idea. The death's-head at the corner diagonally opposite had, in the same manner, the air of a stamp, or seal" (5:128–29). This signature, a phonetic hieroglyph that stands not for the physical object "kid" but, by homonymy, for the proper name "Kidd," turns out to be the key to the cipher. Legrand explains: "In all cases of secret writing—the first question regards the *language* of the cipher; for the principles of solution, so far, especially, as the more simple ciphers are concerned, depend on, and are varied by, the genius of the particular idiom. In general, there is no alternative but experiment (directed by probabilities) of every tongue known to him who attempts the solution, until the true one be attained. But, with the cipher now before us, all difficulty is removed by the signature. The pun on the word 'Kidd' is appreciable in no other language than the English" (5:132).

The distinction between an ideogram and a phonetic hieroglyph that Poe emphasizes in "The Gold Bug" occurs again in "Some Words with a Mummy." The mummy, after the application of several electric shocks from a voltaic pile, is aroused from his cataleptic state. Whereupon Mr. Gliddon, acting as interpreter, speaks to him "in phonetics": "And but for the deficiency of American printing-offices in hieroglyphical type," the narrator adds, "it would afford me much pleasure to record here, in the original, the whole of his very excellent speech" (6:124). Although Gliddon speaks Egyptian as if it were his native tongue, there are certain modern concepts that he has difficulty in making the mummy understand, and he is "reduced, occasionally, to the employment of sensible forms for the purpose of conveying a particular meaning": "Mr. Gliddon, at one period, for example, could not make the Egyptian comprehend the term 'politics,' until he sketched upon the wall, with a bit of charcoal, a little carbuncle-nosed gentleman, out at elbows, standing upon a stump, with his left leg drawn back, his right arm thrown forward, with the fist shut, the eyes rolled up toward Heaven, and the mouth open at an angle of ninety degrees" (6:125).

So closely connected had the hieroglyphics become, since their decipherment, with the problem of Biblical chronology (and thus with the question of human origins) that the conversation with the mummy inevitably turns to the subject of the Creation. Doctor Ponnonner remarks, "Since it is quite clear . . . that at least five thousand years have elapsed since your entombment, I take it for granted that your histories at that period, if not your traditions, were sufficiently explicit on that one topic of universal interest, the Creation, which took place, as I presume you are aware, only about ten centuries before" (6:131). To which the astonished mummy replies: "The ideas you have suggested are to me, I confess, utterly novel. During my time I never knew any one to entertain so singular a fancy as that the universe (or this world if you will have it so) ever had a beginning at all. I remember, once, and once only, hearing something remotely hinted, by a man of many speculations, concerning the origin *of the human race;* and by this individual the very word *Adam,* (or Red Earth) which you make use of, was employed. He employed it, however, in a generical sense, with reference to the spontaneous germination from rank soil (just as a thousand of the lower *genera* of creatures are germinated)—the spontaneous germination, I say, of five vast hordes of men, simultaneously upspringing in five distinct and nearly equal divisions of the globe" (6:132).

Allamistakeo's reply is significant for a variety of reasons. First, he doubts that the question of an absolute origin applies to the universe at all. At any rate, man could have no possible experience of that origin. As to the origin of the human race, Allamistakeo approaches the question etymologically by recalling the roots of the original word for man— "Adam." The implication is that the origin of the word for man is in a sense the origin of man, that language constitutes human self-consciousness. Although Allamistakeo gives the root meaning of the word "Adam" (the Biblical proper name for the first man and the Hebrew generic name for man) as "Red Earth," he says that to his recollection the name was used only generically and not as the proper name of an individual. As posed by the narrator and his friends, the question of the origin of the human race assumes the priority of unity to multiplicity. But the mummy's account suggests the simultaneous constitution of the one by the many and the many by the one—a single human race created by "the spontaneous germination . . . of five vast hordes of men, simultaneously upspringing in five distinct and nearly equal divisions of the globe." Allamistakeo's reply subtly shifts the question of origin from a biological to an epistemological ground; that is, the question of recognizing an original human form is seen to be circumscribed by the more basic question of the origin of recognition itself, the origin of consciousness.

The Biblical story, of course, locates the origin of the human race in a single pair, whose sexual differentiation is God-given, and then accounts for the major physiognomic differences among races as the result of subsequent events, for example, the punishment of Ham. In raising the question of the mythical ancient seat of the human race in *Cosmos*, Alexander von Humboldt prefaced his remarks with a quotation from Johannes Müller's *Physiologie des Menschen* concerning differences in race:

> Families of animals and plants . . . undergo, within certain limitations peculiar to the different races and species, various modifications in their distribution over the surface of the earth, propagating these variations as organic types of species. . . . The

different races of mankind are forms of one sole species, by the union of two of whose members descendants are propagated. They are not different species of a genus, since in that case their hybrid descendants would remain unfruitful. But whether the human races have descended from several primitive races of men, or from one alone, is a question that can not be determined from experience.[10]

Humboldt seems to favor the theory of descent from several primitive races, but the importance of the general shape of the argument from our point of view is that the question of man's origin is phrased as a question of human self-recognition—the physiognomic differences among the various races of men versus the physiognomic similarity that distinguishes the human race. That is, the question of the origin of the human race quickly becomes a matter of reading the essential character of Man from the interplay of sameness and difference in the forms and features of the various races of men, thus suggesting that the true origin of Man, his distinguishing characteristic, is not to be found in a physiological form but in the very power of self-recognition. In this connection, it was particularly appropriate that Poe made George Gliddon a character in his tale, for besides his interest in Egyptology, Gliddon was an ethnologist deeply involved in the pre–Civil War controversy over the monogenetic and polygenetic theories of human origin. The controversy was fueled by the political question of whether certain races were inherently inferior and thus whether it was the right, and even the duty, of a superior race to subject and, if need be, to annihilate inferior races as the superior race worked out its manifest destiny. Proponents of the doctrine of the inherent racial inferiority of blacks and Indians tended to favor the theory of polygenesis as accounting for the original and ineradicable differences (inequalities) between races. The racist proponents of polygenesis were either nonbelievers who dismissed the Genesis account of man's origin as mythic or believers who interpreted the Genesis account as the description of only one of several different human creations, that is, the creation of the Caucasian race—the only race to which pertained the full dignity of humanity as described in Genesis.

In 1854 Gliddon collaborated with Dr. Josiah Nott of Mobile, a noted defender of slavery, polygenesis, and racial inequality, on the popular *Types of Mankind.* Part of the book's argument for polygenesis was based on the evidence of cranial differences among races. Nott was a follower of Samuel G. Morton, one of the most prominent American ethnologists of the day. In 1839 Morton had published *Crania Americana; or, A Comparative View of the Skulls of Various Aboriginal Nations of North and South America. To Which is Prefixed an Essay on the Varieties of the Human Species.* Morton had established in Philadelphia "the world's largest scientific collection of human skulls. Comparing cranial size, capacity, and structure, he posited the existence of races that had always been distinct from physical, not environmental causes. By the end of the 1840s, he contended that there had been various human creations, in different parts of the world."[11] George Combe, the noted phrenologist, wrote an essay on the principles of his science as an appendix to *Crania Americana,* and throughout the monogenesis/polygenesis controversy, phrenology played a part in the analysis of an "original" racial inequality. Thus in Poe's tale the inquiry into human origins leads to a discussion of the phrenological differences between the mummy and his nineteenth-century examiners. After "glancing slightly at the occiput and then at the sinciput of Allamistakeo," Mr. Silk Buckingham ventures "to attribute the marked inferiority of the old Egyptians in all particulars of science, when compared with the moderns, and more especially with the Yankees, altogether to the superior solidity of the Egyptian skull" (6:132). Puzzled by this remark, Allamistakeo asks to what "particulars of science" he refers, and the "whole party, joining voices" detail "at great length the assumptions of phrenology and the marvels of animal magnetism" (6:133). Allamistakeo replies with "a few anecdotes" that make it "evident that prototypes of Gall and Spurzheim had flourished and faded in Egypt so long ago as to have been forgotten" (6:133). The comic technique of the tale is a variation of the battle of the ancients and the moderns. The proudest achievements of the nineteenth century are described by Allamistakeo's questioners as proof of the superiority of the modern American to the ancient Egyptian; but in each case Allamistakeo shows that not only were the moderns anticipated by the ancients in these achievements but that the ancients carried them to even higher levels of accomplishment, so that in comparison the moderns are not only unoriginal but inferior.

The elements of the tale and the structure governing the way in which those elements are combined and transformed here and in related stories can be summarized in this way: If one begins with the image of hieroglyphic writing and the problem of deciphering an inner, hidden meaning from an outer, visible shape by means of a necessary though obscure correspondence between the two, then one is immediately led to the questions of how and why that necessary correspondence became obscure, which in turn leads to the question of the development of writing from its origins, and thus to the origin of language. As the hieroglyphical problem of the relationship between outer shape and inner meaning becomes the question of the origin of man and language, the image of "writing" expands until all physical shapes become obscurely meaningful forms of script, forms of hieroglyphic writing each of which has its own science of decipherment—signature analysis, physiognomy, phrenology, fingerprint analysis, zoology, botany, geology, and so on. If, on the other hand, one starts the scenario with the question of origins, then one main form taken by that inquiry is a movement back through the history of language to discover the original names, to trace words to their etymological roots in order to find the link (either necessary or arbitrary, pictographic or phonetic, depending on the tradition) that originally bound a name to its object, back to that originary act of naming (symbolization) that separated man from the world, the subject from the object.

The attempt to discover the origin of man through language inevitably leads to the hieroglyphics, to that basic form of signification in which the physical shape of the sign is taken directly from—indeed, is like the shadow of—the physical shape of the object that it stands for. For the writers of the American Renaissance, the hieroglyphics and the question of man's origin are implicit in one another; if you start with one, sooner or later you will be led to the other. Furthermore, because in pictographic writing the shape of a sign is in a sense a double of the physical shape of the object it represents, like a shadow or a mirror image, the essays and stories from this period dealing with the hieroglyphics and human origins are always, in one way or another, "double" stories.

Although we can have no direct knowledge of the simultaneous origin of man and language, for many of these writers it was an appealing, indeed a compelling, myth to imagine that origin as a form of "hieroglyphic" doubling in which a prelinguistic creature saw the outline of his shadow on the ground or his reflection in water and experienced both the revelation of human self-consciousness (the differentiated existence of self and world) and the revelation of language, the sudden understanding that his shadow or reflection was a double of himself and yet *not* himself, that it was somehow separate and thus could serve as a substitute that would by its shape evoke recognition of what it stood in place of. This reflexive doubling, then, would be that mutually constitutive act of origination in which the self recognizes its image as at once the same and different, itself and other, and at the same time constitutes itself (that is, unifies, delimits itself) by that very act of recognizing the discrete image as an image of the self. Inasmuch as all human knowledge is a more or less arbitrary unification of experience from the limited perspective of a knowing subject, and inasmuch as all man's ideas of unity ultimately derive from the unity of the human body, the process of knowledge is in a sense man's discovery of the hieroglyphical outline of his shadow on the world, that image of organic unity derived from the limits of his own body that he projects on the world in order to render it intelligible. As Emerson says in *Nature,* "One after another his victorious thought comes up with and reduces all things, until the world becomes at last only a realized will,—the double of the man" (1:40).

Significantly enough, one of the oldest legends of the origin of painting concerns the tracing of the outline of a shadow. In his *Natural History,* the elder Pliny notes that although the geographic "origin of the art of painting is uncertain . . . , all agree that it began with tracing an outline round a man's shadow and consequently that pictures were originally done in this way."[12] Later, in discussing the origin of sculpture, Pliny elaborates on this legend: "[the] modelling [of] portraits from clay was first invented by Butades, a potter of Sicyon, at Corinth. He did this owing to his daughter, who was in love with a young man; and she, when he was going abroad, drew in outline on the wall the shadow of his face thrown by the lamp. Her father pressed clay on this and made a relief, which he hardened by exposure to fire with the rest of his pottery" (9:372–73). As Robert Rosenblum has pointed out, the legend of the Corinthian maid Dibutade, which was recounted in art treatises from the Renaissance to the eighteenth century, appearing in works as various as Leonardo's *Trattato,* Vasari's *Proemio delle Vite,* Diderot's *Encyclopédie,* and d'Origny's *Dictionnaire des origines,* suddenly became, during the fifty-year period from the 1770s to the 1820s, the subject of scores of paintings, drawings, and engravings by European artists like Runciman, Wright of Derby, Girodet, Suvée, and Daumier.

Of particular significance is the connection between this sudden interest in the legend of Dibutade and the beginning of the science of physiognomy and the art of silhouette making. Rosenblum notes:

> The invention and flourishing of the silhouette . . . corresponded to the very years in which the Corinthian maid rose to prominence. . . . In the case of Girodet, a familiarity with the silhouette was more than casual, for his knowledge of Johann Caspar Lavater's physiognomical studies is well documented. But more broadly speaking, the analogy between the silhouette and the legendary antique origin of painting was easily made. In Henry Fuseli's Lectures to the Royal Academy of 1801, for example, the Anglo-Swiss master remarks first how ". . . the amorous tale of the Corinthian maid, who traced the shade of her departing lover by the secret lamp, appeals to our sympathy, to grant it," and then goes on to tell us that "the first essays of the art [painting] were skiagrams, simple outlines of a shade, similar to those which have been introduced to vulgar use by the students and parasites of Physiognomy, under the name of Silhouettes."[13]

Indeed, Lavater himself had suggested that drawing and painting probably originated with the making of shadow outlines or silhouettes.[14] And Winckelmann believed that "the earliest essays, especially in the drawing of figures, have represented, not the manner in which a man appears to us, but what he is; not a view of his body, but the outline of his shadow."[15]

It was not accidental that the renewed artistic interest in the legend of Dibutade and the beginning of the art of silhouette making coincided with the renewed interest in Egyptian art and the hieroglyphics, for all of these were part of "the period's general fascination with a flat, linear style." And it requires no great imaginative leap to see in the tracing of a human shadow outline not only the origin of painting and drawing but the origin of pictographic writing as well, to see that origin as an act of hieroglyphic doubling in which the outline in its fixed presence continues to stand for the object that cast the shadow after both the shadow and the object are absent. Rosenblum points out that the legend of Dibutade was often connected by artists of the period with the legend of Pygmalion and Galatea, for here, "in another erotic Greek myth, a comparable theme—the magical identity of a mimetic image with the object imitated—is encountered, although the situation is, of course, reversed"

(p. 285). In the legend of Dibutade, a woman makes an image of her lover to keep with her during his absence, while in the legend of Pygmalion and Galatea a man makes an image of an ideal woman, falls in love with the image, and then finds that image transformed into a real woman because of his love. These two legends, along with the two main variants of the legend of Narcissus (in Ovid's version he falls in love with his own image in the water; in Pausanias's version he takes the image to be that of his dead, beloved twin sister), form a central Romantic image complex in which the origin of art—of symbolization or representation— is depicted as a form of hieroglyphic doubling.

Section 5
Ends and Origins: The Voyage to the Polar Abyss and the Journey to the Source of the Nile; The Survival of the Manuscript

A myth of hieroglyphic doubling as the simultaneous origin of man and language structures Poe's most subtle transformation of the symbol of the hieroglyphics, the (trans)figuration that forms the ending of the *Narrative of A. Gordon Pym* (1838). In order to understand the puzzling conclusion that Poe has provided for his longest narrative fiction, we must read that conclusion in relation to other Poe tales that bear structural affinities with it. The most obviously related of these is "MS. Found in a Bottle" (1833) which, like the ending of *Pym*, concerns the narrator's voyage to the South Pole, a voyage that becomes a descent into the polar abyss.

The narrator of "MS. Found in a Bottle," journeying by ship from Java to the Sunda Islands, is caught in a sudden storm that wrecks the vessel and leaves him and an old Swede as the only survivors on board the drifting hulk. For five days the ship and its two passengers are driven southward into an area of "pitchy darkness" where they are surrounded by "horror, and thick gloom, and a black sweltering desert of ebony" (2:6). The ocean is churned into huge billows and troughs, and while the wreck is "at the bottom of one of these abysses," the narrator sees a "gigantic ship ... upreared upon the summit of a wave more than a hundred times her own altitude. ... For a moment of intense terror she paused upon the giddy pinnacle, as if in contemplation of her own sublimity, then trembled and tottered, and—came down" (2:7). The ships collide, and the narrator is hurled from the wreck into the rigging of the strange vessel. The narrator's first impulse is to conceal himself from the crew; but soon he discovers that concealment is pointless, for the crew are simply unable to see him. On board this ghost ship the narrator is carried still farther southward "within the influence of some strong current, or impetuous under-tow" (2:12). As the ship nears the pole, it is enveloped by "the blackness of eternal night, and a chaos of foamless water" (2:13) evocative of the descent into the abyss as a return to the primal origin. Though the narrator is appalled by the thought of his approaching destruction, he admits that "a curiosity to penetrate the mysteries of these awful regions, predominates even over my despair, and will reconcile me to the most hideous aspect of death. It is evident that we are hurrying onwards to some exciting knowledge—some never-to-be-imparted secret, whose attainment is destruction. Perhaps this current leads us to the southern pole itself" (2:14).

Earlier in the manuscript, the narrator's unwilling voyage toward this "never-to-be-imparted secret" had been implicitly associated with the act of writing: while sitting on deck "musing upon the singularity" of his fate, the narrator "unwittingly daubed with a tar-brush the edges of a neatly-folded studding-sail" only to find, when the sail was raised, that "the thoughtless touches of the brush" spelled "the word DISCOVERY" (2:10). When the narrator's ship reaches the pole, it is catapulted into a gigantic whirlpool, and the manuscript breaks off just as the ship is going down. In a concluding footnote on the polar abyss, Poe says, "The 'MS. Found in a Bottle,' was originally published in 1831 [1833], and it was not until many years afterwards that I became acquainted with the maps of Mercator, in which the ocean is represented as rushing, by four mouths, into the (northern) Polar Gulf, to be absorbed into the bowels of the earth; the Pole itself being represented by a black rock, towering to a prodigious height" (2:15).

In "The Unparalleled Adventure of One Hans Pfaall" (1835), the narrator's lunar ascent in a balloon, in comic counterpoint to the descent into the abyss, carries him over the North Pole. As Pfaall approaches the pole, he sees at a distance "a thin, white, and exceedingly brilliant line, or streak, on the edge of the horizon," which he takes to be "the southern disc of the ices of the Polar sea," and as he looks at the water beneath him, he notes that the "convexity of the ocean had become so evident, that the entire mass of the distant water seemed to be tumbling headlong over the abyss of the horizon, and I found myself listening on tiptoe for the echoes of the mighty cataract" (2:85–86). When the balloon passes directly over the pole, the narrator observes:

> Northwardly from that huge rim before mentioned, and which, with slight qualification, may be called the limit of human discovery in these regions, one unbroken, or nearly unbroken sheet of ice continues to extend. In the first few degrees of this its progress, its surface is very sensibly flattened, farther on depressed into a plane, and finally, becoming *not a little concave,* it terminates, at the Pole itself, in a circular centre, sharply defined, whose apparent diameter subtended at the balloon an angle of about sixty-five seconds, and whose dusky hue, varying in intensity, was at all times darker than any other spot upon the visible hemisphere, and occasionally deepened into the most absolute blackness. Farther than this, little could be ascertained. (2:88–89).

From "MS. Found in a Bottle" and "Hans Pfaall" we can abstract some of the common features of Poe's description of the polar regions and the abyss—features that he later combined with the symbol of the hieroglyphics to form the conclusion of *Pym.* First, the polar region represents an absolute "limit of human discovery"; it is an area of ultimate knowledge where one learns "some never-to-be-imparted secret, whose attainment is destruction." Second, it is an area where mediation breaks down, a region where the polar opposites have grown so far apart that they can no longer be compared and as a result become indistinguishable. Thus the polar region, though composed of the unrelieved whiteness of ice, snow, and mist, is experienced by the narrator of "MS. Found in a Bottle" as "the blackness of eternal night," while the polar abyss as seen from above by Hans Pfaall is "the most absolute blackness." Third, the Pole itself is an abyss descending into the center of the earth, and the entrance to that abyss is represented as a cataract leading to a whirlpool.

In Poe's other great tale of the whirlpool/abyss, "A Descent into the Maelström" (1841), many of these same descriptive elements are present along with significant additions. In this tale the abyss is not at the pole but off the coast of Norway. As the narrator of "A Descent" looks down from his perch on the mountaintop, he sees "a wide expanse of ocean, whose waters wore so inky a hue as to bring at once to my mind the Nubian geographer's account of the *Mare Tenebrarum*" (2:226–27). (One is reminded by this reference to the *Mare Tenebrarum* that the imaginary letter from the future that Poe quotes at the beginning of *Eureka*—the same letter in which Champollion is presented as an example of the intuitive decipherer—is said "to have been found corked in a bottle and floating on the *Mare Tenebrarum*—an ocean well described by the Nubian geographer, Ptolemy Hephestion, but little frequented in modern days unless by the Transcendentalists and some other divers for crotchets" [16:187–88]. Indeed, what better place than the Sea of Shadows for that narcissistic act of knowledge in which one orders the inchoate ocean of the phenomenal world by casting upon it the shadow of a unified body.)

As the circulation of the maelstrom develops, the narrator describes its interior as "a smooth, shining, and jet-black wall of water" that in its circular movement sends "forth to the winds an appalling voice, half shriek, half roar, such as not even the mighty cataract at Niagara ever lifts up in its agony to Heaven" (2:220). Canvassing the various explanations for the whirlpool, he says:

> The idea generally received is that this, as well as the three smaller vortices among the Feroe Islands, "have no other cause than the collision of waves rising and falling, at flux and reflux, against a ridge of rocks and shelves, which confines the water so that it precipitates itself like a cataract; and thus the higher the flood rises, the deeper must the fall be, and the natural result of all is a whirlpool or vortex, the prodigious suction of which is sufficiently known by lesser experiments."—These are the words of the *Encyclopaedia Britannica*. Kircher and others imagine that in the centre of the channel of the Maelström is an abyss penetrating the globe, and issuing in some very remote part—the Gulf of Bothnia being somewhat decidedly named in one instance. This opinion, idle in itself, was the one to which, as I gazed, my imagination most readily assented. . . . (2:232)

The narrator's guide, a Norwegian fisherman, tells how he and his two brothers were out in their boat one day when a sudden storm, like the one that struck the ship in "MS. Found in a Bottle," drove the vessel into the maelstrom. At first he was terrified, but then, having made up his mind to hope no more, he says: "I became possessed with the keenest curiosity about the whirl itself. I positively felt a *wish* to explore its depths, even at the sacrifice I was going to make; and my principal grief was that I should never be able to tell my old companions on shore about the mysteries I should see" (2:240). Like the narrator of "MS. Found in a Bottle," the fisherman knows that the price of that ultimate knowledge of the abyss is death and consequently that what one discovers is a "never-to-be-imparted secret." But where the narrator of the earlier tale is carried down into the abyss without being able to impart his discovery, the fisherman escapes from the abyss without ever learning its secret: he says that even though the "rays of the moon seemed to search the very bottom of the profound gulf; . . . still I could make out nothing distinctly, on account of a thick mist in which everything there was enveloped, and over which there hung a magnificent rainbow, like that narrow and tottering bridge which Mussulmen say is the only pathway between Time and Eternity (2:242–43). Yet the fisherman's close encounter with the absolute has worked a profound and emblematic change on his person. He tells the narrator, "The six hours of deadly terror which I . . . endured have broken me up body and soul. You suppose me a *very* old man—but I am not. It took less than a single day to change these hairs from a jetty black to white, to weaken my limbs, and to unstring my nerves, so that I tremble at the least exertion, and am frightened at a shadow" (2:225). As the abyss represents the dissolution of mediation in the absolute, so the fisherman's brush with the abyss leaves its mark on him as a confounding of mediation: though the inside of the abyss is a "jet-black wall of water," in a single day it changes the color of the fisherman's hair from "a jetty black to white," a reversal that suggests the way that bipolar opposites (like diametrically opposed points on a wheel) change places, merge, and finally vanish within the rapidly spinning vortex of the absolute.

Linguistic mediation, considered as simply the ability to communicate, is likewise disrupted by the fisherman's encounter with the abyss. Rescued from the sea by some of his friends, he is at first "speechless from the memory of its horror," but beyond that, his physical appearance has been so radically altered by the experience that his features no longer communicate his identity. His friends know him "no more than they would have known a traveller from the spirit-land," for "the whole expression" of his "countenance had changed" (2:247). More disconcerting still, when he regains his speech and tells his friends the story, they refuse to believe him. The fisherman says to the narrator, "I now tell it to *you*—and I can scarcely expect you to put more faith in it than did the

merry fishermen of Lofoden" (2:247). The fisherman has come close
enough to the unspeakable "mysteries" of the abyss for some of their
incommunicability to rub off on his narrative, an incommunicability that
involves, not the dissolution of language or its failure to convey meaning,
but its failure to convey credibility. As the direct confrontation with the
absolute means the ontological undoing of narrator and narrative, so the
mere vicinity of the absolute brings about their logical undoing, the
dissolution of the logical status of discourse.

The essential precariousness, both logical and ontological, of the narrative act is one of Poe's continuing themes, a theme that is especially
evident in a tale such as "MS. Found in a Bottle." The title immediately
directs the reader's attention to the question of the tale's written presence and to the problem of its origin; for if the tale is the narrative of a
voyage that led to "some never-to-be-imparted secret, whose attainment
is destruction," then it is only logical to inquire how the written narrative
returned from a voyage of discovery that neither the narrator nor anyone else survived. The tale obligingly provides the explanation, a fiction
of its own origin as writing, and thus, by implication, raises the question
of the origin of writing itself. The narrator says, "It was no long while
ago that I ventured into the captain's own private cabin, and took thence
the materials with which I write, and have written. I shall from time to
time continue this journal. It is true that I may not find an opportunity
of transmitting it to the world, but I will not fail to make the endeavour.
At the last moment I will enclose the MS. in a bottle, and cast it within the
sea" (2:9–10). Since the manuscript is to be cast into the sea "at the last
moment," the narrative that the manuscript contains must break off
before that moment. The very mechanics of written narration—the
necessity to interrupt the text before the moment of ultimate discovery
in order to dispatch it before the destruction of the narrator—excludes
the written narrative from any access to the absolute.

One is tempted to speculate that the manuscript's fictive origin in the
theft of writing materials from "the captain's own private cabin" is meant
to evoke the invention of writing as a transgression against the father,
the Promethean theft of the father's stylus and the virgin sheet. This
sense of writing's origin as an act of transgression accords with the
mechanics of inscription; for as Emerson remarks in *Nature*, the original,
"concrete" meaning of *transgression* was "the crossing of a *line*," and it is
precisely the crossing of lines, both vertical and horizontal, that forms

one of the differential oppositions constituting the physical presence of writing. Moreover, in Poe the precariousness of narration is characteristically associated with the crossing of previously uncrossed lines in search of an ultimate knowledge. Poe's most explicit references to the possibility of the narrative's permanent interruption or its total loss (its nonexistence for the reader) occur in tales of journeys to unexplored regions, regions that had previously formed the "limit of human knowledge." Thus the narrator of "Hans Pfaall," after one of his narrow escapes from accidental death during his trip to the moon, considers what the fate of his narrative would have been if the circumstances of the accident had been slightly different, and he concludes that "the disclosures now made would have been utterly lost to posterity" (2:59). The crossing of the line between the known and the unknown territories carries with it a sense of the overreaching of human limitations, as if, in the case of the quest for origin, man attempted to confront a forbidden primal scene. The womblike abyss that is the goal of so many of Poe's voyagers bears an Oedipal prohibition.

The Poe tales that raise the dual question of their own written origin and the origin of language pose at the same time the question of personal originality. For these narratives of discovery inevitably concern "the first man," whether he be the first man to reach the moon, the first to discover the South Pole, the first to survive the maelstrom, or, as in the unfinished tale *The Journal of Julius Rodman* (1840), the first civilized man to cross the Rocky Mountains. Poe's fictive editor remarks of Rodman's journal that it "not only embodies a relation of *the first* successful attempt to cross the gigantic barriers of that immense chain of mountains which stretches from the Polar Sea in the north, to the Isthmus of Darien in the south, ... but, what is of still greater importance, gives the particulars of a tour, beyond these mountains, through an immense extent of territory which, *at this day,* is looked upon as totally untravelled and unknown, and which, in every map of the country to which we can obtain access, is marked as '*an unexplored region.*' It is, moreover, the *only* unexplored region within the limits of the continent of North America" (4:9–10).

The notion of "the first man" to reach the South Pole or the first civilized man to cross the Rockies means, of course, the first to make the discovery and return to tell the tale (either in person or in a written narrative, if he is physically unable to return), the first to inscribe the discovery in the written narrative of history. It is writing, then, that constitutes the *originality* of the first man to enter an unknown region, whether that writing is an inscription left on a rock or tree to mark the place and time of discovery or a journal of the expedition brought back to civilization or a narrative written after the explorer's return.

One of the principal activities of the first man to discover a new region is the same as that of the mythic first man in the garden of Eden—to name things as yet unnamed. In *The Journal of Julius Rodman,* the territory under exploration is described as a garden world (4:44), a "terrestrial Paradise" (4:45); and one of the major tasks of Rodman's expedition is to record the landmarks of the region and to name any new species of plant and animal life encountered on the journey. This work of naming, whereby physical nature is translated into phonetic signs, is possible only because nature already possesses a linguistic structure, the structure of a picture language projected upon the world in the mythic originary act of symbolization, of knowledge.

In their journey up the Missouri, Rodman and his party are suddenly brought face to face with the image of nature as man's pictographic double, the image of natural shapes as hieroglyphic writing. Passing a series of cliffs along the river bank, they sight "a high wall of black rock on the south, towering above the ordinary cliffs for about a quarter of a mile along the stream," then, after passing an open plain, "another wall of a light color on the same side," and then, after another open plain, "still another wall of the most singular appearance arises on the north, soaring in height probably two hundred and fifty feet, and being in thickness about twelve, with a very regular artificial character" (4:90). The cliffs on the north bank "are composed of very white soft sandstone, which readily receives the impression of water" (4:90). Rodman notes:

> The face of these remarkable cliffs, as might be supposed, is chequered with a variety of lines formed by the trickling of the rains upon the soft material, so that a fertile fancy might easily imagine them to be gigantic monuments reared by human art, and carved over with hieroglyphical devices. Sometimes there are complete niches (like those we see for statues in common temples) formed by the dropping out bodily of large fragments of sandstone; and there are several points where staircases and long corridors appear.... We passed these singular bluffs in a bright moonlight and their

effect upon my imagination I shall never forget. They had all the air
of enchanted structures, (such as I have dreamed of,). . . . Besides
the main walls there are, at intervals, inferior ones, of from twenty
to a hundred feet high. . . . These are formed of a succession of
large black-looking stones, apparently made up of loam, sand, and
quartz, and absolutely symmetrical in figure . . . , lying one above the
other as exactly and with as perfect regularity as if placed there by
some mortal mason. . . . We regarded the scenery presented to our
view at this portion of the Missouri as altogether the most surprising, if not the most beautiful, which we had yet seen. (4:91–92).

The imagery of "gigantic monuments," "hieroglyphical devices,"
"niches (like those we see for statues in common temples)," "staircases
and long corridors" transforms an account of the rocky cliffs of the
Missouri River into a description of a temple carved out of rock along
the Nile. The analogy between the Nile and the Mississippi/Missouri was
a commonplace in nineteenth-century America, as indicated by the
names of river towns like Memphis, Tennessee (founded in 1819) and
Cairo, Illinois (first settled in 1818 and then resettled in 1837) and by the
name of the wedge-shaped area at the confluence of the Mississippi and
Ohio rivers—"Little Egypt."

Poe's description of the eroded, "hieroglyphic" banks of the Missouri
is part of a tradition of descriptions of natural writing that includes
Thoreau's hieroglyphic musings on the erosion of the sandbank in *Walden* and Emerson's contention in the essay on Goethe that "All things are
engaged in writing their history. The planet, the pebble, goes attended
by its shadow. The rolling rock leaves its scratches on the mountain; the
river its channel in the soil; the animal its bones in the stratum; the fern
and leaf their modest epitaph in the coal. The falling drop makes its
sculpture in the sand or stone"—descriptions that present this writing as
the inscribed record of the natural history of the world, a geo-logic story
of origins and thus a kind of "historical" writing whose counterpart is the
historical narratives of the first men to discover these phenomena. In
Rodman's account the correlation between the phonetic writing of
human history and the hieroglyphic writing of natural history is
suggested by the black/white imagery in the description of the cliffs, for
just as the crossing of vertical and horizontal lines is one bipolar opposition that grounds writing, so the differentiation of black and white is

another. Differentiation involves, of course, a reciprocal act in which two entities are held apart by being held together and are held together by being held apart, in which the two can be seen as different only because there is at least one sense in which they can be seen as the same. Rodman's description of the hieroglyphic cliffs begins with the geo-graphic separation of black and white: first, "a high wall of black rock on the south," then the space of an intervening plain (a distance of some three miles), and then "another wall of a light color on the same side." This is immediately followed by the juxtaposition of black and white: on the north bank are a series of cliffs "composed of very white soft sandstone" with "inferior walls" of "large black-looking stones . . . absolutely symmetrical in figure . . . , as if placed there by some mortal mason," appearing "at intervals" in the white sandstone bank. This interplay of black and white also evokes that original differentiation of light and dark that, according to Genesis, began the orderly work of creation.

What differentiation demands is a humanly perceptible dividing line, an edge. Considered spatially, that dividing line involves the juxtaposition or superimposition of the differentiated entities; while considered temporally, the dividing line involves an oscillation, a scanning back and forth between those entities and across the edge of difference. Yet if the entities cannot both be present to human perception at the same time—either because they naturally alternate in time or because they must be made to alternate in time (their magnitudes being such that either entity exhausts the limits of individual perception, so that the perceiver must physically relocate himself in order to cross the dividing line and confront the other entity at a different time)—then differentiation becomes primarily a matter of temporal oscillation, and the rhythm of that oscillation must itself be within the limits of human perception (neither so fast as to be imperceptible to the senses nor so slow as to be beyond the limits of memory or of a single lifetime). Poe chooses the polar region as the scene for the breakdown of linguistic mediation not only because it is an area where the unrelieved whiteness of ice and snow can literally blind a man, thus obliterating color differentiation, but also because it is an area where the rhythmic oscillation of dark and light begins to collapse, slowing down and separating into extended periods of daylight and darkness. The breakdown of black/white differentiation reaches a problematic extreme at the end of the *Narrative of A. Gordon Pym* in the geo-graphic separation of the island of Tsalal (where nothing white is to be found) from the polar realm of Tekeli-li (where nothing is to be found that is not white).

Before discussing *Pym* and the significance of the separation of Tsalal and Tekeli-li, we must look once more at the passage in Rodman's journal describing the hieroglyphic cliffs along the Missouri, for that passage brings together a number of images that are related to the trope of the hieroglyphics and that form a complex background to the ending of *Pym*. The passage in Rodman's journal describing the hieroglyphic cliffs is based, as are most of the geographical descriptions in the tale, on the journals of the Lewis and Clark expedition. These journals, edited by Paul Allen, were published in 1814 in Philadelphia under the title *History of the Expedition Under the Command of Captains Lewis and Clark, to the Sources of the Missouri, Thence Across the Rocky Mountains and Down the Columbia River to the Pacific Ocean.* The whole point, however, of the elaborate fiction of Rodman's journal is to establish his priority to Lewis and Clark, for Rodman's fictive exploration of the Missouri (1791–94) antedated the Lewis and Clark expedition (1804–06) by more than ten years; but because Rodman's journal was lost and remained unpublished until almost fifty years later, Lewis and Clark were credited with being the first civilized men to explore the region. Clearly, in this tale "originality" is understood to be a function of the written narrative's successful journey back to civilization and into print. In a brief account of the life of Meriwether Lewis prefacing the Allen edition of the journals, Thomas Jefferson quotes the written instructions that he gave Lewis for the journey, instructions that emphasized the precautions Lewis was to take in order to insure that the journals of the expedition returned safely, lest, as Jefferson warned, "in the loss of yourselves we should lose also the information you will have acquired."[16]

Poe's alterations of the passage from the Lewis and Clark journals describing the eroded cliffs of the Missouri give some indication of his intentions. In the Lewis and Clark account, the cliffs are described as "rising pyramidally over each other till they terminate in a sharp point" (1:238–39). Though the word "pyramidally" in the authentic account suggests the image of Egyptian architecture, it is Poe who adds the detail that the eroded cliffs looked as if they were "carved over with hieroglyphical devices" and who thus imposes the image of natural writing on the scene. Among other changes, Poe alters the time of day at which the cliffs are sighted. Lewis and Clark passed the cliffs in broad daylight; but

Rodman's party passes them "in a bright moonlight," and Rodman notes their unforgettable effect on his imagination, their "air of enchanted structures, (such as I have dreamed of)." Earlier, Rodman had commented on the way that the eroded cliffs engaged the imagination, so that "a fertile fancy" could see in them a work of human art rather than of nature. In a traditional Romantic image, Poe evokes the projective, transfiguring power of the imagination through the transfiguring power of moonlight. Echoing the Coleridgean sense of the imagination as both the power in search of origins and the continuing ground of personal originality, Poe adds the final detail that the hieroglyphic cliffs left upon Rodman's "mind an impression of novelty—of singularity, which can never be effaced" (4:92)—"novelty" being one of Poe's favorite terms to describe the effect of the imaginative sublime.

Since *The Journal of Julius Rodman* was never completed, we can only speculate about its final shape and its relationship to *Pym,* published two years earlier. Yet these speculations can take authorial direction from the fact that the completed portion of the tale was closely based on Allen's edition of the Lewis and Clark journals. Thus although the fictitious editor of Rodman's journal presents it as primarily an account of the crossing of the Rockies, it is, more accurately, an account of a journey to discover the origin of a great river, as the title of Allen's edition makes clear (*History of the Expedition . . . to the Sources of the Missouri . . .*). The crossing of the Rockies was only incidental to the primary purpose of the Lewis and Clark expedition, which was to explore the principal river leading into the new territory and then to find the best land portage route to the principal river leading to the Pacific Ocean.

In his introduction to the Allen edition, Jefferson recounts his first attempt to have the region explored. During his residence in Paris, Jefferson encountered "John Ledyard, of Connecticut," who "had accompanied captain Cook on his voyage to the Pacific Ocean; and distinguished himself on that voyage by his intrepidity" (1:ix-x). Jefferson suggested that Ledyard "go by land to Kamschatka, cross in some of the Russian vessels to Nootka Sound, fall down into the latitude of the Missouri, and penetrate to, and through, that to the United States" (1:ix-x). He obtained permission from the Russian empress for Ledyard to travel to Kamschatka, but by the time the explorer had reached the west coast of Russia, the empress had changed her mind. Ledyard was arrested and returned in a closed carriage, journeying night and day, to Poland. Although the fatigue of the trip left his "bodily strength... much impaired," Ledyard embarked on a new adventure, the journey to "the head of the Nile" (1:x–xi). In November 1788 he died in Cairo at the start of the expedition.

We know that Poe was familiar with Jefferson's account of Ledyard's unsuccessful attempt to explore the Pacific Northwest: the fictitious editor of Rodman's journal summarizes that account in his introduction to Rodman's work and notes that "Mr. Jefferson, in speaking of Ledyard's undertaking, erroneously calls it 'the first attempt to explore the western part of our northern continent'" (4:17–18). In Ledyard, Poe would have found a figure who was personally involved in three major explorations: Captain Cook's voyage to the South Seas and the Antarctic regions, a voyage frequently referred to in *Pym* as a predecessor of Pym's journey to the polar regions on board the *Jane Guy;* the failed effort to explore the Pacific Northwest, whose successful achievement by Lewis and Clark formed the factual basis for *The Journal of Julius Rodman;* and finally, the journey to discover the source of the Nile, at the start of which Ledyard died. Whether or not these three explorations had become generally associated with each other in the public mind at this period, they were certainly associated in Poe's mind and in the minds of other writers of the American Renaissance. In Hawthorne's *The Blithedale Romance,* the narrator, Miles Coverdale, remarks: "I felt an inexpressible longing for at least a temporary novelty. I thought of going across the Rocky Mountains, or to Europe, or up the Nile—of offering myself a volunteer on the Exploring Expedition—of taking a ramble of years, no matter in what direction, and coming back on the other side of the world."[17]

The "Exploring Expedition" referred to by Coverdale was the Wilkes Expedition of 1838–42 sponsored by the United States government and commanded by a naval lieutenant named Charles Wilkes, better remembered today as the Union captain who in 1861 stopped the British packet *Trent* and arrested Mason and Slidell, the Confederate commissioners to France and England. The Wilkes Expedition was the culmination of a project that had originally been proposed in 1826 by President John Quincy Adams and Secretary of the Navy Samuel Southard. Congress had been reluctant to finance the expedition, and Adams and Southard had tried to drum up popular support by sending Jeremiah N. Reynolds, a backwoods orator from Clinton County, Ohio, along the

Eastern seaboard to seek petitions from shipowners in favor of the project. In his encounters, Reynolds propounded the theory (inherited from a lecturer named Captain John Symmes) that the earth was hollow and inhabited and that holes leading into the earth's interior were to be found at the poles. When Congress still refused to fund the expedition, Reynolds persuaded private backers to finance an Antarctic voyage in which he took part. A government-sponsored expedition did not materialize during Adams's administration, and though preparations for a major voyage of exploration were started during Jackson's presidency, it was not until Martin Van Buren took office that the project was finally realized. In August 1838 (the preface to *Pym* is dated July 1838), Wilkes and his expedition of six ships set sail from Hampton Roads on a four-year voyage to the South Polar regions, the South Pacific, and the Pacific Northwest.

In *Pym* Poe quotes frequently from a book on Antarctic exploration by "Mr. J. N. Reynolds" (3:167); and in "Autography" Poe includes Reynolds among the famous men whose signatures he analyzes, citing Reynolds's "great and laudable exertions to get up the American South Polar expedition, from personal participation in which he was most shamefully excluded" (15:243–44). Poe had written review essays on the subject of the Polar Exploring Expedition in the August 1836 and January 1837 issues of the *Southern Literary Messenger.* In the lengthy note that ends *Pym,* Poe mentions the Wilkes Expedition in discussing the unfinished state of the manuscript: "The loss of two or three final chapters (for there were but two or three,) is more deeply to be regretted, as, it cannot be doubted, they contained matter relative to the Pole itself, or at least to regions in its very near proximity; and as, too, the statements of the author in relation to these regions may shortly be verified or contradicted by means of the governmental expedition now preparing for the Southern Ocean" (3:243).

Beginning the voyage that will ultimately lead him to the Antarctic, Pym, stowed away on board the *Grampus,* passes his time by reading an account of "the expedition of Lewis and Clarke to the mouth of the Columbia" (3:25), and later in a nightmare he dreams that he "stood, naked and alone, amid the burning sand-plains of Zahara" (3:28). One can understand, considering the analogy between the Nile and the Mississippi/Missouri, how the expedition of Lewis and Clark up the Missouri (one of whose goals was to locate "the most northern source" [Allen, 1:xvi] of the Mississippi) became associated with explorations to discover the source of the Nile, but it is not so easy to see how the explorations of these two rivers could become associated with a voyage to the Pole. The answer is to be found in a nexus of traditional images of origin that was reworked during the Romantic period, under the pressure of recent historical events. In light of that image complex, a work like *The Journal of Julius Rodman,* considered as an account of a journey up a river in search of its source rather than an account of the crossing of the Rockies, becomes immediately recognizable as a Romantic genre piece, and its relationship to the ending of *Pym* becomes clear.

There is, of course, in Western literature a long-standing tradition of imaging the origin of poetry, or imagination, or language as a remote, hidden, or inaccessible fountain that is the source of a periodically overflowing river. One thinks of the Heliconian fount, Hippocrene, and of all the hidden springs that feed underground rivers in Romantic poems. But one also thinks of the Nile, as in Wordsworth's description of the source of the imagination in book 6 of *The Prelude* (1850):

> Imagination—here the Power so called
> Through sad incompetence of human speech,
> That awful Power rose from the mind's abyss
> Like an unfathered vapour that enwraps,
> At once, some lonely traveller. I was lost;
> Halted without an effort to break through;
> But to my conscious soul I now can say—
> 'I recognise thy glory:' in such strength
> Of usurpation, when the light of sense
> Goes out, but with a flash that has revealed
> The invisible world, doth greatness make abode,
> There harbours; whether we be young or old,
> Our destiny, our being's heart and home,
> Is with infinitude, and only there . . .
> Under such banners militant, the soul
> Seeks for no trophies, struggles for no spoils
> That may attest her prowess, blest in thoughts
> That are their own perfection and reward,
> Strong in herself and in beatitude
> That hides her, like the mighty flood of Nile
> Poured from his fount of Abyssinian clouds
> To fertilise the whole Egyptian plain.[18]

This passage—in which Wordsworth says, among other things, that the true nature of the imagination is beyond human speech, that it has its origin in "the mind's abyss," that it is "like an unfathered vapour" and involves a "strength of usurpation" in which light becomes darkness—directly follows the account of Wordsworth's unconscious act of "transgression" when, during his journey, he crossed the Alps without realizing it. It is the crossing of this barrier in the Simplon Pass section of the poem that brings him, within the narrative, to the contemplation of the origin of imagination symbolized as the Abyssinian source of the Nile. Having transgressed a natural limit to confront within the poem a primal scene of inspiration/insemination (the overflowing of the imagination / the Nile's fertilizing of the Egyptian plain), Wordsworth descends into a womblike chasm in the Gondo Gorge passage and is given a prefiguration of the merging of opposites in the absolute:

> Tumult and peace, the darkness and the light—
> Were all like workings of one mind, the features
> Of the same face, blossoms upon one tree;
> Characters of the great Apocalypse,
> The types and symbols of Eternity,
> Of first, and last, and midst, and without end.
>
>   (p. 211)

In the passage on the imagination, Wordsworth balances the opening image of the Power rising "from the mind's abyss / Like an unfathered vapour" against the concluding image of the Nile rising to "fertilise the whole Egyptian plain," and in the latter instance as in the former, the origin of that rising is a vapor from the abyss: the river is poured from the "fount of Abyssinian clouds." Besides evoking, in the image of the rising of a river, the roots of the words "origin" (L. *origo, originis* from *oriri,* "to rise") and "source" (L. *surgere,* "to rise"; literally, a spring or fountain, the starting point of a stream), Wordsworth plays on the etymological relationship of the words "abyss" and "Abyssinia" and on the classical tradition of treating Abyssinia—the mysterious source of the Nile, the unexplored lower region of the classical world—as if it were literally an abyss. Thus in book 10 of Lucan's *The Civil War,* Julius Caesar tells the Egyptian priest Acoreus: "There is nothing I would rather learn than the causes, concealed through such long ages, that account for the Nile, and the secret of its source. Give me an assured hope to set eyes on the springs of the river, and I will abandon civil war."[19] In his lengthy reply Acoreus discusses the various learned conjectures about "the hidden founts of the Nile" (p. 605): "Some think that there are air-passages in the earth, and great fissures in its hollow frame. In these, far below the surface, water travels and moves to and fro invisibly, and is summoned from the cold North [*ab Arcto*] to the Equator, whenever the Sun is directly above Meroe and the parched earth attracts water thither; the Ganges and the Po are thus conveyed through a hidden region of the world; and then the Nile, discharging all rivers from a single source, carries them by many mouths to the sea" (p. 609). Acoreus tells Caesar that Alexander, Sesostris, and Cambyses had all tried to discover the source of the Nile and had failed because "Nature has revealed to none his hidden source, nor has it been permitted to mankind to see the stripling Nile; she has concealed his hiding-places, preferring that the nations should marvel at them rather than know them.... He alone is permitted to stray through both hemispheres [*solique vagari / Concessum per utrosque polos*]. In one hemisphere his source is unknown, in the other his final goal" (p. 613).

Neither Caesar nor his emissaries discovered the source of the Nile, and the river's origin remained a mystery for Western civilization until the beginning of the seventeenth century. In 1615 a Portuguese missionary, Father Pedro Paez, was shown by the Abyssinians the fountains that are the source of the Blue Nile, and ten years later another Portuguese missionary, Father Jeronimo Lobo, visited these same fountains. One version of the accounts of Paez and Lobo was written by the tireless Athanasius Kircher. An English version, done by Sir Peter Wyche, was published by order of the Royal Society in 1669. During the next century there were many who doubted the authenticity of this discovery, and one of these, the Scot James Bruce of Kinnaird, after an arduous journey of more than two years, arrived in November 1770 at the site of the Abyssinian fountains that are the head of the Blue Nile and were believed at the time to be the legendary *caput Nili*. Bruce published the account of his journey in *Travels to Discover the Source of the Nile, 1768–73* (Edinburgh, 1790). Bruce's *Travels* was one of the most popular books of the late eighteenth and early nineteenth centuries. Besides inspiring countless other explorers to seek out the fountains that are the Blue Nile's source, and thereby fostering a series of nineteenth-century expeditions leading to the discovery of the source of the White Nile, Bruce's book had an important effect on the literature of the period.

John Livingston Lowes has shown the influence of Bruce's *Travels* on

Romantic poetry, particularly on the work of Coleridge. Describing the *Travels* as "one book of the day which everybody who read at all was reading," Lowes notes that Bruce's work "was the topic of discussion in April, 1794, in Coleridge's circle at Cambridge. On Christmas Eve, 1794, Coleridge quoted one of its purple patches in a note to his 'Religious Musings,' and thirteen years later we find Dorothy Wordsworth writing to Lady Beaumont: 'Coleridge says that the last edition of Bruce's "Travels" is a book that you ought by all means to have.'"[20] Coleridge's use of the *Travels* is most apparent in "Kubla Khan," and Lowes has demonstrated how the creation of that poem was so closely intertwined with the creation of *The Rime of the Ancient Mariner* that Bruce's account of his journey to the fountains of the Nile became in Coleridge's mind associated with, and then began to merge into, those accounts of polar expeditions that Coleridge had used as background material for the ancient mariner's voyage to the South Polar regions.

We can see how these two explorations became associated in the poet's imagination if we consider again one of the theories concerning the origin of the Nile mentioned by the Egyptian priest in Lucan. According to that theory, "there are air-passages in the earth, and great fissures in its hollow frame. In these, far below the surface, water travels and moves to and fro invisibly, and is summoned from the cold North [*ab Arcto*] to the Equator." Granting the image of an opening in the earth at each pole (like the one described in the final footnote to "MS. Found in a Bottle"), one could easily imagine a circular system in which water rushed into the earth at the polar abysses, was conveyed through subterranean passageways to the equator, and then issued from the earth again through fountains like those that form the source of the Nile. The fountains of the Nile and the polar abyss would be, respectively, the beginning and the end, the first and the final cause; and since in a circular system the beginning and the end are one, the journey to the source of the Nile and the voyage to the pole would be complementary quests for origins.

That Coleridge connected the journey up the Nile with the quest for origins, particularly linguistic origins, is clear from a notebook entry he made in 1801: "N. B. to make a detailed comparison in the manner of Jerome Taylor between the searching for the first Cause of a Thing and the seeking the fountains of the Nile—so many streams each with their junction, etc., etc.—at last, it all comes to a name—."[21] Commenting on the etymology of the name "Mount Abora" in "Kubla Khan," Leslie Brisman notes: "Even in its purely linguistic associations, 'Abora' points to first things. Coleridge, who was fascinated by the way the Hebrew *ab-ba* seems to father language (the sounds bringing forth the alphabet) as well as signify 'father,' delighted generally in the potential insights of word-sources. 'In disciplining the mind,' he advised, 'one of the first rules should be, to lose no opportunity of tracing words to their origin.'"[22] The sacred river in "Kubla Khan" is, of course, the Alph (aleph, alpha-bet), and what Coleridge sees in his dream vision is the river's origin in a "deep romantic chasm":

> And from this chasm, with ceaseless turmoil seething,
> As if the earth in fast thick pants were breathing,
> A mighty fountain momently was forced:
> Amid whose swift half-intermitted burst
> Huge fragments vaulted like rebounding hail,
> Or chaffy grain beneath the thresher's flail:
> And 'mid these dancing rocks at once and ever
> It flung up momently the sacred river.[23]

He adds that he once saw in a vision "an Abyssinian maid, / And on her dulcimer she played, / Singing of Mount Abora" (1:298).

Beyond the appropriateness of calling the spot of linguistic origin *ab ora,* with the dual sense of a human mouth and the mouth of a river, here is what Coleridge would have found in Bruce's *Travels* on the etymology of the Abyssinian names for the Nile:

> Among the Agow, a barbarous and idolatrous nation, it is called Gzeir, Geesa, Seir; the first of these names signifying *God;* it is also called Abba, or Ab, *Father.* . . .
>
> . . . now, the name of the river in Amharic is Abay . . . , and the sense of that word so wrote in Geez, as well as Amharic, is "the river that suddenly swells, or overflows, periodically with rain."
>
> . . . the next name by which the Nile went was Siris. . . . This name the Greeks thought was given to it, because of its black colour during the inundation, which mistake presently produced confusion; and we find, according to this idea, the compiler of the Old Testament . . . has translated Siris, the black river, by the Hebrew, Shihor; but nobody ever saw the Nile black when it overflowed; and it would be a very strong figure to call it so in Egypt, where it is always white during the whole of the inundation.

... I would pass over another name, that of Geon, which some of
the fathers of the church have fondly given it, pretending it was one
of the rivers that came from the terrestrial paradise, ... whilst, for
this purpose, they bring it two thousand miles by a series of miracles,
as it were, under the earth and under the sea.[24]

As one of the names of the Nile is Abba, "Father," so Bruce theorizes
that the annual flooding of the Nile, its fertilization of the Egyptian
plain, had originally fathered the invention of the hieroglyphics. Remarking that it is "impossible to avoid saying something ... of the origin
of languages" in his account of Abyssinia, he devotes an entire chapter to
the beginning of writing. Discounting the legend that writing was invented by the Egyptian king Osiris and his secretary Tot, he presents his
own theory:

Thebes was built by a colony of Ethiopians from Sirè, the city of
Seir, or the dog Star. Diodorus Siculus says, that the Greeks, by
putting O before Siris, had made the word unintelligible to the
Egyptians: Siris, then, was Osiris; but he was not the Sun, no more
than he was Abraham, nor was he a real personage. He was Syrius,
or the dog-star, designed under the figure of a dog, because of the
warning he gave to Atbara, where the first observations were made
at his heliacal rising, or his disengaging himself from the rays of the
sun, so as to be visible to the naked eye. He was the Latrator Anubis,
and his first appearance was figuratively compared to the barking of
a dog, by the warning it gave to prepare for the approaching inun-
dation. I believe, therefore, this was the first hieroglyphic; and that
Isis, Osiris, and Tot, were all after inventions relating to it. ...

It is not to be doubted, that hieroglyphics then, but not as-
tronomy, were invented at Thebes. ... (1:412–13)

Bruce also speculates about the origin of phonetic characters: "It
seems ... probable, that the first alphabet was Ethiopic, first founded on
hieroglyphics, and afterwards modeled into more current, and less
laborious figures" (1:420). He goes on to discount the belief that letters
are of divine origin:

... it appears from scripture there were two different sorts of
characters known to Moses, when God spoke to him on Mount Sinai.
The first two tables, we are told, were wrote by the finger of God, in

what character is not said, but Moses received them to be read to the people, so he surely understood them. But, when he had broken these two tables, and had another meeting with God on the mount on the subject of the law, God directs him specially not to write in the Egyptian character or hieroglyphics, but in the current hand used by the Ethiopian merchants, *like the letters* upon a signet; that is, he should not write in hieroglyphics by a *picture,* representing the *thing,* for that the law forbids; and the bad consequences of this were evident; but he should write the law in the current hand, by characters representing sounds, (though nothing else in heaven or on earth,) or by the letters that the Ishmaelites, Cushites, and India trading nations had long used in business for signing their invoices, engagements, etc. and this was the meaning of being *like the letters of a signet.*

Hence, it is very clear, God did not invent letters, nor did Moses, who understood both characters before the promulgation of the law upon Mount Sinai, having learned them in Egypt, and during his long stay among the Cushites, and Shepherds in Arabia Petrea. Hence it should appear also, that the sacred character of the Egyptian was considered as profane, and forbid to the Hebrews, and that the common Ethiopic was the Hebrew sacred character, in which the copy of the law was first wrote. (1:421)

According to Bruce, then, not only were the hieroglyphics originally invented by the descendants of the Ethiopian founders of Thebes as a means of recording the flooding of the Nile (and thus doubly Abyssinian in origin, since both the source of the river that gave rise to the invention and the ancestors of the inventors were Abyssinian), but the first phonetic writing was Ethiopic as well, having derived from the hieroglyphics and still showing that origin in the shape of some of its letters. Further, in his speculation on the way in which Hebrew writing was borrowed from Ethiopic, Bruce clearly relates hieroglyphic writing to a transgression against the father. God forbids Moses (his spiritual son) to inscribe the tablets containing the prohibitions "in hieroglyphics by a *picture,* representing the *thing,*" for that type of writing is contrary to one of the laws to be inscribed, that is, the prohibition against making graven images. Instead, the laws are to be written in "characters representing sounds, (though nothing else in heaven or on earth)." The implication

seems to be that hieroglyphic writing is forbidden because it blasphe-
mously aspires to write in that script of physical objects in which God
originally inscribed the world, a form of blasphemy for which the Hebrews showed their inclination when they made the golden calf. It would
be difficult for an imaginative reader of the *Travels* not to be left with the
image of Bruce's journey to the Abyssinian fountains of the Nile as an
expedition to the original source of written language, a journey fraught
with perils and the danger of death precisely because it evoked an ancient transgression and an ancient prohibition by which man is exiled
from his origins.

Poe undoubtedly knew Bruce's book. Travel books were among his
favorite reading, and Bruce's work was, in Richard Garnett's words, "the
epic of African travel." Poe would also have been familiar with the
Travels from references and allusions to it in the Romantic poets, especially in Coleridge and Shelley, whose influence on Poe's work is well
known. Thus, for example, in *Religious Musings* Coleridge describes a
"sun-scorched waste, / Where oft majestic through the tainted noon /
The Simoom sails, before whose purple pomp / Who falls not prostrate
dies!" (1:118–19), and as an explanatory footnote to the image of the
Simoom, he quotes the following passage from Bruce:

> At eleven o'clock, while we contemplated with great pleasure the
> rugged top of Chiggre, to which we were fast approaching, and
> where we were to solace ourselves with plenty of good water, Idris
> cried out with a loud voice, 'Fall upon your faces, for here is the
> Simoom'. I saw from the S. E. an haze come on, in colour like the
> purple part of the rainbow, but not so compressed or thick. It did
> not occupy twenty yards in breadth, and was about twelve feet high
> from the ground.—We all lay flat on the ground, as if dead, till Idris
> told us it was blown over. The meteor, or purple haze, which I saw,
> was indeed passed; but the light air that still blew was of heat to
> threaten suffocation. Bruce's *Travels*, vol. 4, p. 557 . . . (1:119)

During his voyage from Java, the narrator of Poe's "MS. Found in a
Bottle" notices one evening "a very singular, isolated cloud, to the N.
W. . . . remarkable, as well for its color, as from its being the first we had
seen since our departure from Batavia" (2:2). As the sea becomes unusu-
ally "transparent" and the air "intolerably hot," the narrator remarks,
"Every appearance warranted me in apprehending a Simoom" (2:3).

That it is a simoom which swamps the narrator's vessel and starts him on his voyage to the polar abyss might seem to be an insignificant detail, until we recall that the simoom is a dust-laden desert wind of North Africa and that the narrator's ship is on a voyage "from the port of Batavia, in the rich and populous island of Java . . . to the Archipelago of the Sunda islands" (2:2). However inappropriate it is in terms of meteorology to have a North African simoom strike a ship in the middle of the Pacific Ocean, the symbolic appropriateness of having the wind that destroys the narrator's vessel and drives him to the polar abyss be the same dangerous wind that struck Bruce and his party on the journey to the source of the Nile must, in view of the complementary nature of the journeys, have appealed to Poe.

As a trope of poetic inspiration, the violent wind that overwhelms the writer's "vessel" and carries him off into the sublime is a common Romantic counterpart of the image of a hidden fountain or overflowing stream. That wind is the inspiring breath of the god that Shelley addressed in the "Ode to the West Wind" as "destroyer and preserver." Shelley's is the appropriate name in this context, for the image of the poet's vessel overcome by the afflatus and driven across the sea to the abyss of the sublime pervades his work. One thinks immediately of "My soul is an enchanted boat" from *Prometheus Unbound* or of the ending of *Adonais:*

> The breath whose might I have invoked in song
> Descends on me; my spirit's bark is driven,
> Far from the shore, far from the trembling throng
> Whose sails were never to the tempest given;
> The massy earth and spherèd skies are riven!
> I am borne darkly, fearfully, afar;
> Whilst, burning through the inmost veil of Heaven,
> The soul of Adonais, like a star,
> Beacons from the abode where the Eternal are.[25]

Earlier in the poem, Shelley implicitly compares the dead Adonais to Narcissus, saying that Echo is now voiceless because "she can mimic not his lips, more dear / Than those for whose disdain she pined away / Into a shadow of all sounds" (p. 478), and Shelley consoles himself with the thought that Adonais' "pure spirit shall flow / Back to the burning fountain whence it came" (p. 484). The fountain of poetic creation, the mirroring stream or pool, and the figure of Narcissus fatally in love with his own image are part of a Romantic image complex that evokes the narcissistic doubling lying at the heart of artistic creation. In his long poem *Alastor,* Shelley combined these tropes with the images of the divine wind, the overwhelming of the poet's vessel, the whirlpool/abyss, and the hieroglyphics to produce a work whose structure Poe obsessively repeated in his double stories and tales of the abyss.

In *Alastor* the young poet leaves his "alienated home" to "seek strange truths in undiscovered lands" (p. 18). A Narcissus-figure who ignores the virgins who "have pined / And wasted for fond love of his wild eyes" (p. 17), he goes in search of the origin of things, in particular the origin of poetry. This quest leads him to Egypt and Abyssinia and to the origin of writing:

> His wandering step,
> Obedient to high thoughts, has visited
> The awful ruins of the days of old:
> Athens, and Tyre, and Balbec, and the waste
> Where stood Jerusalem, the fallen towers
> Of Babylon, the eternal pyramids,
> Memphis and Thebes, and whatsoe'er of strange
> Sculptured on alabaster obelisk,
> Or jasper tomb, or mutilated sphynx,
> Dark Aethiopia in her desert hills
> Conceals. Among the ruined temples there,
> Stupendous columns, and wild images
> Of more than man, where marble daemons watch
> The Zodiac's brazen mystery, and dead men
> Hang their mute thoughts on the mute walls around,
> He lingered, poring on memorials
> Of the world's youth, through the long burning day
> Gazed on those speechless shapes, nor, when the moon
> Filled the mysterious halls with floating shades
> Suspended he the task, but ever gazed
> And gazed, till meaning on his vacant mind
> Flashed like strong inspiration, and he saw
> The thrilling secrets of the birth of time.
>
> (Pp. 18–19)

(One is reminded of the hieroglyphic cliffs viewed by moonlight that resemble a ruined temple in *The Journal of Julius Rodman,* or the passage in "MS. Found in a Bottle" where the narrator describes the ghost ship that is carrying him to the abyss: "The ship and all in it are imbued with the spirit of Eld. The crew glide to and fro like the ghosts of buried centuries; their eyes have an eager and uneasy meaning; and when their fingers fall athwart my path in the wild glare of the battle-lanterns, I feel as I have never felt before, although I have been all my life a dealer in antiquities, and have imbibed the shadows of fallen columns at Balbec, and Tadmor, and Persepolis, until my very soul has become a ruin" [2:13].)

The "secrets of the birth of time" that the poet learns by gazing at the hieroglyphics concern the narcissistic doubling that is the mythic origin of symbolization and that grounds the human self-consciousness we call "time"; for what he sees "on the mute walls" where "dead men / Hang their mute thoughts" are "daemons" and "floating shades"—man-made shadow outlines, human doubles that have become "wild images / Of more than man." Wandering on, he reaches the valley of Cashmire where he has a dream-vision of "a veilèd maid . . . herself a poet," whose voice "was like the voice of his own soul / Heard in the calm of thought" (p. 19). A Psyche-figure, the veiled maiden is a female double of the poet, reflecting his self-love for the objectified other of the work of art. The maiden evokes as well the self-destructive aspect of that narcissistic love, for the poet's dream is a punishment: "The spirit of sweet human love has sent / A vision to the sleep of him who spurned / Her choicest gifts. He eagerly pursues / Beyond the realms of dream that fleeting shade" (p. 20).

At the end of a long, vain search for the dream maiden, the poet arrives at the Chorasmian shore. He has begun to suspect that as he had first seen the maiden in his sleep, so he will only be reunited with her in the final sleep of death. At the shore he finds a small boat: "A restless impulse urged him to embark / And meet lone Death on the drear ocean's waste; / For well he knew that mighty Shadow loves / The slimy caverns of the populous deep" (pp. 22–23). Driven by a whirlwind to the foot of the Caucasian cliffs, the boat rushes into a cavern, follows its winding passages, and arrives finally at a chasm filled with a gigantic whirlpool that, like the vortex in Poe's "Descent into the Maelström," is equally capable of spinning an object up towards its edge or down into the abyss. "Seized by the sway of the ascending stream" (p. 24), the boat rises to "the extremest curve," where a breeze catches it and bears it out of the vortex and into a placid brook. Following the brook, the poet reaches a dark glen containing a fountain/well, whose depths are like a "liquid mirror" (p. 26). In Shelley, the whirlpool/abyss and the fountain, instead of being at the pole and the equator respectively, are within a short distance of each other and are visibly linked by a stream. Further, both the abyss and the fountain are narcissistic mirrors: in the middle of the vortex is "a pool of treacherous and tremendous calm . . . reflecting, yet distorting every cloud" (p. 24), while the fountain/well reflects the poet's face "as the human heart, / Gazing in dreams over the gloomy grave, / Sees its own treacherous likeness there" (p. 26).

As masculine and feminine symbols, the fountain and the vortex taken in conjunction represent a forbidden primal scene of origin, and the compulsion to view that primal scene is the poet's narcissistic fate—his fatal discovery of the illusory (that is, symbolic) nature of the self. Looking into the "dark fountain," the poet's eyes see the reflection of "their own wan light." Later, "when his regard / Was raised by intense pensiveness, . . . two eyes, / Two starry eyes, hung in the gloom of thought, / And seemed with their serene and azure smiles / To beckon him" (pp. 26-27). (One thinks of Poe's "Ligeia.") "Obedient to the light / That shone within his soul," he follows the stream that issues from the fountain, hoping to discover its ultimate end. The stream, which the poet says images his life, increases to a river, and at a precipice that seems "to overhang the world," the river falls "into that immeasurable void / Scattering its waters to the passing winds" (p. 28). On the precipice there is a nook where the dead leaves collect, "the haunt / Of every gentle wind," and here the poet, the first ever to penetrate "the stillness of its solitude" (p. 29), expires—the "leaves" of *Alastor* his only memorial.

The *Narrative of A. Gordon Pym* begins with an interesting variation of the "overwhelming of the vessel," a trope that serves as the allusive context for the book's other shipwreck episodes. The youthful Pym and his friend Augustus Barnard, after a party at which both have become "not a little intoxicated," decide to go for a midnight sail in Pym's boat, appropriately named the *Ariel*. In a "kind of ecstasy" Pym and Augustus put to sea, even though it is "blowing almost a gale" (3:7). But what begins as ecstatic intoxication turns into a drunken nightmare once they are at sea. (In "MS. Found in a Bottle" we are given a hint about the form

of intoxication that overwhelms the vessel when the narrator remarks
that the ship's cargo includes "a few cases of opium" [2:2].) In the teeth
of the gale, Pym finds that his friend's rational appearance earlier "had
been the result of a highly concentrated state of intoxication—a state
which, like madness, frequently enables the victim to imitate the outward
demeanour of one in perfect possession of his senses" (3:8–9). When
Augustus passes out, Pym realizes that by himself he is "incapable of
managing the boat, and that a fierce wind and strong ebb tide" are
hurrying them to destruction (3:9). Like the battered hulk run down by
the ghost ship in "MS. Found in a Bottle," the *Ariel* is cut in two during
the gale by a whaling vessel, and Pym and Augustus are hauled from the
sea more dead than alive. When Pym regains consciousness on board the
whaler, he doesn't know what happened or how he got there; but, he
says, "the mystery of our being in existence was now soon explained"
(3:11). That remark could serve as an ironic epigraph for the whole
book, since the mystery of Pym's "being in existence," which the book
poses in terms of the mechanics of its own composition, is never explained.

The mystery arises from Pym's preface, the unfinished state of the
narrative, and the closing note. The preface is dated "New York, July,
1838"—some ten years after the point at which the narrative breaks off
as Pym and Dirk Peters, in a canoe moving "with a hideous velocity"
(3:241), are about to enter a chasm at the South Pole. The opening
paragraph of the final note "explains" the interruption in the writing:
"The circumstances connected with the late sudden and distressing
death of Mr. Pym are already well known to the public through the
medium of the daily press. It is feared that the few remaining chapters
which were to have completed his narrative, and which were retained by
him, while the above were in type, for the purpose of revision, have been
irrecoverably lost through the accident by which he perished himself.
This, however, may prove not to be the case, and the papers, if ultimately found, will be given to the public" (3:243). At the point where the
narrative is interrupted, Pym and Peters are about to descend into the
abyss and discover that "never-to-be-imparted secret, whose attainment
is destruction." And yet that seems not to have happened, for ten years
later Pym is still alive and back again in the civilized world, writing his
book. What is uncanny, however, about the composition of that book is
that Pym's sudden death during the process of readying the manuscript

for publication interrupts the narrative at the exact point where the
entry into the abyss would have interrupted the voyage. And more uncanny still, the unnamed accident that takes Pym's life takes the last
chapters of his book as well. That Pym's voyage to the pole is a symbolic
quest for the origin of writing, a quest embodied in the written narrative's own oblique questioning of its origin (its unexplained "being in
existence"), is subtly evoked by Poe's displacment of the dangers of the
abyss from the act of exploring to the act of writing. It is not that the
writing stops with the interruption of the voyage but that the voyage
stops with the interruption of the writing. Writing in search of its origin
is the self-dissolving voyage to the abyss.

In "MS. Found in a Bottle," *The Journal of Julius Rodman,* and "Hans
Pfaall," the narrative provides the fiction of its own presence, the fiction
of its return from the unknown region to the civilized world. But that
"fiction of its own presence" is just what, for all its apparatus of preface
and closing note, *Pym* refuses to provide; in fact, it is the apparatus that
serves to point up the absence of that fiction. In the preface Pym says
that he had only returned "to the United States a few months ago, after
the extraordinary series of adventure in the South Seas and elsewhere,
of which an account is given in the following pages" (3:1). But that
account, which breaks off at the point where Pym appears to be headed
for certain destruction (an appearance confirmed by Pym's subsequent
death at just this point during the writing), raises the question of how we
come to be reading this narrative at all, how its author survived to write
it, who could not even survive the writing of it. For unlike "MS. Found in
a Bottle," Pym's narrative was not written during the course of the journey so as to provide, in the event of the narrator's sudden destruction, an
already existing record that could survive that destruction. Pym tells us
in the preface that he had been reluctant to write this account upon his
return because he had "kept no journal during a greater portion of the
time" in which he was absent and consequently would not be able "to
write, from mere memory, a statement so minute and connected as to
have the *appearance* of that truth it would really possess" (3:1). Another
deterrent was that "the incidents to be narrated were of a nature so
positively marvelous, that, unsupported as my assertions must necessarily be (except by the evidence of a single individual, and he a half-breed
Indian), I could only hope for belief among my family, and those of my
friends who have had reason, through life, to put faith in my veracity—

the probability being that the public at large would regard what I should put forth as merely an impudent and ingenious fiction" (3:1–2).

Like the fisherman in "A Descent into the Maelström," Pym has an incredible truth to tell, and he must try to present it in writing so that it will have the *appearance* of truth, so that it will be self-proving, self-evidently convincing. For Pym understands that if the writer does not solve the problem of producing a self-evidential statement, then an incredible truth becomes an incommunicable truth, and the abyss suddenly yawns between the writer and all other minds. The narrator of "MS. Found in a Bottle" poses the question of the narrative's credibility within the larger epistemological problem of the uncertainty of all human knowledge:

> Beyond all things, the study of the German moralists gave me great delight; not from any ill-advised admiration of their eloquent madness, but from the ease with which my habits of rigid thought enabled me to detect their falsities. I have often been reproached with the aridity of my genius; a deficiency of imagination has been imputed to me as a crime; and the Pyrrhonism of my opinions has at all times rendered me notorious. . . . Upon the whole, no person could be less liable than myself to be led away from the severe precincts of truth by the *ignes fatui* of superstition. I have thought proper to premise thus much, lest the incredible tale I have to tell should be considered rather the raving of a crude imagination, than the positive experience of a mind to which the reveries of fancy have been a dead letter and a nullity. (2:1–2)

The narrator's skepticism as to the certainty of any knowledge (even direct sense perception), his habitual incredulity, is presented here as a warrant for the credibility of his "incredible tale." The self-evidence for his statement is the evidence of a credible (that is, skeptical) self, the personal credit of the narrator; or as Pym phrased the problem, "I could only hope for belief among my family, and those of my friends who have had reason, through life, to put faith in my veracity." But that is exactly the kind of credit that a fictive writer never has in advance of his text, a narrator in advance of his story, precisely because for the reader it is the narrative that constitutes the narrator's self. Consequently, the narrator's credibility cannot be logically advanced as evidence of the narrative's truth; rather, it is the self-evidence of the narrative's credibility (involving not so much truth as the *appearance* of truth, to use Pym's phrase) that is the evidence of a credible self. A narrative is an unverified statement that strives to be self-verifying. Yet paradoxically, the mark of the narrative's success will be a masking of itself, a reversal in which the credibility of the narrative will appear to derive from the credibility of the narrator's self.

What we referred to earlier from the writer's point of view as the logical precariousness of the narrative act is this same problem of certainty or credibility or self-evidence seen from the reader's point of view. As a truth beyond language interrupts communication for the writer, so an incredible truth interrupts it for the reader. Yet the Romantic writer frequently had to testify to a personal brush with, or intimation of, the sublime or supernatural or suprarational, one of those privileged "spots of time" that would seem incredible to his readers. The narrator of Melville's *Mardi* says, "A thing incredible is about to be related; but a thing may be incredible and still be true; sometimes it is incredible because it is true."[26] By Poe's day the question of certainty or credibility had become the great corrosive question of man's knowledge of the world. As Emerson stated it in the essay "Experience":

> It is very unhappy, but too late to be helped, the discovery we have made that we exist. That discovery is called the Fall of Man. Ever afterwards we suspect our instruments. We have learned that we do not see directly, but mediately, and that we have no means of correcting these colored and distorting lenses which we are, or of computing the amount of their errors. Perhaps these subject-lenses have a creative power; perhaps there are no objects. Once we lived in what we saw; now, the rapaciousness of this new power, which threatens to absorb all things, engages us. Nature, art, persons, letters, religions, objects, successively tumble in, and God is but one of its ideas. Nature and literature are subjective phenomena; every evil and every good thing is a shadow which we cast. (3:75–76)

In Poe, the dual problem of the precariousness of narration and the credibility of the narrative becomes a synecdoche for the larger epistemological problems of whether the mind is a self-verifying apparatus and the book of nature a self-evidential text, in that Poe's works continu-

ally put in question the concept of self-evidence (as well as the component concepts of self and evidence) common to these problems of narration and knowledge.

Section 6
Certainty and Credibility—Self-
Evidence and Self-Reference;
Nietzsche and Tragedy—Whitman
and Opera; The Open Road

In a realist epistemology the substantial existence of nature is a self-evident
first principle. The self-evidence of its
existence is its presence (within a tra-
dition that understands Being as presence), its unconcealment to sight,
its visibility. It is self-evident because it shows itself in the light; it is there
for all to see, and no one would ever think to doubt it. But once (willfully)
one does "think" to doubt it (inasmuch as doubt can be defined here as
thought about thought, a self-willed exercise of the power of mind over
the world of objects) and the critique of knowledge begins by one of those
characteristic separations such as presence-to-sight from presence-to-
mind, the real from the ideal, the phenomenal from the noumenal, appearance from reality (with a consequent instability in the privileging of
one term over another within the pairs), then the question of what constitutes self-evidence, what it means to convince by presence, what
constitutes presence, becomes a central issue.

In *Nature* Emerson says: "Whenever a true theory appears, it will be its
own evidence. Its test is, that it will explain all phenomena" (1:4). That is,
it will render the opaque object transparent, illuminate it, make the
object's meaning visibly present, make the real and the ideal coincide. In
Emerson's thought, transparency is synonymous with spirit. In "Experience" he remarks, "The definition of *spiritual* should be, *that which is its*
own evidence" (3:53). But here self-evidence as a visible presence that
causes immediate conviction seems to depend upon an immediate or
unmediated presence that suddenly renders the mediate world "fluid,"
to use another favorite Emersonian word, and the problem that vexed
Emerson all his life still remains: what is the direction of that immediate,
fluid presence—outer to inner or inner to outer, world to mind or mind
to world? Or is transparency a matter of a momentary synchronization
of rhythms, a reciprocal oscillation, an alignment of polarized light
waves? In *Nature* he uses the polarization of light as an image for the
relation between mind and world: "The problem of restoring to the
world original and eternal beauty is solved by the redemption of the

soul. The ruin or the blank that we see when we look at nature, is in our own eye. The axis of vision is not coincident with the axis of things, and so they appear not transparent but opaque" (1:73). Compare this with a recent explanation of the opacity of phenomena from the physicist Steven Weinberg's book *The First Three Minutes: A Modern View of the Origin of the Universe* (1977): "Nature now exhibits a great diversity of types of particles and types of interactions. Yet we have learned to look beneath this diversity, to try to see the various particles and interactions as aspects of a single unified gauge field theory. The present universe is so cold that the symmetries among the different particles and interactions have been obscured by a kind of freezing; they are not manifest in ordinary phenomena, but have to be expressed mathematically, in our gauge field theories. That which we do now by mathematics was done in the very early universe by heat—physical phenomena directly exhibited the essential simplicity of nature. But no one was there to see it."[27]

For Weinberg the original transparency of nature is a function of matter's incandescent fluidity at high temperatures, while nature's present opacity is a function of the hardening of matter caused by cooling. According to Emerson, however, the defect is not in the physical world but in the instrument of perception, a defect that can be corrected by the working of spirit. Earlier in *Nature* Emerson observes that nature "always speaks of Spirit. . . . It is a great shadow pointing always to the sun behind us. . . . the noblest ministry of nature is to stand as the apparition of God. It is the organ through which the universal spirit speaks to the individual, and strives to lead back the individual to it" (1:61–62). But Emerson adds that this is not the whole story, and he goes on to affirm the contrary: spirit "does not act upon us from without, that is, in space and time, but spiritually, or through ourselves: therefore, that spirit, that is, the Supreme Being, does not build up nature around us, but puts it forth through us, as the life of the tree puts forth new branches and leaves through the pores of the old" (1:64). Of this view Emerson remarks that it "carries upon its face the highest certificate of truth, because it animates me to create my own world through the purification of my soul" (1:64). (But does this quality of carrying "upon its face the highest certificate of truth" constitute self-evidence? Apparently not, if the next word in the sentence has to be "because," if we have to be given a reason to choose it.)

Between his statements of these two positions, Emerson rehearses the idealist critique of the substantial existence of nature and says of this view: "The heart resists it, because it balks the affections in denying substantive being to men and women. . . . this theory makes nature foreign to me" (1:63). Yet a theory that redefines nature as wholly apparential would seem to make nature not foreign to the perceiver but uniquely personal to him. And it is difficult to see how Emerson's theory that spirit "does not build up nature around us, but puts it forth through us" can avoid "denying substantive being to men and women," for as he maintains elsewhere in *Nature,* everything that is not the individual mind (including one's own body and other men and women) must be considered, in relation to that mind, as part of nature, and thus other men and women as part of nature would be put forth by spirit operating through each individual mind and so would have only an apparential being.

From this abyss of world-dissolving thought about thought, the only escape would seem to be some kind of self-evidential sign able to evoke immediate conviction. But the problem implicit in the logical concept of self-evidence remains that of whose self is being evidenced—the in-itself or the for-itself. In order for a self-evidential sign really to operate, it would have to suspend or abrogate thought in a kind of mystical immediacy. A self-evidential sign would have to be an unmediated sign, a self-interpreting sign, since any mediation would involve the uncertainty of interpretation. But with the concept of an unmediated sign, epistemology reaches the borders of mysticism. One thinks of Wittgenstein's written statements in the *Tractatus Logico-Philosophicus* (1921):

4.1212   What *can* be shown, *cannot* be said.[28]

And:

6.51   Scepticism is *not* irrefutable, but obviously nonsensical, when it tries to raise doubts where no questions can be asked.
            For doubt can exist only where a question exists, a question only where an answer exists, and an answer only where something *can be said.*

6.52   We feel that even when *all possible* scientific questions have been answered, the problems of life remain completely untouched. Of course there are then no questions left, and this itself is the answer.

6.521   The solution of the problem of life is seen in the vanish-
           ing of the problem.
           (Is not this the reason why those who have found after a
           long period of doubt that the sense of life became clear to
           them have then been unable to say what constituted that
           sense?)

6.522   There are, indeed, things that cannot be put into words.
           They *make themselves manifest.* They are what is mystical.
                                                              (Pp. 149–51)

What does it mean to *write* words like those? What could be understood
as the common ground between writer and reader for that written testimony? Within this rigorous contraction of the ground of philosophy,
what is left to, or left of, a writer (a written self) who says that "the
problems of life remain completely untouched" and that, having experienced "the sense of life," one is "unable to say what constituted that
sense"? What could the word "sense" mean in that sentence?

Certainly the question of self-evidence, of a self-evidential sign, is one
of central importance for a writer. For it is not just that an author (one
who seeks to write with authority) derives that authority from the authenticity of his writing, from that stylistic self-authentication that evokes
immediate conviction through the mastery of language, it is that the
writer as a written self exists only as words on the page, words that
achieve authenticity (convince) by authenticating (evidencing) a self who
in turn authenticates (unifies, gives a context to, provides the speaker of)
the words in an endlessly oscillating grounding of one by the other.
Because in writing the speaker himself must be spoken, a written sign is
in one sense, then, self-evidential insofar as it stylistically evidences a self,
insofar as it renders the writer's self (the written self) as an embodied
presence for the reader. Style is a "physical" gesture. In "Song of Myself"
Whitman writes:

> Writing and talk do not prove me,
> I carry the plenum of proof and every thing else in my face,
> With the hush of my lips I wholly confound the skeptic.
>   (7:55)

And in "Song of the Open Road":

> (I and mine do not convince by arguments, similes, rhymes,
> We convince by our presence.)
>   (7:155)

The kind of immediately convincing presence that Whitman has in mind is not the presence of a speaking voice but of a visible body. "The plenum of proof" is in his face, Whitman says, and the original 1855 edition of *Leaves of Grass* had a drawing of Walt Whitman as its frontispiece in accordance with the physiognomic/pictographic presence that the book was meant to embody. Whitman's poems are intended to be outlines of the body—hieroglyphic gestures. In "A Song of the Rolling Earth," he writes:

> Human bodies are words, myriads of words,
> (In the best poems re-appears the body, man's or woman's,
>   well-shaped, natural, gay,
> Every part able, active, receptive, without shame or the
>   need of shame.) . . .
>
> A healthy presence, a friendly or commanding gesture, are words,
>   sayings, meanings,
> The charms that go with the mere looks of some men and women,
>   are sayings and meanings also.
>
> (7:220)

Underlying Whitman's sense that "in the best poems re-appears the body" is the image of writing as hierogylphic doubling, the image of the work of art as the writer's inscribed other self. And certainly part of the immense symbolic importance of the Egyptian hieroglyphics for the writers of the American Renaissance is that the hieroglyphics represent the archetypal form of writing in which the outline of a body is rendered visibly present. Wherever the question of certainty or credibility arises (in fact two distinct questions—one pertaining to knowledge, the other to belief—inextricably mingled in the writers of this period), the hieroglyphics are never far away, for considered as pictographs, they are constantly employed as a symbol of that ideal condition in which the physical shape of writing is self-evidential. Obviously, neither Whitman nor any of his contemporaries wrote in pictographs. They employed an arbitrarily stylized written notation of equally arbitrary spoken phonetic signs. Yet the symbolic use of the hieroglyphics constantly raised the practical question of how phonetic writing could hope to achieve the visible presence, the self-evidence, of pictographic signs.

To understand what is at issue here, we must consider for a moment

two different senses of "presence" in regard to language. First, we tend
to identify speech with presence, the presence of the living voice, the
evident context, the meaningful intonation, and so on, while writing
involves the absence of all these. Speech is primary, writing ancillary,
simply a means of recording speech. In this context, self-evidence pertains to the presence of the speaking self and not to the presence of the
referent of the speech. But if we consider the referent, then speech and
writing as phonetic signs that are discontinuous with their referents and
only arbitrarily linked to them represent an absence when compared to
the presence of a pictograph, the visible presence of the referent in the
pictograph's physical shape. A poet, a writer of phonetic script whose
poetic self consists of that very script, faces, then, a double absence in the
use of phonetic signs—the absence both of the live speaking voice and of
the referent.

Whitman's poetic strategy was to merge these two absences and
thereby transform them into a metaphoric presence. If we take "Song of
Myself" as the paradigm, we find that the steps in the process show the
economy of genius. First, Whitman makes the poetic self the sole referent of the poem. But since the poetic self is, as Whitman makes clear,
a visible self—an inscribed, imaged self constituted by the poem's written
words—that act makes the poem its own referent. As a result, the absence of the poem's referent is circumvented. Further, because in writing the speaker is spoken by the words, Whitman's identifying the poetic
self with the written words of the poem circumvents the absence of the
live speaking voice as well: there never was a live speaker whose voice the
phonetic script of the poem transcribes; the writing created its theoreti-
cal speaker, a written self whose living voice was never absent because it
never was, a self who can never be any more present than the written
words. Whitman's making the poetic self the sole referent of the poem
does not, as one might expect, turn out to be a disastrously limiting
maneuver, for at the same time in a kind of cosmic consciousness he
merges the whole universe into that linguistic self. The next step is to
identify that universal poem/self with song, with words arranged to produce a rhythm and a melody, an absolute music that transcends the
mediation of words; for Whitman's poem/self aspires to that condition of
music in which matter and form, inner and outer, blend—a condition in
which "presence" is simply that absence of an external referent that we
call self-referentiality. What Whitman seeks is the immediacy of music,

its power to create immediate conviction. But Whitman is not a composer or a singer, he is a writer; and what he gives us, as he never tires of pointing out, is a book, not something audible but something visual—something visual that aspires not to the opaque (mediate, referential) audibility of spoken words but to the transparent (immediate, self-referential) audibility of music.

In the poem, then, phonetic writing tries to overcome the absence of its referent and achieve the self-evidential presence of a pictograph, not by arranging itself into pictographic shapes on the page, but rather by trying to overcome that prior absence of the referent from phonetic speech that phonetic writing simply transcribes, trying to overcome it by turning phonetic words into a music whose immediacy is, in terms of the force of conviction, the equivalent of the visible presence of a pictograph. In Whitman's poetry phonetic writing seeks to attain the self-evidential quality of a pictograph by achieving the self-referential quality of music.

In *The World as Will and Representation* (1819) Schopenhauer describes the immediacy of music in terms that shed light on Whitman's musical solution:

> ... we may regard the phenomenal world, or nature, and music as two different expressions of the same thing, which is therefore itself the only medium of their analogy, so that a knowledge of it is demanded in order to understand that analogy. Music, therefore, if regarded as an expression of the world, is in the highest degree a universal language. ... All possible efforts, excitements, and manifestations of will, all that goes on in the heart of man and that reason includes in the wide, negative concept of feeling, may be expressed by the infinite number of possible melodies, but always in the universal, in the mere form, without the material, always according to the thing-in-itself, not the phenomenon, the inmost soul, as it were, of the phenomenon without the body. ... We might, therefore, just as well call the world embodied music as embodied will; and this is the reason why music makes every painting, and indeed every scene of real life and of the world, at once appear with higher significance, certainly all the more, in proportion as its melody is analogous to the inner spirit of the given phenomenon. Therefore

we are able to set a poem to music as a song, or a visible representation as a pantomine, or both as an opera.[29]

Elsewhere in the work, Schopenhauer says that "music is as *immediate* an objectification of the whole *will* as the world itself is, indeed as the Ideas are, the multiplied phenomenon of which constitutes the world of individual things. Therefore music is by no means like the other arts, namely a copy of the Ideas, but a *copy of the will itself,* the objectivity of which are the Ideas."[30]

Like Kant, Schopenhauer believes that the absolute essence of things, the thing-in-itself, is unavailable to discursive reason, but since he understands that absolute reality as will, the same will that each human being bears within himself, then there does exist a means of access to the thing-in-itself through immediate intuition. Since the human will and the will whose mediate representation is the world of visible objects are essentially the same, and since music is an immediate representation of the human will whereby the will makes itself available to aesthetic contemplation, then music is the means of immediate intuition of that thing-in-itself whose phenomenal representation is the world. Further, insofar as music is the means by which the will immediately represents itself to itself, music's "self-referentiality," its being without an external referent, is an immediate representation of the will as *that which is always its own referent, that which refers only to itself* and consequently as *that which is always its own evidence,* the ground of immediate conviction. This self-referentiality of music explains, then, how music as a re-presentation can be im-mediate, for music's self-referentiality involves its having as its sole referent the self as will, as that which refers only to itself and that to which the representation is always made. Music's lack of an external referent exactly mirrors the will's lack of an external referent. Thus Whitman's making the self the sole referent of the poem necessarily involves his identifying the poem/self with music, for what Pater meant when he said that all art aspires to the condition of music (that condition in which "the end is not distinct from the means, the form from the matter, the subject from the expression") is that all art aspires to the self-referentiality of the Romantic self, the self as pure will, as pure motion/emotion.

The structure of the will, then, immediately intuited, is musical, but that immediate intuition of the will has its differentiated existence as one pole of a constitutive opposition whose other pole is that mediate knowledge of the will in its phenomenal representation as the physical world. Since in mutually constitutive oppositions the opposites are implicit in one another, the act of listening to music, as an immediate intuition of the will, necessarily involves, as Schopenhauer maintains in *The World as Will and Representation*, a simultaneous internal visualization of phenomena: "Whoever gives himself up entirely to the impression of a symphony, seems to see all the possible events of life and the world take place in himself" (p. 102). And conversely, the phenomenal world is only apprehended in its true significance as mediate representation, as "the adequate objectivity of the will," that is, the referential as opposed to the self-referential, when juxtaposed to music: "Suitable music played to any scene, action, event, or surrounding seems to disclose to us its most secret meaning, and appears as the most accurate and distinct commentary upon it" (p. 102), and this is because music as "an immediate copy of the will itself . . . complements everything physical in the world and every phenomenon by representing what is metaphysical, the thing in itself" (p. 102). In a bipolar opposition will (music) and the phenomenal world (plastic art) constitute each other as inner and outer, intensity and extensity, immediate and mediate, self-referential and (nonself-) referential, temporal and spatial, audible and visual, and so on.

In imagining the structure of a bipolar opposition, we should think of it not as static but dynamic: as an equilibrium or equivalence of opposing forces on the model of electrical polarity—a balancing of mutual attraction and repulsion in which the opposites are simultaneously held together and held apart in that oscillation of sameness and difference that constitutes differentiation, oscillation in the sense of a flickering in or hovering about of one opposite in the other. For Schopenhauer, this dynamic equilibrium of music and phenomenon (visual image) in which each reveals the deepest meaning of the other reaches the height of aesthetic contemplation in opera and its two component arts, song and mime. In song, music is balanced against verbal imagery (the Ideas abstracted from the visual images of phenomena); in mime it is balanced against the visual images themselves; and in opera it is juxtaposed to both verbal imagery and visual images at once.

In *The Birth of Tragedy from the Spirit of Music* (1872), Nietzsche, elaborating his own bipolar opposition between the visual and the musi-

cal, the Apollonian and Dionysian arts considered at the high point
of their mutual interaction in Greek tragedy, approaches the question
from his own grounding in Wagnerian opera and the writings of
Schopenhauer: "What aesthetic effect results when the essentially separate art-forces, the Apollinian and the Dionysian, enter into simultaneous activity? Or more briefly: how is music related to image and concept?
Schopenhauer, whom Richard Wagner, with special reference to this
point, praises for an unsurpassable clearness and clarity of exposition,
expresses himself most thoroughly on the subject."[31] Nietzsche quotes at
length from Schopenhauer's discussion of music in *The World as Will and
Representation* and then gives his own interpretation of Schopenhauer's
insights as they apply to the Apollonian/Dionysian opposition:

> According to the doctrine of Schopenhauer ... we understand
> music as the immediate language of the will, and we feel our fancy
> stimulated to give form to this invisible and yet so actively stirred
> spirit-world which speaks to us, and we feel prompted to embody it
> in an analogous example. On the other hand, image and concept,
> under the influence of a truly corresponding music, acquire a
> higher significance. Dionysian art therefore is wont to exercise two
> kinds of influences on the Apollinian art faculty: music incites to
> the *symbolic intuition* of Dionysian universality, and music allows the
> symbolic image to emerge in *its highest significance.* From these
> facts, ... I infer the capacity of music to give birth to *myth* (the most
> significant example), and particularly the *tragic* myth: the myth
> which expresses Dionysian knowledge in symbols. ...
>   It is only through the spirit of music that we can understand the
> joy involved in the annihilation of the individual. For it is only in
> particular examples of such annihilation that we see clearly the
> eternal phenomenon of Dionysian art, which gives expression to
> the will in its omnipotence, as it were, behind the *principium indi-
> viduationis,* the eternal life beyond all phenomena, and despite all
> annihilation. The metaphysical joy in the tragic is a translation of
> the instinctive unconscious Dionysian wisdom into the language of
> images: the hero, the highest manifestation of the will, is negated
> for our pleasure, because he is only phenomenon, and because the
> eternal life of the will is not affected by his annihilation. "We believe
> in eternal life," exclaims tragedy; while music is the immediate idea

of this life. Plastic art has an altogether different aim: here Apollo overcomes the suffering of the individual by the radiant glorification of the *eternity of the phenomenon:* here beauty triumphs over the suffering inherent in life; pain is obliterated by lies from the features of nature. (Pp. 103–104)

Commenting on his interpretation of tragedy, Nietzsche admits:

... the meaning of tragic myth set forth above never became clear in transparent concepts to the Greek poets, not to speak of the Greek philosophers: their heroes speak, as it were, more superficially than they act; the myth does not at all obtain adequate objectification in the spoken word. The structure of the scenes and the visual images reveal a deeper wisdom than the poet himself can put into words and concepts....

With respect to Greek tragedy, which of course presents itself to us only as word-drama, I have even intimated that the lack of congruity between myth and expression might easily lead us to regard it as shallower and less significant than it really is, and accordingly to attribute to it a more superficial effect than it must have had according to the testimony of the ancients: for how easily one forgets that what the word-poet did not succeed in doing, namely, attain the highest spiritualization and ideality of the myth, he might very well succeed in doing every moment as creative musician! (P. 105)

Nietzsche's explanation of "how music is related to image and concept" in Greek tragedy forms an illuminating counterpoint to Whitman's own poetic strategy in dealing with the same post-Kantian epistemological dilemma that had evoked Schopenhauer's (and Nietzsche's) doctrine of music as the mode of immediate intuition. For Nietzsche, Greek tragedy is a Heraclitean play of opposites (*play,* in the sense of both game and drama) like that which he describes in the section on Heraclitus in *Philosophy in the Tragic Age of the Greeks:*

In this world only play, play as artists and children engage in it, exhibits coming-to-be and passing away, structuring and destroying, without any moral additive, in forever equal innocence. And as children and artists play, so plays the ever-living fire. It constructs and destroys, all in innocence.... Not hybris but the ever self-renewing impulse to play calls new worlds into being.... Only aesthetic man can look thus at the world, a man who has experienced in artists and in the birth of art objects how the struggle of the many can yet carry rules and laws inherent in itself, how the artist stands contemplatively above and at the same time actively within his work, how necessity and random play, oppositional tension and harmony, must pair to create a work of art.[32]

The world is, then, a play (game) of opposites (will and phenomena, the ever-living fire and illusion) that is raised to the level of aesthetic contemplation in another play (tragic drama) of opposites (Dionysian music and Apollonian visual image). In Nietzsche's conception, the world will is a pure self-renewing energy continually creating and destroying forms, continually objectifying itself in phenomena. Imaged as the "ever-living fire" of Heraclitus, the world will is that ceaseless Becoming which in the ceaselessness of its becoming constitutes Being; it is that continual (temporal) difference in phenomena that, by always being different, constitutes what Nietzsche was later to call the "eternal recurrence of the same." According to Nietzsche, the joy that we experience in tragic drama derives from a simultaneous glimpse of the eternal from two opposing viewpoints: the Dionysian unfolding of the will's omnipotence and "the eternal life beyond all phenomena" and the Apollonian "glorification of the *eternity of the phenomenon*" in its ceaseless "coming-to-be and passing away." Why the experience of the "eternal" is necessarily joyful is, however, not explained.

Nietzsche's understanding of Greek tragedy as an interplay of the Apollonian/Dionysian opposition is, of course, a retrospective interpretation of tragic drama in the light of Wagnerian opera and, in particular, of Wagner's revelation of the musical structure of myth, a revelation that underpins Nietzsche's inference of "the capacity of music to give birth to *myth* . . . , and particularly the *tragic* myth." The actual role of music in Greek tragedy would have been largely a matter of conjecture for Nietzsche, as he implicitly acknowledges when he says that Greek tragedy "presents itself to us only as word-drama." His interpretation of tragedy is an imaginative reconstruction meant in part to account for the intense effect that tragedy "must have had according to the testimony of the ancients," an effect that he cannot now educe simply from the written words of the drama ("their heroes speak, as it were, more superficially than they act"). His explanation locates the intense tragic effect recorded by the ancients in the simultaneous presence, along with the verbal imagery, of Apollonian visual images ("the structure of the scenes and the visual images reveal a deeper wisdom than the poet himself can put into words and concepts") and Dionysian music ("how easily one forgets that what the word-poet did not succeed in doing, namely, attain the highest spiritualization and ideality of the myth, he might very well succeed in doing every moment as creative musician").

Nietzsche's sense of "the lack of congruity between myth and expression" in the written text of the drama, his sense that "the myth does not at all obtain adequate objectification in the spoken word," springs from his understanding of the written drama as an abstract—and thus weakened or obscured—expression of the Apollonian/Dionysian interplay. For him the written text of the tragedy is a combination of verbal imagery (the "words and concepts" abstracted from visual images) with a mythic structure (the rhythmic/melodic structural repetitions abstracted from music), a combination that can only achieve its deepest significance, that paradoxical state of simultaneous "adequate objectification" and "highest spiritualization and ideality," when in performance the verbal imagery and mythic structure are juxtaposed to the visual images and music from which they were derived, thus allowing the written drama's Apollonian/Dionysian interplay of imagery and myth to be at once visibly objectified in the actors and scenes and invisibly idealized by the music.

Nietzsche's sense of the inadequacy of words, an inadequacy solved by the addition of visual image and music, was the same inadequacy that Whitman felt in the use of phonetic signs when he wrote, "I swear I begin to *see* little or nothing in *audible* words" (italics mine). And just as the opera for Schopenhauer, and the Greek tragedy conceived on the model of Wagnerian opera for Nietzsche, represented the highest expression of that interplay of verbal imagery, visual image, and music in which the true significance of the phenomenal world and the will was revealed, so too for Whitman opera represented that simultaneous "adequate objectification" and "highest spiritualization and ideality"— the state of projecting at once the visible presence of a self-evidential sign and the immediate intuitive conviction of music—that he wished his poetry to achieve.

Whitman's love of opera is well known: his frequent attendance at Italian operas in New York during the 1850s, the numerous references to opera in both his poetry and prose, the comments of his friends and critics on his operatic method of composition come readily to mind. In "Proud Music of the Storm," Whitman, telling how from the time he was a small child "all sounds became music" to him, either describes or names most of his favorite operas, including his favorite opera singer, Marietta Alboni. At the end of the poem he says that the various forms of music he has described are not the sounds of nature, "Nor vocalism of sun-bright Italy, / Nor German organ majestic, nor vast concourse of voices, nor layers of harmonies," but

> ... to a new rhythmus fitted for thee,
> Poems bridging the way from Life to Death, vaguely wafted
>   in night air, uncaught, unwritten,
> Which let us go forth in the bold day and write.
>
> (7:410)

Discussing the influence of Italian opera on his work, Whitman remarks in *Good-Bye My Fancy* that his friends have claimed "that the new Wagner and his pieces belong far more truly to me, and I to them. Very likely. But I was fed and bred under the Italian dispensation, and absorb'd it, and doubtless show it" (9:694).

Perhaps Whitman's most important use of opera as a symbol for the type of mingled presence and immediacy that he wants his poetry to achieve occurs in section 26 of "Song of Myself," directly following his statement that "writing and talk do not prove me...":

> I hear the violoncello, ('tis the young man's heart's complaint,)
> I hear the key'd cornet, it glides quickly in through my ears,
> It shakes mad-sweet pangs through my belly and breast.
>
> I hear the chorus, it is a grand opera,
> Ah, this indeed is music—this suits me.
>
> A tenor large and fresh as the creation fills me,
> The orbic flex of his mouth is pouring and filling me full.
>
> I hear the train'd soprano (what work with hers is this?)
> The orchestra whirls me wider than Uranus flies,
> It wrenches such ardors from me I did not know I possess'd them,
> It sails me, I dab with bare feet, they are lick'd by
>   the indolent waves,

> I am cut by bitter and angry hail, I lose my breath,
> Steep'd amid honey'd morphine, my windpipe throttled
>   in fakes of death,
> At length let up again to feel the puzzle of puzzles,
> And that we call Being.
>
>   (7:56)

In his interpretation of Greek tragedy, Nietzsche sees in the interplay between the tragic hero and the chorus an embodiment of the Apollonian/Dionysian opposition. The chorus represents the Dionysian universality (will, music) from which the tragic hero as the Apollonian *principium individuationis* (phenomenon, visual image) emerges. The tragic drama plays itself out, then, as "a translation of the instinctive unconscious Dionysian widsom into the language of images: the hero, the highest manifestation of the will, is negated for our pleasure, because he is only phenomenon, and because the eternal life of the will is not affected by his annihilation." In Whitman's poetry this Apollonian/Dionysian opposition is dramatized in the scenario of the solitary singer by the sea. The singer represents the Apollonian principle of individuation as melody, while the sea represents the Dionysian universality as rhythm. Thus in "Out of the Cradle Endlessly Rocking," the song of the bird, "the lone singer," is an "aria," while the sound of the sea waves is an incessant rhythmic "undertone" (7:251). Together the bird's song and the sea's chant resemble a Wagnerian Liebestod: the bird, seeking its dead mate, sings, "*loved! loved! loved! loved! loved!*" and the sea, indicating the only mode of the pair's reunion, replies, "death, death, death, death, death." Whitman wrote "Out of the Cradle Endlessly Rocking" in the late 1850s, the same period during which Wagner was working on *Tristan und Isolde* and the swelling/receding, oceanic cadences of its Liebestod. "Out of the Cradle Endlessly Rocking" appeared in the 1860 edition of *Leaves of Grass*, while *Tristan und Isolde* had its world premiere in 1865. This is not to suggest that there was a direct influence of one work on the other but rather that Whitman and Wagner were both influenced by the same operatic tradition.

In Whitman's symbolic use of opera in the passage quoted from "Song of Myself," the Apollonian/Dionysian interplay is represented in the distinction between the operatic chrous and the lead singers (tenor and soprano); and the effect of that interplay, the overwhelming of the individual by the universal imaged as a drowning in the ocean ("lick'd by the indolent waves"), an "expiration" in song ("I lose my breath"), a loss of consciousness ("Steep'd amid honey'd morphine"), is experienced by Whitman as an ecstatic brush with death from which he returns "to feel the puzzle of puzzles . . . that we call Being"—returns to write the poem, just as Poe's Pym and Melville's Ishmael return to tell the tale of a near-drowning in the abyss of undifferentiated Being, but without being able to tell of that ultimate confrontation which would have rendered all telling impossible.

Whitman's sense of the Apollonian/Dionysian interplay as a joyous affirmation of the eternity of the will in its willing seems to parallel Nietzsche's interpretation of the ultimate meaning of tragedy: "In Dionysian art and its tragic symbolism the same nature cries to us with its true, undissembled voice: 'Be as I am! Amid the ceaseless flux of phenomena I am the eternally creative primordial mother, eternally impelling to existence, eternally finding satisfaction in this change of phenomena!'" (p. 104). In Whitman's "As I Ebb'd with the Ocean of Life," the Dionysian sea is described as "the fierce old mother" who is always casting new "types" (of which the poet is one) upon the shore and at the same time "endlessly" crying "for her castaways" to return to her (7:253–54). Yet if the *expressed* purpose of the Dionysian impulse in Whitman's poetry is the reabsorption of the individual self into the cosmic float, we as readers should never forget that the actual method of the poetry is just the opposite, in that the generic "I" of Whitman's poems is based on the absorption of the cosmos into the individual, the identification of the world with the self. Whitman's avowed Dionysian impulse is simply a reversed, veiled statement of his true Romantic impulse. A particularly transparent instance of this type of reversal occurs at the end of Poe's cosmological prose-poem *Eureka*, when Poe admonishes the reader to "think that the sense of individual identity will be gradually merged in the general consciousness—that Man, for example, ceasing imperceptibly to feel himself Man, will at length attain that awfully triumphant epoch when he shall recognize his existence as that of Jehovah" (16:314–15). One of Poe's editors has remarked: "The pain of the consideration that we shall lose our individual identity ceases at once when we further reflect that the process, as above described, is neither more or less than the absorption by each individual intelligence of all other intelligences (that is, of the Universe) into his own. That God may be all in all, each must become God."[33]

The main difference between Nietzsche and Whitman regarding the way in which the interplay of Apollonian visual image and Dionysian music solves the inadequacy of words is that for Nietzsche the interplay is understood to take place literally in the performance of the tragedy, while for Whitman the interplay is always figurative. Neither a composer of music nor a writer of opera, Whitman has only words with which to achieve that interplay of visual presence and musical immediacy that is meant to solve the inadequacy of words. As we said, Whitman's solution is not a visual one; he is not an emblem poet like Quarles nor an experimenter with typography like Cummings. Rather, his is a musical solution. In attempting to raise words to the condition of music, that is, in trying to approximate musical effects by means of the rhythm and melody of verse, the musiclike self-referentiality of the poem, and the musical repetitive structure of myth, he is relying on that mutually constitutive opposition between Apollonian visual image and Dionysian music (the implicit presence of the opposites in one another) to raise at the same time the verbal imagery of his poetry to the level of visual image through the juxtaposition of that verbal imagery to the poetry's verbal music within the poetic line, raise it to the level of visual image not literally but in terms of an equivalence of force. That is, if he can achieve through the musical effects of his poetry that immediacy of intuitive conviction associated with real music, then, because of the dynamic equilibrium of force between musical immediacy and visual presence in the Dionysian/Apollonian opposition, he can confer on his verbal imagery through its constitutive opposition to the poem's verbal music a force equivalent to the self-evidential presence of a visual image. Nietzsche, in attempting to convey the sense of Dionysian universality through the precise verbal imagery of his own text, explicitly compares that attempt to the transformation of music into a visual image:

> Under the charm of the Dionysian not only is the union between man and man reaffirmed, but nature which has become alienated, hostile, or subjugated, celebrates once more her reconciliation with her lost son, man. Freely, earth proffers her gifts, and peacefully the beasts of prey of the rocks and desert approach. The chariot of

Dionysus is covered with flowers and garlands; panthers and tigers walk under its yoke. *Transform Beethoven's "Hymn to Joy" into a painting;* let your imagination conceive the multitudes bowing to the dust, awestruck—then you will approach the Dionysian. . . . Now, with the gospel of *universal harmony,* each one feels himself not only united, reconciled, and fused with his neighbor, but as one with him, as if *the veil of māyā* had been torn aside and were now merely fluttering in tatters before the mysterious primordial unity. (Italics mine)[34]

The self-referential, musical sense of "universal harmony" causes a visual piercing of the veil—the self-evidence of unmediated vision.

As a poet of the absolute self, Whitman is necessarily a poet of the will, and what we see in his poetry is the way in which the music of the will (the ceaselessly mobile energy of internal time-consciousness) strives to create its own phenomenal world, as if, to use Schopenhauer's phrase, when a person gives himself to this music, he "seems to see all the possible events of life and the world take place in himself." The internal music of the will evokes the visual image in the mind, the self-referential grounds the self-evidential. For Whitman, poetic singing and poetic see-ing are a mutually constitutive opposition, and throughout the poems the words "I sing" and "I see" constantly give way to one another in an oscillating equivalency. As a poetic descendant of Whitman's was to write some seventy years later in his own version of the solitary singer walking beside the "ever-hooded, tragic gestured sea" amid "theatrical distances, bronze shadows heaped on high horizons":

> She was the single artificer of the world
> In which she sang. And when she sang, the sea,
> Whatever self it had, became the self
> That was her song, for she was the maker. Then we,
> As we beheld her striding there alone,
> Knew that there never was a world for her
> Except the one she sang and, singing, made.[35]

The way that Nietzsche uses Schopenhauer's concept of music in for-mulating the Dionysian/Apollonian interplay shows the transvaluation of universal doubt (to which the doctrine of immediate intuition responds) from an affliction into a power. In order for there to be an immediate intuition, that which is to be intuited must exist in an accessible unmediated form: it must exist within the self. Thus Schopenhauer posits the continuity of the world will (the thing in itself) and the human will; the world will can only be understood by analogy with the human will. But when Nietzsche explains the tragic joy that we derive from observing the eternal overwhelming of phenomena in the Dionysian/Apollonian interplay, the drama that he implicitly describes is the substitution of the human will for the world will. What Nietzsche gives us is a parable of "the will in its omnipotence," for the way in which the world will expresses its power by the creation and annihilation of phenomena is a projection of the way in which the human will expresses *its* power by means of a universal doubt that annihilates a "real world" and creates a purely "phenomenal world" in its place. By making the flux of phenomena something joyful, by making ceaseless Becoming the true Being, a dynamic Being, Nietzsche relocates all value in the essential quality of the will—motion. The will is a principle of restless, mobile energy, ceaselessly striving to actualize all possibilities, creating, destroying, and creating again; it is the never-to-be-satisfied desire for more or other that Schopenhauer called the "will to live" and sought to negate through asceticism, and that Nietzsche called the "will to power" and sought to apotheosize in "the eternal recurrence of the same." Nietzsche transvalues universal doubt by reinterpreting it, by seeing it not as a weak, passive uncertainty about our knowledge of the real world but as the strong, active mode through which the will-to-power as knowledge asserts its omnipotence over the real world by denying the world its independent reality, by making the world simply an effect of knowledge and thus of the will.

That sense of the will as restless mobility, as a never-to-be-satisfied desire, becomes in Whitman the image of the open road, the image of limitless possibility, of an infinite "second chance" or new beginning, one of whose historical manifestations was the idea of the expanding frontier. Yet we will never quite understand Whitman's open road and the idea of an endless frontier unless we see it as one pole of an opposition whose other pole is the voyage to the abyss. For just as the idea of the open road makes man's goal the endlessness of beginning again, so the voyage to the abyss as a quest for an ultimate origin (a quest for a beginning beyond which one cannot go and thus for a beginning that is an end) reveals that quest to be *abyssos,* bottomless, nonclosable, just like the interrupted "ending" of *Pym* that doesn't really end and that symbolizes the endlessness of the quest for origins, the limitlessness of seeking an ultimate limit.

This opposition of the open road and the voyage to the abyss is an expression of that deeper opposition that lies at the heart of the American dream—the opposition between endless optimism and ultimate desperation. It expresses the American dream as the *last* hope of a *new* start, a paradoxical condition in which hope is born out of hopelessness and then by becoming nonclosable turns out to be hopeless (that is, hope without an end or goal). The American dream, the dream of achieving an ultimate earliness, was a European dream, a late dream, reflecting the experience of those first settlers who left the Old World only to find that the Edenic virgin continent, the green world, the first world, is the oldest world of all—the paradoxical experience that the attempt to free oneself from the burden of history (the Old World's corruption, its political systems, its fixed social hierarchy) by returning to the origin and starting over is simply to begin history once again, and that if one seeks to void the burden of history, then one is committed to an endless series of beginnings again, committed to a future that is an endless quest for the oldest thing in the past, the point where/before history began.

Fitzgerald evokes the oscillation between endless optimism and ultimate desperation that lies at the core of the American dream, when, at the end of *The Great Gatsby*, Nick Carraway imagines how Long Island, Whitman's Paumanok, must have looked to the first Dutch sailors who saw it:

> . . . a fresh, green breast of the new world. Its vanished trees, the trees that had made way for Gatsby's house, had once pandered in whispers to the last and greatest all human dreams; for a transitory enchanted moment man must have held his breath in the presence of this continent, compelled into an aesthetic contemplation he neither understood nor desired, face to face for the last time in history with something commensurate to his capacity for wonder.
>
> And as I sat there brooding on the old, unknown world, I thought of Gatsby's wonder when he first picked out the green light at the end of Daisy's dock. He had come a long way to this blue lawn, and his dream must have seemed so close that he could hardly fail to

grasp it. He did not know that it was already behind him, somewhere back in that vast obscurity beyond the city, where the dark
fields of the republic rolled on under the night.

Gatsby believed in the green light, the orgiastic future that year by
year recedes before us. It eluded us then, but that's no matter—
tomorrow we will run faster, stretch out our arms farther . . . . And
one fine morning—

So we beat on, boats against the current, borne back ceaselessly
into the past.[36]

The American dream of "the orgiastic future," of endless tomorrows
in which one can always go back to the beginning, void history's foreclo-
sure of possibilities, and start over, in the same way that Gatsby tried to
repeat the past, is "the last and greatest of all human dreams," a dream
of beginning that grows out of a sense of lateness, a sense that something
is happening "for the last time in history." In "Passage to India" and
"Prayer of Columbus," Whitman suggests that the real discovery of
America was the understanding that East and West are polar opposites
joined by a circular path, that the journey's end leads back to its beginning. Yet the peculiar dilemma of the American condition is that though
spatial movement on the surface of a sphere will reverse itself and return
to the point of origin, temporal movement is irreversible. Even if one
returns to the starting place, it is always a different, a later, time. The
past cannot be repeated; the temporal point of origin is inaccessible. But
for a people whose country began with the idea that there is a spatial
solution to temporal (historical) problems, that moving to a new place
means making a new beginning, the realization of the irreversibility of
time must be rejected. Tomorrow we must run faster and stretch out our
arms farther, even though what we seek is always behind us—indeed,
because what we seek is always behind us. The restless mobility of the
American will to power is at once impelled and baffled by the irreversibility of time.

Section 7
*Writing Self / Written Self; The Dark
Double; The Overwhelming of the Vessel*

It may seem at this point that, starting
with the mingled question of the credibility of narration and the certainty
of knowledge in Poe and pursuing it into the problem of a self-evidential
sign in Emerson and on into the balancing of visual presence with the

intuitive immediacy of music in Whitman, we have wandered far away from Pym and his voyage to the Pole. But as with our earlier digression into the Romantic poets' symbolic use of the journey to the source of the Nile, the present digression has been a circular path leading us back to Pym and his voyage, a necessary detour in order to continue that voyage with some sense of its full significance. For just as we cannot understand Pym's voyage as a quest for linguistic origins unless we see that the imagery of the search for the Abyssinian source of the Nile has been superimposed on the voyage to the polar abyss, nor understand the meaning of that superimposition unless we grasp the relationship between the whirlpool/fountain imagery and narcissistic doubling, so we will never understand the ending of Pym's voyage unless we grasp the connection between narcissistic doubling and hieroglyphic (pictographic) writing; nor comprehend the importance of the symbol of the hieroglyphics for the writers of the American Renaissance unless we see it within the context of the mingled question of epistemological certainty and narrative credibility; nor understand the hieroglyphics as the symbol of self-evidential visual presence in writing unless we see them in a reciprocal relationship with music as the symbol of immediate intuitive conviction.

For Poe the interaction of verbal imagery, music, and intuition represents the essence of poetry in both theory and practice, a fact that illuminates the curious split between Poe's poetry and fiction in regard to two different senses of intuition. What Poe praises in Champollion and embodies in Dupin is scientific intuition, an extraordinary combination of analytic method and imagination. Yet it is clear from the tales that scientific intuition is not what we would call immediate intuition, not something that arrests discursive reasoning, but rather a power that carries reasoning to a degree of complexity that seems suprarational to ordinary men. Poe says of Dupin that his solutions to problems exhibit "a degree of *acumen* which appears to the ordinary apprehension preternatural," that his results, "brought about by the very soul and essence of method, have, in truth, the whole air of intuition." Scientific intuition dictates the structure of those tales in which the climax and denouement of a seemingly insoluble problem or mystery is an apparently intuitive solution followed by an ingenious rational explanation—the archetypal detective story scenario.

Opposed to this merely apparent intuition is the intuitive mode that

Poe associates with the musical aspect of poetry and with the experience of the sublime as the *indefinite*. In the "Letter to B＿＿＿" (originally the preface to his *Poems* of 1831), he observes that a poem "is opposed to a work of science by having, for its *immediate* object, pleasure, not truth; to romance, by having for its object an *indefinite* instead of a *definite* pleasure, being a poem only so far as this object is attained; romance presenting perceptible images with definite, poetry with *in*definite sensations, to which end music is an *essential,* since the comprehension of sweet sound is our most indefinite conception. Music, when combined with a pleasurable idea, is poetry; music without the idea is simply music; the idea without the music is prose from its very definitiveness" (7:xliii). In a letter written in 1844 to James Russell Lowell, Poe says, "Music is the perfection of the soul, or idea, of Poetry. The *vagueness* of exaltation aroused by a sweet air (which should be strictly indefinite and never too strongly suggestive) is precisely what we should aim at in poetry."[37] And in "The Poetic Principle," written at the very end of his life, he returns to the subject once more: "Contenting myself with the certainty that Music, in its various modes of metre, rhythm, and rhyme, is of so vast a moment in Poetry as never to be wisely rejected—is so vitally important an adjunct, that he is simply silly who declines its assistance, I will not now pause to maintain its absolute essentiality. It is in Music, perhaps, that the soul most nearly attains the great end for which, when inspired by the Poetic Sentiment, it struggles—the creation of supernal Beauty. It *may* be, indeed, that here this sublime end is, now and then, attained *in fact*" (14:274).

Poe operates in a long-standing tradition linking the sublime and the indefinite, a tradition whose most eloquent eighteenth-century statement in English is the section on obscurity in Edmund Burke's *A Philosophical Enquiry into the Origin of our Ideas of the Sublime and Beautiful* (1757). Contrasting the different effects of painting and poetry, Burke says, "It is one thing to make an idea clear, and another to make it *affecting* to the imagination. . . . the most lively and spirited verbal description I can give, raises a very obscure and imperfect *idea*" of visual objects, but such a description raises "a stronger *emotion*" than could "the best painting. . . . so far is clearness of imagery from being absolutely necessary to an influence upon the passions, that they may be considerably operated upon without presenting any image at all, by certain sounds adapted to that purpose; of which we have a sufficient proof in the acknowledged and powerful effects of instrumental music."[38] And he adds, "The images raised by poetry are always of this obscure kind; . . . in nature dark, confused, uncertain images have a greater power on the fancy to form the grander passions than those have which are more clear and determinate" (p. 62).

Inasmuch as the experience of the sublime involves an intuition of undifferentiated Being, it is necessarily an indefinite experience, an experience beyond words and images that can only be approximated by that sense of the indefinite that *can* be conveyed in words and images. But the question is whether the indefinite is to be evoked by a figure/ ground opposition between the clearly defined verbal image and the indefinite verbal music, the sharp limits of one outlining the vague realm of the other, or by a fusion of the two in which the indefiniteness of the verbal music blurs the verbal imagery. The latter method is that of Poe's poetry, while the former influences the structure of many of the tales, texts in which the rule seems to be that the more incredible the story or the more indeterminate the experience to be evoked, then the more "scientifically" exact the narrative and descriptive apparatus, so that, by defining its own boundaries in the clearest possible imagery, linguistic discourse defines as well the opposing limits of what lies beyond language and reason.

Poe's treatment of scientific intuition also evokes the way in which reason at its highest pitch can reverse into its opposite and become either madness or that skepticism which, having experienced the arbitrariness and relativity of knowledge, uses reason to undermine all certainty in disillusioned reaction. The genius/madman and the genius/hoaxster are two types of narrators that Poe frequently employs in thematizing the dual question of epistemological certainty and narrative credibility. Since in a narrative the certainty of our knowledge seems to rest upon the credibility of the narrator, putting the latter in question puts the former in question, thereby directing our attention to the coincidence between the limits of knowledge and the limits of the written discourse. The inability of the mind to test its knowledge by any other apparatus than that by which the knowledge was acquired, the question of whether the world has a substantial existence apart from the mind or is simply an illusion, become in Poe's narratives the reader's inability to verify the truth of what the narrator says (since the narrator is the sole source of information) and the question of how the narrative is to be taken:

whether in its fictionality the narrative is to be understood as the story of something that is supposed to have actually happened or as an hallucination, a dream, a hoax; or whether it is not to be understood as fiction at all, but as a factual account. All of these possibilities are to be found in Poe's tales—from the ending of "The Fall of the House of Usher" (where the narrator, under the influence of Roderick's hysteria, seems to be having an hallucination); to the conclusion of "Hans Pfaall" (where the narrator reports that after the publication of Pfaall's letter from the moon, popular gossip decried "the whole business as nothing better than a hoax," but then he adds, "Hoax, with these sort of people, is, I believe, a general term for all matters above their comprehension" [2:102]); and on to Poe's "The Balloon-Hoax" (first published in the April 13, 1844 issue of *The New York Sun* and of which Poe subsequently noted: "The subjoined *jeu d'esprit* . . . was originally published, as matter of fact, in the 'New York Sun,' a daily newspaper, and therein fully subserved the purpose of creating indigestible aliment for the *quidnuncs*. . . . The rush for the 'sole paper which had the news,' was something even beyond the prodigious" [5:224]).

Poe is, of course, a master at creating narrators who in the attempt to establish the credibility of their narratives manage to unravel their own efforts. In "MS. Found in a Bottle," the narrator offers his habitual incredulity as evidence of the fact that "no person could be less liable" than himself "to be led away from the severe precincts of truth," and yet he remarks that his only inducement to make the sea voyage was "a kind of nervous restlessness which haunted me as a fiend." When he then adds that the ship's cargo contains "a few cases of opium" and that the "stowage was clumsily done, and the vessel was consequently crank" (2:2), we are left wondering whether this narrative is to be understood as a psychotic episode, an opium dream, or the tall tale of a crackpot.

Typically, Poe's narrators, having an incredible tale to tell, try to disarm the reader's skepticism by the candor with which they acknowledge the problem of credibility. That same candor leads them to tell us something of themselves as evidence of their reliability, their normality, until, becoming too candid, they add a detail that arouses our distrust, usually a revelation of doubleness. The narrator of "The Murders in the Rue Morgue," after describing a "double Dupin—the creative and the resolvent," volunteers, "What I have described in the Frenchman, was

merely the result of an excited, or perhaps of a diseased intelligence"
(4:152), thus giving the impression that the real split and doubling in
Dupin may be less between the creative and the resolvent than between
the genius and the madman. Indeed, the narrator, commenting on the
life that he and Dupin led together in their "time-eaten and grotesque
mansion" in the Faubourg St. Germain, says: "Had the routine of our
life at this place been known to the world, we should have been regarded
as madmen—although, perhaps, as madmen of a harmless nature. Our
seclusion was perfect. We admitted no visitors. . . . We existed within
ourselves alone" (4:151).

Similarly, Pym, in the preface to his narrative, makes a series of unwitting admissions that render the logical status of the narration permanently ambiguous. Acknowledging the problem of credibility involved in
a narrative whose incidents are "of a nature so positively marvellous," he
laments that his assertions are unsupported "except by the evidence of a
single individual, and he a half-breed Indian" (3:1). The half-breed in
American literature is, of course, a stock fictional type of someone whose
word is not to be trusted, an in-between person suspect by both races to
which he belongs. But the half-breed (whether a mixture of white and
Indian, or white and black), besides being a symbol of doubleness, is also
one of the most common forms of the double in American fiction, and in
the latter half of *Pym* it is precisely this role of the dark other self that the
half-breed Dirk Peters plays in relation to the narrator.

Yet the most significant instance of doubling in the preface is not that
of Pym and Peters, the narrator and his ambiguous verifier, but that of
Pym and Poe, the fictive narrator and the real writer. Pym says that
lacking a journal of the voyage to aid him in giving his account "the
appearance of that truth it would really possess," and distrusting his own
abilities as a writer, he felt that anything he published would be regarded
by the public "as merely an impudent and ingenious fiction" (3:2). But
he adds that among the many people who expressed an interest in the
story of his adventures was a "Mr. Poe, lately editor of the Southern
Literary Messenger," who was intrigued with that portion "which related
to the Antarctic Ocean" (3:2). Poe advised Pym to publish his account,
but when Pym still refused, Poe suggested as an alternative that he (Poe)
should "draw up, in his own words, a narrative of the earlier portion" of
Pym's adventures, "publishing it in the Southern Messenger *under the*

garb of fiction" (3:2). Pym agreed to this, and accordingly, "two numbers of the pretended fiction appeared . . . in the Messenger for January and February (1837)" (3:2).

The doubling of Poe and Pym suggests the constitutive opposition between the writing self and the written self, the problematic doubling of the writer and his book. The narrator, a fictive self created by the words of the narrative, pretends by the very convention of his role to be the real self who writes the words; and this reversal is carried a step further when, in the preface that Poe's surrogate Pym is supposed to have written, the real writer appears as a character who offers to serve as a surrogate for the writing of Pym's story. This reversal of roles evokes the imaginative writer's feeling that his real self is the written self (the body of his work), in comparison with which the writing self is a fiction. Call it the writer's atavistic sense of the omnipotence of thought or his aesthetic sense of the primacy of the world of the imagination, it is the feeling that the opposition between the writer and his book, the creator and his creation, conceived as a master/slave relationship, is reversed at some point during the writing, so that the creation becomes the master and the writer becomes its servant: that to write is to be possessed or overpowered by a daemon or, as the narrator of "MS. Found in a Bottle" says, to be haunted by a fiend.

In Pym's preface the polarities of truth and fiction, reality and art, oscillate in relation to the writing self and the written self. According to the fictive narrator, Poe suggests that Pym's lack of art in writing will give his story "all the better chance of being received as truth" (3:2). And when Pym agrees to let Poe write the tale and publish it "*under the garb of fiction,*" the only stipulation is that Pym's "real name be retained" in the story, but "in order that it might certainly be regarded as fiction, the name of Mr. Poe was affixed to the articles in the table of contents of the magazine" (3:2). As if this oscillating relationship were not complex enough, Poe adds one further reversal that links the opposition of writing self and written self to the question of a self-evidential sign and the mingled issues of credibility and certainty. Commenting on the public's unexpected reaction to the story, Pym says, "I found that, in spite of the air of fable which had been so ingeniously thrown around that portion of my statement which appeared in the Messenger (without altering or distorting a single fact), the public were still not at all disposed to receive it as fable, and several letters were sent to Mr. P.'s address, distinctly pressing a conviction to the contrary" (3:3). Pym virtually claims for his work the status of a self-evidential sign: that the facts of the narrative are "of such a nature as to carry with them sufficient evidence of their own authenticity" (3:3). And he makes this claim on the basis of a practical test: that even when the narrative was published as a fiction, the public refused to accept it as such, so evident was its truth. Feeling that he has "little to fear on the score of popular incredulity" (3:3), Pym, the fictive writer of self-evident truths, dismisses Poe, the real writer of ingenious fictions, and takes over the writing of his own narrative.

Having set out to evoke the reversibility of the constitutive opposites *writing self / written self*, Poe adds to the structure of the preface a moment of indeterminacy that dissolves the whole, a sight of the abyss upon which this differential opposition rests. Pym concludes: "This *exposé* being made, it will be seen at once how much of what follows I claim to be my own writing; and it will also be understood that no fact is misrepresented in the first few pages which were written by Mr. Poe. Even to those readers who have not seen the Messenger, it will be unnecessary to point out where his portion ends and my own commences; the difference in point of style will be readily perceived" (3:3). If the style is the man, then that point in the act of writing where one man stops and another begins is defined by a difference in styles, a visible limit. But what happens when, as in this case, the two "men" to be differentiated are the writing self and the written self (the latter being represented here by the fictive narrator who exists *in* and *as* the words of his narrative)? For if it is true that the self *as written* is wholly an affair of words, is that any less true of the self *as writer?* What Poe evokes is the paradox of mutually constitutive oppositions, the way in which difference constitutes identity.

That the interplay of sameness and difference in self-identity was a continuing concern of Poe's is indicated by a remark made by the narrator of "Morella" (1835): "That identity which is termed personal, Mr. Locke, I think, truly defines to consist in the sameness of a rational being. And since by person we understand an intelligent essence having reason, and since there is a consciousness which always accompanies thinking, it is this which makes us all to be that which we call *ourselves*—thereby distinguishing us from other beings that think, and giving us our personal identity. But the *principium individuationis*—the notion of that identity *which at death is or is not lost forever,* was to me—at all times, a

consideration of intense interest."[39] Implicit in the concept of personal
identity as "the sameness of a rational being" is the sense of sameness as a
persistence through change, a repetition in difference, so that to conceive of the sameness of the self with itself is implicitly and simultaneously to conceive of the difference of the self from itself, to conceive of
the unified self as double and of unity as split. The self as self-conscious
identity, as the awareness of unity with itself, consists in the ability to
perceive itself as simultaneously one and more than one, that is, another
one (doubling), and as one and less than one (splitting). That act of
symbolization in which the shadow, recognized as the self's *own*, stands
as an image of self, of *ownness* (part for whole), and in which its inscription, the tracing of the shadow outline, stands as the self's image in the
self's absence (the substitution of one for another), gives (as splitting and
doubling) the two basic modes of metonymy and metaphor by which
man and language constitute one another in their essentially relational
condition. For if it is true that language is a continuous system of differences, an interlocking network of mutually constitutive oppositions,
of pure relationships in which the related entities have no existence prior
to or apart from the relationship, and if it is also true that those constitutive oppositions themselves exist only in relation to an observer (that is,
the self), then it is equally true that the self is only the sum of those
relationships as they intersect in a point. The self that speaks is simultaneously spoken by language, the self that writes is simultaneously written by its words. Language is an effect of the self, and the self is recip-
rocally an effect of language.

The paradox here involves the way in which a mutually constitutive
opposition simultaneously depends upon and dissolves the notion of a
limit, whether that limit be internal or external. Like a Möbius strip in
which a two-sided surface is turned into a one-sided surface but is still
experienced as if it had two sides, a mutually constitutive opposition
involves the same bewildering interpenetration of one and two, so that it
is felt at once to be both one and two, and neither one nor two. It is as if
we asked whether a spot on the globe was to our left or to our right and,
upon receiving the reply "Both," suddenly realized that the answer, in
dissolving the "or" of the question, dissolved the question, dissolved the
ground of perception on which it was based. In a mutually constitutive
opposition we confront what seems like a stupid mystery: for what does
it mean, on the one hand, to speak of inseparable, differentiated entities,

of entities that are always implicit in one another, or on the other hand, to speak of the opposing aspects of a single entity, aspects whose very opposition constitutes the entity? Questions of priority are, of course, meaningless here, for what sense does it make to ask whether left came before right, up before down, subject before object, or man before language? In a mutually constitutive opposition, if both of the opposites do not come into existence together, then neither comes into existence, for it is their coming-together that constitutes their being-apart, just as their being-apart constitutes their coming-together. Like a Möbius strip stared at too long, constitutive oppositions thought upon too long make us feel dizzy, as if we were losing our orientation, as if we were seeing the boundaries and limits of the world vanish before our eyes, so that finally it is impossible to say whether the concept of a limit has been rendered indeterminate or whether we have come up against the concept of an indeterminate limit.

When Pym characterizes the difference between himself and Poe within the text as a "difference in point of style" that "will be readily perceived," this is in line with Poe's usual practice in double stories of locating the origin of an external doubling in an internal split—in this case, the technical division between author and narrator internal to the written text. Yet that "difference in point of style" is precisely what is *not* to be perceived within the text of *Pym*. Though the difference between the writing self and the written self, between the writer and his self-constituting, inscribed image, is certainly one that we experience and use, it is not likely to be a difference that we can locate with any accuracy, nor one to which the question of an undivided origin will apply. The dividing line between the self and its language is indeterminate precisely because the difference between the two is an oscillating, self-reversing difference: where one is, the other is, and where the Other is, One is. We can know the One from the Other (the self from its double), but we cannot know the One *apart from* the Other, for without the Other there is no One.

It is within the context of this problematic doubling between Poe and Pym, as it is evoked in the preface, that the subsequent doublings, first between Pym and Augustus and then between Pym and Dirk Peters, are to be understood. The reversibility of self and other is made explicit at the very start of the narrative when Pym, noting Augustus's uncanny ability to enter "into my state of mind," explains, "It is probable, indeed, that our intimate communion had resulted in a partial interchange of character" (3:18). The interplay of Pym and his doubles is, of course, the main narrative device for objectifying that split in the self that leads to the overwhelming of the rational by the irrational in the various shipwreck episodes.

In the first episode (the running down of the sailboat *Ariel*) the cause of the literal overwhelming of the boat is the figurative overpowering of the vessel of reason by a drunkenness that is "like madness," and the method of this overthrow is especially significant. Though both Pym and Augustus have become "not a little intoxicated" at the party, it is not Pym who proposes the midnight sail in the storm, but Augustus, the irrational double who carries Pym off by counterfeiting the appearance of sober reason. In response to Augustus's suggestion, Pym says:

> I was never so astonished in my life, not knowing what he intended, and thinking that the wines and liquors he had drunk had set him entirely beside himself. He proceeded to talk very coolly, however, saying he knew that I supposed him intoxicated, but that he was never more sober in his life. He was ... determined to get up and dress, and go out on a frolic with the boat. I can hardly tell what possessed me, but the words were no sooner out of his mouth than I felt a thrill of the greatest excitement and pleasure, and thought his mad idea one of the most delightful and most reasonable things in the world. (3:6–7)

The language of the passage—Pym's suspicion that intoxication had set Augustus "entirely beside himself," his own wonder at what "possessed" him to think a "mad idea one of the ... most reasonable things in the world"—evokes both the internal split / external doubling of daemonic possession and the reciprocal oscillation by which rational and irrational are constituted. This sense of the presence of the opposites in one another, of the way that the irrational reflects the antithetical image of the rational, is emphasized when Augustus loses consciousness during the storm and Pym realizes that his friend has been in "a highly concentrated state of intoxication ... which, like madness, frequently enables the victim to imitate the outward demeanour of one in perfect possession of his senses" (3:8–9). Seeing Augustus's reversal from rational appearance to irrational reality, Pym immediately shifts roles and comes to his senses.

In the second overwhelming-of-the-vessel episode (the mutiny and shipwreck of the *Grampus*), Dirk Peters, the half-breed Indian, replaces Augustus as Pym's double. As in the first episode, the ultimate cause of the *Grampus*'s wreck is an irrational uprising, the drunken overwhelming of the enlightened, human side of the self by its dark, animal side. The irrational animal in man is, of course, a frequent culprit in Poe's double stories—from the perverse self of "William Wilson" to the savage ape of "The Murders in the Rue Morgue." In the mutiny on the *Grampus*, the dark, animal side of the self is embodied first by the Negro cook who methodically butchers the bound crew members with an axe and throws them overboard. The cook is about to make Augustus his next victim when he is prevented by a sudden reversal of character among the mutineers:

> ... the four remaining prisoners, together with my friend, who had been thrown on the deck with the rest, were respited while the mate sent below for rum, and the whole murderous party held a drunken carouse.... They now fell to disputing in regard to the fate of the survivors.... Upon some of the mutineers the liquor appeared to have a softening effect, for several voices were heard in favor of releasing the captives altogether, on condition of joining the mutiny and sharing the profits. The black cook, however (who in all respects was a perfect demon, and who seemed to exert as much influence, if not more, than the mate himself), would listen to no proposition of the kind.... Fortunately, he was so far overcome by intoxication as to be easily restrained by the less blood-thirsty of the party, among whom was a line-manager, who went by the name of Dirk Peters. (3:51)

In the dialectic of rational and irrational, of light self and dark self, it is the in-between figure, the half-breed Dirk Peters, who changes sides in the mutiny, saves the lives of both Augustus and Pym, and eventually enables them to regain control of the vessel. After the capsizing of the *Grampus* in the storm and Augustus's death, Peters becomes Pym's inseparable companion for the rest of the narrative and saves his life once again on the island of Tsalal when the two narrowly escape being massacred by the black islanders. Yet although Peters saves Pym's life on at least two occasions, the role he plays in relation to Pym is clearly that of the dark other, the daemonic opposing self that at once threatens and sustains. Pym's first description of Peters emphasizes both his animal nature and his daemonic appearance:

> Peters himself was one of the most ferocious-looking men I ever beheld. He was short in stature—not more than four feet eight inches high—but his limbs were of Herculean mould. His hands, especially, were so enormously thick and broad as hardly to retain a human shape. His arms, as well as legs, were *bowed* in the most singular manner.... His head was equally deformed, being of immense size, with an indentation on the crown (like that on the head of most negroes), and entirely bald. To conceal this latter deficiency ... he usually wore a wig formed of any hair-like material which presented itself—occasionally the skin of a Spanish dog or American grizzly bear. At the time spoken of he had on a portion of one of these bear-skins; and it added no little to the natural ferocity of his countenance.... To pass this man with a casual glance, one might imagine him to be convulsed with laughter—but a second look would induce a shuddering acknowledgement, that if such an expression were indicative of merriment, the merriment must be that of a demon. (3:51–52)

The simian Peters with his bowed arms and legs and his bearskin toupée resembles less a human being than the ape of "The Murders in the Rue Morgue," and the resemblance is not without meaning; for as the sailor's loss of control over his pet orangutan in the Dupin story results in the commission of a crime marked by such prodigious physical strength and animal savagery that the narrator concludes it must have been done by "a madman, ... some raving maniac, escaped from a neighboring *Maison de Santé*" (4:181), so the apelike sailor Peters seems to Pym always to be in danger of lapsing into a state of animal irrationality in which his exceptional strength will work indiscriminate destruction. Pym says that there were many anecdotes about Peters "prevalent among the seafaring men of Nantucket. These anecdotes went to prove his prodigious strength when under excitement, and some of them had given rise to a doubt of his sanity" (3:52). And when Pym and Augustus consider the possibility of regaining control of the ship with Peters' help, Augustus urges "the necessity of the greatest caution in making the attempt, as the conduct of the hybrid appeared to be instigated by the most arbitrary caprice alone; and, indeed, it was difficult to say if at any moment he was of sound mind" (3:73-74). Peters himself tells Pym that if he is ever arraigned for his part in the mutiny, he depends on "getting acquitted upon trial, on the score of insanity (which he solemnly averred had actuated him in lending his aid to the mutiny)" (3:80).

After his initial lengthy description of Peters, Pym explains that he has gone into such detail because Peters "proved the main instrument" in saving their lives and because "I shall have frequent occasion to mention him hereafter in the course of my narrative," but then, as if sensing how incredible the description of Peters has been, he adds, "a narrative, let me say, which, in its latter portions, will be found to include incidents of a nature so entirely out of the range of human experience, and for this reason so far beyond the limits of human credulity, that I proceed in utter hopelessness of obtaining credence for all that I shall tell, yet confidently trusting in time and progressing science to verify some of the most important and most improbable of my statements" (3:53). The implication is that if the reader thinks the description of the daemonic Peters is incredible, it will soon seem, through Pym's method of constitution by opposition, the most believable thing in the world compared to what follows.

Pym obviously finds Peters' presence in the narrative troubling; for as Pym is a written self who has, within this text, supposedly reversed roles with the writing self by taking over the writing of the narrative from Poe and reducing the actual writer to the status of a character, so Peters, the only living witness to the incredible events that Pym narrates, is capable of carrying out the same reversal in relation to Pym. Poe emphasizes Peters' status as a written character in a book when he has Pym tell us that the book he read on board the *Grampus* concerned "the expedition of Lewis and Clarke to the mouth of the Columbia" (3:25), and then has Pym begin his description of Peters a few pages later with the following account of the half-breed's origin: the "man was the son of an Indian woman of the tribe of Upsarokas, who live among the fastnesses of the Black Hills near the source of the Missouri. His father was a fur-trader, I believe, or at least connected in some manner with the Indian trading-posts on Lewis river" (3:51).

Since Peters exists for us as a written self within a narrative whose fictive writing self is Pym, it is only appropriate that Peters' place of origin should be located in the written text that Peters' "author" has most recently read, thus dissolving the question of the author's originality versus the character's, the question of which came first—writing self or written self. For the reader, Peters is a man made out of words, the words of the supposed writer Pym; but Pym, who is also a man made out of words, is himself a reader, and by locating Peters' place of origin in a book that Pym has just read, Poe suggests that Pym's writing is the rewriting of his reading and, conversely, that his reading is the (self-projective/self-reflective) rereading of his writing. This is simply another way of stating the paradox that writing self and written self, the self and its hieroglyphic double, mutually constitute one an-other, that though we can know one from the other, we cannot know one apart from the other. Pym can write Peters only because Peters is, in some sense, *already written*. The self can constitute the other as the image of the self, which simultaneously constitutes the self as image, only because the self is originally other to itself—another way of saying that an internal split grounds an external doubling at the same time that an external doubling grounds an internal split, that the origin is simultaneously split and doubled.

Since it is specifically in his role as the dark double that Peters accompanies Pym to the abyss, and since that voyage to the limits of differentiation is evoked as a quest for the simultaneous origin of man and language by superimposing upon the polar voyage a traditional figure of the search for linguistic origins (the journey to the *Abyss*inian source of the Nile, and its American equivalent, the journey to the source of the Missouri/Mississippi), it is particularly appropriate that the dark Peters—a man whose real origin, as Poe implies, is linguistic—should have his fictitious place of origin located "among the fastnesses of the Black Hills near the source of the Missouri"—the geographic source of the Lewis and Clark journals that are Peters' graphic source. For Peters, the quests for a linguistic origin and a personal origin coincide as the images of the voyage to the abyss and the journey to the source of the Missouri merge.

As a half-breed, a mixture of light and dark, Peters doubles the constitutive opposition of rational and irrational, light self and dark self, man and animal, within Pym at the same time that he evokes Pym's linguistic status as a man made of words, a self constituted by the black/white opposition of print on paper. To call Peters Pym's dark self or dark other is not to imply, then, that Peters is devoid of rational, human qualities or conversely to imply that Pym is devoid of irrational, animal traits. Rather, it is to indicate that in Peters the irrational animal predominates over the rational man, while in Pym it is the reverse, and that the relation between Pym and his double begins by opposing the dominant aspect of each as the basis for subsequent reversals. Pym feels for Peters a simultaneous attraction and repulsion precisely because he senses how much the half-breed's animal nature embodies something deep and powerful in his own person and thus something to which he himself is only partially opposed, something that could, under Peters' influence, overwhelm his rational nature.

Section 8
Cannibalism and Sacrifice; Metaphors of the Body—Transfiguration, Transubstantiation, Resurrection, and Ascension

The most significant instance of this feared reversion to animality occurs after the wreck of the *Grampus* when Pym, Augustus, Peters, and a seaman named Parker have been drifting for days without food and water. Parker suggests to Pym that the only solution to their extremity is cannibalism: "Parker turned suddenly towards me with an expression of countenance which made me shudder. There was about him an air of self-possession which I had not noticed in him until now, and before he opened his lips my heart told me what he would say. He proposed, in a few words, that one of us should die to preserve the existence of the others" (3:123). At this point the chapter ends; and in the instant before the next chapter begins, the reader cannot help but think that if Pym knew in his heart what Parker would say, it can only be because Pym himself had considered the same possibility. At the start of the next chapter, Pym admits, "I had, for some time past, dwelt upon the prospect of our being reduced to this last horrible extremity, and had secretly made up my mind to suffer death in any shape or under any circumstances rather than resort to such a course" (3:124). Pym tries to reason with Parker, "begging him in the name of everything which he held sacred" to abandon the idea and not mention it to Augustus or Peters. Parker agrees that "to resort to such a course was the most horrible alternative which could enter into the mind of man; but that he had now held out as long as human nature could be sustained; that it was unnecessary for all to perish, when, by the death of one, it was possible, and even probable, that the rest might be finally preserved" (3:124).

Pym discovers to his horror that both "Augustus and Peters, who, it seems, had long secretly entertained the same fearful idea which Parker had been merely the first to broach, joined with him in his design, and insisted upon its immediately being carried into effect" (3:126). Pym had hoped that one of the two "would be found still possessed of sufficient strength of mind" to side with him against Parker; but finding this not to be the case, he says: "It became absolutely necessary that I should attend to my own safety, as a further resistance on my part might possibly be considered by men in their frightful condition a sufficient excuse for refusing me fair play in the tragedy that I knew would speedily be enacted. I now told them I was willing to submit to the proposal" (3:126). When one recalls that this is the same Pym who had said only a few paragraphs earlier that he had made up his mind "to suffer death in any shape or under any circumstances rather than resort to such a course," one can only wonder how straightforward Pym's account of his motives has been. When it is decided that they will draw straws to pick the sacrificial victim and that Pym will hold them, he confides, "I . . . thought over every species of finesse by which I could trick some one of my fellow-sufferers to draw the short straw," but he adds in his defense, "Before any one condemn me for this apparent heartlessness, let him be placed in a situation precisely similar to my own" (3:128). The short straw falls to Parker, and Peters stabs him in the back. After cutting off Parker's head, hands, and feet, they devour the rest of the body piecemeal over the next four days. Pym says that it was "a scene which, with its minutest details, no after events have been able to efface in the slightest degree from my memory, and whose stern recollection will embitter every future moment of my existence" (3:126–27).

Poe has constructed the cannibalism episode so that it bears a dual significance reflecting the essential doubleness of signification in relation to the abyss as ground. On the one hand, because the prohibition against cannibalism (the sameness of eating one's own kind) is, in terms of human culture, almost as universal a principle of differentiation between "man" and "animal" as the incest taboo (the sameness of mating with the members of one's own family), the cannibalism episode would indicate that Pym and his doubles have reverted from reason to instinct, from human to animal behavior, after having, in Parker's words, "held out as long as human nature could be sustained." Their cannibalism would appear, then, to be a confounding of differentiation. Yet, on the other hand, this episode is presented from the very start as a type of sacrifice. Parker proposes that one of them "should die to preserve the existence of the others," and when Pym argues with him, he replies that it is "unnecessary for all to perish, when, by the death of one" it is possible "that the rest might be finally preserved." Parker enunciates one of the two principles that constitute the symbolic order—metonymic reduction (part for whole): one member shall die as a sacrificial substitute for the death of the entire group. The other principle of the symbolic order, metaphoric substitution (one whole for another), usually takes, within a sacrificial context, the form of the scapegoat, the animal that is substituted for the human victim. In the cannibalism episode, it would seem that although the metonymic principle is in play, the metaphoric is not, since it is precisely the lack of an animal to use for food (an animal which would be substituted for the human victim in a sacrifice) that drives the starving men to cannibalism. Yet this absence of the metaphoric principle can only be an apparent absence; for metonymy and metaphor, internal splitting and external doubling, are mutually constitutive, and if the metonymic principle is present, then the metaphoric must be as well, even though its operation may be masked.

In order for Parker's cannibalization to be presented as a sacrifice, as a metonymic reduction, there must be in operation a metaphoric substitution whereby the four shipwrecked seamen are understood to form a whole, a communal "body" of related members. Earlier, in discussing the way that man unifies the world by casting his shadow upon it, we remarked that all ideas of unity are ultimately derived from the human body, from a physical, organic whole of articulated parts whose natural double is its shadow. That individual human beings, independent organic wholes, are able to consider themselves as parts of a larger whole conceived as a metaphoric body not only evokes the paradoxical way in which doubleness (multiplicity) constitutes unity but also suggests the thematic connection between the cannibalism episode and the doubling of Pym and Peters, for it is precisely the metaphor of the body and the process of embodiment that is at issue in their doubling.

As Pym's shadow self, Peters represents the irrational aspect of human nature, an aspect that, as Poe implies in relating the half-breed's erratic behavior to his apelike physiognomy, is essentially a function of man's animal body. But the paradox to which the doubling of Pym and Peters draws our attention is that though Peters stands for the bodily,

instinctual half of man as differentiated from the rational self, it is precisely the *metaphor of the body* that constitutes the self-conscious, nonphysical entity called the self. For what we mean by the word "self" in this
context is an internal psychic unity that persists through the continual
change of intensive states, an immaterial entity that manifests a continuity analogous to the spatial continuity and organic unity of the body.
The self's difference from the body is grounded, then, on its sameness
with the body, grounded on a recognition of the self as a metaphoric
body. In "Morella" Poe quotes Locke's definition of personal identity as
consisting in "the sameness of a rational being," but in *Pym* he draws our
attention to the paradoxical fact that the sameness of a rational being,
that personal identity which is supposed to survive the destruction of the
body, is always imagined as being like the sameness of a body, the continuous unity of a physical whole.

Earlier, in discussing the mythic origin of man and language as an act
of hieroglyphic doubling, we said that it is only when a nameless creature
without language first recognizes its own shadow on the ground or its
own reflection in a pool—that is, recognizes itself as *image*—that it recognizes an image of its *self*. We are now in a better position to appreciate
the conceptual difficulties involved in the notion of a simultaneously
split and doubled origin that this statement tries to evoke, for obviously
the statement contains what seems to be a contradiction. To say that this
nameless creature becomes self-conscious by recognizing its shadow, by
recognizing an image as *its own*, is to imply by the words "its own" that
this as yet unselfconscious creature is already conscious of itself, of its
ownness. What this points up is that simultaneously present with the
metaphor of the body *as a unified whole* is a metonymic relationship in
which the body is seen *as part of a larger whole*. We might, then, rephrase
the myth of origin as follows: the prelinguistic creature notices a correlation between the shape of its body and the shape of a dark figure on the
ground. Sometimes the dark figure is there, sometimes it isn't; but
whenever it *is* there, it always has a special relationship to the body, a
relationship best revealed by motion. Whatever movement the body
makes, the dark figure makes the same movement *at exactly the same time*.
The dark figure parallels or doubles the body. This phenomenon would
present the unselfconscious creature with two possibilities: either the
dark figure is a part of the body, or it is another like the body. There
would be sense perceptions to support each view. As in the case of a

separate being, the dark figure's comings and goings are not under the direct control of the unselfconscious creature's body. At night or on a cloudy day, the dark figure is not there, and there is nothing the body can do about it. But when the dark figure *is* there, its shape and movement are under the body's immediate sway; it responds as if it were part of the body. The two possibilities regarding the dark figure (a part of the body; another like body) can be phrased as an either/or or as a both/and relationship. Indeed, the essence of this special relationship between the body and its shadow is that both ways of phrasing the two possibilities (either the dark figure is a part of the body or it is another like the body; the dark figure is both a part of the body and another like the body) are simultaneously maintained in existence. The mind oscillates between the two. (Whose mind? That of the unselfconscious creature who as yet has no mind?)

The point at which the unselfconscious creature becomes conscious of itself within this mythic scenario of the origin of man and language is the moment when it senses, feels, sees (what verb should we use?) that the external relationship between the body and its shadow corresponds to another relationship between the body and something internal to the body. The shadow that the body casts is simultaneously introjected and reprojected outward again. The shadow is understood to be an image of the body at the very moment and in the very act in which the relationship body/shadow is understood as an image of the relationship body/self. That is, the body/shadow relationship is understood to be a metonymic, whole/part relationship at the very instant and in the very act in which the body/shadow–body/self equation is understood as a metaphoric, one-for-another substitution; and simultaneously, the body/self relationship is understood to be a metonymic, part/whole relationship at the very instant and in the very act in which the equation of shadow and self is understood as a metaphoric substitution. The metaphor of the body as an organic whole is thus grounded on a metonymic relationship of body to self as part to whole, and the metaphoric substitution of shadow for self is based on the paradoxical *symbolic* equation "part equals whole."

Though the word "self" is frequently used to refer to the total human personality, the combination of mind and body, I have used it in the constitutive opposition body/self (rather than a word like "mind" or "psyche") in order to evoke through its specific character as a reflexive, intensive pronoun the crucial aspect of that immaterial entity that opposes itself to the body. When we speak of self-consciousness, we mean the presence of the self to itself—self-possession; and it is precisely this sense of reflexiveness, intensiveness, possession, ownness, of belonging to, that the word "self" conveys. The self sees a self-constituting image of itself, that is, sees itself as image, at the moment that it sees, in gazing at the relationship between the body and its shadow image, that the self's ownness, its oneness, is precisely the dualness of being that entity whose essence *is its constitutive relatedness to an image of itself*. The self is pure reflexiveness, *an imaged presence to itself as image,* a primariness that is always already a secondariness, a mirror image of a mirror image of a mirror image. We could say, then, that the simultaneous origin of man and language, the mutual, instantaneous constitution of the symbolic order, involves a triangular structure of self, body, and shadow (image of the body) with the three points of the triangle related by three mutually constitutive, bipolar oppositions (body/shadow, body/self, self/shadow). Self-consciousness occurs at the instant when all possible relationships of splitting and doubling between the three points of the triangle simultaneously come into play.

It is time to pause in this arabesque and point out some of the obvious difficulties in the language that we have been using to describe this mythic origin of language. First of all, in trying to evoke the essence of the self as pure reflexiveness, language necessarily becomes circular, sentences tend to double back on themselves, words and thoughts seem to spin with ever-increasing speed around a central void. Perhaps it is just this dizzying sensation of thought about thought that underlies the image of the whirlpool/abyss. The second difficulty is that in trying to discuss self-consciousness, we are faced with something so basic, pervasive, and familiar that it is almost invisible, something that is so intimately involved with the nature of language that it always seems to evade the attempt to evoke it in language. As a result, our language must become progressively more complex, more distorted, in order to render the familiar unfamiliar, in order to put what is closest to the self at some distance so that we can see it. The third difficulty arises in trying to talk about the simultaneity of mutually constitutive oppositions—not just the fact that, being mutually constitutive, neither opposite can have temporal or logical priority over the other, but the fact that the symbolic order is constituted by a network of these bipolar oppositions coming into existence *simultaneously* (left and right, up and down, light and dark, and so on). The difficulty is that though one can use the word "simultaneous" to describe the process of mutual constitution, when one then goes on to discuss this process, the very temporal, discursive structure of a sentence will demand that one opposite be placed syntactically before another, that one pair of opposites precede another in the discussion, so that language will thus seem to give priority to one opposite, or to privilege one pair, over another. As a result, one's language must suffer the distortions required to thwart this apparent contradiction of simultaneity.

The final and most pervasive linguistic difficulty that we face in talking about the simultaneous origin of man and language arises from the fact that we are dealing with an alogical myth. As we noted earlier, man can have no real knowledge of the origin of language, for such knowledge would require that one know that undifferentiated condition from which language is distinguished. It would require that one express in language the condition of no-language, that one think the absence of thought. And yet as surely as man can have no real knowledge of the origin of language, just as surely he is impelled by his self-defining nature to that impossible, delimiting knowledge. Consequently, his myths of origin, as reasonable explanations of the unexplainable, implicitly reveal their own alogicality: the irrationality of an unknowable ground of knowing, an unsymbolizable ground of symbolization. In speaking of his origins, man paradoxically grounds his words upon an essential wordlessness. That is, language, as a continuous network of differential oppositions, can only treat what lies beyond language by making it part of an opposition: differentiated/undifferentiated. Yet the essence of the undifferentiated is precisely that it cannot be made part of an opposition. Consequently, the opposition differentiated/undifferentiated is not just an opposition like any other; it is an illusory opposition that grounds the rationality of differentiation on the alogic of treating what is essentially unrelatable *as if* it could be incorporated into a differential relationship.

Words like "alogical" or "undifferentiated" do not, of course, name what lies beyond language. Rather, they evoke the distortions or warps that occur within language when it tries to speak of its origin—the warp in thought that results, for example, from treating what is beyond language as if it were simply a negation of the characteristics of language and thus could be named by prefixing an *a-* or *un-* to words like "logical" or "differentiated." Yet negation is itself a linguistic category. Even the phrase "beyond language" implies a deceptive spatial relationship between language and what lies "beyond" it. Yet if what lies beyond language is not available to language, how would we ever become aware that there is anything beyond language? The answer would seem to be: only by its contradictory, logic-dissolving effect on thought, its distortion of language whenever language tries to approach its limit, its origin—the kind of warping effect that has been present at numerous points in our discussion of *Pym*.

The myth of hieroglyphic doubling as the origin of man and language manifests its alogical core when we pursue the logical consequences of the scenario in which an act of simultaneous projection/introjection of the shadow raises a prelinguistic creature to the level of self-consciousness. For in order to explain such an operation, we must at some point attribute to that unselfconscious creature characteristics and aptitudes that are incompatible with its being truly unselfconscious, precisely because we cannot explain an absolute beginning of self-consciousness, cannot grasp within the self-conscious medium of language what unselfconsciousness involves, and so must conceive of the creature as if it were already in possession of abilities of perceiving, correlating, and differentiating that necessarily imply self-consciousness. The alogical core of myths of linguistic origin, the way in which these myths ground the logic of their terms, their rational linguistic explanation of language as *ratio*, on a violation of logic, a violation masked by a linguistic sleight of mind (like the opposition differentiated/undifferentiated), is the result of thought's inability to conceive of either an absolute limit or its alternative, infinity. It is in light of this paradox—the grounding of a system upon an act that confounds the logical distinctions of the very system that it founds—that we can grasp the full significance of Parker's cannibalization.

What Poe focuses on in the cannibalism episode is the oscillation between a metaphoric body and a literal body, an oscillation that enables a single act to bear two opposing significances, to be a con-founding foundation in which mutually constitutive oppositions are simultaneously phrased as both/and and either/or relationships. Since it is a metaphoric body (the shadow outline) that provides an image of unity for the self, thereby differentiating human from animal, the opposition animal/human hinges upon an opposition between a physical body and the image of a body. Poe evokes this oscillation between literal and symbolic in the dual significance (cannibalism and sacrifice; cannibalism or sacrifice) of a single act of dismemberment and reassimilation. If Parker, as a human being, has a dual nature (animal and man, literal body and imaged body) whose two aspects can be related both metonymically (as two halves of a whole: a both/and relationship: splitting) and metaphorically (as two separate wholes: an either/or relationship: doubling), then we can phrase the significance of Parker's death in the following possible ways. First, either Parker is a man or an animal: If Parker is a man, then for his fellow men to devour him is an act of cannibalism, a reversal of human conduct that transforms these men into "animals," into instinctual creatures who devour their own kind. Yet it was Parker who, in suggesting that cannibalism was the solution to their extremity, first put aside his human nature and became an animal. And if Parker is an animal, then devouring him is in a sense not cannibalism. He can thus be used as a sacrificial substitute, a scapegoat made to bear the full responsibility for the "animal" impulse to cannibalism that is to be exiled from the community of men by his destruction. Indeed, Parker's fate, even though it is arbitrarily determined by the drawing of lots, is interpreted by Pym as springing directly from Parker's renunciation of his human nature. Pym sees "the consummation" of the episode "in the death of him who had been chiefly instrumental in bringing it about" (3:129). The community of men rids itself of a dangerous creature in its midst; it amputates a mortifying member of the communal body. (It is worth noting in this regard that Augustus's subsequent death on board the drifting hulk results from the mortification of his unamputated wounded arm. When Peters throws Augustus's corpse overboard, the putrefied body literally comes apart in his hands, and Pym and Peters watch in horror as the floating body is devoured by sharks.)

The second possible way of phrasing the significance of Parker's death is that Parker is both a man and an animal and that as a man he willingly offers his physical body as a sacrifice to preserve the life of the communal body of men. Because of the episode's ambiguous structure, there is as much textual evidence to support a sacrificial interpretation as there is to support a purely cannibalistic one. Thus, although Parker suggests the inhuman recourse of cannibalism, he proposes it for a humane reason and in terms of human rationality (that it is illogical for all to perish when by the death of one the rest may be saved). And when the lot falls on him, he willingly accepts his fate and submits to his death without resistance—in clear contrast to Pym's deliberation about how he could trick one of his fellow men into choosing the short straw. In presenting his cannibalization as a voluntary sacrifice, Parker's human self offers up its animal body to sustain, to physically ground, the metaphoric communal body of men by nourishing the members of that body. What then occurs in the sacrificial cannibalization of Parker is a dismemberment and reassimilation. Parker's "membership" in this body of men presumes a part/whole relationship between his individual metaphoric body (his personal self) and the communal metaphoric body, while the dismemberment, his separation from the communal body of men (his otherness to it), depends upon a one-for-another substitution of his physical body for his personal metaphoric body. By an act of personal choice, Parker divests his physical body of that aura of sacredness cast over it by the both/and relationship of body and self, and presents it as a literal flesh-and-blood organism capable of being eaten and of sustaining life in other organisms. The sacrificial dismemberment of Parker from the metaphoric communal body is thus based on the alogical simultaneous phrasing of the opposition body/self (animal/human) as an either/or and a both/and relationship. In this simultaneous phrasing, the self's control over the body rests on a metonymic, part/whole relationship of body and self, a control that is used against itself in order to replace the part/whole relation with a metaphoric, one-for-another relationship whereby the literal animal body as an independent unit is substituted for the human self and is thus cut off from the communal body of men.

Parker's symbolic dismemberment from the communal body is followed by the literal dismemberment of his physical body, and the process of Parker's reassimilation into the communal body—that reincorporation whereby a physical whole is divided into parts that are ingested and assimilated by other physical wholes that are in turn members of the symbolic body of men—depends on the same interplay of metaphor and metonymy. Unlike sacrifices in which the victim is driven out of the community never to return or in which the act of sacrificial destruction is meant to render the victim physically unusable to the community as a sign of its being offered up to a higher, nonphysical power, Parker's sacrifice is intended to render the victim available to the community in all his physicality as an edible body.

The issues that Parker's cannibalization raises regarding the relation-

ship of the symbolic order to the constitutive interplay of a literal and a
metaphoric body are made even more problematic by the fact that Poe
implicitly sets Parker's death within the context of another cannibalistic
sacrifice. Trying to prevent Parker from mentioning the idea of cannibalism to the others, Pym begins by "mentally praying to God for
power to dissuade him from the horrible purpose he entertained" and
then begs Parker "in the name of everything which he held sacred . . . to
abandon the idea" (3:124). The mention of God and the appeal "in the
name of everything which he held sacred" remind us that for Pym and
his companions the sacredness of the body and the prohibition against
cannibalism would be formulated as part of the Christian religion, whose
central act, reenacted through time as the bond of the Christian community, is a cannibalistic sacrifice—the devouring of the body of a slain
god. At the Last Supper, Christ transubstantiates bread and wine into his
body and blood, breaks the bread into pieces, and distributes his dismembered body to his disciples to eat. The offering up of Christ's body
at the Last Supper, a self-sacrifice that is consummated the following day
with his death on the cross, appeases the wrath of the Father for Adam's
sin and redeems man from eternal death. Unlike Parker's sacrifice in
which the body that is eaten becomes part of the person who eats it, in
Christ's sacrifice the person who eats the body becomes part of what is
eaten: he is incorporated into the mystical body of Christ. By eating the
dismembered parts of Christ's body, the disciples become members of
that body; and after their own deaths when their physical bodies have
decayed, that membership will be the means by which they are remembered by Christ and saved from everlasting destruction.

In Parker's sacrifice and in Christ's, the life of a communal,
metaphoric body is grounded on the death of an individual, physical
body. But in Parker's case it is the communal body's physical life that is
preserved, while in Christ's it is its spiritual life. This difference in the
type of life sustained in each instance corresponds to the two different
pairs of opposites that are simultaneously phrased as both/and and
either/or in the two sacrifices. With Parker, the paired opposites are
animal/human. With Christ, they are human/divine, simultaneously
phrased as "Christ is both man and God" and "Christ is either man or
God." (All of these alternatives are to be found among the early strains
of Christianity: thus, the Arians denied Christ's divinity, and the
Docetists denied his humanity; while the orthodoxy of the Nicene Creed

settled the matter by proclaiming Christ to be true God and true man.) If Parker's sacrifice is concerned with that metaphorizing of a body that differentiates the human self from an animal organism, Christ's sacrifice is concerned with that apotheosizing of an image that differentiates the immortal soul from the human self. In the person of Christ, God becomes man—the Supreme Being takes on a human body. And in Christ's sacrifice, man becomes like a god—Christ's death gives man a share in eternal life, a persistence of the personal self beyond death.

By placing Parker's sacrifice within the context of Christ's sacrificial death, Poe evokes the way in which one half of a mutually constitutive opposition becomes privileged over the other half, the way in which the human self that is differentiated from the body by whose physical life it exists becomes separated from the body to exist by a spiritual life of its own, a life retrospectively conceived as prior to, and independent of, the body. The poet in Shelley's *Alastor*, gazing at the hieroglyphic images of gods and daemons on the temple walls, sees that they are man-made "images of more than man." What he sees is the self-dissolving reversal implicit in the symbolic order. For in the process of its apotheosis, the body's image becomes progressively more bodiless—from being an image that is differentiated from the body, to being an image that is independent of and prior to the body, to being finally an image that so transcends the body that in its *ultimate bodilessness* it has become *essentially imageless*.

Two moments in the New Testament—the transfiguration and the transubstantiation—point up this progression. At the transfiguration, Christ takes Peter, James, and John "up into a high mountain" and allows them to see an image of his apotheosized body, the human body become radiant with divine life: "And [he] was transfigured before them: and his face did shine as the sun, and his raiment was white as the light [Rheims-Douay: . . . became white as snow; King James Version of Mark 9:3: And his raiment became shining, exceeding white as snow . . .]. And, behold, there appeared unto them Moses and Elias talking with him. . . . behold, a bright cloud overshadowed them: and behold a voice out of the cloud, which said, This is my beloved Son, in whom I am well pleased: hear ye him. . . . And as they came down from the mountain, Jesus charged them, saying, Tell the vision to no man, until the Son of man be risen again from the dead" (Matthew 17:2–9). What the apostles see is Christ's human body glorified by the life of the divine spirit, a "life" that transcends the physical life of the body and that will reanimate Christ's body after his physical death. But if what the apostles see on the mountain is the *image of an apotheosized body,* what we see in the text is the *apotheosized image of a body.* In order to give the apostles a "vision" of his divinity, Christ shows them an image that they will recognize as both himself and more than himself: Christ presents himself in conversation with Moses and Elias, both of whom had died centuries before and whose bodies have presumably been reanimated by the same nonbodily life that transfigures Christ. (But are these the physical bodies of Moses and Elias or disembodied images?) Further, Christ's body, shining like the sun, emits a radiance that threatens to interrupt its own visibility, to abolish its own image by blinding the observers. Indeed, one senses that Christ's transfigured body conceals more of the radiance of the Godhead than it reveals, that it masks a radiance whose unmediated vision would kill the apostles. God the Father, without a physical body to mediate his effulgence, veils himself in a cloud.

Clearly, the notion of a "spiritual" life separate from the body, which we find in the transfiguration, is conceived by analogy with the "life" of a mental image and its separate existence from the physical object it pictures. We are familiar with the way that in Plato, for example, the mental life of an image is deified to become the eternal life of an Ideal Form. In the preface to *Alastor,* Shelley describes the generation of an Ideal Being in the Platonic poet's quest for his apotheosized double. The young poet

> drinks deep of the fountains of knowledge, and is still insatiate. . . .
> So long as it is possible for his desires to point towards objects . . .
> infinite and unmeasured, he is joyous, and tranquil, and self-
> possessed. But the period arrives when these objects cease to suffice.
> His mind is at length suddenly awakened and thirsts for inter-
> course with an intelligence similar to itself. He images to himself the
> Being whom he loves. Conversant with speculations of the sublimest
> and most perfect natures, the vision in which he embodies his own
> imaginations unites all of wonderful, or wise, or beautiful, which the
> poet, the philosopher, or the lover could depicture. . . . He seeks in
> vain for a prototype of his conception. Blasted by his disappoint-
> ment, he descends to an untimely grave.[40]

The Ideal Being who "unites all of wonderful, or wise, or beautiful" convicts all mere human beings of shameful inadequacy in comparison;

and instead of becoming a generative force to raise the level of human existence, the Ideal destroys the poet who created it.

The Nietzschean critique of a morality based on the Platonic valorizing of ideal forms and its life-negating quality focuses on that reversal of cause and effect whereby the mental image derived from an object's physical appearance is transformed into the Eternal Image from which the object is derived. In *The Will to Power,* Nietzsche calls Plato "a great Cagliostro . . . ; he wanted to have *taught* as absolute truth what he himself did not regard as even conditionally true: namely, the separate existence and separate immortality of 'souls.' "[41] And he adds that with Plato, "moral judgments are torn from their conditionality, in which they have grown and alone possess any meaning, from their Greek and Greek-political ground and soil, to be denaturalized under the pretense of sublimation. The great concepts 'good' and 'just' are severed from the presuppositions to which they belong and, as liberated 'ideas,' become objects of dialectic. One looks for truth in them, one takes them for entities or signs of entities: one *invents* a world where they are at home, where they originate" (pp. 234–35). Yet what is most interesting for our purposes is the way in which the Hebraic idea of a personal God who is essentially imageless (his specific commandment to the Hebrews not to make images of him is a revelation of his invisible nature) becomes the Christian idea of a God who assumes a human body in order to obtain personal immortality for men. For if that immortality is conceived as a sharing in the divine life, then it inevitably leads, within the Judeo-Christian tradition, to a condition of imagelessness that, inasmuch as it represents the dissolution of the image of a body, represents as well the dissolution of anything that we could understand by the term "personal self." This alogical core, in which immortality means the annihilation of the self-as-image, is encrypted in the notion of Christ's resurrection as a proof of his divine life, for this proof of a nonbodily life beyond death can only be "shown" in the restoration of life to a dead body, that is, the visual evidence of a nonbodily life must be the appearance of bodily life (the only context in which the word "life" has any meaning).

But appearance in what sense? The Gospel descriptions of the various appearances that Christ makes to his disciples during the period between his resurrection and ascension indicate the ambiguous status of his body. On the one hand, his resurrected body shows many of the characteristics of a living physical entity. It is solid and touchable: In Matthew, the women who first meet Jesus after his resurrection take hold of his feet and worship him (28:9). In Luke, Christ says to the disciples, "Behold my hands and my feet, that it is I myself; handle me, and see; for a spirit hath not flesh and bones, as ye see me have" (24:39). In John, the doubting apostle Thomas puts his hand into Christ's wounds (20:26-29). Like a living body, Christ's takes nourishment (Luke 24:41-43). But on the other hand, his body also shows the characteristics of a mental image. It suddenly appears and vanishes (Luke 24:31-36); it is not hindered by material obstructions (John 20:19); it must not be touched (John 20:17); it alters its shape (Mark 16:12). In this last regard, Christ's body seems to have undergone, in the process of death and resurrection, a transfiguration sufficient to require in many cases a further sign to reveal his identity. Thus when Christ appeared to the two disciples on the road to Emmaus, "their eyes were holden that they should not know him . . . And it came to pass, as he sat at meat with them, he took bread, and blessed it, and brake, and gave to them. And their eyes were opened, and they knew him; and he vanished out of their sight" (Luke 24:13-31). Later, the two disciples tell the others "how he was known of them in breaking of bread" (Luke 24:35). In this instance the sign that reveals Christ's identity beneath his transfigured appearance is, appropriately enough, his reenactment of the transubstantiation (the breaking of bread), for the concept of transubstantiation—that under the same appearance (bread) there exists a different substance (Christ's body)—carries within it the concept of transfiguration—that under a different appearance there exists the same person. Transfiguration and transubstantiation are two ways of expressing the same thing: the destruction of the necessary relationship between a body and its image, between substance and appearance.

In a characteristic reversal, the apotheosized immortal self becomes more "substantial" than the physical body; and the proof of its eternal substantiality, of its independence and transcendence of an insubstantial (because corruptible) corpse, is that for this self, which originally derived from a physical appearance, physical appearance no longer signifies. The revelation of the apotheosized self's essential imagelessness is that, if it chooses, it can be substantially present under any appearance, precisely because no appearance, no image, necessarily pertains to it. What has been created in the concepts of transfiguration and transubstantiation is the notion of a personal unity that is wholly emptied of both the mental image and the physical appearance of a body. At the transubstan-

tiation when Christ takes bread and says "This is my body" and gives the
bread to his disciples to eat, he transforms a physical body into a mystical
body by making the word "body" cease to signify the mental image of a
body at the very instant and in the very act of making the physical
appearance of bread cease to signify anything at all. What they stand for
is the absence of an image, the presence of the abstract Word. And what
we find in the Gospel accounts of Christ's resurrected body is precisely
the sense of that body's oscillation between being a literal, physical entity
and a mental image, an oscillation between either/or and both/and that
culminates in the neither/nor of the ascension in which the body and its
image both vanish.

What the New Testament accounts of the resurrection and ascension
say is that after three days in the tomb, Christ rose from the dead,
"shewed himself alive after his passion by many infallible proofs, being
seen of them forty days . . ." (Acts 1:3), and at the end of that time, while
in the midst of his disciples, "was taken up; and a cloud received him out
of their sight" (Acts 1:9). But what the New Testament accounts of the
ascension *do* is to effect a massive reversal of their own sense of the
resurrection as visible proof. For the disciples, within the text, the proof
of a nonbodily life after death is the presence of Christ's resurrected
body, but for the readers of the text, the proof of that life will be,
through the device of the ascension, the absence of Christ's resurrected
body. The visible sign of an imageless, nonbodily life will be, henceforth,
that Christ's body is no longer visible. The readers of the New Testament
are not to look for Christ's resurrected body in this world; it has withdrawn to another "world," leaving the promise of an infinitely deferred
return. What the New Testament stories do is to rename an absence as a
presence, to call physical death "eternal life" by making a subtle shift in
the absence they rename; for what the New Testament explains as the
absence of a resurrected body is literally the absence of a corpse. And
that absence can be renamed as visible proof that Christ has returned to
life and ascended into heaven precisely because it preempts the major
proof to the contrary—the presence of a dead body.

The imagery of the transfiguration sheds light on this renaming of the
absence of a corpse. Christ directly connects the significance of the transfiguration with the resurrection when, after the transfiguration, he admonishes the apostles, "Tell the vision to no man, till the Son of man be
risen again from the dead" (Matthew 17:9)—a statement that at the time

mystifies them: "And they kept that saying with themselves, questioning one with another what the rising from the dead should mean" (Mark 9:10). The detail in the transfiguration that is most significant for our purposes is the appearance of Moses and Elias talking with Christ. Beyond indicating that the nonbodily life that transfigures Christ is the same force that reanimated Moses and Elias and will reanimate Christ after his death, the vision calls to mind the disposition of the bodies of the two Old Testament figures. When Moses died, God buried his body secretly "in a valley in the land of Moab, over against Bethpeor: but no man knoweth of his sepulchre unto this day" (Deuteronomy 34:6). When Elias reached the end of his days, he was taken up bodily into heaven in a fiery chariot (2 Kings 2:11). These two possibilities in the disposition of a body (secret burial and ascension into heaven), evoked by the presence of Moses and Elias at the transfiguration, come together in the New Testament accounts of Christ's resurrection and ascension. In Matthew's version, when the guards at the tomb tell the chief priests what has occurred, the priests and elders give "large money unto the soldiers, Saying, Say ye, His disciples came by night, and stole him away while we slept. . . . So they took the money, and did as they were taught: and this saying is commonly reported among the Jews until this day" (Matthew 28:12-15). In opposition to this rumor that Christ's disciples had stolen his body and secretly buried it, the New Testament tells the story of Christ's resurrection and ascension. Yet the chief priests' story and the New Testament explanation are both meant to account for the same physical fact—the absence of a corpse.

In the ascension's reversal of the sense of "proof" as visible presence, we recognize not only the way in which Christianity culminates the imaged self's relationship to the imageless God of Hebrew tradition, but also the way in which the Judeo-Christian concept of personal immortality forms one pole of an opposition whose other pole is the Egyptian notion of personal survival. As the empty tomb and the vanished body evoke the Judeo-Christian concept of an immortal self that is independent enough of the body to have dispensed with even a bodily image, so the monumental pyramid and the mummified corpse express the Egyptian sense that the immortality of the personal self is constitutively linked to the preservation of such an image. The mummified corpse is meant to have the same physical durability as the stone pyramid that encloses it. Among those aspects of an individual's being that the Egyptians differentiated from the physical body, the notion of the ka is perhaps most revealing of the Egyptian concept of personal survival. Gardiner says that the term ka "appears to embrace the entire 'self' of a person regarded as an entity to some extent separable from that person."[42] Yet the ka as the "entire 'self'" was not considered by the Egyptians to be independent of the body. The ka, "which required, even after death, food and drink, and the satisfaction of sensuous needs," was "supposed to be born together with the person to whom it belonged, and on the very rare occasions when it was depicted, wears his exact resemblance."[43]

This sense of the ka as an exact bodily resemblance and of the ka's dependence on the physical care of the corpse expresses the Egyptian concept of the self as an imaged double of the body, their awareness that the self has no meaning apart from the concept of an image and that an image is always grounded on a bodily appearance. Through mummification the corpse becomes a kind of permanently sculpted image of the deceased much like the sculpted image on the front of the sarcophagus in which the mummy is encased. (One thinks of Queequeg's coffin in *Moby-Dick,* inscribed, like a second skin, with the same hieroglyphics that were tattooed on Queequeg's body.) Significantly, the hieroglyph for the ka is a pair of uplifted hands ($\bigsqcup$) suggesting the Egyptian sense that the relationship between body and self is like the mutually constitutive opposition between left and right. Further, if we oppose, as images of the Judeo-Christian and Egyptian concepts of immortality, the vanished body and the mummified corpse, we can see that, within the context of the self as a linguistic entity, the contrast between the Egyptian hieroglyphics and the Christian imageless Word is simply the difference between the visible presence and the visible absence of the referent in the opposition pictographic writing / phonetic speech—the opposition between god as graven image and god as disembodied voice.

One might speculate that the historical crossing point between the Egyptian and the Judeo-Christian concepts of personal immortality is the Egyptian pharaoh Akhenaten, one of whose followers, so Freud theorized in *Moses and Monotheism,* was a man bearing the Egyptian name (   )-*mose* ([   ]-*a-child,* as in Thot-mose or Ra-mose) whom the Jews called "Moses."[44] Suffice it to say that Akhenaten, in the midst of a polytheistic culture obsessed with making physical images of the gods and with preparing for an afterlife of the self that was dependent on the preservation of an image of a physical body, proposed the worship of a single true god, Aten, of whom it was forbidden to make any graven image because the god, so Akhenaten said, was without a form. The religion of Aten evinced, as far as records show, no interest in the traditional Egyptian concept of an afterlife dependent on the survival of a bodily image.[45]

It is worth recalling in this context that Freud suggests in *Moses and Monotheism* that Christ's cannibalistic sacrifice was an unconscious retribution for, a reversal of, an often-repeated prehistoric scenario in which the father of the primal horde was killed and cannibalized by his sons. Freud further theorizes that the unconscious guilt of this primeval murder and cannibalization was revived by the Israelites' murder of Moses in the desert, an act whose memory was wholly repressed within Hebrew tradition but remained the hidden core of the Mosaic law and culminated in Christianity's cannibalistic sacrifice of the son as atonement to the father. According to Freud's speculations, then, cannibalistic sacrifice lies at the very heart of the Judeo-Christian tradition and its moral valorization of the symbolic order.

By placing Parker's cannibalization within the context of Christ's sacrifice, Poe evokes the alogical apotheosis by which a metaphoric communal body made up of individual physical bodies becomes an imageless mystical body of equally imageless souls—the paradox of a symbolic order based on the sacrificial death of the literal that attempts to deal with a realm whose essence is the obliteration of the literal. If what occurs in death is that an animated subject becomes an inert object—that the spirit departs, leaving the literal body behind—then what occurs in sacrifice is the ritual slaying of death, the active offering up of the physical body so that it can be reborn as an image. In sacrifice, man attempts to transform death from something passively suffered into something actively controlled. By incorporating death into a ritual, man attempts to change the meaninglessness of death as obliteration, as the absolute external limit of the personal self, into the meaningfulness of death as translation, as an internal limit between one state of life and another. If the literal (the physical body) is death, then the slaying of death is rebirth, the reanimation of the corpse as an image. But the death of the literal is in no sense the obliteration of the literal; for in their mutually constitutive opposition, when the literal vanishes, the symbolic vanishes along with it. Even in Parker's cannibalistic sacrifice, where the physical body is consumed to sustain the communal body, thereby allowing the self of the victim to survive as an image in the transpersonal memory of the group, the symbolic life (the life of a metaphoric body) is still grounded on the physical life of the mortal bodies of its members who are nourished by the victim's flesh. In the symbolic order, the sacrificial death of the literal always conserves the literal. But in Christ's sacrifice the image of a body is voided and the corpse vanishes precisely because the life to which this sacrifice admits the self is wholly independent of the literality of a physical body. And because this life is not the subjective immortality of an image in the communal memory but the objective immortality of a personal nonbodily self in a condition of imagelessness, the sacrifice that gives access to this life does so by alogically dissolving the meaning of sacrifice and of symbolization through the vanishing of the literal.

Section 9
Narcissus and the Illusion of Depth

In examining the interplay of a body and the image of a body in Parker's sacrifice and then in tracing that interplay through Christ's transfiguration, transubstantiation, resurrection, and ascension, we have established a context in which to consider the imagery of the final passage in Pym's narrative. Pym, drifting in a canoe with Peters and a black native of Tsalal, approaches the curtain of ashy vapor that shrouds the polar abyss:

> *March 22.* The darkness had materially increased, relieved only by the glare of the water thrown back from the white curtain before us. Many gigantic and pallidly white birds flew continuously now from beyond the veil, and their scream was the eternal *Tekeli-li!* as they retreated from our vision. Hereupon Nu-Nu stirred in the bottom of the boat; but upon touching him, we found his spirit departed. And now we rushed into the embraces of the cataract, where a chasm threw itself open to receive us. But there arose in our path-way a shrouded human figure, very far larger in its proportions than any dweller among men. And the hue of the skin of the figure was of the perfect whiteness of the snow. (3:242)

The magnified human figure against the curtain of mist that hides the ultimate mystery evokes the transfiguration's figure/ground opposition between Christ's apotheosized body ("his face did shine as the sun: and his garments became white as snow" [Matthew 17:2]) and the cloud that veils the imageless godhead of the Father. Further, as the significance of Christ's transfiguration lies in its revelation (Latin *revelare*, "to draw back the veil") of the nonbodily life that will reanimate his corpse at the resurrection, so the final passage in *Pym* subtly raises the question of resurrection, of the survival of the self as bodily image, in relation to the shrouded human figure. For as the canoe rushes into the polar chasm, Pym is obviously on the point of learning that "never-to-be-imparted secret, whose attainment is destruction." The imminence of death is clear: the black man Nu-Nu dies at this point in the adventure, and Pym dies at this point in the writing almost ten years later. Yet it is precisely the displacement of Pym's death from the actual journey to the act of writing that poses the question of Pym's mysterious "resurrection," of his survival beyond the break in the writing and his subsequent return to begin the narrative. From his vantage point of almost a decade later, the returned voyager Pym, writing the *Grampus* episode, mentions the "nine long years" that lay ahead of him at that point in the action, years "crowded with events... of the most unconceived and unconceivable character" (3:109). That the events were of an "unconceived and unconceivable character" is literally true, for that nine-year period represents the hiatus between the year in which the narrative of the voyage breaks off (1828) and the year in which the preface to the narrative is written (1838). But Poe also suggests, through the expected pun, that the "character" of Pym is unconceived and unconceivable, precisely because we cannot conceive of a written self, an inscribed image, returning from or being born out of an imageless abyss. The narrative we read is a text that, according to its own story, could never have existed. What Poe has done here as well is to raise, within the context of the Judeo-Christian notion of personal immortality, the question of an author's "immortality" in his writings (the survival of the writing self encrypted in the written self). For if the Judeo-Christian notion involves the alogical translation of the body's image into the condition of imagelessness, then the inscribed immortality of an author whose writing seeks to confront the simultaneous origin of man and language in the abyss of undifferentiated Being will involve the same self-dissolving translation.

The transformation of Poe the writer into *Poe* the written corpus considered as the means of the self's personal survival underlies Pym's problematic double role as fictive writing self and real written self, as perishing narrator and enduring narrative. For the author in the act of writing, the opposition writing self / written self is an opposition between living subject and dead object. The writing self is progressively sacrificed to, devoured by, the written self as living, subjective experience is transformed into lifeless, objective print. But that cannibalization of the writer's life is a self-sacrifice meant to slay death, for at the writer's death the polarity writing self / written self considered as life/death, spirit/letter, is reversed. The writing self is now related to the written self as lifeless corpse to living corpus: the progressive sacrifice of the life of the writing self has so vivified the dead letter that in comparison to the corpse, the written corpus is now a living entity capable of sustaining the dead writing self as an image in the communal memory. In *Pierre* (1852) Melville describes in terms of both doubling and vampirism this process whereby a writer sacrifices himself to his book:

> . . . that which now absorbs the time and life of Pierre, is not the book, but the primitive elementalizing of the strange stuff, which in the act of attempting that book, has upheaved and upgushed in his soul. Two books are being writ; of which the world shall only see one, and that the bungled one. The larger book, and the infinitely better, is for Pierre's own private shelf. That it is, whose unfathomable cravings drink his blood: the other only demands his ink. But circumstances have so decreed, that the one can not be composed on the paper, but only as the other is writ down in his soul. And the one of the soul is elephantinely sluggish, and will not budge at a breath. Thus Pierre is fastened on by two leeches:—how then can the life of Pierre last? Lo! he is fitting himself for the highest life, by thinning his blood and collapsing his heart. He is learning how to live, by rehearsing the part of death.[46]

The paradox of Pym's role as a fictive writing self in pursuit of its own linguistic origin in the abyss is that in the course of the narrated action, the manuscript that constitutes Pym's written self would have had to share the fate of the writing self lost in the abyss *before* its written text could ever have presented him to the reader as its fictive writer. Pym's manuscript testifies not to the progressive dying of its writer during the act of composition but to his prior death. Besides staging the alogic of confronting within language the ultimate origin of language and the self, Pym's mysterious vanishing, resurrection, and death (whose sequence reverses the New Testament order of death, resurrection, and ascension) obliquely dismantles the principal rite-of-passage scenario for the crossing of major internal limits in the development of the self from childhood to maturity—the scenario of symbolic death and rebirth. Yet to understand the full implications of Pym's vanishing, resurrection, and death, we must read the apotheosized figure in the mist at the narrative's end in relation to the mysterious writing on the chasm wall that Pym and Peters discover on the island of Tsalal, an inscription whose decipherment is the chief concern of the note that follows the interrupted narrative.

The discovery of this writing occurs during the third overwhelming-of-the-vessel episode, an episode that begins when Pym and Peters, after the cannibalization of Parker and the death of Augustus, are rescued from the drifting hulk of the *Grampus* by the schooner *Jane Guy*. On board this ship, Pym and his dark double start their voyage toward the South Pole, and from this point on in the narrative the written character of Pym's journey becomes increasingly explicit. A few pages deep into the *Jane Guy* episode, Pym begins to introduce into his narrative the observations of previous Antarctic explorers. The islands sighted by the *Jane Guy* on its journey southward are precisely located by latitude and longitude, and brief histories of their first discovery are given. At the point where Captain Guy decides "to push on toward the pole," Pym says, "Before entering upon this portion of my narrative, it may be as well, for the information of those readers who have paid little attention to the progress of discovery in these regions, to give some brief account of the very few attempts at reaching the southern pole which have hitherto been made" (3:165). Pym summarizes Captain Cook's explorations in 1772–73, quotes from J. N. Reynolds, "whose great exertions and perseverance have at length succeeded in getting set on foot a national expedition, partly for the purpose of exploring these regions" (3:167), and then discusses at length the voyages of Kreutzenstern and Lisiausky (1803), Captain James Weddell of the British Navy (1822), Captain Benjamin Morrell of the American schooner *Wasp* (1823), and Captain Briscoe "in the employ of the Messieurs Enderby, whale-ship owners of London" (1831–32).

Besides indicating the books that Poe used as background for this episode, Pym's résumé of previous Antarctic explorations is meant to place his own narrative within that tradition of written accounts in which the act of discovery (the penetration of *terra incognita* and the consequent extension of the limits of human knowledge) is a function of inscription. When Pym summarizes "the progress of discovery in these regions," he begins with Captain Cook's expedition precisely because it is "the first of which we have any distinct account" (3:165). What "discovery" means in this context is the Antarctic's entrance into the written memory of Western historical man, that being whose cultural self-consciousness is a function of contemplating his inscribed image through the course of recorded time. In the same sense, Champollion's decipherment of the hieroglyphics was hailed in his day as the discovery of ancient Egypt.

This sense of the word "discovery" is, of course, unaffected by the fact that the regions discovered were often already inhabited by men, as when we say that Columbus discovered America. At one point the *Jane Guy* comes upon an uncharted island on which the crew finds "near the shore, half buried in a pile of loose stones, a piece of wood, which seemed to have formed the prow of a canoe," and on this apparent marker Captain Guy makes out the carved figure of a tortoise. Pym, however, dismisses this evidence of earlier human visitors and remarks that upon reaching the island they "had now advanced to the southward more than eight degrees farther than any previous navigators" (3:177). Earlier, when the *Jane Guy* had anchored at Desolation Island in the southern Indian Ocean, Captain Guy had left a marker of his own—a sealed letter in a bottle placed on one of the highest peaks on the island. Pym says, "It is probable that his design was to leave the letter on that height for some vessel which he expected to come after him" (3:157).

Clearly, Captain Guy's letter cannot be an historical marker meant to claim discovery of the island, for Pym had already mentioned that the island "was first discovered in 1772, by the Baron de Kergulen, or Kerguelen, a Frenchman" and that it was visited in 1777 by Captain Cook who gave it its present name (3:152). Yet, granting the connection in Poe's work between the manuscript in a bottle and the voyage to the polar abyss, we cannot help but be struck both by the introduction of this incident into Pym's narrative and by the way in which Pym, having once introduced it, glosses it over, ignoring its obvious significance. For this incident shows the way in which a written manuscript can survive a voyage that the writer of that manuscript does not himself survive; it points to the kind of explanation of the manuscript's existence that is given in "MS. Found in a Bottle" and that is called for by the nature of Pym's journey but is not given. Because Pym's existence as fictive narrator is a function of a written narrative whose content points to the impossibility of his having written the text that grounds his existence, Pym must be, by the very terms of his narrative act, blind to the significance of this incident of the letter in the bottle, with its potential revelation of his own contradictory status. In the later episode on the uncharted island where Pym dismisses the evidence of the carved prow that has apparently been left by someone as an inscribed marker during the course of a voyage, this blindness is once again at work.

Yet there is another factor involved in the dismissal, for Pym in ignoring this evidence of previous visitors to the island is denying not so much that living beings have set foot there before as that these beings were "men" in his sense of the word, that is, historically self-conscious beings within a tradition that understands the individual self as the mnemic inscription of a personal history. Pym's sense that full humanity involves a written memory, an historically inscribed self-consciousness, is only what one would expect in this quest for the simultaneous origin of man and language as an act of hieroglyphic doubling, as the double inscription of the image of a body.

In the confrontation between the white crew of the *Jane Guy* and the black islanders of Tsalal, the equation of Man and written history intersects the monogenesis/polygenesis controversy. Pym says that the islanders' initial reaction to the crew made it "quite evident that they had never before seen any of the white race—from whose complexion, indeed, they appeared to recoil (3:182). And his final judgment, after the massacre of the crew by the islanders, is that the Tsalalians "appeared to be the most wicked, hypocritical, vindictive, bloodthirsty, and altogether fiendish race of men upon the face of the globe" (3:234). Although Pym characterizes both white and black as races of "men," his descriptions of the islanders emphasize their animality, their subhuman or nonhuman qualities, so that one would expect to account for the radical differences between these races that possess a common human form but not a common humanity by a polygenetic theory that posited a separate origin for each race. Yet if the opposition of the white crew and the black islanders seems to present the question of human origin (the differentiation of human from nonhuman) in biological terms, the equation of Man and written history (the symbolic interplay of white and black personified by the relationship of the writing self and the written self, the white Pym and his dark double) reminds us that the problem of recognizing an original human form in the interplay of physiognomic sameness and difference is circumscribed by a more basic epistemological problem— the origin of differential self-consciousness, of recognition itself. In the confrontation between the white crew and the black islanders, Poe is less interested in theories of biological origin and racial difference than in relating the primal differentiation within Judeo-Christian *written* tradition (the original opposition of light and dark in Genesis) to the concept of a bounding surface or differentiating edge, specifically, the human skin as the indeterminate boundary, the ambiguous limit, between inner and outer, subject and object, self and other.

This interest in the notion of a bounding surface is part of the book's attempt to deal with the concept of an absolute limit, to understand death as the final boundary of human knowledge and the symbolic order. Yet what is significant in Poe's treatment of the bounding surface (the differentiating edge or limit or line that distinguishes one entity from another, that separates figure from ground) is that this edge is always presented as the visual border between different colors. One of the most explicit instances of this occurs on the island of Tsalal when Pym and the crew notice that the water of the streams is purple in hue. Pym remarks:

> I am at a loss to give a distinct idea of the nature of this liquid, and cannot do so without many words. Although it flowed with rapidity in all declivities where common water would do so, yet never, except when falling in a cascade, had it the customary appearance of *limpidity*. It was, nevertheless, in point of fact, as perfectly limpid as any limestone water in existence, the difference being only in appearance. At first sight, and especially in cases where little declivity was found, it bore resemblance, as regards consistency, to a thick infusion of gum Arabic in common water. But this was only the least remarkable of its extraordinary qualities. It was *not* colourless, nor was it of any one uniform colour—presenting to the eye, as it flowed, every possible shade of purple, like the hues of a changeable silk. This variation in shade was produced in a manner which excited as profound astonishment in the minds of our party as the mirror had done in the case of Too-wit. Upon collecting a basinful,

and allowing it to settle thoroughly, we perceived that the whole
mass of liquid was made up of a number of distinct veins, each of a
distinct hue; that these veins did not commingle; and that their
cohesion was perfect in regard to neighbouring veins. Upon passing
the blade of a knife athwart the veins, the water closed over it immediately, as with us, and also, in withdrawing it, all traces of the
passage of the knife were instantly obliterated. If, however, the
blade was passed down accurately between the two veins, a perfect
separation was effected, which the power of cohesion did not immediately rectify. (3:186–87)

The liquid is a medium internally divided into veins of color that do
not commingle; and the boundaries, the dividing lines between each of
these veins, can be precisely located and a separation effected, as with
the insertion of the knife blade, because of this difference in hue. Yet
this precision of differentiation within the medium is linked to an indeterminacy at its surface, an uncertainty as to whether the medium is
limpid or not. Pym says that "except when falling in a cascade," the liquid
never had "the customary appearance of *limpidity*." But he then reverses
himself and affirms that "in point of fact" it was "as perfectly limpid as
any limestone water in existence, *the difference being only in appearance*"
(italics mine). The puzzled reader can only shake his head at this and ask,
"But what is limpidity or transparency except an appearance?" If under
certain circumstances a liquid appears not to be transparent, and if
transparency is itself only a visual appearance, then under those circumstances the liquid is "in point of fact" not transparent.

Poe suggests that this perceptual ambiguity concerning the limpid/
nonlimpid appearance of the water is really an uncertainty about
whether the liquid's surface is transparent or reflective, whether the
surface allows vision to pass through it or turns vision back upon itself in
the form of a mirror image. Pym says that looking at the liquid "excited
as profound astonishment in the minds of our party as the mirror had
done in the case of Too-wit," the native chief who had first seen his own
reflection in a mirror on board the *Jane Guy.* Pym's description of that
incident makes the reference especially significant:

There were two large mirrors in the cabin. . . . Too-wit was the first
to approach them, and he had got in the middle of the cabin, with
his face to one and his back to the other, before he fairly perceived

them. Upon raising his eyes and seeing his reflected self in the glass, I thought the savage would go mad; but, upon turning short round to make a retreat, and beholding himself a second time in the opposite direction, I was afraid he would expire upon the spot. No persuasion could prevail upon him to take another look; but, throwing himself upon the floor, with his face buried in his hands, he remained thus until we were obliged to drag him upon deck. (3:183)

The liquid, with its internal division through differences in color and its surface division (in the sense of perceptual ambiguity) through two opposing appearances (transparent/nontransparent), is explicitly linked with a mirror and the effect of external doubling through reflection (underlined in the incident on board ship by Too-wit's seeing himself successively in two facing mirrors on opposite walls). This equation of the water that is internally split by a color difference and the mirror that externally doubles a dark figure suggests the internal split / external doubling of Narcissus and his image in the pool or the constitutive opposition of self and shadow. The attempt to divide a mutually constitutive opposition and completely separate the opposing terms from each other always turns into a splitting/doubling, as if one tried to separate the north and south poles of a bar magnet by sawing the bar in half, only to find that instead of separating the poles one had produced two new bar magnets, each with its own north and south poles. Or to phrase it another way, the splitting of a mutually constitutive opposition is like the dividing of an amoeba: halving is doubling. Thus, the "half-breed" Peters is Pym's dark double because he is Pym's dark half. It is this simultaneous internal splitting / external doubling that renders the notion of a limit problematic in a mutually constitutive opposition. For example, in the opposition between body and shadow, there is an essential (that is, original) uncertainty as to whether the dividing line between the two should be interpreted as an internal or an external limit, whether the line should be read metonymically (as the internal boundary between two halves of a whole—splitting) or metaphorically (as the external boundary between two similar wholes—doubling).

It is this same uncertainty about whether a differentiating edge should be interpreted as an internal or an external boundary that is at issue in the transparent/nontransparent appearance of the purple water on Tsalal. For if the water is transparent, if vision passes through the surface, then in terms of perception that surface boundary is an external limit between what lies below the surface and what lies above it. But if the water is not transparent—if, as the comparison with the mirror suggests, it is reflective, not allowing vision to pass through but rather turning vision back upon itself—then the surface boundary is an internal limit between what lies above the surface and its own reflected image—an ambiguous image, a surface reflection that gives the illusion of depth (of another world below the surface), that represents the same *as if* were separate and another. The indeterminacy of this bounding surface lies in the dizzying realization that this internal limit *is* the self's external limit, that the self as image cannot pass the reflecting surface, cannot pass the image as boundary.

It is precisely this ambiguity that is evoked by the three key moments in Narcissus's contemplation of his image in the pool. According to Ovid, Narcissus at first mistakes his image for another person, either another youth swimming in the pool or some inhabitant of a world below the surface that is the counterpart of the world above it. Narcissus addresses the youth, reaches out to touch him, finds his gestures reciprocated; and yet when his hand meets the water, the youth vanishes. Narcissus complains of the elusive, indefinite character of the border between them:

> "I am charmed, and I see; but what I see and what charms me I cannot find"—so serious is the lover's delusion—"and, to make me grieve the more, no mighty ocean separates us, no long road, no mountain ranges, no city walls with close-shut gates; by a thin barrier of water we are kept apart. He himself is eager to be embraced. For, often as I stretch my lips towards the lucent wave, so often with upturned face he strives to lift his lips to mine. You would think he could be touched—so small a thing it is that separates our loving hearts."[47]

The second key moment in the episode occurs when Narcissus eventually notices that though all his gestures and facial expressions are doubled by the youth, there is one major difference: when the youth's lips move in speech, there is no sound corresponding to Narcissus's voice. And with that observation, Narcissus realizes the truth—what he sees is his own image:

> "Oh, I am he! I have felt it, I know now my own image. I burn with love of my own self; I both kindle the flames and suffer them. What shall I do? Shall I be wooed or woo? Why woo at all? What I desire, I

have; the very abundance of my riches beggars me. Oh, that I might
be parted from my own body! and, strange prayer for a lover, I
would that what I love were absent from me!" (1:157)

But this second moment, this realization that it is himself that he sees,
does not void the first moment in which he mistook his image for
another person. Rather, these two moments are combined and balanced
in a third in which Narcissus treats his image *as if* it were another person
in order to reveal that difference in sameness that constitutes the true
otherness of the reflected image:

"Death is nothing to me, for in death I shall leave my troubles; I
would he that is loved might live longer; but as it is, we two shall die
together in one breath."
   He spoke and, half distraught, turned again to the same image.
His tears ruffled the water, and dimly the image came back from the
troubled pool. As he saw it thus depart, he cried: "Oh, whither do you
flee? Stay here, and desert not him who loves thee, cruel one! Still
may it be mine to gaze on what I may not touch, and by that gaze
feed my unhappy passion." (1:157, 159)

The paradox experienced by Narcissus is that although his image is
other, it is not *an other;* although his body and his image both inhabit the
visual order, his image does not, like his body, inhabit the tactile order.
Narcissus can see both his physical body and his reflected body, and he
can touch his physical body, but when he reaches out toward his reflected body, he touches only formless water. Narcissus can never be
united with his image; his physical body can never be conjoined with his
reflected body. For though his reflected body gives the illusion of depth
and thus seems to promise the possible penetration of a boundary, yet at
the first touch, at the first attempt to cross that boundary, the image
vanishes.
   The three moments in the Narcissus episode represent an original
oscillation between self and other, between body and image, which can
be rephrased in this way: in the first moment Narcissus mistakes the
image of his own body for another person (difference); in the second
moment he recognizes that what he sees is the image of his own person
(sameness); and in the third moment he realizes the difference between
a body and an image, between himself and his reflection (sameness as

difference). Narcissus and his image are too close ever to be joined; the price of his image's visual sameness is its tactile otherness. (In one sense the Narcissus episode is a parable of the self's attempt to make love to its own thoughts, to make love to what can be seen in the mirror of the mind but can never be embraced. The artistic form of this impulse, the artist's forever frustrated desire to make love to the work of art, achieves its fantasized fulfillment in the myth of Pygmalion and Galatea, where the artist marries the living embodiment of his own creative conception, the statue turned woman.) What Narcissus clearly exhibits in the third moment, by treating his image *as if* it were another person even though he knows it is not, is the essential (original) otherness of the self to itself, the indeterminate status of self-reflection as both a part of the body and a double of the body and as either a part of the body or a double of the body. What the third moment expresses is that if the self is at once both a cause and a function of self-consciousness, if it is one pole (one half) of a mutually constitutive opposition (whose other pole is the visual image of a body) and is at the same time the entity that reflects upon that opposition (that is, doubles it in self-reflective thought), then the origin of the self is a union that differentiates, a coming together to hold apart; and as such that origin inscribes within the self's mirroring of the mutually constitutive opposition of self and image the destructive illusion of reunion—destructive because the original union was a differentiation, while the illusory reunion is always an attempt to merge what was originally held apart, an attempt that results not in reunion but in dissolution.

The illusion of reunion is based on the illusion of depth, the mistaking of a shadow or a reflected image for a physical body; and it is this illusion of reunion in its most extended metaphysical form (the belief in reunion with God after death) that Poe focuses on at the end of *Pym,* where the movement toward the womblike abyss of undifferentiation is also the movement toward that apotheosized image of a body in a cloud which, within Christian tradition, represents the reunion of the personal self with an imageless God as a translation into the condition of imagelessness, that vanishing of the image of a body that results when Narcissus tries to be reunited with his own reflection. This vanishing occurs twice in the story of Narcissus: first, when he touches the water and his image shatters, and again when, pining for himself, he wastes away, leaving not a corpse but a flower in his place.

The way in which Poe treats the illusion of reunion in *Pym* evokes the mythic, original differentiating union of self-consciousness (which the reunion seeks to repeat as a fusing of opposites) as the intersection of a series of mutually constitutive oppositions: self/image, body/shadow, black/white (the differentiating edge as the boundary between different planes of color), figure/ground (the privileging of one color over another), horizontal/vertical. It is in the notion of origin as the simultaneous intersection of precisely these oppositions which explicitly structure the scene Pym traverses on his way to the polar abyss, that we perceive in its profoundest (because most superficial and thus most easily overlooked) sense the written character of Pym's voyage, for it is just these oppositions that constitute the physical presence, the visibility, of writing in general and of Pym's written narrative in particular.

Consider what that physical presence amounts to. There is the color opposition of black ink and white paper. There is the figure/ground opposition in which the shapes of the written characters are perceived against the blank background of the page, a focusing process (both visual and mental—a reciprocal focusing of the eye and focusing of attention) in which the background is suppressed or made indefinite, so that the significant shape becomes the black outline of the letter rather than the white space that surrounds it. There is the horizontal/vertical opposition both in the intersecting lines of the letters (whose differences in shape are seen as significant in terms of a horizontal/vertical grid) and in the act of reading, which moves downward along a vertical axis by moving back and forth along a horizontal axis (the scanning process on which the focusing process rides). There is the self/image opposition in which writing is viewed as the visible track of one's ever-altering mental and emotional states, as the external image of the self's internal principle of continuity—the memory trace. There is the body/shadow opposition in which writing is viewed not as the immediate image of hidden thought, of mental pictures, but as the image of the body in motion considered as the surface of expressivity, the boundary at which inner becomes outer, at once the blank surface that is written upon and the source of the expressive shapes of feature and gesture that are inscribed upon that surface. In the light-skin/dark-skin, writing self / written self opposition of Pym and Peters, Poe projects upon this surface the intersection of the world-founding differentiation of light and dark from Genesis and the man-founding differentiation of self and image.

Melville is even more explicit than Poe in treating the body's surface as the inscribed/inscribing boundary where the light/dark opposition intersects the self/image opposition. In *Moby-Dick*, Queequeg (the dark double and fictive written self of the narrator Ishmael) has "hieroglyphic" tattoos all over his body. And these same hieroglyphics are carved on his coffin, which floats to the surface after the *Pequod* sinks into the vortex (the *vor*-textual abyss) and which serves as a lifebuoy for Ishmael, who returns to produce the book in which Queequeg survives as a written character. At one point in the act of writing the narrative, Ishmael says that the dimensions of a whale he is describing "are copied verbatim from my right arm, where I had them tattooed; as in my wild wanderings at that period, there was no other secure way of preserving such valuable statistics."[48] And he adds, "I was crowded for space, and wished the other parts of my body to remain a blank page for a poem I was then composing—at least, what untattooed parts might remain (p. 376).

In the story of Narcissus, the reflecting surface of the water and the surface of the human body are both indeterminate boundaries, ambiguous limits between inner and outer, precisely because the mirroring of the body's surface on the surface of the water implicitly equates these two surfaces and the two different bipolar oppositions connected with them—the opposition between intensity and extensity (between internal time-consciousness and external spatiality) that pertains to the body's surface as the limit between inner and outer, and the spatial opposition between depth and surface that pertains to the water's surface as the limit between inner and outer. The problem with this equation is that while extensity and outer surface are the same, intensity and inner depth are not. It is this identification of inner depth and intensity that constitutes what we have called the illusion of depth—the illusion, as in the case of Narcissus, that the spatial depth lying below his image on the surface of the water corresponds to the self-conscious "inner" being that "lies below" the surface of his body, the illusion that a physical penetration of the surface of the water provides a means of spatial access to a "depth" or "inner space" that is itself not spatial at all, but temporal—the metaphoric "inner space" of thought. In light of the regressive character of narcissism, we can recognize in this scenario the basic structure of the return to the womb—the wish/fantasy that there exists an inner depth to which one can physically journey as if it were a point in space but that in fact would be a point in time, the point where/before time began for the individual consciousness at birth. It is this same structure that we find in the voyage to the abyss as a quest for the origin of the self and language.

The identification of depth and intensity is based on the illusion that inner depth, being the opposite of outer surface, is somehow not itself a surface, when in fact depth is simply the surface below the surface, as is shown in the incident of the purple water on Tsalal, where the insertion of the knife blade between the veins of color (a penetration from surface to depth) causes a temporary separation of the immiscible veins, thus revealing that the inner depth is made up of surfaces. As Melville says in *Pierre:*

> The old mummy lies buried in cloth on cloth; it takes time to un-wrap this Egyptian king. Yet now, forsooth, because Pierre began to see through the first superficiality of the world, he fondly weens he has come to the unlayered substance. But, far as any geologist has yet gone down into the world, it is found to consist of nothing but surface stratified on surface. To its axis, the world being nothing but superinduced superficies. By vast pains we mine into the pyramid; by horrible gropings we come to the central room; with joy we espy the sarcophagus; but we lift the lid—and no body is there!— appallingly vacant as vast is the soul of a man! (Pp. 284–85)

Within the world of human consciousness, there is no surface whose penetration frees us from surfaces any more than there is an absolute limit whose crossing frees us from limits, though there is an absolute limit whose crossing frees us from consciousness. The original indeterminacy as to whether the surface of the body is an internal or an external limit of the self accounts, of course, for the necessary slippage in the use of the word "self," its referring at some moments to a whole made up of mind, body, shadow, reflected image and dramatic role, and referring at other moments to one part of that whole as distinguished from another part, as in the opposition self/image. This slippage reflects that basic sense of the self as simultaneously both part and whole and either part or whole, as being *both* one half of a mutually constitutive opposition *and* that which doubles the whole opposition in self-reflective consciousness, and at the same instant, *either* the image in the mirror *or* the mirror itself.

Section 10
Self-Recognition; Deciphering a
Mnemic Inscription; Historical
Amnesia and Personal Anamnesis

As the narrative of the *Jane Guy* episode progresses, those oppositions whose intersection constitutes the physical presence of writing come more and more to be the dominant features of the polar world. As Pym approaches the origin of language in the abyss, the physical qualities of his written text are projected onto the scene that the text describes, that it creates out of words. Thus the black/white opposition of ink and paper and the self/image opposition of writer and text, from their intersection in the opposition between Pym and Peters, expand to the human/subhuman opposition between the white crew and the black islanders (where "Man" is distinguished from the inhuman savages by the possession of a written memory), and ultimately extend to the geo-graphic opposition between the island of Tsalal (where "nothing *white* was to be found") and the polar realm of Tekeli-li (where nothing was to be found that was not white). The black/white opposition of writing even manages, during the course of the *Jane Guy* episode, to establish its ascendancy over the primordial light/dark opposition of day and night. From the point at which Captain Guy decides to head southward to the pole, Pym begins to cast his narrative in the form of a journal, a method of composition that is governed by the passage of days, by the alternation of light and dark. Yet Pym points out that with their entrance into the polar latitudes the alternation of light and dark had long since broken down:

> The terms *morning* and *evening*, which I have made use of to avoid confusion in my narrative, as far as possible, must not, of course, be taken in their ordinary sense. For a long time past we had no night at all, the daylight being continual. The dates throughout are according to nautical time, and the bearings must be understood as per compass. I would also remark, in this place, that I cannot, in the first portion of what is here written, pretend to strict accuracy in respect to dates, or latitudes, having kept no regular journal until after the period of which this first portion treats. In many instances I have relied altogether upon memory. (3:179)

Pym adopts the journal format for his narrative not because he actually began to compose the narrative on a day-to-day basis at this point in the journey; rather, he adopts the form for reasons that are internal to his text, reasons that pertain to the text's ontological status as a narrative whose content questions the possibility of its ever having been written. Since the quest for the origin of language in the abyss has been displaced from the actual polar journey onto the act of writing the account of that journey, the narrative, as it approaches the moment when it will break off, must be cast in a form *that appears to progress at the same daily rate* as the voyage it narrates, a form that, by the very mechanism of its composition, seems necessarily blind to any foreknowledge of the narrative's alogical ending. Yet although the final portion of Pym's story takes the form of a journal, the entire narrative, as Pym makes clear in the preface, *was written only after he had returned from the voyage*, a claim so much at odds with the nature of the journey to the abyss that it can only be meant to call attention to the alogical status of writing in pursuit of its own origin.

Besides allowing the superimposition of the black/white polarity of writing, of narrated time, upon the light/dark alternation of natural time, the journal format also permits the projection upon physical nature of the horizontal/vertical opposition of inscribed lines. Most of the journal entries contain a record of the ship's position (as of the entry's date) given in terms of latitude and longitude, those intersecting horizontal and vertical lines inscribed on a map that represent the crossing of imaginary circles on the globe. And just as the successive journal entries are based on a passage of days that is no longer indicated by the natural alternation of light and dark, but rather, one assumes, by the movement of a man-made recording device, the ship's chronometer, so too the latitudes and longitudes he gives are based not on an observation of physical nature such as a sextant reading but on dead reckoning ("the bearings must be understood as per compass"), that is, on the ship's estimated position as computed from its inscribed track on a map using such data as speed, compass heading, and elapsed time.

The other oppositions whose intersection constitutes the physical presence of writing (body/shadow and figure/ground) are projected onto the physical world of Pym's journey in two related key scenes—the appearance of the figure in the mist at the end (where the notion of "projection" in both the literal and the metaphoric senses and the notion of a "ground" in both the perceptual and the ontological senses are rendered mutually problematic) and the earlier discovery on Tsalal of the writing carved on the chasm wall (where the two different senses of "presence" associated with pictographic and phonetic scripts are simultaneously put in play).

The scene in the chasm—certainly the most explicit instance within the narrative of writing physically inscribed on the external world—occurs after the black islanders have killed most of the *Jane Guy*'s crew by trapping them in an avalanche. Only moments before the landslide, Pym, Peters, and another crew member had separated from the group in order to explore a fissure in the rocky defile. Because of their distance from the rock fall, Pym and Peters escape being crushed to death, though their companion is killed. Fearing at first that the avalanche has left them permanently entombed, they discover that the rock fall in blocking one end of the fissure has opened a passageway at the other end, and after a dangerous climb up the passageway they reach the hilltop above the ravine where the crew is buried. They find the series of wooden levers and ropes by which the islanders had been able to hurl "the whole face of the hill, upon a given signal, into the bosom of the abyss below." Pym adds: "The fate of our poor companions was no longer a matter of uncertainty. We alone had escaped from the tempest of that overwhelming destruction. We were the only living white men upon the island" (3:209). It is worth noting that Pym refers to the ravine, in which he and Peters had narrowly avoided the fate of the ship's crew, as the "abyss," and that his words upon exiting ("We alone had escaped from the tempest of that overwhelming destruction") are echoed more than a decade later when Ishmael, another voyager from Nantucket, avoids the fate of the *Pequod's* crew in the vortex's abyss ("And I only am escaped alone to tell thee"). It is also significant that Pym, who refers to Peters in both the narrative and the preface as "a half-breed Indian," describes him at this point, in opposition to the black islanders who threaten them, as a white man.

Exploring the hilltop, Pym and Peters discover a "chasm of black granite," whose structure suggests that it is not "altogether the work of nature" (3:221). On descending into this chasm, which Pym variously calls an "abyss" (3:222) and a "gulf" (3:223), they find that it consists of three interconnecting caverns. These Pym describes in minute detail, even going so far as to reproduce in the text drawings of the general outline of each cavern, which he prefaces with the remark, "The precise formation of the chasm will best be understood by means of a delineation taken upon the spot; for I had luckily with me a pocket-book and pencil, which I preserved with great care through a long series of subsequent adventure, and to which I am indebted for memoranda of many subjects which would otherwise have been crowded from my remembrance" (3:223). This is the only point in the narrative where Pym describes himself as writing, *during the journey itself,* a memorandum of an event in the journey, and it is also the only point where he explicitly raises the question of preserving a manuscript through the course of a dangerous voyage—both of which facts suggest that Pym's descent into the "abyss" of the chasm and his face-to-face confrontation with the characters inscribed on the chasm wall are a foreshadowing of his descent into the polar abyss ("where a chasm threw itself open to receive us") and his confrontation with the apotheosized figure in the mist.

It is in the third of the three connecting caverns that Pym and Peters find the writing on the wall:

> We were about leaving this fissure, into which very little light was admitted, when Peters called my attention to a range of singular looking indentures in the surface of the marl forming the termination of the *cul-de-sac.* With a very slight exertion of the imagination, the left, or most northern of the indentures might have been taken for the intentional, although rude, representation of a human figure standing erect, with outstretched arm. The rest of them bore also some little resemblance to alphabetical characters, and Peters was willing, at all events, to adopt the idle opinion that they were really such. I convinced him of his error, finally, by directing his attention to the floor of the fissure, where, among the powder, we picked up, piece by piece, several large flakes of the marl, which had evidently been broken off by some convulsion from the surface where the indentures were found, and which had projecting points exactly fitting the indentures; thus proving them to have been the work of nature. (3:225)

Pym then reproduces in the text a copy of the markings on the wall:

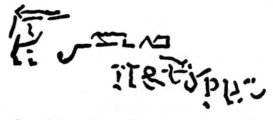

One of the first things that strikes the reader in this episode is the emphasis placed on Pym's and Peters' uncertainty about the natural or human origin of the chasm and its markings. On entering the chasm, Pym says that they "could scarcely . . . believe it altogether the work of nature." Moreover, Peters thinks that some of the characters on the wall are alphabetical, though Pym disparages this opinion by pointing out what he considers to be physical evidence that the markings were caused by a natural fragmentation of the "surface where the indentures were found." Pym's argument, however, seems suspect, for if the markings had been chipped into the wall by some crude man-made tool such as a flint chisel, there would also have been left on the cavern floor fragmentary chips whose shapes would correspond to the indentations on the wall. Furthermore, Pym had noted in his progress through the chasm that in each of the passageways connecting the caverns there was a "vast heap" (3:223) of "white arrowhead flints" (3:224). As the author of the concluding note points out, "Nothing *white* was to be found at Tsalal"— by which he means that nothing white *naturally occurred* on Tsalal. Any white object on the island, like the pocket handkerchief that terrified the black islander Nu-Nu, had been brought there from someplace else. Thus the presence of the white arrowhead flints in the chasm would seem to be a strong indication that the shapes of the caverns and the markings on the wall were both man-made. That Pym records the presence of obvious human artifacts (apparently digging or carving tools) without ever questioning how white arrowhead flints found their way into a chasm made of marl and black granite seems to be of a piece with his earlier dismissal of the carved prow of a ship discovered on Bennet's Islet—a kind of inherent blindness on Pym's part to the traces of previous human presence.

Poe emphasizes the uncertainty about whether the markings in the chasm are natural or man-made in order to call attention to the two opposing notions of linguistic origin evoked by the two different forms of writing on the wall. The first type of writing is hieroglyphic: a pictographic ideogram described as "the intentional, although rude, representation of a human figure standing erect, with outstretched arm." The second type is phonetic—"alphabetical characters." The first type of writing, which copies the script of natural objects, has its ultimate origin in the Author of nature, while the second type, an arbitrary and conventional sign system, is wholly man-made. The first type evokes an original transparency of meaning that is wholly masked by phonetic signs but that can still be dimly perceived in the universally recognizable natural shapes of pictographic script. Thus Pym has no trouble at all in identifying the pictograph as "the representation of a human figure," whereas he dismisses Peters' suggestion that the other markings are alphabetical characters, probably because the characters—given the conventional and culturally varying nature of phonetic signs—differ so radically in shape from those of his own language that he simply does not recognize them as being human writing. (We are told in the concluding note that the two words written on the wall are in Arabic and Coptic scripts respectively, and that the designs of the three caverns reproduce the shapes of letters in Ethiopic script).

Yet Pym's and Peters' uncertainty about whether the markings are natural or man-made reflects a deeper uncertainty inherent in the very opposition between nature and art—a constitutive uncertainty that the markings in the chasm are intended to exhibit. Though the hieroglyphic figure on the wall evokes a language whose characters are necessary, natural shapes rather than arbitrary, man-made signs, the very fact that the hieroglyph in this case is the representation of a human figure tends to make the "natural/man-made" distinction problematic. For it suggests, on the one hand, that since man is as naturally occurring an object as trees or rocks or rivers, his arbitrary designs, the traces of his movements, are just as much natural shapes as are leaves or fissures or erosions; and it suggests, on the other hand, that the concept of the "natural," as a function of the differential opposition "natural/man-made," is itself something man-made.

This latter position is especially evident in the two different senses of the natural that are implicit in the chasm episode, for the natural as distinguished from the man-made can mean either the necessary as opposed to the arbitrary or the random as opposed to the arbitrary. Obviously, not all naturally occurring shapes are interpreted as "necessary" shapes (in the sense of inherently meaningful), but only those that, like the shape of a leaf or the outline of an animal body, show a *recurring form* (the very fact of whose recurrence indicates a purposive design by the Author of nature). Natural shapes that are produced in a nonrecurring fashion are classified as random or meaningless. Thus Pym dismisses Peters' suggestion that some of the marks on the wall are man-made alphabetical characters by arguing that the marks had been caused "by some convulsion from the surface where the indentures were found," that they were the accidental "work of nature." Yet Pym apparently classifies the shapes on the wall as "natural" (in the sense of random) less on the basis of the physical evidence he educes than on the basis of his not recognizing among these "alphabetical" characters any familiar, recurring form. (Would Pym have been so sure that the markings were the random work of nature if he had been acquainted with the Arabic and Coptic scripts?) On the other hand, the hieroglyphic indentation, though it would presumably have been formed, according to Pym's view, by the same random "convulsion from the surface," is, "with a very slight exertion of the imagination," immediately identified as the representation of a human body simply because the marking possesses a familiar shape. But does this then imply that the surface convulsion that produced this necessary shape was neither man-made nor accidental, but of divine origin?

Pym's interpretive response to the enigmatic markings suggests the way in which human art or arbitrariness, the "exertion of the imagination," arbitrates between the two senses of the natural, drawing out of the same ground (reading against the same background) the differential opposition between the necessary and the random, the meaningful and the meaningless, on the basis of the human capacity for re-cognition: the repetitive structure of memory. More important still, it shows the way in which this act of human arbitration between the two senses of the natural masks itself from itself, by attributing to the Author of nature (the apotheosized ground of meaning, the superhuman) those "necessary" shapes whose recurrence suggests a purposive design like that of human repetition, and by attributing to chance or accident, to the nonhuman, those shapes that are unique and unfamiliar. Thus Pym, looking at the writing on the wall, makes the distinction between meaningful and meaningless, recurring and nonrecurring "natural" shapes within an interpretive act the condition of whose functioning is the nonrecognition of these shapes as man-made, that is, the nonrecognition of a human presence in the very concept of the natural—a nonrecognition at the very moment when Pym stands looking at the hieroglyphic shadow outline of a human body that evokes the mythic original language of nature. It is as if the arbitrary, the necessary, and the random were three corners of an equilateral triangle: man, standing at the angle of the arbitrary, sees before him the necessary and the random in a bipolar opposition without seeing that that polar relationship is a function of his own position at once in between and above the polar opposites. Pym's stance in interpreting the markings on the cavern wall exhibits the doubleness of man's relationship to nature: the fact that man as a self-conscious entity is simultaneously within the natural world and above the natural world, at once part of it and separate from it. It is an aspect of this same doubleness that we confronted earlier in the indeterminate status of the body's surface as the dividing line between inner and outer, between the self and the natural world.

Most significant of all, Pym's stance in interpreting the markings on the wall exhibits that necessary absence of the self to itself on which self-consciousness, as the imaged presence of the self to itself, is grounded. Standing at the bottom of a chasm (a word derived from the same Greek root as the word "chaos"—*chainein*, "to yawn, gape") that he describes as an "abyss" and a "gulf," a chasm like the one in which the crew of the *Jane Guy* met the death from which he and Peters narrowly escaped, standing beside his dark double (a character created by Pym's narrative, a fictive written self to Pym's fictive writing self) and facing the inscribed outline of a human body (evocative of that confrontation between man and his shadow image that is the origin of the symbolic order), Pym denies that the markings on the wall are man-made—a denial of human presence that is symbolic of that death of the self to itself in opposition to which self-conscious life is differentiated, a death that is not simply the external limit of self-consciousness but its internal limit as well, a death lying at the core of self-consciousness and inhabiting the objective otherness of the inscribed image. In order to grasp the dual sense of that death, which is at once continuous and discontinuous with self-consciousness, at once its outer limit of dissolution and its internal limit of differentiation, we must understand the way in which Pym's confrontation with the hieroglyphic human figure in the cavern *foreshadows* his final confrontation with the apotheosized human figure in the mist, and we must then read the two episodes together as if solving a simultaneous equation, an equation in which neither episode by itself would give us enough information to decipher the meaning.

As a first step in this process, let us consider for a moment one possible source of the chasm episode, a source that would have been readily available to Poe. Earlier, we commented on Alexander von Humboldt's lengthy treatment of the Aztec hieroglyphics in his *Researches, Concerning the Institutions and Monuments of the Ancient Inhabitants of America.* Humboldt observes that while in other areas of the world hieroglyphic writing developed by progressive stages into phonetic writing, "no native people of America had attained that analysis of sounds, which leads to the most admirable, we might say the most miraculous of all inventions, an alphabet" (p. 149). In defending his theory that the transition from pictographic ideograms to arbitrary phonetic signs never occurred among the natives of America, Humboldt discusses some of the best known examples of rock inscriptions in America in order to show either that the inscriptions are not alphabetic or that they were not produced by native Americans. At one point he says:

I have carefully examined the four drawings of the celebrated stone of Taunton river, which Mr. Lort published in London in the Memoirs of the Antiquarian Society. Far from recognizing a symmetrical arrangement of simple letters and syllabic characters, I discover a drawing scarcely traced, like those that have been found on the rocks of Norway, and in almost all the countries inhabited by the Scandinavian nations. In this sketch we distinguish, from the form of the heads, five human figures, surrounding an animal with horns. . . .

In the voyage made by M. Bonpland and myself to ascertain the communication between the rivers Orinoco and Amazon, we were told of an inscription, which it was asserted was found in a chain of granitic mountains, that, in the seventh degree of latitude, extends from the Indian village of Uruana, or Urbana, as far as the western banks of the Caura. A missionary, Ramon Bueno, a Franciscan monk, having accidentally entered a cavern formed by the separation of some ledges of rocks, beheld in the middle of the cave a large block of granite, on which he saw what he believed to be characters formed into various groups, and ranged on the same line. . . . The missionary gave me a copy of part of these characters, of which the following is an engraving.

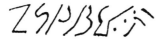

Some resemblance to the Phoenician alphabet may be discovered in these characters; but I much doubt whether the good monk, who seemed to be but little interested about this pretended inscription, had copied it very carefully. It is somewhat remarkable, that out of seven characters there were none several times repeated....

It is also remarkable, that in this savage and desert country, where P. Bueno found letters engraven in granite, are a great number of rocks, which at considerable heights are covered with figures of animals, representations of the sun, the moon, and the stars, and other hieroglyphical signs. The natives relate, that their ancestors, in the time of the *great waters,* came in canoes to the top of these mountains: and that the stones were then in so plastic a state, that men could trace marks on them with their fingers. This tradition indicates a tribe in a different state of civilization from that of the people by which it was preceded, discovering an absolute ignorance of the use of the chisel, and every other metallic tool. (Pp. 152–54)

As we know, Poe borrowed from a wide variety of works in creating *Pym.* Whether or not this passage from Humboldt represents another of Poe's sources, the similarities between it and the chasm episode suggest the general characteristics of those contemporary anthropological speculations that Poe's fictive episode draws upon and in relation to which that episode must be understood. Just as Pym, confronting the markings on the chasm wall, recognizes the hieroglyphic outline of a human figure but not the alphabetic characters beside it, so Humboldt, in the case of "the celebrated stone of Taunton river," fails to recognize the "symmetrical arrangement of simple letters and syllabic characters" that others had claimed to find there, but finds instead a "drawing scarcely traced" showing "five human figures, surrounding an animal with horns." In each case the inscribed outline of the human body is immediately transparent for the writer, while the phonetic script is considered either opaque or nonexistent. Further, in Humboldt's version of the chasm episode, the dismissal of the inscribed characters as inauthentic is based on the same principle implicit in Pym's dismissal of the alphabetic characters—the absence of a recurring form. Whereas Pym acknowledges that the markings on the wall bear "some little resemblance to alphabetical characters" but then decides that they cannot be man-made phonetic script, apparently because none of them repeats the shape of phonetic characters he is familiar with, Humboldt acknowledges that the markings discovered by the missionary show "some resemblance to the Phoenician alphabet" but then casts doubt on their authenticity by adding, "It is somewhat remarkable, that out of seven characters there were none several times repeated." Indeed, if this criterion of repeated characters *within* an inscription were applied to the markings discovered by Pym, they too would appear inauthentic, since no character occurs more than once in any of the three scripts. The nonrepetition of characters within the inscription discovered by the missionary would, of course, have been vexing to Humboldt for reasons inherent in, but unacknowledged by, his argument, for without a character repeated, either within the inscription or between this inscription and some other written text, there would be no hope of deciphering the writing, thus confronting the scientist with the problem of human knowledge lost and now irrecoverable.

In this regard the most interesting part of Humboldt's chasm episode, because of the way it undercuts the episode as a whole, is the brief addendum on forgetting, on the faultiness of historical consciousness considered as collective human memory. Humboldt comments that the natives' curious myth concerning the origin of the "hieroglyphical signs" carved on the rocks "indicates a tribe in a different state of civilization from that of the people by which it was preceded, discovering an absolute ignorance of the use of the chisel, and every other metallic tool." The remark is interesting for two reasons: first, because Pym's nonrecognition of the alphabetic characters also involves a kind of "ignorance of the use of the chisel" insofar as he records, but then draws no conclusion from, the presence of the white arrowhead flints in the chasm; and second, because the notion of a people later in time who are at a lower stage of development than a people earlier in time whom they have supplanted in a geographic area calls into question one of Humboldt's anthropological assumptions.

As a nineteenth-century scientist, Humboldt participated in the ongoing, post-Enlightenment work of elaborating the concept of Man through the reconstruction of his historical past, and specifically the concept of Man as a historically conscious being who leaves throughout the world inscribed traces of his self-conscious presence, a being who possesses a written memory. Implicit in this scientific notion of a universal memory called history, made up of man's various inscriptions (writing, artifacts, landscaping, and so on), is the sense of the progressive accumulation of human knowledge through the course of time and the consequent intellectual superiority of man at a later period in history to man at an earlier period. One form that this sense of superiority takes in the era of Western European voyages of discovery and scientific exploration is the assumption that journeys to distant lands are journeys into the past, that the natives of these lands are men in an earlier state of cultural development than the Europeans who visit them.

Obviously, what the phrase "cultural development" means in this context is scientific development. The sense of cultural superiority rests on the fact that it was the Europeans who, because of their technological advancement, journeyed to far-off lands, subdued them, made their inhabitants objects of scientific study, expropriated their artifacts to fill museums, and incorporated them into Western history as "discoveries." There were, of course, no Aztec expeditions to Spain, no Chinese explorations of Portugal, no Indian invasions of England. And the Western assumption has been, since at least the late Middle Ages, that the man who explores new regions and studies other men is inherently superior to the man who is "discovered" and studied. Yet Humboldt's closing comment on the discontinuity in knowledge between the earlier and the later inhabitants of the same region undermines the concept of a progressive human development based on the gradual accumulation of knowledge throughout the course of history. As we noted earlier, it is this same sense of historical progress that Poe satirizes in "Some Words with a Mummy." The notion that the ancient Egyptians had achieved a level of cultural and scientific development far surpassing that of nineteenth-century America implies, of course, that at some point in history there occurred a wholesale loss of knowledge, a radical break in the continuity of historical memory, a collective act of forgetting so massive as to constitute not merely cultural amnesia but a kind of death of the collective Human Self to itself. And it is just such an act of forgetting that is suggested by Humboldt's comment on the discontinuity between the people who made the rock inscriptions and their successors who did not even understand the use of a chisel.

What these periodic losses of memory involve is not the loss of the physical inscriptions of historical memory (writing, artifacts, and so on) but the loss of the ability to read or recognize these inscriptions, the ability to interpret them correctly. And what these collective lapses ultimately suggest is that forgetting, in its constitutive opposition to memory, possesses a dual aspect corresponding to that double sense of death as self-conscious life's internal limit of differentiation and external limit of dissolution. The traditional connection between death and forgetting is clear enough: if the personal self's psychic principle of continuity is memory, then the death of the personal self is equivalent to the destruction of memory. From the point of view of the person who dies, death is an act of total and irrevocable forgetting. In one of those reversals characteristic of homeopathic magic, man memorializes the dead—particularly by images and inscriptions carved in rock—in the hope that if the memory of the deceased survives in the memories of other men, then by the principle of like producing like, the deceased's personal self *qua* memory may survive through a kind of reciprocal mnemic relationship. That is, if death is not an act of forgetting on the part of those who knew the deceased, then perhaps death is not an act of forgetting on the part of the deceased either.

As the absolute forgetting that results from memory's destruction corresponds to the sense of death as the self's external limit, so there is a forgetting that is internally constitutive of memory that corresponds to the sense of death as the self's internal limit, its principle of differentiation. For memory functions by means of the very forgetting that appears to be memory's negation: we are able to remember some things precisely *because* we forget most things. This forgetting is not a passive but an active mechanism; it is a form of that essential abbreviation or reduction of experience on which all human sign systems are based. Moments in an individual's past are able to live on in consciousness, are able to survive over the long term as memories, because the vast majority of moments that the individual has experienced are dead to consciousness—forgotten and irrecoverable.

In his tale "Funes the Memorious," Borges, the modern writer who most resembles Poe, evokes the way in which forgetting constitutes memory as a signifying system through the abbreviation of experience, by showing how signification would dissolve if one were cursed with a memory that never forgot anything. After a riding accident that leaves him paralyzed, the young Ireneo Funes finds that his memory has suddenly become so retentive that he can remember everything he has ever experienced. But the result is that Funes begins to deteriorate as a linguistic being; it becomes increasingly difficult for him to grasp the meaning of the narrator's conversation. As the narrator describes the phenomenon:

> Locke, in the seventeenth century, postulated (and rejected) an impossible language in which each individual thing, each stone, each

bird and each branch, would have its own name; Funes once projected an analogous language, but discarded it because it seemed too general to him, too ambiguous. In fact, Funes remembered not only every leaf of every tree of every wood, but also every one of the times he had perceived or imagined it. He decided to reduce each of his past days to some seventy thousand memories, which would then be defined by means of ciphers. He was dissuaded from this by two considerations: his awareness that the task was interminable, his awareness that it was useless. He thought that by the hour of his death he would not even have finished classifying all the memories of his childhood. . . .

He was, let us not forget, almost incapable of ideas of a general, Platonic sort. Not only was it difficult for him to comprehend that the generic symbol *dog* embraces so many unlike individuals of diverse size and form; it bothered him that the dog at three fourteen (seen from the side) should have the same name as the dog at three fifteen (seen from the front). His own face in the mirror, his own hands, surprised him every time he saw them. . . .

With no effort, he had learned English, French, Portuguese and Latin. I suspect, however, that he was not very capable of thought. To think is to forget differences, generalize, make abstractions. In the teeming world of Funes, there were only details, almost immediate in their presence.[49]

Although Funes is only nineteen, "he seemed to me," the narrator says, "as monumental as bronze, more ancient than Egypt, older than the prophecies and pyramids" (p. 66).

Because Funes remembers each individual experience in all its details, the category of sameness begins to break down, and with it the possibility of signification; for if each thing is retained in full detail, in its unique difference, then no one thing can be made to stand as a sign for any other, nor, in a consciousness where minutely remembered details constitute unique differences among objects, can a single sign, such as the word *dog*, be made to stand for a class of objects, since the category of classes, of sameness, would simply not exist. A memory that retained every detail would require a language in which each perception of each individual object "would have its own name," but such a language could never communicate anything. Lacking the abbreviation essential to a

symbolic system, it would be a linguistic model of the world exactly equal
in size and detail to the world of which it was a model. It would be, to use
an example Borges often cites, like the map of natural size described by
the German professor in Lewis Carroll's *Sylvie and Bruno Concluded*, a
map that the cartographers in his native land made on a scale of a mile to
the mile: "'It has never been spread out, yet,' said Mein Herr: 'the
farmers objected: they said it would cover the whole country, and shut
out the sunlight! So now we use the country itself, as its own map, and I
assure you it does nearly as well.'"[50] The map of natural size is a sign that
totally displaces the object it stands for: when the map is unfolded, the
country disappears. (One is reminded of the curious closing verse of
John's Gospel: "And there are also many other things which Jesus did,
the which, if they should be written every one, I suppose that even the
world itself could not contain the books that should be written.")

Since it exhausts all available space, the map leaves no margin between
sign and referent wherein symbolization can occur. Similarly, the kind of
"language" required by a memory incapable of forgetting would exhaust
all available space, not the external space of nature as with the map, but
the internal space of consciousness. Normal forgetting clears a working
space in consciousness for speculation, but as more and more of Funes's
conscious life is given over to remembering things in minute detail, he
gradually becomes incapable of thought, and his memory, needing more
room to expand, extends its borders from the daytime world into the
nocturnal space reserved for dreams: "It was very difficult for him to
sleep. To sleep is to turn one's mind from the world; Funes, lying on his
back on his cot in the shadows, could imagine every crevice and every
molding in the sharply defined houses surrounding him. (I repeat that
the least important of his memories was more minute and more vivid
than our perception of physical pleasure or physical torment)" (p. 66).
Funes's memory, which finally exhausts the space of consciousness, ex-
tinguishes consciousness, for when every detail is equally significant,
equally memorable, then nothing is significant, nothing can be made to
stand for precisely because nothing *stands out*—there exists no figure/
ground relationship.

Within Borges's work the mnemic reciprocal of Funes is the minotaur
Asterion: where Funes's photographic memory registers only details,
only unique differences, Asterion's memory tends to elide all differences. "Bothersome and trivial details," he says, "have no place in my
spirit, which is prepared for all that is vast and grand; I have never

retained the difference between one letter and another. A certain generous impatience has not permitted that I learn to read" (p. 139). In attempting to bring about an absolute separation of sameness and difference, Asterion and Funes are extremes that meet: with each, signification breaks down, and consciousness finally evaporates. Where Funes's self is gradually absorbed into the uniqueness of a minutely detailed world, Asterion absorbs the world into the uniqueness of the self. "The fact is that I am unique," Asterion says. "I am not interested in what one man may transmit to other men; like the philosopher, I think that nothing is communicable by the act of writing" (p. 139). The titular "House of Asterion"—ostensibly the labyrinth—is Asterion's own mind. In words that recall the map of natural size, he says, "The house is the same size as the world; or rather, it is the world" (p. 139).

In the case of both Funes and Asterion, the breakdown of the reciprocal relationship between sameness and difference (as one or the other is pushed to an absolute extreme) is presented in terms of the hieroglyphic doubling that grounds the self. The narrator says that Funes's "own face in the mirror, his own hands, surprised him every time he saw them"; while Asterion, who plays imaginary games in a dreamlike state, thinks, "Of all the games, I prefer the one about the other Asterion. I pretend that he comes to visit me and that I show him my house" (p. 139). But since the house is Asterion's mind, the imaginary game of showing the other Asterion his house is one that he plays *literally* in the very act of imagining it. The game and the dream of the game are indistinguishable. He says, "Perhaps I have created the stars and the sun and this enormous house, but I no longer remember" (p. 140).

A memory that retains everything and a memory that retains almost nothing amount finally to the same thing—the collapse of signification. For language to function there must be a partial forgetting that creates a blank background for figuration. This forgetting is the self's internal limit of differentiation; it is a death that exists at the very core of self-conscious life. The ambiguous relationship between this *forgetting as death* and that *death as forgetting* which forms the self's external limit of dissolution is clearly exhibited in scenarios like the chasm episode in *Pym* and the story of the mysterious cavern inscription in Humboldt's *Researches*. It is not just that writing carved in stone is inevitably associated with death, with the self-conscious attempt to trace memory on a ground so permanent that it outlasts the individual life, nor just that the Egyptian hieroglyphics, as the archetypal form of monumental writing in Western tradition, inevitably call up the image of a civilization so obsessed with death and personal survival that its foremost cultural occupation seems to have been the construction of inscribed funerary monuments—pyramids, tombs, obelisks, stelae, sarcophagi, and so on. Rather, it is that prior to the series of nineteenth-century decipherments of ancient languages that began with Champollion's reading of the hieroglyphics, the scenario of an explorer confronting a rock-hewn inscription in a mysterious ancient tongue presented modern Western man with the disturbing image of a language that was dead in a dual sense—not simply a language no longer spoken because lacking a living community of speakers, but one literally unspeakable because unintelligible, undecipherable. The writing carved in rock had survived the men who carved it, but the ability to read the writing had not survived. Such inscriptions seemed to reverse the basic sense of an immortal memorializing through writing in stone, for what an undecipherable inscription preserves is the memory of that forgetting which forms memory's external limit of dissolution, that death which obliterates signification.

An undecipherable inscription is disturbing precisely because here writing seems to commemorate its own inability by itself to transmit memory, its status not as a substitute for memory but simply as an aid to memory. And this raises a series of doubts about the plausibility of historical consciousness *per se;* it suggests the possibility of radical discontinuities in history, large unbridgeable gaps in the collective human memory on the far side of which civilizations superior to any of the present may have arisen and then vanished without their accumulated knowledge or even the fact of their existence having survived. Whitman expresses his sense of this in one of his prose fragments:

The most immense part of ancient history is altogether unknown. . . . There were . . . nations on all the continents of the earth at intervals through the stretch of time from ten thousand years ago down to twenty-six hundred years ago—signs and materials of them remain. Of their literature, government, religions, social customs and general civilization—silence. No one can now tell the names of those nations. . . . Time, the passage of many thousands of years, the total vacuity of our letters about them, their places blank upon the

map, not a mark nor a figure that is demonstrably so. With all this
they lived as surely as we do now.... The Ruins in North
America— ... the mounds in the valley of the Mississippi—the vast
ruins of Central America, Mexico and South America—grand temple walls &c., now overgrown with old trees—all prove beyond cavil
the existence, ages since, in the Western World, of powerful, populous and probably civilized nations, whose names, histories and even
traditions had been lost long before the discovery of Columbus and
Vespucius.[51]

Such a possibility plays havoc with the quest for a linguistic or a biological
origin (a *lingua humana* or a missing link) as well as with the nineteenth-
century notion of progress (the sense of a temporal or geographic direction to history), because it points to a basic instability in the concept of
recognition.

To recognize something can mean to identify it as previously known
or as the same as that which was previously known, but it can also mean
to acknowledge the existence, validity, or genuineness of something, to
constitute it as an object of knowledge. The oscillation between these two
senses of recognition is apparent in nineteenth-century anthropological
speculations where the work of elaborating the concept of Man as an
historically conscious being can either mean identifying or not identifying an inscription or artifact, a custom or race, as "human" on the basis
of its resemblance to previously known (generally Western) criteria, or
else can mean granting the validity, the very existence, of an object as
"human" (even though it may be totally unfamiliar to the observer) by
simply extending the concept of Man, by applying the same name to
something different. Thus an explorer confronting an Australian
aborigine may find the native's customs so different from his own that he
denies the aborigine is human and treats him like an animal, or he may
acknowledge the aborigine as a man, thereby revising his own notion of
the range of humanity.

The act of recognizing the "human" is never merely a biological identification, a simple recognition of the shape of a body. It is rather a
cultural recognition: "humanity" is something *willfully* conferred or
withheld by an act of naming. Thus, for example, the modern anthropological task of recognizing a missing link is one that began at a
specific point in Western culture with the application of the idea of

historical progress to biology. It was a task literally unimaginable as long as Western man believed that he had been created in the physical image and likeness of God; and it remains a task whose "successful" conclusion will ultimately depend less on the discovery of some new fossilized skeleton than on how much further man is willing to expand the concept of the human. The task assumes a historical continuity of biological forms, a series of links connecting man and ape; yet this quest for a biological beginning, for the first recognizably human body, is not at all the same as the quest for a human origin, that original act of recognizing the image of a body that constitutes self-recognition. No continuity of biological forms between man and animal can lead "back" to that original act of discontinuity that differentiates man and animal. The confusion of a biological beginning with a human origin is one way that the originating ground of human consciousness, of time, veils its alogical (atemporal) character in the logical concept of a temporal starting point.

The belief in a historical continuity of biological forms—a continuity archaeologically inscribed through fossilized remains, a kind of natural writing in stone—is a willed projection of the individual self's mnemic continuity onto a physical world indifferent to such continuity, a world that can be made to preserve markings but not meanings. Western historical consciousness treats the physical world as if it were a self, man's gigantic Other, as if it possessed the continuity of an individual memory. Clearly, one of the cultural purposes of history is to assure the individual that the dead past (the world prior to his birth) is continuous with the living present, that no matter how far back in time one goes—even beyond the advent of man, as in the study of natural history—the world remains humanly recognizable. But the deeper purpose of this retrospective continuity is to ground a sense of prospective continuity, a sense that the world after one's death will show the same continuity with the living present that the world before one's birth has shown through history. And this sense of prospective continuity applies not just to the physical world—whose presumed continuance after death gives meaning to life by assuring the individual that the mark he has left on the world will not be obliterated or rendered undecipherable by his passing, that he will live on in memory—it applies as well to that "other world" into which the individual presumably enters at death, a world somehow continuous with the living present, a world at once humanly recognizable and recognizably human where the individual will survive not simply *in* memory but *as* memory, a realm in which the individual through the persistence of his personal memory will continue to recognize himself. In light of this deeper purpose we can see why an undecipherable inscription is so disturbing, for in raising the specter of a discontinuous past, of a wholesale loss of human memory, it raises as well the possibility of a discontinuous future, an absolute loss of memory at death, a vanishing of that ability to recognize oneself that constitutes personal survival.

We must keep in mind, however, the dual sense of "recognition" involved here and the instability that occurs when the recognition of the human (self-recognition) is confused with the recognition of the outline of a body. When Pym sees the outline of a human figure on the chasm wall, he recognizes it in one sense but not in another: he identifies the outline as resembling a previously known bodily form, but he refuses to acknowledge the markings as man-made, he refuses to recognize the shape as a symbol, intentional and meaningful. Pym's nonrecognition, his *withholding* of recognition, emphasizes the fact that recognizing the outline of a human body, identifying a familiar visual shape, does not constitute the recognition of the human. Indeed, many animals can recognize previously known shapes. What the recognition of the human involves is the granting or willing of significance, the acknowledging of a visual shape as a sign of something that is unseen and, most basically, of something that is unseen precisely because that something is, by the very nature of sight, always looking away from itself. *Self-recognition is a reflected mirroring, a foreshadowed doubling, that allows vision to turn back on itself and recognize its own state of nonrecognition, to remember its own forgetfulness, to know death.* As with the three moments in the Narcissus scenario, the second moment, in which the image is recognized, does not obliterate the first moment of nonrecognition; rather, the two moments are balanced in a third, where the interplay of sameness and difference between body and image is seen to be that condition of in-betweenness we call the self.

Self-consciousness is, then, the recognition (in both senses of the word) of nonrecognition, the simultaneous constitution of both a polar opposition and the condition of mediation. When Pym sees the outline of a human figure on the chasm wall, he reverses the first two moments of the Narcissus scenario by first recognizing the outline as resembling the image of a body and then not recognizing it as symbolic—a displacement that allows the reader, the hidden observer of the scene, to enact for himself the third moment (the recognition of the human), allows him to see the omnipresent, arbitrary willing of significance through Pym's arbitrary withholding of significance. Meaning is what man necessarily adds to every scene, but Pym constantly withholds meaning, and not just in an obvious sense as with the letter in the bottle on Kerguelen's Island, or the carved prow on Bennet's Islet, or the arrowhead flints and the inscribed figure on Tsalal. Just prior to the letter-in-the-bottle incident, Poe, with fine irony, has Pym comment on the near human behavior of the penguins he has observed on the island: "Nothing can be more astonishing than the spirit of reflection evinced by these feathered beings, and nothing surely can be better calculated to elicit reflection in every well-regulated human intellect" (3:157)—a reflection that is never elicited in Pym by the traces of human intellect that he keeps stumbling over.

Section 11
*Repetition; Symbolic Death and
Rebirth; The Infinite and the Indefinite;
The Mechanism of Foreshadowing*

Throughout the narrative Pym is characterized by his inability to recognize repetition. For all Pym's talk about memory, he has written a book that is apparently without a memory. It is not merely the fact that nothing seems to be carried over in terms of reflective experience from one incident to another (as when Pym says of the cannibalizing of Parker that it was "a scene which, with its minutest details, no after events have been able to efface in the slightest degree from my memory, and whose stern recollection will embitter every future moment of my existence" [3:126], and then never refers to it again), nor just that the blitheness of Pym's outlook remains unaffected by any of the hair-raising events that continually befall him. It is rather that Pym enacts over and over again the same scenario without ever becoming aware of it. One could say that for Pym difference is simply the nonrecognition of the same. Not only is the overwhelming-of-the-vessel episode repeated three times, but in each episode the symbolic overwhelming of the human vessel always involves at some point a loss of consciousness on Pym's part. When the *Ariel* is run down in the storm, Pym has his first fainting spell: "Never while I live shall I forget the intense agony of terror I experienced at that moment. My hair stood erect on my head—I felt the blood congealing in my veins—my heart ceased utterly to beat, and without having once raised my eyes to learn the source of my alarm, I tumbled headlong and insensible upon the body of my fallen companion" (3:10).

Stowed away in the hold of the *Grampus,* Pym faints a second time when the air in the coffinlike box where he is hiding becomes so foul that he is almost asphyxiated; and when he regains consciousness only to find that the trapdoor leading from the hold to Augustus's cabin has been sealed, he says: "In vain I attempted to reason on the probable cause of my being thus *entombed.* I could summon up no connected chain of reflection, and, sinking on the floor, gave way, unresistingly, to the most gloomy imaginings, in which the dreadful deaths of thirst, famine, suffocation, and *premature interment,* crowded upon me as the prominent disasters to be encountered" (3:33, italics mine). Later, on the island of Tsalal, when Pym and Peters are buried alive by the landslide, Pym describes the experience in familiar terms: "For a long time we gave up supinely to the most intense agony and despair, such as cannot be adequately imagined by those who have never been in a similar situation. I firmly believed that no incident ever occurring in the course of human events is more adapted to inspire the supremeness of mental and bodily distress than a case like our own, of living inhumation" (3:204–05). After escaping from their entombment and exploring the chasm with the carved inscription, Pym and Peters are in the process of descending a steep cliff on the island when Pym faints for the third time:

> ... I found my imagination growing terribly excited by thoughts of the vast depth yet to be descended.... It was in vain I endeavoured to banish these reflections, and to keep my eyes steadily bent upon the flat surface of the cliff before me. The more earnestly I struggled *not to think,* the more intensely vivid became my conceptions, and the more horribly distinct. At length arrived that crisis of fancy, so fearful in all similar cases, the crisis in which we begin to anticipate the feelings with which we *shall* fall—to picture to ourselves the sickness, and dizziness, and the last struggle, and the half swoon, and the final bitterness of the rushing and headlong descent. And now I found these fancies creating their own realities, and all imagined horrors crowding upon me in fact.... There was a ringing in my ears, and I said, "This is my knell of death!" And now I was consumed with the irrepressible desire of looking below. I could not, I would not, confine my glances to the cliff; and, with a wild,

indefinable emotion, half of horror, half of relieved oppression, I threw my vision far down into the abyss. For one moment my fingers clutched convulsively upon their hold, while, with the movement, the faintest possible idea of ultimate escape wandered, like a shadow, through my mind—in the next my whole soul was pervaded with a *longing to fall;* a desire, a yearning, a passion utterly uncontrollable.... Now there came a spinning of the brain; a shrill-sounding and phantom voice screamed within my ears; a dusky, fiendish, and filmy figure stood immediately beneath me; and, sighing, I sunk down with a bursting heart, and plunged within its arms.

I had swooned, and Peters had caught me as I fell.... On recovery, my trepidation had entirely vanished; I felt a new being, and, with some little further aid from my companion, reached the bottom also in safety.

We now found ourselves not far from the ravine which had proved the tomb of our friends.... (3:229-30)

Since *Pym* presents itself on the most basic level as the story of a young man's passage from adolescence to maturity, and since the structure most common to rites of passage or initiation rites is one of symbolic death and rebirth, often involving a momentary loss of consciousness that represents the young man's death to a lower state of life and rebirth to a higher state,[52] Pym's repeated faintings during the course of his journey are not difficult to account for. What does require explanation is the fact that Pym, for all the symbolic deaths and rebirths he experiences, never seems to pass into a higher state of consciousness.

The central issue in male initiation rites is the overcoming of the fear of death.[53] An adolescent becomes an adult, or an adult becomes a shamanistic visionary, by passing through a ritual test in which he demonstrates his fearlessness of death, his understanding that death is not an end to life but the price of and portal to a higher form of life that one can never reach as long as one is afraid to pass through that narrow gate. But the rite of passage also serves another, less obvious, purpose, for it is a means by which the community as a whole protects itself against the fear of death. By making the structure of the rite a symbolic death and rebirth, the community transforms death from a senseless alien force within whose grip man is essentially passive into a meaningful stage of human life, a stage over which man exercises active control through a ritual repetition. By incorporating it into a ritual, the community is able to make death, which attacks each man separately, subject to communal action, as if it were a stalking predator that could be hunted by the whole tribe. More important still, what the structure of a symbolic death and rebirth ritually reenacts for the community, what it offers visible evidence of, is not that the death of the child in a man necessarily leads to the birth of the adult, but rather that the state that follows real physical death is continuous with life, is another state of life in just the same way that childhood and adulthood are continuous states of life. The deepest significance of the rite-of-passage scenario is, then, not that it imprints the structure of a symbolic death and rebirth onto the passage from adolescence to maturity, but rather that by a kind of reverse transference it surreptitiously imprints upon physical death the sense of a passage between states of life. By its incorporation into a ritual, death is represented as an internal limit of human life rather than its external limit.

Clearly, Pym's repeated losses of consciousness are meant to be symbolic deaths. But we should keep in mind that his fainting spells generally occur in response to the imminence of death; they are, and are the result of, the imaginative anticipation of death. Faced with the permanent loss of consciousness, Pym characteristically suffers a temporary loss of consciousness caused by fright. This fear of death, so intense that it ultimately creates what it fears, is one of Poe's obsessive themes. In "The Fall of the House of Usher" (1839), Roderick Usher says, "I have, indeed, no abhorrence of danger, except in its absolute effect—in terror. In this unnerved—in this pitiable condition—I feel that the period will sooner or later arrive when I must abandon life and reason together, in some struggle with the grim phantasm, FEAR" (3:280). And the manner of death that Poe fears most is, of course, death by premature burial—an embodiment of that imaginative anticipation of death that puts the living in the place of the dead. Roderick's terrifying realization that he has entombed his twin sister Madeline while she is still alive and Madeline's real or imagined return from the grave unite finally to frighten Roderick to death. And Pym, after his own premature burial, observes that the "blackness of darkness which envelops the victim, the terrific oppression of the lungs, the stifling fumes from the damp earth, unite with the ghastly considerations that we are beyond the remotest confines of hope, and that such is the allotted portion of *the dead*, to carry into the human heart a degree of appalling awe and horror not to be tolerated—never to be conceived" (3:205). Yet with that last phrase—"never to be conceived"—the entire passage is undercut, for one suddenly realizes that the terrors of the grave Pym has described are *not* the allotted portion of the dead but of the living. If death is the absolute extinction of individual consciousness, then the dead are conscious of nothing, they have no "allotted portion." And even if one believes in personal immortality, the very separation of body and soul at death would preclude the soul's experiencing after death any "bodily distress" such as "the terrific oppression of the lungs" or "the stifling fumes from the damp earth." Someone who is dying may have these sensations, but someone who is dying is still alive.

During Pym's descent of the precipice, Poe once again calls our attention to the impossibility of conceiving of one's own death, of thinking the absence of thought. Pym says that from his position on the cliff he threw his "vision far down into the abyss." But what waits at the bottom of the abyss cannot be foreseen; it is the "never-to-be-imparted secret, whose attainment is destruction." And Pym is of two minds about this ultimate knowledge that consumes the knower: part of him seeks the experience, but part wants to survive. And as one would expect, these opposing states of mind (which exhibit the essential division between hero and narrator) tend to oscillate, the movement toward one pole inevitably bringing a reversal into the opposite. Thus, on the precipice Pym is "excited by thoughts of the vast depth yet to be descended," but when he tries to resist the attraction of the abyss, the method he chooses turns out to be an image of that very extinction of consciousness he wants to avoid—"I struggled *not to think.*" In order to banish his "reflections" on the abyss, he refuses to look down; instead he keeps his eyes on "the flat surface of the cliff," apparently hoping that the visual image of a blank wall will help void any mental images. But for someone who is conscious, it is impossible not to think, and what Pym finds is that the very effort to make his mind a void renders his conceptions "more intensely vivid . . . , more horribly distinct." The abyss, as it exists within conscious life, seems to call forth images to fill it, until those very anticipatory images of death create "their own realities," thereby threatening to void themselves as images once and for all in the destruction of the imagination.

What this oscillation subtly directs our attention to is the odd equation of death and the abyss. The abyss is, after all, the endless, the limitless— it is infinity; while death is the absolute limit of human consciousness.

What accounts for this equation is the fact that an absolute limit and the absolutely limitless are equally impossible for the human mind to conceive. In his discussion of infinity in *Eureka*, Poe says that the word "infinity," like the words "God" and "spirit," is "by no means the expression of an idea—but of an effort at one. It stands for the possible attempt at an impossible conception. Man needed a term by which to point out the *direction* of this effort—the cloud behind which lay, forever invisible, the *object* of this attempt. A word, in fine, was demanded, by means of which one human being might put himself in relation at once with another human being and with a certain *tendency* of the human intellect. Out of this demand arose the word, 'Infinity;' which is thus the representative but of the *thought of a thought*" (16:200).

Taking the infinity of space as an example, Poe refutes the argument that the human mind entertains the idea of infinity "through the greater *difficulty* which it finds in entertaining" (16:200) the idea of an absolute limit. He points out that there can be no question of the relative difficulty of the two ideas, since both are impossible to conceive, and that consequently it makes no sense to claim that one impossible conception is entertained because it is less difficult than another impossible conception. Poe then shows that the same argument that is used to establish infinity is also used to establish its opposite, the existence of an ultimate origin, since it is precisely "the superior difficulty" which the mind experiences "in conceiving cause beyond cause without end" that is invoked by theologians as the basis for believing in a First Cause: "And what is a First Cause? An ultimate termination of causes. And what is an ultimate termination of causes? Finity—the Finite. Thus the one quibble, in two processes, by God knows how many philosophers, is made to support now Finity and now Infinity" (16:202).

Poe argues that in order actually to conceive of infinity, of "point still beyond point" (16:203), the conceptual act itself would have to continue for an infinite amount of time to match the infinity of space. But since the finite life span of any individual thinker precludes that infinite continuance of thought, infinity is inconceivable. What usually masks this inconceivability is that the completion of the thought of infinity, which overthrows the concept of the infinite precisely by terminating it, "by resting upon some one ultimate and therefore definite point" (16:203), simultaneously turns the mind away from the overthrown concept through the cessation of the thought. Poe maintains that in using a term like "infinity," anyone

> who has a right to say that he thinks *at all*, feels himself called upon, *not* to entertain a conception, but simply to direct his mental vision toward some given point, in the intellectual firmament, where lies a nebula never to be resolved. . . . The finest quality of Thought is its self-cognizance; and, with some little equivocation, it may be said that no fog of the mind can well be greater than that which, extending to the very boundaries of the mental domain, shuts out even these boundaries themselves from comprehension.
>
> It will now be understood that, in using the phrase, "Infinity of Space," I make no call upon the reader to entertain the impossible conception of an *absolute* infinity. I refer simply to the "*utmost conceivable expanse*" of space—a shadowy and fluctuating domain, now shrinking, now swelling, in accordance with the vacillating energies of the imagination. (16:203–04)

Poe's rhetorical strategy is ingenious. Establishing an analogy between the outer space of physical nature and the inner "space" of temporal consciousness so as to equate the thought of infinity with the infinity of thought, Poe demonstrates that the two spaces are incommensurable. But then on the basis of this analogy (and because the infinite is inconceivable), Poe suggests a substitution of inner space for outer space, of the "boundaries of the mental domain" for the boundless universe. He says that in using "the phrase, 'Infinity of Space' " he does not expect the reader to entertain "the impossible conception of an *absolute* infinity"; rather, he asks him to imagine simply the " '*utmost conceivable expanse*' of space." To the impasse between infinite space and finite mind, between the limitlessness of eternal life and the absolute limit of death, Poe brings a third term—the indefinite; for what he intends to substitute for both the absolutely limitless and the absolutely limited (that is, for the inconceivable) is indeterminacy and the undecidable. The mental domain is not boundless, but what boundaries it has are "shadowy and fluctuating." Indeed, these boundaries may even reverse themselves, since they ultimately depend upon "the vacillating energies of the imagination." The great advantage of the indefinite over the infinite is that, while it may be undecidable, it is not inconceivable. The notion of a shifting or reversible limit, though difficult to imagine, is still not impossible to grasp in an image—the Möbius strip, for example.

In undermining Pym's anticipatory images of his own death, Poe obliquely points out that all of man's images of death, his images of the imageless, are based on the substitution of the undecidable for the inconceivable, of the uncertain for the unknowable. This substitution involves a subtle shift between two different aspects of death in that the split and doubled self images its own death *as if* it were the death of another person. Yet the very act of *witnessing* a death always implies the persistence of the observer's consciousness beyond that death. By its very nature, then, any *image* of death (even the image of oneself as a corpse) bears within it the notion of the survival of consciousness, the survival of oneself as *observer of the image.* But one's own death is the destruction of observing.

In his "Sonnet—Silence" (1840), published two years after the appearance of *Pym,* Poe depicts the difference between another's death and one's own in terms of the constitutive opposition of a double silence:

> There are some qualities—some incorporate things,
>   That have a double life, which thus is made
> A type of that twin entity which springs
>   From matter and light, evinced in solid and shade.
> There is a two-fold *Silence*—sea and shore—
>   Body and soul. One dwells in lonely places,
>   Newly with grass o'ergrown; some solemn graces,
> Some human memories and tearful lore,
> Render him terrorless: his name's "No More."
> He is the corporate Silence: dread him not!
>   No power hath he of evil in himself;
> But should some urgent fate (untimely lot!)
>   Bring thee to meet his shadow (nameless elf,
> That haunteth the lone regions where hath trod
> No foot of man,) commend thyself to God!
>
>   (7:85)

Death, though bodiless (an "incorporate" thing), is treated here as if it possessed an image, while the paradoxical "double life" that death has within human consciousness is made a "type" of the split and doubled relationship of body and image. The body/shadow opposition that begins the poem becomes by the sixth line the body/soul opposition, implicitly equating shadow and soul and thus suggesting the ambiguous significance of the shadow as both harbinger of death and immortal self. The death of another, "the corporate Silence," is portrayed through the communal rites surrounding the interment of a corpse, rites that apparently include some kind of mnemic inscription in stone ("human memories and tearful lore") and a naming that renders terrorless the alien force of death by domesticating it in language, by making it an internal limit of consciousness. Opposed to this is one's own death, marked in the poem by the sudden appearance of the second person and direct address ("But should some urgent fate . . . / Bring thee to meet his shadow . . . / . . . commend thyself to God!"). Unlike the death of another, it cannot be domesticated in language; it is "nameless," the very dissolution of naming. As the self's external limit, this death inhabits "the lone regions where hath trod / No foot of man," the regions that Pym traverses at the polar abyss.

Because this quality with "a double life" is invisible, Poe likens it to something on the level of sound (the level of invisible presence), even though he represents the quality in a visual figure. Yet he also makes clear that what this quality resembles on the sonic level is absence. The notion of a visual image of an absent sound suggests phonetic script; and in the tradition that considers speech prior to writing, the tradition in which "writing" always means phonetic transcription, the body/shadow opposition is not an unusual figure for the speech/writing opposition. Thus, for example, Edmund Fry in the preface to *Pantographia* (1799) says that of the two most useful methods of conveying ideas (speech and writing): "The first method was rendered more complete by the invention of the second, because it opened a door to the communication of ideas, through the sense of *sight,* as well as that of *hearing.*—Speech may be considered as the substance; and writing, as the shadow that follows it."[54] In this trope the invisible, ephemeral realm of speech is, paradoxically, identified with the substantial and bodily, while the visible, enduring realm of writing is identified with its insubstantial shadow. Yet it is precisely this application of a figure of pictographic doubling to the relationship between speech and phonetic script that is at issue. For this trope (which evokes man's desire to give the ephemeral flow of consciousness the enduring stability of a visual image) determines in its specific manner of linking the visual and the vocal the various possible modes of the self's imagined survival after death.

The distinction that Poe makes between the two kinds of silence corresponds to a basic difference between phonetic and pictographic script. Like the "corporate Silence," phonetic script is the silent image of a sound that was once present but now is "no more,"—it is the image of *absent sound*. But since a pictographic ideogram (as a visual double of its referent) does not depend on the spoken word in order to communicate an idea, pictographic script, like the incorporate silence, is "nameless"—not the image of an absent sound but the image of *an original absence of sound*. And in the poem, this original absence of sound seems to pose the question of the self's survival wholly in terms of an image rather than a voice. Yet the last line of the poem says that on meeting the shadow—the image of one's own death, of that which has no image— one must commend oneself to God, that is, *invoke* that Being who is essentially imageless. But with this prospective passage from image to imagelessness (a foreshadowed movement into a condition of absence on the visual level that is the equivalent of an original silence on the vocal level), the poem makes its final paradoxical turn, bringing us back to an ultimate dependence on voice. For as Poe says in *Eureka*, the word "God" does not express an idea but an effort at one; it indicates the direction of human thought. And what allows this "possible attempt at an impossible conception" is precisely the fact that the spoken word need not be related to a visual or mental image any more than pictographic script need be related to speech. Like the Biblical image of God, the word is a "cloud" behind which lies, "forever invisible, the *object* of this attempt." At the very point, then, where the poem seems to discount the possibility of the personal self's survival as a voice, staging that possibility instead in terms of a projected image, Poe indirectly recalls, by the use of the word "God," that within the Judeo-Christian tradition, the ground of man's hope for survival after death (the imageless Deity) is available to human thought only through the voice's ability to free itself from any dependence on the visible, to free itself through that very indefiniteness of sound which allows the phonetic sign to stand for the inconceivable. In Poe's "The Colloquy of Monos and Una" (1841), one of several sketches that imagine possible modes of the self's survival, the female half of a disembodied, twin entity whose two names both mean "one," says, "In Death we have both learned the propensity of man to define the indefinable" (4:201).

The analogy that the poem draws between three sets of relationships—absent sound and an original absence of sound, another's death and one's own, phonetic and pictographic script—must finally be understood in light of the governing image that Poe provides for the linking of each pair: the doubling of body and shadow. Poe makes one of the meanings of the body/shadow relationship explicit in his brief tale "The Imp of the Perverse" (1845). The narrator, discussing that "radical, . . . irreducible" principle of opposition within the self which he calls the perverse, says, "We tremble with the violence of the conflict within us,—of the definite with the indefinite—of the substance with the shadow. But, if the contest have proceeded thus far, it is the shadow which prevails,—we struggle in vain" (6:148-49). The narrator elaborates this opposition between the definite and the indefinite in a passage that recalls the imagery of Pym's descent of the precipice on Tsalal and of his confrontation with the figure in the mist:

We stand upon the brink of a precipice. We peer into the abyss—we grow sick and dizzy. Our first impulse is to shrink from the danger. Unaccountably we remain. By slow degrees our sickness, and dizziness, and horror, become merged in a cloud of unnameable feeling. By gradations, still more imperceptible, this cloud assumes shape, as did the vapor from the bottle out of which arose the genius in the Arabian Nights. But out of this *our* cloud upon the precipice's edge, there grows into palpability, a shape far more terrible . . . and yet it is but a thought . . . the idea of what would be our sensations during the sweeping precipitancy of a fall from such a height. And this fall—this rushing annihilation—for the very reason that it involves that one most ghastly and loathsome of all the . . . images of death and suffering which have ever presented themselves to our imagination—for this very cause we do now the most vividly desire it. And because our reason violently deters us from the brink, *therefore,* do we the more impetuously approach it. . . . To indulge for a moment, in any attempt at *thought,* is to be inevitably lost; for reflection but urges us to forbear, and *therefore* it is, I say,

that we *cannot.* If there be no friendly arm to check us, or if we fail
in a sudden effort to prostrate ourselves backward from the abyss,
we plunge, and are destroyed. (6:149–50)

The passage begins with two images that Poe characteristically associates with the abyss: first, the image of a mist or vapor that represents
the indefinite substituted for the inconceivable ("a cloud of unnameable
feeling"), an image usually connected with a sense of extreme mental
perplexity expressed as dizziness or drowsiness; and second, the image
of a human figure emerging or taking shape from the mist, a figure that
functions as an ambivalent counterself at once threatening and sustaining, the shadow of death and the shadow of hope. Poe says that this
demonic shape is "but a thought, ... the idea of what would be our
sensations during the sweeping precipitancy of a fall from such a
height." Descending the precipice on Tsalal, Pym looks down into the
"abyss" with an "indefinable emotion" followed by "a spinning of the
brain." In this cloudy state he says that "the faintest possible idea of
ultimate escape wandered, like a shadow, through my mind," but he
adds that this shadow image of survival is immediately succeeded by "*a
longing to fall;* ... a passion utterly uncontrollable." Pym is saved from
this overwhelming attraction to the abyss by the sudden appearance of
his daemonic shadow self Dirk Peters who, though he seems in Pym's
dizzy state to be a "phantom," "a dusky, fiendish, and filmy figure,"
provides "the friendly arm to check" his fall. For both Pym and the
narrator of "The Imp of the Perverse," the edge of the abyss threatens a
destructive reversal of polarity in which the rational thought of self-
preservation evokes an irrational or suprarational impulse directly opposed to it, an impulse to perversely overrule or sublimely transcend
reason, that can only lead to the annihilation of reason. Moreover, in
each instance the injunction not to think is symptomatic of that self-
dissolving abyss of thought about thought, of thought seeking its own
origin by trying to conceive of the condition of nonthought that preceded it.

Considering the network of images that Poe groups around the abyss,
we can see that the repeated rite-of-passage scenario with its symbolic
death and rebirth—and in particular, the three incidents on Tsalal:
Pym's burial in the ravine, his exploration of the chasm, and his descent
of the precipice—are meant to foreshadow Pym's final descent into the

polar abyss and his death at this point during the writing; but even more important, we can see that what this scenario foreshadows is precisely *the mechanism of foreshadowing*, of projecting an image of the self into the infinite void beyond death. That act of imaginative projection requires first of all that a background be established in the void against which a shadow image can be cast in a figure/ground relationship. The establishment of such a background means, of course, putting a bottom to the abyss, placing within the abyss a screen or curtain of mist that at once limits vision (making the void no longer infinite) and bears the projected image. Moreover, the indefiniteness of the mist is characteristically transferred to the shadow image projected upon it, not in the sense that the shape is amorphous (were that the case, there would be no distinguishing between figure and ground, and thus no image at all), but rather in the sense that the shape is indeterminate, that one cannot decide with any certainty whether the figure is a real body or an image, and if an image, whether it is another's or one's own. This act of foreshadowing, which projects the rebirth of the self-as-image after death, repeats the structure of that mythic original birth of the self conceived as an act of hieroglyphic doubling.

Section 12
The Unfinished Narrative; The Cavern Inscription on Tsalal; Survival in an Image

The anonymous note, which follows the break in the narrative, immediately directs our attention from the figure in the mist back to the inscription on the chasm wall, thus initiating a rereading of the two episodes that turns upon the mechanism of foreshadowing in both its spatial and temporal aspects. After explaining that the narrative is unfinished due to Pym's accidental death, the author of the note reports that the "gentleman whose name is mentioned in the preface" (Poe) was asked to complete the narrative ("to fill the vacuum," as the notewriter says) but that he declined—in part because of "his disbelief in the entire truth of the latter portions" (3:243). The anonymous author adds that Dirk Peters "is still alive, and a resident of Illinois," and though he cannot presently be located, he may at some time in the future "afford material for a conclusion of Mr. Pym's account" (3:243). In its juxtaposition of Poe and Peters—the writing self who refuses to finish the work, thereby releasing it to lead its own life, and the written self who still lives and may yet continue the work—the note suggests that the task of completing the unfinished text is an image of the narrative's continued survival in an act of interpretation, indeed that the task is a synecdoche for interpretation itself, the effort to "complete" any text through an analytic reading, an effort that, by the very fact that it is a continuation of the text, enacts the deferral of such completion. It is precisely the writing self's refusal to add anything and the written self's unavailability (its resistance to exact determination) that opens the gap that the anonymous commentator himself begins to fill. For what starts out as simply a notice of Pym's death becomes within a few paragraphs an interpretation of Pym's narrative. Although the anonymous author's ostensible aim is to decipher the markings in the chasm, he admits that the philological information he has provided opens "a wide field for speculation and exciting conjecture," and he urges the reader to interpret the data "in connection with some of the most faintly-detailed incidents of the narrative; although in no visible manner is this chain of connection complete" (3:245). Acknowledging the incompleteness of his own interpretation, the author of the note leaves the continuation of his task to the reader.

Significantly, the method that the anonymous commentator employs in carrying out his interpretation is in its own way a continuation of the narrative's attempt to present the abyss in language; for if the break in the narrative represents language's entrance into the abyss, the closing note represents language's recoil from that ultimate limit—but a recoil that has, through its proximity to the abyss, absorbed the circularizing influence of the vortex. In directing our attention "to the chasms found on the island of Tsalal, and to the whole of the figures upon pages 222, 224, 225" (3:243), the commentator returns us to a specific point in the printed text and to an obviously problematic figuration. But the anonymous author is Poe himself, and the fictitious closing note, which presents itself as a separate commentary on Pym's unfinished narrative, is, of course, the real ending of Poe's narrative. As part of Poe's text, the closing note curves the narrative line back into itself, for since the depths of the abyss lie beyond language, the only presence that the abyss can have *within* language is as a reversible limit—a negative presence that, as an illusion of plenitude (the mistaking of one's own image for the Other's body), warps the narrative line and doubles it back in the opposite direction. Within language the abyss of undifferentiated Being is (re)present(ed) as ταὐτολόγος, tautology, the same words (circled) about the Same. Thus the note returns the reader to the chasm episode, presumably to retrace the narrative line to the final break in the text, and then on to the note which sends him back to the chasm episode, and so on.

This skewed circularizing of the narrative line points to the only kind of immortality that writing can confer on the author's self: not an endless persistence of the self-as-image in the infinite void beyond death, but an indefinite repetition of the author's inscribed self through the act of (re)reading. As one of the characters in Borges's "The Garden of the Forking Paths" says: "I had questioned myself about the ways in which a book can be infinite. I could think of nothing other than a cyclic volume, a circular one. A book whose last page was identical with the first, a book which had the possibility of continuing indefinitely. I remembered too that night which is at the middle of the Thousand and One Nights when Scheherazade (through a magical oversight of the copyist) begins to relate word for word the story of the Thousand and One Nights, establishing the risk of coming once again to the night when she must repeat it, and thus on to infinity" (p. 25). Such a narrative is not infinite; rather, it is unbounded or, as in *Pym's* case, "unfinished," in that the narrative line, by leading back into itself, erases its endpoint.

The anonymous commentator begins the work of deciphering the chasm inscription by recalling Pym's belief that the markings on the wall were definitely not alphabetical characters and by noting that the authenticity of the inscribed characters even "escaped the attention of Mr. Poe" (3:244). In presenting his philological data as an insight that has eluded both the fictive writing self and the real writing self, the notewriter seems to make the text's independence of its author (the written self's subversion of authorial control through its power to mean in ways the author was unaware of) the paradoxical "authorization" of his own commentary—a notion of authority as negative presence that is wholly appropriate to the fictive writing self's loss in the abyss. Referring to Pym's drawings in the text, the author of the note points out that the shapes of the chasms, "when conjoined with one another in the precise order which the chasms themselves presented, ... constitute an Ethiopian verbal root—the root $\mathbf{\mathcal{R}}\mathbf{\Lambda}\mathbf{\mathcal{P}_{\ast}}$ 'To be shady'—whence all inflections of shadow or darkness" (3:244). As to the markings on the wall, he observes:

it is more than probable that the opinion of Peters was correct, and that the hieroglyphical appearance was really the work of art, and intended as the representation of a human form. The delineation is before the reader, and he may, or may not, perceive the resemblance suggested; but the rest of the indentures afford strong confirmation of Peters's idea. The upper range is evidently the Arabic verbal root ⟨ＡＬＡＯ⟩ "To be white," whence all inflections of brilliancy and whiteness. The lower range is not so immediately perspicuous. The characters are somewhat broken and disjointed; nevertheless, it cannot be doubted that, in their perfect state, they formed the full Egyptian word **ΠＡ℧ΥΡＨＣ** , "The region of the south." It should be observed that these interpretations confirm the opinion of Peters in regard to the "most northwardly" of the figures. The arm is outstretched towards the south. (3:244–45)

At first glance one might think that the note's philological information is a typical Poe hoax. But we should remember that Poe plays at least two different kinds of hoaxes. In the more obvious kind he takes false information and makes it look authentic; in the less obvious, of which the philological data are an example, he takes authentic information and makes it look slightly suspicious. In this type of hoax, the reader is duped if he fails to take Poe's learning seriously and thus fails to pursue the implications of the data that Poe provides. For in fact the linguistic information in the note is as accurate and authentic as the scholarship of Poe's day was capable of producing. Sidney Kaplan has suggested that Poe's principal source for the philological material was Edward Robinson's *A Hebrew and English Lexicon of the Old Testament from the Latin of William Gesenius* (Boston, 1836).[55] This is certainly possible, though in his review of John Lloyd Stephens' *Travels in Arabia Petraea* in the *New York Review* for October 1837, Poe, commenting on the Hebrew text of Ezekiel 35:7, cites Gesenius (10:18) not in Robinson's translation, but in Christopher Leo's translation entitled *A Hebrew Lexicon to the Books of the Old Testament* (Cambridge, 1825). Poe received the philological information on Ezekiel 35:7, as well as the citation of Gesenius in the Leo translation, in a letter (17:42–43) dated June 1, 1837 from Charles Anthon, "the well-known Jay professor of the Greek and Latin languages in Columbia College, New York" (15:34), as Poe describes him in "The Literati of New York City." It is possible that Poe simply reproduced the data that Anthon provided without actually examining Leo's translation for himself; and since Anthon had been so helpful in this instance,

Poe may also have consulted him about the data contained in the closing note to *Pym*. But whether in the Leo or the Robinson translation or in the original Latin (and with or without Anthon's assistance), Poe's ultimate source for the philological information contained in the closing note to *Pym* was undoubtedly Gesenius's *Lexicon*.

The Ethiopic script (**ጸላማ**) is the verb *ṣlm* (*ṣalma*, the *ṣ* being pronounced like "ts"), meaning "to be shady, obscure, dark," and is found in Robinson's translation of Gesenius under the Hebrew root *ṣlm*.[56] The Arabic script (صحر) is the verb *ṣhr* (*ṣahar*), meaning "to be bleak, sand-colored, desert-like."[57] In Robinson's translation, the Arabic *ṣahar* appears under the Hebrew root *ṣhr* (p. 865), meaning "to be dazzling white," the connection apparently being for Gesenius that the Arabic word means to be colored like the desert sand and that one of the more common hues of desert sand is a brilliant white. The verb *ṣahar* is related to the Arabic noun *ṣahrā* ("desert"), whose English form is the name of the desert through which the Nile flows, the Sahara. Poe would have found this link between *ṣahar* and desert in Robinson's translation as well. The word **ΠⲀⲐⲨⲢⲎⲤ** (Robinson's translation, p. 853), which Poe identifies as Egyptian, is more accurately the Coptic form (Pathures) of the Egyptian word *p3-t3-rśy*, meaning literally "the (*p3*) land (*t3*) southern (*rśy*)" or "the region of the south," as Poe has it.

The name Pathures appears in the Rheims-Douay Version of the Bible as "Phatures" and in the King James Version as "Pathros." Thus in Ezekiel 29:14 God says, "I will bring again the captivity of Egypt, and will cause them to return into the land of Pathros, into the land of their habitation; and they shall be there a base kingdom." (The Rheims-Douay Version translates "into the land of their habitation" as "in the land of their nativity.") And in Ezekiel 30:14, God says that He will "make Pathros desolate." Gesenius identifies Pathros as Upper Egypt—the portion of Egypt south of Memphis including part of Nubia or northern Abyssinia. It is worth noting that Ezekiel 29:14 designates Pathros as the Egyptians' place of origin, to which they will ultimately be returned for the completion of God's vengeance, and that Ezekiel 30:13–14 associates the desolation of Pathros with the imageless God's destruction of images. The offense that God singles out as the cause for his punishment of the Egyptians is Pharaoh's blasphemous pride in asserting "My river is mine own, and I have made it for myself" (Ezekiel 29:3)—the river in question is, of course, the Nile. (The Rheims-Douay translation renders Pharaoh's words as "The river is mine and I made myself"—which could easily be misread as associating the Nile with the origin of the self, thus making Pharaoh claim the godlike quality of being his own origin.)

The fact that the Tsalalian chasm inscriptions pointing the way to the polar abyss are written in Ethiopic, Arabic, and Egyptian, the languages of the Nile Valley, and that Pathros, the name applied to the South Polar region, is the name of southern Egypt and northern Abyssinia, is simply part of Poe's conflation of the journey to the Abyssinian source of the Nile and the voyage to the polar abyss as reciprocal quests for the linguistic origin of the self. Thus the philological connection between the Arabic verb meaning "to be white" (ṣaḥar) and the name of the desert surrounding the Nile is prefigured early in the narrative when Pym, stowed away in the hold of the *Grampus,* reads the journals of the Lewis and Clark expedition up the Missouri and then falls asleep to dream of "deserts, limitless, and of the most forlorn and awe-inspiring character": "I stood, naked and alone, amid the burning sand-plains of Zahara." There is, of course, an obvious connection between the Sahara and the Antarctic—both are lonely wastes of dazzling whiteness where the extremes of temperature produce similar desolation.

In light of the desolation associated with Pathros in Ezekiel and the application of the name Pathros to the barren South Polar region, it is worth noting that the image of desolation is characteristically associated in Poe's work with silence and the image of the shadow. In the sonnet "Silence," the shadow of one's own death haunts "the lone regions where hath trod / No foot of man," an image that recalls the desolation prophesied for Egypt in Ezekiel 29:11: "No foot of man shall pass through it" and the desolation of Mount Seir in Ezekiel 35:7, which Poe, under Anthon's tutelage, had translated in his review as "And I will give mount Seir for an utter desolation, and will cut off from it him *that passeth and repasseth therein*" (10:18). In Poe's short fantasy entitled "Silence—A Fable" (1838), a "Demon" tells the narrator a story set in "a dreary region in Libya, by the borders of the river Zaire" (2:220). In this wasteland the Demon discovers "a huge gray rock" with "characters engraven in the stone . . . and the characters were DESOLATION" (2:221–22). He sees a man standing on the summit of the rock: "the outlines of his figure were indistinct—but his features were the features of a deity" (2:222). The Demon observes the man in secret, and after failing to disturb his solitude with the curse of tumult, the Demon, growing angry, curses the region "with the curse of *silence,*" so that there is no "shadow of sound throughout the vast illimitable desert" (2:223–24): "And I looked upon the characters of the rock, and they were changed;—and the characters were SILENCE" (2:224). The narrator says that of all the stories ever known, the "fable which the Demon told me as he sat by my side in the shadow of the tomb, I hold to be the most wonderful of all! And as the Demon made an end of his story, he fell back within the cavity of the tomb and laughed" (2:224).

Just after Pym's descent of the precipice on Tsalal, that prefigurative descent into the abyss during which the "idea of ultimate escape" wanders "like a shadow" through his mind, he comes upon an almost Biblical scene of desolation:

> We now found ourselves not far from the ravine which had proved the tomb of our friends. . . . The place was one of singular wildness, and its aspect brought to my mind the descriptions given by travellers of those dreary regions marking the site of degraded Babylon. . . . The surface of the ground . . . was strewn with huge tumuli, apparently the wreck of some gigantic structures of art; although, in detail, no semblance of art could be detected. . . . Of vegetation there were no traces whatsoever throughout the whole of the desolate area within sight. (3:230–31)

For Poe the image of desolation inevitably evokes an image of the tomb and the absolute solitude of one's own death (the self alone with itself in the void), as well as the idea of judgment or vengeance, an idea that recurs at the end of the closing note. After giving the philological data on the chasm inscription, the anonymous author continues:

> Tekeli-li! was the cry of the affrighted natives of Tsalal upon discovering the carcass of the *white* animal picked up at sea. This also was the shuddering exclamation of the captive Tsalalian upon encountering the *white* materials in the possession of Mr. Pym. This also was the shriek of the swift-flying, *white*, and gigantic birds which issued from the vapoury *white* curtain of the South. Nothing *white* was to be found at Tsalal, and nothing otherwise in the subsequent voyage to the region beyond. It is not impossible that "Tsalal," the appellation of the island of the chasms, may be found, upon minute philological scrutiny, to betray either some alliance with the chasms themselves, or some reference to the Ethiopian characters so mysteriously written in their windings.

"*I have graven it within the hills, and my vengeance upon the dust within the rock.*" (3:245)

If we subject the name "Tsalal" to the "minute philological scrutiny" the author suggests—which amounts in this case simply to looking up the Hebrew root *ṣll* in Gesenius—we find first of all that in the *Lexicon ṣll* immediately precedes the Hebrew root *ṣlm*, under which Poe found the Ethiopic root **ጸልመ፡** (*ṣalma* or *tsalma,* meaning "to be shady or dark"); second, that one of the meanings of the Hebrew root *ṣll* is "to be shaded, dark" and that under the entry for *ṣll* in Gesenius's *Thesaurus*[58] there is given an Ethiopic root **ጸለለ፡** (*ṣalala* or *tsalala*) also meaning "to be dark"; third, that both *ṣlm* and *ṣll* are related to the Hebrew root *ṣl,* meaning "shadow," so that the anonymous author of the note is correct in linking *ṣalma* to "all the inflections of shadow or darkness"; fourth, that the Hebrew root *ṣlm* also means "image" or "likeness," as in Genesis 1:26, "And God said, Let us make man in our image, after our likeness"; fifth, that either *ṣll* or *ṣlm* is the root of the Hebrew word *ṣalmāwet,* meaning "death-shadow," a word characterizing the world of the dead; and sixth, that one of the meanings of the Hebrew root *ṣll,* besides "to be dark," is "to sink or be submerged," the unique Biblical use of *ṣll* in this sense being in Exodus 15:10, where Moses praises the Lord for causing Pharaoh's army to sink "as lead in the mighty waters." One further bit of philological information can be garnered in this context concerning the name of the ruler of Tsalal which Pym transcribes as *Tsalemon* or *Psalemoun* (3:239). Under the root *ṣlm* Poe would have found an entry for the proper name *Ṣalmon,* a word meaning "dark" or "shady" that, besides being a personal name, is the name of a mountain in Samaria, mentioned, as Gesenius points out, in Psalm 68:14: "When the Almighty scattered kings in it, it was white as snow in Salmon"—the kind of black/white reversal that would have appealed to Poe.

In associating the black/white opposition of Tsalal and Tekeli-li with both the epistemological and the moral opposition of dark and light, the closing note might almost be an illustration of Emerson's remark that "every word which is used to express a moral or intellectual fact, if traced to its root, is found to be borrowed from some material appearance." Yet what Poe's etymological exercise puts in question is the Emersonian sense of the moral fact's priority to the material appearance. Focusing on two opposing perceptual terms (white and black) whose differentiation is synonymous in our tradition with the origin of the basic moral categories of good and evil ("And God saw the light, that it was good: and God divided the light from the darkness," Genesis 1:4), Poe traces these terms for "moral facts" back to their roots in the figure/ground opposition between a shadow image and the light. In so doing he suggests that the notion of an ideal, spiritual world as the standard for moral judgments of the physical world derives from, and thus ultimately depends upon, the material structure of image projection: that the very notion of judgment as the comparison of something to its archetypal model is meaningless apart from a visual perception of the necessary correspondence between an object and its shadow image.

With the outline of a human figure carved on its wall and the shapes of its caverns spelling out the Ethiopic root "whence all the inflections of shadow or darkness," the Tsalalian chasm, besides alluding to the Classical myth of the afterlife as a subterranean world of shades, evokes another scenario from the Classical world having to do with shadows in a cave—Plato's allegory of the cave from book 7 of the *Republic*. Using the body/shadow opposition as a paradigm of image projection, Plato effects a massive reversal of values in which the objects of this world become shadows and their shadow outlines become eternal objects—a reversal that causes a shift in the hierarchy of the upper and lower worlds. In Classical mythology the realm of shadows is an underworld to the world of physical objects; but in Plato our world of objects becomes a cavern, an underworld in relation to the world of unchanging shadow images. Man's destiny involves, then, not a descent into darkness but an ascent into the light. One must escape from the cavern of shadows and, like the man whom Plato describes, rise by degrees "into the intelligible region" until one sees "the idea of the good," which is the cause "of all that is right and beautiful, giving birth in the visible world to light, and the author of light and itself in the intelligible world being the authentic source of truth and reason" (pp. 749–50). The Platonic progress from the dark cavern to the bright vision is undoubtedly one of the allusive backgrounds for Pym's journey from Tsalal to Tekeli-li.

The allegory of the cave also effects, by implication, a color reversal, for the shadow outline, translated into the realm of intelligible light, changes from a dark silhouette into a bright, transparent image, an ideal form. Plato's realm of ideal forms was, of course, a model for the Chris-

tian conception of heaven and for that color-value reversal whereby the
shadow of death became the shining immortal soul. The Christian notion of an afterlife retained the Classical underworld as part of its structure, though the lower world of darkness, which in Classical mythology
was the common destiny of good and bad alike became, in accordance
with Christianity's black/white revenge morality, the exclusive dwelling
place of the wicked. Where the Old Testament God created the light,
saw that it was good, and divided it from the darkness, the Platonic God
of the New Testament is himself the intelligible light and the good (as in
John 1:1–5). Through their identification with pure Being, the light and
the good are privileged absolutely over their opposites, so that within
Judeo-Christian tradition what begins as the differentiation of beneficent light from chaotic darkness in Genesis ends, under the Platonic
influence, as the absolute separation of good from evil in Revelations.

Inasmuch as the black islanders of Tsalal are identified with evil and
degradation, the fiction of Tsalal and Tekeli-li—that whiteness can be
wholly separated from any trace of darkness—is a fiction of moral non-
contamination, which is to say, a fiction of spiritual transcendence: the
notion of the separate, wholly independent existence of a world of ideal
images that is synonymous with the light and the good and that serves as
the unchanging ground of morality. And it is precisely this moral fiction
which the episodes of Tsalal and Tekeli-li subtly undermine on epistemological grounds. For though Pym says that they "noticed no light-
colored substance of any kind on the island" and though the anonymous
author of the note adds that "nothing *white* was to be found at Tsalal,
and nothing otherwise in the subsequent voyage to the region beyond,"
Pym himself points out the white arrowhead flints in the chasm. And just
as whiteness lies at the core of the dark realm of Tsalal, so darkness must
be present in the white realm of Tekeli-li, otherwise there could be no
color boundary, no figure/ground differentiation, no signification. The
shadow image haunts the lone regions of Tekeli-li—whether Pym recognizes it or not.

Carved into the black granite chasm (presumably by means of the
white arrowhead flints), the hieroglyphic human figure with its arm
"outstretched towards the south" points to the word Pathros ("region of
the south") and beyond to that other human figure that Pym will confront in the abyss. And this hieroglyph, whose pictographic doubling of
the body's shape is in turn phonetically doubled by the shape of the

chasm spelling the root of the word "shadow," not only foreshadows (that is, temporally doubles) the appearance of the giant figure in the mist but also points to the fact that that figure is itself a spatial double, a white shadow that has undergone the color reversal characteristic of the opaque image's translation into the immortal soul. The concept of an immortal soul, the "idea of ultimate escape" from the annihilation of the self in death, is an idea of the self as Platonic Idea, as deified mental image. Combining the senses of both spirit and temporal infinity, the notion of the soul represents "the possible attempt at an impossible conception, . . . a term by which to point out the *direction* of this effort— the cloud" behind which lies, "forever invisible, the *object* of this attempt," just as the dark hieroglyph in the chasm points out the direction of the bright figure and the curtain of mist that veils the objectless object of this attempt. What the ending of *Pym* acts out, then, is "a certain *tendency* of the human intellect" (inscribed within it by the very structure of its birth) to try to survive death by projecting an image of itself (the self as image) into the infinite void of the abyss.

Section 13
The White Shadow; Imaging the Indefinite; Reading the Spirit from the Letter; The Finality of Revenge; The Alogical Status of the Self

That the figure at the pole is a white shadow, indeed, that it is Pym's own shadow, which he does not recognize, seems more than likely when one considers the similarities between the ending of *Pym* and the numerous examples of the trope of the white shadow in Romantic tradition (particularly among authors whom Poe admired). Thus in Coleridge's poem "Constancy to an Ideal Object" (1828), the speaker is haunted by a "yearning Thought" that "liv'st but in the brain," the thought of an idealized woman who is synonymous with home. Yet this ideal can only be realized when "Hope and Despair meet in the porch of Death!" (1:455–56). Without this companion, any place where the speaker dwells is like "a becalméd bark, / Whose Helmsman on an ocean waste and wide / Sits mute and pale his mouldering helm beside" (1:456). The poem concludes with the speaker's acknowledgment that this ideal object is an unrecognized shadow image that he himself has projected:

> And art thou nothing? Such thou art, as when
> The woodman winding westward up the glen

At wintry dawn, where o'er the sheep track's maze
The viewless snow-mist weaves a glist'ning haze,
Sees full before him, gliding without tread,
An image with a glory round its head;
The enamoured rustic worships its fair hues,
Nor knows he makes the shadow, he pursues!

(1:456)

In James Hogg's *The Private Memoirs and Confessions of a Justified Sinner*
(1824), the scenario of the white shadow in the mist is part of a classic
double story—the murder of the good George Colwan by his evil half-
brother, Robert Wringhim. The malicious Wringhim dogs his brother's
every movement like "the shadow ... cast from the substance, or the ray
of light from the opposing denser medium."[59] To escape Wringhim's
constant shadowing, George goes for a walk at daybreak in the mist and
beholds "to his astonishment, a bright halo in the cloud of haze, that rose
in a semicircle over his head like a pale rainbow" (p. 38). He realizes that
"the lovely vision" is "his own shadow on the cloud" with "a halo of glory
round a point of the cloud ... whiter and purer than the rest" (p. 44).
Seating himself "on the pinnacle of the rocky precipice," George believes
that he has finally escaped from his brother's annoying presence, unaware that Wringhim has followed him and is at that instant approaching from behind to push him off the cliff:

> The idea of his brother's dark and malevolent looks coming at that
> moment across his mind, he turned his eyes instinctively to the right,
> to the point where that unwelcome guest was wont to make his
> appearance.... What an apparition was there presented to his view!
> He saw, delineated in the cloud, the shoulders, arms, and features
> of a human being of the most dreadful aspect. The face was the face
> of his brother, but dilated to twenty times the natural size. Its dark
> eyes gleamed on him through the mist.
> ... he took it for some horrid demon ... that ... in taking on
> itself the human form, had miscalculated dreadfully on the size, and
> presented itself thus to him in a blown-up, dilated frame of em-
> bodied air, exhaled from the caverns of death or the regions of
> devouring fire. He was farther confirmed in the belief that it was a
> malignant spirit on perceiving that it approached him across the
> front of a precipice, where there was not footing for thing of mortal
> frame. (Pp. 39–40)

As the apparition continues to approach, George turns to flee, but "the very first bolt that he made in his flight he came in contact with a *real* body of flesh and blood.... George then perceived that it was his brother; and being confounded between the shadow and the substance, he knew not what he was doing or what he had done" (p. 40).

Whether or not the image of George's brother is the apparition of a malignant spirit, there is certainly nothing supernatural about the white shadow in the mist. In Poe's day one of the best known examples of this phenomenon was the gigantic spectre of the Brocken in north Germany. Coleridge had climbed the Brocken on Whitsunday 1799, with a group of English students from Göttingen, but failed to see the phantom; while in 1845 DeQuincey described the spectre in one of the "Suspiria de Profundis" articles in *Blackwood's,* a description based not on a real ascent of the Brocken but on an ascent "executed in dreams ... under advanced stages in the development of opium."[60] The best contemporary scientific account of the phenomenon was in David Brewster's *Letters on Natural Magic* (1832), a book that Poe quotes at length in his essay "Maelzel's Chess-Player" (14:7–8) published in April 1836. In his chapter on natural optical illusions, Brewster recounts two separate sightings of the spectre of the Brocken in 1797 and 1798 and explains the physical circumstances causing the appearance:

The spectre of the Brocken and other phenomena of the same kind ... are merely shadows of the observer projected on dense vapour or thin fleecy clouds, which have the power of reflecting much light. They are seen most frequently at sunrise, because it is at that time that the vapours and clouds necessary for their production are most likely to be generated; and they can be seen only when the sun is throwing his rays horizontally, because the shadow of the observer would otherwise be thrown either up in the air, or down upon the ground.... The head will be more distinct than the rest of the figure, because the rays of the sun will be more copiously reflected at a perpendicular incidence; and as from this cause the light reflected from the vapour or cloud becomes fainter farther from the shadow, the appearance of a halo round the head of the observer is frequently visible.[61]

In *Walden* Thoreau gives us his own version of the white shadow and then cites Benvenuto Cellini's account of a similar experience as evi-

dence of the phenomenon's relation to the angle of light and the atmospheric diffusion of moisture common in the early morning:

> As I walked on the railway causeway, I used to wonder at the halo of
> light around my shadow, and would fain fancy myself one of the
> elect.... Benvenuto Cellini tells us in his memoirs, that, after a
> certain terrible dream or vision which he had during his confine-
> ment in the castle of St. Angelo, a resplendent light appeared over
> the shadow of his head at morning and evening, ... and it was
> particularly conspicuous when the grass was moist with dew. This
> was probably the same phenomenon to which I have referred,
> which is especially observed in the morning, but also at other times,
> and even by moonlight. Though a constant one, it is not commonly
> noticed, and, in the case of an excitable imagination like Cellini's, it
> would be basis enough for superstition. (P. 202)

One of the places where natural optical illusions occur most frequently, as Brewster points out, is in the polar seas during temperature
inversions, the kind of temperature inversion that Pym experiences
when the atmosphere begins to grow warmer the closer he gets to the
pole. During the final stage of the journey, Pym associates the polar
region, and in particular the curtain of vapor, with extraordinary optical
appearances: "Many unusual phenomena now indicated that we were
entering upon a region of novelty and wonder. A high range of light
gray vapour appeared constantly in the southern horizon, flaring up
occasionally in lofty streaks, now darting from east to west, now from
west to east, and again presenting a level and uniform summit—in short,
having all the wild variations of the Aurora Borealis" (3:238). Of the two
physical conditions that are required for the appearance of the white
shadow, one is obviously present in the polar regions—the curtain of
vapor. As to the position of the sun, Pym notes after leaving Tsalal that
there was continual daylight, but as they journey farther to the south he
says that the "Polar winter appeared to be coming on" and that a "sullen
darkness now hovered above us" (3:240–41). The date on which Pym
sees the figure in the mist, March 22, is one day after the autumnal
equinox in the Southern Hemisphere. Consequently, in the South Polar
region, the sun would be at the horizon for the full twenty-four hours of
that day. It would be like a day-long sunrise, with half of the sun's disk
always visible above the earth's edge. The sun would make a circuit of
the horizon, continually throwing its rays along a horizontal plane in

precisely the manner required to cast a shadow on the vapor. Further, the fact that Pym describes the shape in the mist as "a shrouded human figure" whose skin is "of the perfect whiteness of the snow" suggests that he is distinguishing between the body of the figure, the portion that would presumably be "shrouded," that is, indistinct, and its head where the whiteness of the skin would normally be exposed—a differentiation that coincides with Brewster's remark that the shadow's head with its luminous halo "will be more distinct than the rest of the figure."

In addition to the essay on natural optical illusions, Poe would have found in Brewster's work a discussion of spectral illusions that compares the physiological bases of visual, mental, and hallucinatory images—a discussion that Poe may have found especially interesting, since many of the incidents that Brewster describes involve the appearance of human figures shrouded in their grave-clothes. Brewster maintains that spectral apparitions "are nothing more than ideas or the recollected images of the mind, which in certain states of bodily indisposition have been rendered more vivid than actual impressions; or to use other words, that the pictures in the 'mind's eye' are more vivid than the pictures in the body's eye" (p. 53). He proposes "to show that the 'mind's eye' is actually the body's eye, and that the retina is the common tablet on which both classes of impressions are painted" as well as "all ideas recalled by the memory or created by the imagination," so that "they receive their visual existence according to the same optical laws" (p. 53). He continues:

> In the healthy state of the mind and body, the relative intensity of these two classes of impressions on the retina are [*sic*] nicely adjusted. The mental pictures are transient and comparatively feeble, and in ordinary temperaments are never capable of disturbing or effacing the direct images of visible objects. . . .
>
> In darkness and solitude, when external objects no longer interfere with the pictures of the mind, they become more vivid and distinct; and in the state between waking and sleeping, the intensity of the impressions approaches to that of visible objects. With persons of studious habits, who are much occupied with the operations of their own minds, the mental pictures are much more distinct than in ordinary persons. . . . (Pp. 54–55)

According to Brewster, a hallucinatory image involves a reversal of energy that alters the relative intensities of visual images and mental images on the retina, with the result that a mental image becomes vivid

enough to be taken for a visual image, indeed becomes so vivid at times
as to blot out a visual image. Brewster associates a less energetic form of
this reversal with that state between waking and sleep which the Romantics considered the special province of the creative imagination. As Pym's
canoe approaches the curtain of vapor, he and his companions drift into
a liminal state of consciousness. Pym says, "I felt a *numbness* of body and
mind—a dreaminess of sensation. . . . Peters spoke little, and I knew not
what to think of his apathy" (3:240–41); meanwhile the black man
Nu-Nu succumbs to "drowsiness and stupor" (3:240). In Pym's case, this
state lies between waking consciousness and the final sleep of the abyss.
In the *Marginalia* Poe describes his own experience of drifting into the
state between waking and sleep in words that have special significance
for Pym's situation:

> There is . . . a class of fancies, of exquisite delicacy, which are *not*
> thoughts, and to which, *as yet,* I have found it absolutely impossible
> to adapt language. I use the word *fancies* at random, and merely
> because I must use *some* word; but the idea commonly attached to
> the term is not even remotely applicable to the shadows of shadows
> in question. They seem to me rather psychal than intellectual. They
> arise in the soul (alas, how rarely!) only at its epochs of most intense
> tranquillity . . . and at those mere points of time where the confines
> of the waking world blend with those of the world of dreams. I am
> aware of these "fancies" only when I am upon the very brink of
> sleep, with the consciousness that I am so. I have satisfied myself
> that this condition exists but for an inappreciable *point* of time—yet
> it is crowded with these "shadows of shadows"; and for absolute
> *thought* there is demanded time's *endurance.* (16:88)

There is obviously a connection between these "fancies," which Poe
describes as "shadows of shadows," and such notions as God, spirit, and
infinity, which he calls "thoughts of thought." As the fancies are "*not*
thoughts," so God, spirit, and infinity are "by no means the expression of
an idea, but of an effort at one." Poe says that he is aware of these fancies
in that in-between state where sleeping and waking blend—"upon the
very brink of sleep, with the consciousness that I am so"—a state similar
to that of imagining one's own death as if it were the death of another, so
that at the same time one is both dead and yet conscious that one is dead.
Poe adds that he regards "the visions, even as they arise, with an awe

which, in some measure, moderates or tranquilizes the ecstasy—I so regard them, through a conviction (which seems a portion of the ecstasy
itself) that this ecstasy, in itself, is of a character supernal to the Human
Nature—is a glimpse of the spirit's outer world; and I arrive at this
conclusion—if this term is at all applicable to instantaneous intuition—by
a perception that the delight experienced has, as its element, but *the
absoluteness of novelty*" (16:89). One recalls in this regard Pym's charac-
terization of the polar sea as "a region of novelty and wonder."

The visions to which Poe testifies in the *Marginalia* are clearly not
external visual images, but rather something arising from within his own
mind at the edge of waking consciousness, something that, because of its
absolute novelty (its being beyond words), he describes as "supernal to
Human Nature . . . a glimpse of the spirit's outer world." Yet the words
he uses to describe his reaction to these fancies—"a conviction (which
seems a portion of the ecstasy itself)," "instantaneous intuition"—make
one wonder whether these "visions" have any distinct visual component
at all, whether they are not rather a matter of indefinite feeling or mood,
an immediate intuition of the will as motion/emotion, whose most accurate representation is music and in relation to which visual images and
words must always seem unsatisfactory. At any rate, Poe says that "so
entire is my faith in the *power of words,* that, at times, I have believed it
possible to embody even the evanescence of fancies such as I have attempted to describe" (16:89):

> I have proceeded so far . . . as to prevent the lapse from *the point* of
> which I speak—the point of blending between wakefulness and
> sleep—as to prevent at will, I say, the lapse from this border-ground
> into the dominion of sleep. Not that I can *continue* the condition—
> not that I can render the point more than a point—but that I can
> startle myself from the point into wakefulness—*and thus transfer the
> point itself into the realm of Memory*—convey its impressions, or more
> properly their recollections, to a situation where (although still for a
> very brief period) I can survey them with the eye of analysis.
>
> . . . nothing can be more certain than that even a partial record of
> the impressions would startle the universal intellect of mankind, by
> the *supremeness of the novelty* of the material employed, and of its
> consequent suggestions. In a word—should I ever write a paper on
> this topic, the world will be compelled to acknowledge that, at last, I
> have done an original thing. (16:90)

The main problem that these fancies present is their evanescence: they supplant one another so quickly that they never achieve the level of persistence required for the definiteness of an image. Although Poe says that he can transfer the point between waking and sleeping into the realm of memory, he seems to be able to bring into waking consciousness not the impressions themselves, but only some attenuated "recollections," perhaps memories of his own emotional response to the fleeting impressions. The fancies cannot be anything as simple as dream images, since it would be no "original thing" to embody such images in words. The extreme temporal mobility of the fancies would again suggest something musical rather than visual, or perhaps some blending of the two that reflects the "blending between wakefulness and sleep," some visual music. As Pym nears the curtain of mist, he says, "At intervals there were visible in it wide, yawning, but momentary rents, and from out these rents, within which was a chaos of flitting and indistinct images, there came rushing and mighty, but soundless winds, tearing up the enkindled ocean in their course" (3:241–42). This vision combines a glimpse of "flitting and indistinct images" with a traditional image of natural audibility (a rushing wind) and thus of natural musicality (as in the trope of the Aeolian harp), but with the musical component rendered "soundless" and thus visually represented by the fleeting indistinctness of the images. Elsewhere in the *Marginalia* Poe remarks: "I *know* that indefinitiveness is an element of the true music—I mean of the true musical expression. Give to it any undue decision—imbue it with any very determinate tone—and you deprive it, at once, of its ethereal, its ideal, its intrinsic and essential character. You dispel its luxury of dream. You dissolve the atmosphere of the mystic on which it floats" (16:29).

Whatever the status of Poe's "fancies," one thing is clear: his desire to make a fully conscious incursion into the unconscious realm of sleep and return with a written record of his impressions—that "paper" which would compel the world to acknowledge that he had "done an original thing"—parallels the desire to journey into the abyss of origin and return to the world of consciousness with some original word about the unconscious realm of death. Indeed, one might speculate that the latter is a projection of the former and that the notion of the survival of images in the unconscious state of death is derived from those images that we see in the unconscious state of sleep. It is worth recalling in this regard the traditional link between the hieroglyphics and dream interpretation, a connection that Bishop Warburton summarizes in *The Divine Legation of Moses Demonstrated:*

> The *Egyptian priests,* the first interpreters of dreams, took their rules for this species of DIVINATION, from their *symbolic* riddling, in which they were so deeply read: a ground of interpretation which would give the strongest credit to the art; and equally satisfy the diviner and the consulter: for by this time it was generally believed that their gods had given them *hieroglyphic writing.* So that nothing was more natural than to imagine that these gods, who in their opinion gave *dreams* likewise, had employed the same mode of expression in both revelations. This, I suppose, was the true original of *oneirocritic,* or the interpretation of those dreams called allegorical; that is, of dreams in general. . . . the *oneirocritics* borrowed their art of deciphering from symbolic hieroglyphics.[62]

In *A Week on the Concord and Merrimack Rivers* (1849), Thoreau remarks that "In the mythus a superhuman intelligence uses the unconscious thoughts and dreams of men as its hieroglyphics to address men unborn."[63] The notion that dream images are a pictographic script to be deciphered like hieroglyphics was the opinion of the preeminent modern interpreter of dreams as well. Freud writes: "If we reflect that the means of representation in dreams are principally visual images and not words, we shall see that it is even more appropriate to compare dreams with a system of writing than a language. In fact the interpretation of dreams is completely analogous to the decipherment of an ancient pictographic script such as Egyptian hieroglyphs. . . . The ambiguity of various elements of dreams finds a parallel in these ancient systems of writing" (13:177).

Now whether one interprets the gigantic shape that Pym sees in the mist as a natural optical illusion (a white shadow) or a spectral illusion (a mental image that, by a reversal of intensity in a liminal state, appears to have the independent status of a visual image), the figure displays in either case a shadowy character in the sense of being unrecognizedly self-projected. It exhibits the uncertainty of the boundary between observer and phenomenon, that condition of indeterminacy in which the observer in part creates the phenomenon he observes and thus ends by observing his own presence in a kind of veiled narcissism. Yet the characteristic human response to any disembodied self-animating image,

whether natural phenomenon or spectral illusion, is to consider it as
some form of spiritual appearance, some visible evidence of the unseen
world. Thus, for example, Wordsworth, in his own version of the giant
shadow in the mist from book 8 of *The Prelude,* describes his reaction to
the extraordinary appearance of a shepherd remembered from his boy-
hood:

> When up the lonely brooks on rainy days
> Angling I went, or trod the trackless hills
> By mists bewildered, suddenly mine eyes
> Have glanced upon him distant a few steps,
> In size a giant, stalking through thick fog,
> His sheep like Greenland bears; or, as he stepped
> Beyond the boundary line of some hill-shadow,
> His form hath flashed upon me, glorified
> By the deep radiance of the setting sun:
> Or him have I descried in distant sky,
> A solitary object and sublime,
> Above all height! like an aerial cross
> Stationed alone upon a spiry rock
> Of the Chartreuse, for worship.

> (Pp. 285, 287)

Wordsworth says that the shepherd seemed to be a creature "spiritual
almost / As those of books, but more exalted far; / Far more of an imaginative form / Than the gay Corin of the groves, who lives / For his own
fancies" (p. 287). The direction of the passage is clear: from an extraordinary natural phenomenon (the shepherd's gigantic shadow in the
mist), Wordsworth moves toward an apotheosis of the human form, first
"glorified" by the sun and then transformed, through its association with
the "aerial cross," into an image of that divine Good Shepherd who is the
archetype of all pastoral care. When Wordsworth speaks of the shepherd
as "an imaginative form," "spiritual almost as those of books," he implicitly acknowledges that in this passage he has been engaged in reading
the book of nature, in making what is all too plainly a personal interpretation of the script of natural forms whereby the literal becomes the
spiritual. He anticipates this objection in the remarkably defensive passage that follows the description of the shepherd:

> Call ye these appearances—
> Which I beheld of shepherds in my youth,
> This sanctity of Nature given to man—
> A shadow, a delusion, ye who pore
> On the dead letter, miss the spirit of things;
> Whose truth is not a motion or a shape
> Instinct with vital functions, but a block
> Or waxen image which yourselves have made,
> And ye adore! But blessed be the God
> Of Nature and of Man that this was so;
> That men before my inexperienced eyes
> Did first present themselves thus purified,
> Removed, and to a distance that was fit.
>
>   (Pp. 287, 289)

Wordsworth applies to the book of nature that revisionary, New Testament principle of interpreting scripture which Paul enunciates in 2 Corinthians. Comparing individual Christians to "the epistle of Christ . . . written not with ink, but with the Spirit of the living God; not in tables of stone, but in fleshy tables of the heart," Paul says that he is a minister of this "new testament; not of the letter, but of the spirit: for the letter killeth, but the spirit giveth life" (3:3–6). And he adds, "But if the ministration of death, written and engraven in stones, was glorious, so that the children of Israel could not steadfastly behold the face of Moses for the glory of his countenance; which was to be done away: How shall not the ministration of the spirit be rather glorious?" (3:7–8). Paul says that the Jews' "minds were blinded: for until this day remaineth the same vail untaken away in the reading of the old testament; which vail is done away with in Christ. . . . But we all, with open face beholding as in a glass the glory of the Lord, are changed into the same image from glory to glory, even as by the Spirit of the Lord" (3:14, 18).

For both Wordsworth and Paul, man's being is inscribed. It is a writing that can be read according to either the dead letter or the living spirit, a figure that can be interpreted either as the dark shadow of the mortal body (an inanimate "block / Or waxen image," the "ministration of death, written and engraven in stones") or as a bright reflection in a glass ("the glory of the Lord," a shining image that reverses the usual relationship between the body and its mirror double in that the beholder becomes a reflection of the image). (The word "glory," besides its general meaning of "radiance" or "splendor," has as well the specific meaning of "halo." What occurs at Christ's transfiguration, when the splendor of divinity shining through his body makes his face radiant as the sun and his garments white as snow, is known in theology as "the clarity of glory.") Clearly, the opposition of dead letter and living spirit in both Paul and Wordsworth is an image governed by the moralized black/white opposition of writing. The letter is dead because it is dark, the lithic shadow of an inanimate literality, like the engraving on a tombstone; while the meaning that must be interpreted or translated from the dark script, the quickening sense that hovers about the writing like the white page about the black outline of the characters or the nimbus about the body, is the radiant spirit.

That the figure that Pym sees in the mist is a white shadow, his own shadow unrecognized, seems especially likely when we consider the figure's association with Christ's transfiguration and resurrection, and the fact that the only narrated instance of Pym's seeing his own image in a mirror occurs during a mock resurrection in which he purposely transfigures his appearance. After the mutiny on the *Grampus,* Pym and his friends, seeking some means to overcome the numerical superiority of the mutineers and regain control of the ship, hit on the idea of dressing Pym in the clothes of a dead seaman named Hartman Rogers, who was apparently poisoned by the leader of the mutiny. Disguised as the resurrected corpse, Pym is to enter the dimly lit cabin where the mutineers have been drinking, and in the resulting confusion his friends are to overpower them. Peters adds the finishing touches to Pym's transfiguration by rubbing Pym's face "with white chalk, and afterward splotching it with blood" from a cut in his finger (3:87). The fact that Pym's face is powdered a ghostly white by his shadow self Peters points to the subsequent reversal in which Pym's dark shadow becomes the misty figure whose skin is "of the perfect whiteness of the snow." Disguised as the dead man, Pym chances to see his reflection in the cabin mirror: "I was so impressed with a sense of vague awe at my appearance and at the recollection of the terrific reality which I was thus representing, that I was seized with a violent tremour, and could scarcely summon resolution to go on with my part" (3:88). Pym's disguise is so successful that his unexpected appearance in the midst of the mutineers literally frightens their leader to death. And if the crew could mistake Pym's transfigured body for "a visitant from the world of shadows" (3:92), it is not surprising that Pym could later mistake his own transfigured shadow in the mist for a real body.

Pym notes that "the intense effect" caused by a "sudden apparition" is often due "to a kind of anticipative horror, lest the apparition *might possibly be* real" rather "than to an unwavering belief in its reality" (3:92)—a remark that is more an oblique comment on Pym's anticipatory losses of consciousness (and on the relationship of these symbolic deaths to his playing the role of a resurrected corpse) than a description of the mutineers' reaction to his appearance. Indeed, he says that "in the minds of the mutineers there was not even the shadow of a basis upon which to rest a doubt that the apparition of Rogers was indeed a revivification of his disgusting corpse, or at least its spiritual image" (3:92). Although Pym suggests that for the mutineers this apparition has removed any uncertainty about personal survival after death, his own words recast the shadow of doubt at the very moment that they claim to dispel it. The mutineers were sure, he says, that the apparition was *either* a revivified corpse *or* its spiritual image. Yet it is precisely the uncertainty between these two alternatives that is at issue. The notion of resurrection or revivification depends upon the idea of a soul that can exist independently of the body, so as to reanimate the corpse at some later time; but the mutineers' uncertainty as to whether the apparition is a body or an image points up man's inability to conceive of the soul independently of the body, his inability to imagine the soul as anything but a self-animating, disembodied image of the body. The emptiness of any notion of the soul apart from the body—the basic uncertainty of survival—is further emphasized by the fact that what the mutineers see is, as we know, neither a revivified corpse nor a spiritual image but a disguised living body, a hoax.

Pym's mock resurrection evokes as well the necessary link between the concept of resurrection and the reversal of values inherent in a black/white revenge morality. Within Christian tradition the general resurrection is synonymous with the last judgment. Body and soul are reunited as part of the definitive separation of good and evil. That separation is the ultimate revenge, a repetition and reversal of the worldly order: "So the last shall be first and the first last" (Matthew 20:16). But this bringing low of the mighty is also understood to be a destruction; it is the absolute separation of the wicked from the source of spiritual life, "the second death," as the Bible says. It is not, however, an annihilation of the wicked. After this second death their souls survive in hell, condemned to eternal punishments in which, according to Dante, the evildoer is made to passively endure what he had actively dealt out during life. Clearly, Pym's mock resurrection is part of a revenge scenario in which the good destroy the wicked and restore the order of rank that the mutineers had overturned. The fact that the leader of the mutiny is frightened to death by the "apparition" of the seaman he murdered is indicative of the precise balance of this reversal.

One of the major difficulties posed by the Christian concept of the last judgment as a final revenge is that since revenge necessarily involves repetition and reversal, any retribution that allows the wicked to remain in self-conscious existence in order to suffer eternal punishment seems incompatible with absolute finality, with the permanent arresting of repetition. That is, if the taking of revenge is an affront that imprints the desire for revenge upon the person who suffers it, an act that leaves a scar on the memory demanding its own repetition and reversal in turn, then the only revenge that would not beget this desire is one in which the victim's memory was obliterated. But such an annihilation of mnemic continuity is precisely what the last judgment does not involve; and since the wicked do not forget the affront of that "final" revenge, it must be assumed that, being wicked, neither do they forgive it. Yet if the finality of revenge at the last judgment is not constituted by an obliteration of the victim's memory, then perhaps it is achieved by an obliteration of the victim's will. The obvious objection to this is that the notion of a personal self without a will is as inconceivable as the notion of a personal self without a memory. Further, since the wicked are to suffer eternally, and since action and passion are modes of the will, personal suffering is equally inconceivable without a will.

The alternative, then, is to suppose that the revenge meted out at the last judgment leaves the evildoer's memory and will intact, thirsting for some future revenge of his own but forever prevented from carrying it out by the power of God. But again, conceptual difficulties arise; for if, according to Christian doctrine, willing evil is as much an offense against God as doing evil, then the damned soul with memory and will intact can continue to resist God's will, refusing to acknowledge His right to mastery and thus achieving a triumph of the individual will in its own personal mastery. Such resistance would transvalue the punishment and amount to a revenge of creature on Creator. This impulse to resist God's mastery as long as the individual will and memory exist is the essence of Milton's Satan, and, closer to home, of Melville's Ahab addressing the "clear spirit" whose "right worship is defiance": "I own thy speechless, placeless power; but to the last gasp of my earthquake life will dispute its unconditional, unintegral mastery in me. In the midst of the personified impersonal, a personality stands here.... Light though thou be, thou leapest out of darkness; but I am darkness leaping out of light, leaping out of thee!" (p. 417). This determination to remain the master of one's own will no matter what external force is applied or punishment inflicted (so long as that force leaves the self in existence), this impulse of the will to be a rule unto itself, to be its own God, is what it means to be wicked, to be in Satanic rebellion against the divine will. The orthodox Christian position, which holds that after the last judgment the wicked have no desire for revenge because they see and acknowledge the perfect justice of God's action, simply empties wickedness of any meaning. It is precisely because the wicked acknowledge the authority of no one's will but their own, because they refuse to admit that anyone has the right to judge of their actions, that they are punished. The contradictory impulse underlying the last judgment is to have the souls of the wicked be both dead and alive at once—alive enough to experience the suffering of punishment but dead enough not to experience the joy of willed defiance.

Every attempt to understand the finality of revenge at the last judgment leads in the same direction—to words emptied of significance, to words whose apparent meanings are found upon closer examination to be inconceivable. But perhaps this absence of significance is itself the meaning insofar as it indicates that the afterlife is without significance because it is without signs. Paul says that here "we see through a glass darkly" but there "face to face" (1 Corinthians 13:12); here we know by means of signs and symbols, but there signs and symbols have ceased to exist. The difficulty is that human consciousness is itself the dark glass, the self being at once the image reflected in the mirror and the mirror of self-reflection, and that to speak of the self's survival in a realm devoid of signs and images makes no sense. The orthodox believer's reply would be that it is senseless for the finite human intellect to make itself the measure of the infinite, to make the limits of human self-consciousness the rule for conceiving of a realm wholly beyond those limits. A valid enough argument, were it not precisely a question of the persistence of *human* self-consciousness within the realm of the imageless; for although the limitations of the self cannot be made the measure of what lies beyond those limits, they remain the rule for the self's own existence, for any mnemic continuity after death. As a symbolic entity the self could not exist in an asymbolic realm.

One might argue that the notion of the self as a linguistic entity whose persistence depends on a stable mnemic inscription like the writing in a book is simply foreign to the Biblical sense of personal identity, except for the fact that this is one of the commonest Biblical images of the self, particularly in passages dealing with divine judgment and personal survival. Thus, for example, in Revelations 20:

> 12 And I saw the dead, small and great, stand before God; and the books were opened: and another book was opened, which is the book of life: and the dead were judged out of those things which were written in the books, according to their works.
>
> 13 And the sea gave up the dead which were in it; and death and hell delivered up the dead which were in them: and they were judged every man according to their works.
>
> 14 And death and hell were cast into the lake of fire. This is the second death.
>
> 15 And whosoever was not found written in the book of life was cast into the lake of fire.

The mnemic continuity of the self in this world, its personal history, is represented by one set of books in which are recorded the self's good and bad deeds—account books for the great settling of scores at the last judgment—while the mnemic continuity of the self in the next world is represented by the book of life in which one's name is inscribed if, in the accounting, the good deeds outweigh the bad. The image of the "book of life" or the "book of the living" runs through both the Old and New Testaments. In Malachi 3:16 it is called "a book of remembrance" for the Lord, a designation that indicates its doubly mnemic character; for the survival of the individual's ability to remember his personal history and connect those memories with the image of his body and his name depends upon God's preserving of the individual's name, image, and history in His own memory, the ground of all being.

It is in light of *Pym*'s juxtaposition of the kind of written survival possible for an author with the personal survival promised by Christianity that we can understand the full meaning of Poe's speculation on the origin and end of the universe in *Eureka*. In his prefatory remarks, Poe describes the life of *Eureka* after its author's death in terms of the resurrection of the body, corpus substituting for corpse:

> To the few who love me and whom I love—to those who feel rather than to those who think—to the dreamers and those who put faith in dreams as in the only realities—I offer this Book of Truths, not in its character of Truth-Teller, but for the Beauty that abounds in its Truth; constituting it true. To these I present the composition as an Art-Product alone:—let us say as a Romance; or, if I be not urging too lofty a claim, as a Poem.
>
> *What I here propound is true:*—therefore it cannot die:—or if by any means it be now trodden down so that it die, it will "rise again to the Life Everlasting."
>
> Nevertheless it is as a Poem only that I wish this work to be judged after I am dead. (16:183)

If, in this scenario, the first death is that of the writing self Poe, then the second death would be that of the written self *Eureka*, a death that would result from an unfavorable judgment of the work by readers such that the book and its author would be forgotten. Poe seeks to ensure the resurrection of the body of his work, its survival in the collective human memory, by indicating the terms on which it should be judged—not as the logical truth of external reality but as the aesthetic truth of the internal reality of the imagination, that "tendency of the human intellect" in its moments of highest aspiration (as exhibited in pre-Socratic cosmologies, in Plato's *Timaeus*, in the Book of Genesis, and in numerous other myths of origin) to project itself into the void prior to its birth and after its death. Such cosmologies, though they may not be true in terms of empirical science, represent a deeper truth, for they exhibit the fundamental character of cosmology as an imposition of human structures upon a material universe indifferent to meaning. All cosmologies, from the pre-Socratic to the post-Newtonian, anthropomorphize, aestheticize, the material universe. In one basic sense, then, a modern scientific cosmology is as alogical as an aesthetic cosmology like *Eureka*, in that it aspires to describe a primal event, prior to the existence of man and the universe, as if there were a human bystander watching the event take place, though at that point there existed no place for the event to take nor any place for the bystander to stand. In relation to such an event the notion of human observation is meaningless. Yet the alogical impulse to know of an ultimate origin cannot be dismissed as merely illogical, as simply a flaw in the process of reasoning, as if there existed either a logical mode for such knowledge or the alternative of abandoning the quest. The impulse of human consciousness to transcend itself, to attain that knowledge which dissolves both the knower and the concept of "knowing," is not some accidental, dispensable aspect of self-consciousness but is fundamentally constitutive of it. Thus when Poe subtly exhibits the logical emptiness of the Christian notion of spiritual survival in *Pym*, he does so not because he feels that this demonstration frees us from the desire to know of an ultimate human destiny beyond death or because he has some more logical theory to propose in its place. The myth of the self's origin as an act of hieroglyphic doubling is just as alogical, in its pretension to know the undifferentiated and in its inability to conceive of the transition from the unselfconscious to the self-conscious, as is the Christian notion of personal survival. In using an alogical myth of the self's origin to put in question an alogical notion of the self's survival, Poe directs our attention to the problematic quality of all self-conscious existence, the fundamentally alogical status of the self.

Acknowledging the inherent contradictoriness of man's attempt to represent the origin of the universe in a linguistic discourse, Poe offers *Eureka* to "those who feel rather than to those who think." This split between thought and feeling, mind and body, which the preface of *Eureka* associates with the constitutive opposition between writing self and written self, is, in its ultimately unanalyzable, irreducible character, a microcosm of that opposition between sameness and difference, unity and multiplicity, simplicity and complexity that Poe in his cosmology attempts (unsuccessfully) to reduce to a primal Oneness, the origin and the ultimate destiny of the universe. What the poem *Eureka*, at once pre-Socratic and post-Newtonian, asserts is the truth of the feeling, the bodily intuition, that the diverse objects which the mind discovers in contemplating external nature form a unity, that they are all parts of one body which, if not infinite, is so gigantic as to be beyond both the spatial and temporal limits of human perception. In *Eureka*, then, Poe presents us with the paradox of a "unified" macrocosmic body that is without a totalizing image—an alogical, intuitive belief whose "truth" rests upon Poe's sense that cosmologies and myths of origin are forms of internal geography that, under the guise of mapping the physical universe, map the universe of desire. Like the other writers of the American Renaissance, Poe finds himself in the uncertain region between knowledge and belief, waking and dreams, between what compels him intellectually and what moves him emotionally; and like his contemporaries Poe has begun, in the very act of asserting his beliefs, to subordinate those beliefs in crucial and irrevocable ways to his knowledge by allowing that knowledge to dictate the discursive form and logical status of his assertion.

Section 14
The Return to Oneness; Breaking the Crypt; The Limits of Interpretation; The Ultimate Certainty

An assumption common to cosmologies and myths of origin is that origin and end are one, that the ultimate destiny of man and the universe is a return to the undifferentiated ground from which each sprang—an assumption of which *Pym* and *Eureka* are, at least superficially, microcosmic and macrocosmic versions within Poe's work. Yet one of the difficulties that the origin of the universe poses for logical thought is its dual, contradictory status: at once independent of and yet dependent upon the origin of human consciousness. Obviously, the physical origin of the universe precedes man's existence; yet it is only the existence of human consciousness that opens up the physical universe to the question of origin at all. In Genesis one of the things that the name "God" represents is the presence of consciousness to the originating act, as indicated by the depiction of that act as one of illumination. What Poe faced in both *Pym* and *Eureka* was the problem of representing in language an undifferentiated ground. In *Eureka* he says that the starting point of his discussion must be the Godhead, but he adds, "Of this Godhead, *in itself,* he alone is not imbecile . . . who propounds—nothing." In such a situation, man must rely on intuition, which Poe defines as *"the conviction arising from those inductions or deductions of which the processes are so shadowy as to escape our consciousness, elude our reason, or defy our capacity of expression"* (16:206). Poe asserts: "An intuition altogether irresistible, although inexpressible, forces me to the conclusion that what God originally created—that that Matter which, by dint of His Volition, he first made from his Spirit, or from Nihility, *could* have been nothing but Matter in its utmost conceivable state . . . of *Simplicity.* . . . *Oneness,* then, is all that I predicate of the originally created Matter" (16:206–07). Elsewhere in *Eureka* Poe describes the "essentiality" of the source of all "*heterogeneity*" as an original condition of "*no-difference*" (16:212).

If the giant figure in the mist at the end of *Pym* is, beneath its deific associations, simply Pym's unrecognized shadow, then we can understand Poe's characterizing as "shadowy" those intuitive processes that seem to give access to the supernal. Such an interpretation of the figure would, of course, also govern our interpretation of the veil of mist. For if the giant figure is a real body emerging from the mist, then the vapor is like a theater curtain, veiling from sight what lies behind it; but if the figure is a shadow projected upon the mist, then the vapor is like a movie screen, providing a background against which the figure stands out, and veiling, in this case, the abyss of the infinite in which vision is lost. If we adopt the latter interpretation, which the text certainly allows, then we can read the mist as a composite trope in which Poe has tried to solve, on the one hand, the problem of representing within language an undifferentiated ground (language's limit), and on the other hand, the problem of the separate origins of the universe and human consciousness, of being and thinking.

The problem of representation involves finding an entity definite enough to have an image, yet indefinite enough to serve as an image of the undifferentiated. As Pym approaches the vapor, he tells us that it "began to assume more distinctness of form," so that it resembled "a limitless cataract, rolling silently into the sea from some immense and far-distant rampart in the heaven," a "gigantic curtain ranged along the whole extent of the southern horizon" (3:241). On drawing nearer, however, he describes the mist as "a chaos of flitting and indistinct images" (3:241–42). Obviously, the most accurate linguistic representation of the undifferentiated is provided by the narrative's sudden termination as Pym enters the mist, the emptiness of the white page imaging the blankness of the white curtain (the darkening of individual consciousness). Yet this absence of language can be described as a "linguistic representation" only because the verbal image of the mist, which immediately precedes the break, projects *its* meaning onto the sudden blankness of the final page—a paradoxical reversal in which the blank background becomes a figure. The mist's indefiniteness and its quality of simultaneously revealing and veiling make it a particularly appropriate representation of that undifferentiated sublime which, as Poe claims in another context, is experienced in "brief and indeterminate glimpses" (14:274) through the musical element of poetry—the presentation of "perceptible images with . . . *in*definite sensations" (7:xliii). When Poe in the *Marginalia* discusses "indefinitiveness" as an element of "the true musical expression" and refers to "the atmosphere of the mystic" on which the "luxury of dream" floats, he might almost be describing that misty atmosphere which serves as the (back)ground for the self-projected image at the edge of the abyss. By identifying the mist with both the indefiniteness of the sublime (the ontological ground) and the indefiniteness of the background in a figure/ground relationship (the epistemological ground), Poe tries to unify the origins of being and thought in a single image: the ground upon which one's individuated being stands is the background against which one's being stands out as distinct.

Yet this effort to image the presence of consciousness *ab origine* poses a major difficulty in conceiving of that ultimate return of man and the universe to an original condition of oneness. At the beginning of *Eureka* Poe says, "*In the Original Unity of the First Thing lies the Secondary Cause of All Things, with the Germ of their Inevitable Annihilation*" (16:186). The problem is that individual self-consciousness would seem to be one of those secondary things whose fate is annihilation. Poe's solution is to posit a return to unity such that each individual consciousness absorbs all other things into itself, each consciousness in effect becoming God:

No thinking being lives who, at some luminous point of his life of thought, has not felt himself lost amid the surges of futile efforts at understanding, or believing, that anything exists *greater than his own soul*. The utter impossibility of any one's soul feeling itself inferior to another; the intense, overwhelming dissatisfaction and rebellion at the thought;—these, with the omniprevalent aspirations at perfection, are but the spiritual, coincident with the material, struggles towards the original Unity—are, to my mind at least, a species of proof far surpassing what Man terms demonstration, that no one soul *is* inferior to another—that nothing is, or can be, superior to any one soul—that each soul is, in part, its own God—its own Creator:—in a word, that God—the material *and* spiritual God— *now* exists solely in the diffused Matter and Spirit of the Universe;

and that the regathering of this diffused Matter and Spirit will be
but the re-constitution of the *purely* Spiritual and Individual
God. . . .

"Think that the sense of individual identity will be gradually
merged in the general consciousness—that Man, for example, ceasing imperceptibly to feel himself Man, will at length attain that
awfully triumphant epoch when he shall recognize his existence as
that of Jehovah. . . ." (16:312–15)

Such a unified "general consciousness" would, in terms of human
knowledge, be incomprehensible; for since the material universe, in
being absorbed into this single intelligence, would presumably return to
its original condition of *"no-difference,"* this unique intelligence would
have no differentiated objects of knowledge and so could not, in any
sense of the word, be an "intelligence." Yet this meaningless conclusion
seems to follow inevitably from the notion of an ultimate reunion of man
and the universe in a common origin of being and thought.

If Poe's deification of human consciousness to save it from an annihilating return to oneness is, in our tradition, logically implicit in that
prior deification of consciousness (its presence *ab origine*) in Genesis,
then Poe's assertion that man, in his return to origin, will "recognize his
existence as that of Jehovah" need not be interpreted as an unqualified
prophecy of some ultimate cosmic consciousness. Rather, the assertion
can be seen as one pole of an opposition between belief and doubt whose
other pole is the ending of *Pym* with its skeptical sense of what it means
to recognize the self as God. By interpreting the misty figure with its
aura of divinity as Pym's unrecognized shadow, the reader recognizes/
acknowledges that "God" has always been a self-projected, idea-lized
image of man, a personification of man's alogical desire for a form of
consciousness released from the constraints of the body, time, and death,
made omniscient and ubiquitous, primordially creative and eternally
existent. If the ending of *Pym* exhibits a truth of knowledge, the ending
of *Eureka* exhibits a truth of belief, a truth of the will: the desire of
individual self-consciousness to expand until it encompasses everything,
so that there remains no change or movement external to itself in relation to which it could grow old and die. Such is eternity—but such is
oblivion as well.

Poe's "proof" that man will ultimately become God, that "each soul is, in part, its own God—its own Creator" is his intuition of the indomitable strength of his own will—"a species of proof far surpassing what Man terms demonstration"—his "feeling" that nothing exists "greater than his own soul," his "intense, overwhelming dissatisfaction and rebellion" (Satanic rebellion?) "at the thought" that he is "inferior to another." In the tale "Ligeia" (1838), Poe suggests that man succumbs to death only through the failure of his will. Ligeia, a Psyche-figure for the narrator, is described as a creature of "gigantic volition" (2:253); and so that the significance of her return to life will not be missed, the same quotation (attributed to Joseph Glanvill but apparently written by Poe himself) is repeated four times within the brief tale: "And the will therein lieth, which dieth not. Who knoweth the mysteries of the will, with its vigor? For God is but a great will pervading all things by nature of its intentness. Man doth not yield himself to the angels, nor unto death utterly, save only through the weakness of his feeble will" (2:248). Yet in asserting a belief in personal survival, Poe always leaves himself a way out, for Ligeia's return from the dead may be only an hallucination of the narrator, who admits that after Ligeia's death he had "become a bounden slave in the trammels of opium" (2:258).

If it is true that the foreknowledge of one's inevitable death is a mark of the human, it is also true that every man has felt at some time in his life that he will live forever, has felt on the one hand the invincibility of his own will and on the other the literal inconceivability of his own death. A writer—who wills fictive worlds into existence, who creates himself in the act of writing and endows that written self with the power to survive death—is particularly subject to such presentiments of immortality. Perhaps that is the deepest meaning of the quotation that ends *Pym*, for though the quotation sounds like the word of God ("*I have graven it within the hills, and my vengeance upon the dust within the rock*"), Poe's readers, familiar as they were with Scripture, would have known that these words are not from the Bible. And Poe would have known that his readers would immediately register that fact. Certainly, the question we are meant to ask is, who is the author of these godlike words? Not the Creator of the physical universe, but the creator of the written world of *Pym*. Suddenly one understands the significance of the stylistic and logical discontinuity between the quotation and the paragraph that precedes it. The quotation is not simply the final paragraph of the note; it belongs to a different formal level, a different mode of signification. It is an encrypted signature—the author's signature for the whole work. Clearly, the words are meant to be an acknowledgment of authorship—"*I have graven it within the hills*"—an acknowledgment that the hills themselves have been graven in this world made of words. But perhaps a more specific allusion is intended here to the inscribed caverns on Tsalal. Critics have noted that the shapes of the caverns, which spell the Ethiopic root *ṣlm,* also bear a crude resemblance, when connected by the "lateral branches" that serve "as a means of communication between the main chambers," to the initials "e a p" ( ). Certain it is that in drawing the shapes of the caverns Poe has purposely distorted the shapes of the Ethiopic letters— perhaps to invest the characters with the same indeterminacy that shrouds the figure in the mist.

If the shapes of the caverns are meant to suggest the author's initials, then the final quotation is a veiled signature that points to another veiled signature, a cipher whose breaking leads to another cipher, a surface whose penetration brings us to the next surface. One thinks of Melville's image in *Pierre* of the world as "nothing but surface stratified on surface" (p. 285), and one recalls that this image metamorphoses into a description of crypt breaking: "By vast pains we mine into the pyramid; by horrible gropings we come to the central room; with joy we espy the sarcophagus; but we lift the lid—and no body is there!—appallingly vacant as vast is the soul of man!" (p. 285). Breaking the crypt (in the sense of both tomb and cipher) is one of the commonest images in the American Renaissance for the attempt to decipher the meaning of death, the riddle of survival. In "The Fall of the House of Usher," the noise that Madeline makes in breaking out of the crypt counterpoints the action of, and thus serves to decrypt, the story that the narrator reads to Roderick: Ethelred's breaking into the hermit's cell and his slaying of the dragon—the hero's descent into the maw of the grave and his overcoming of the fear of death. In Emerson's poem "Bacchus" (1846), the intoxicated seer says that he will "unlock / Every crypt of every rock" (9:126) to show that nothing in the universe is dead or inanimate. (The verb "unlock" suggests the related image of cipher and key.) Yet Poe, and certainly Melville, had begun to suspect that the crypt was unbreakable precisely because the self as a linguistic entity could never break through some ultimate surface of language to an asymbolic realm, that the cipher was an empty cipher because there existed no supernatural world of *pure significance* corresponding to the natural world of signs. One penetrates

the inscribed rock of the pyramid and the inscribed wood of the sarcophagus only to find that there is no body, no substance within; such
emptiness, such illusory substance is man's soul, his dream of survival
beyond the body. Or as Ishmael says, "Some certain significance lurks in
all things, else all things are little worth, and the round world itself but
an empty cipher, except to sell by the cartload, as they do hills about
Boston, to fill up some morass in the Milky Way" (p. 358); and that final
image recalls Ishmael's most potent reason for the terrifying quality of
whiteness: "Is it that by its *indefiniteness* it *shadows forth* the heartless voids
and immensities of the universe, and thus stabs us from behind with the
thought of annihilation, when beholding the white depths of the milky
way?" (p. 169, italics mine).

Is the writing on the wall within the tomblike, letter-shaped caverns of
Tsalal a crypt within a crypt, like the inscribed sarcophagus within the
inscribed pyramid? Pym's recognition of the carved figure's human
form, followed by his failure to recognize it as a work of art rather than
of nature, prefigures his subsequent recognition of the misty figure's
human shape and his failure to recognize it as his own shadow rather
than a supernatural appearance. In Pym's case, nonrecognition of the
human origin of these shapes grounds an illusory decipherment of
death, a breaking of the crypt (in the sense of both a decoding of an
ultimate meaning and a breaking out of the tomb through personal
survival); for this nonrecognition allows the illusion of a necessary correspondence between "natural" shapes (the figure on the wall) and a
"supernatural" being (the figure in the mist) who created the universe in
his own image. But that skeptical sense of recognizing the self as Jehovah,
suggested for the readers of *Pym* by Poe's veiled signatures as god of this
written world, frames and forms a commentary upon Pym's nonrecognition of the human. To recognize oneself as God in this sense means to
find the self's image or signature wherever one looks, to find nothing
but the self, so that the crypt of death is unbreakable because it is
circular, self-enclosed: language cannot penetrate its own surface to
learn of the self's survival after death because that symbolic surface *is* the
self.

Within Judeo-Christian tradition, death is deciphered as divine vengeance for an original transgression against the Father. But within the
context of this skeptical recognition of the self as God, that "*vengeance
upon the dust within the rock*" (the corruption of the body in the tomb)

assumes another meaning—it refers not to death as revenge, but to a revenge against death, the revenge that man attempts to take, through art, against time, change, and mortality, against the things that threaten to obliterate all trace of his individual existence. The revenge of art—the inscribing of the crypt—is the impulse to grave one's image or name in enduring stone, to leave a permanent memory. In Melville's *Mardi* the sage Babbalanja speculates that death "may be an utter lapse of memory concerning sublunary things," so that one could say of the dead that "they themselves be not themselves" (p. 210). But King Media maintains that the only form of personal survival possible after death is the persistence of one's memory in the minds of others, and he asks Babbalanja, "How may I best perpetuate my name?" (p. 211). To which the sage slyly answers, "Carve it, my lord, deep into a ponderous stone, and sink it, face downward, into the sea; for the unseen foundations of the deep are more enduring than the palpable tops of the mountains" (p. 211). Babbalanja's suggestion for safeguarding the inscription subtly points out that the carving on the stone's surface is ultimately subject to the same obliterating effects of time and change that the self is subject to. Considered in this light, then, Babbalanja's notion of survival as "an utter lapse of memory concerning sublunary things" would seem to be an alogical attempt to dissociate the idea of the self from the concept of an inscribed mnemic surface, so as to free the self from the erosion that all surfaces experience. Significantly, his manner of safeguarding the inscription images this alogical dissociation as a surface penetration that plunges the inscribed self into an unseen (imageless), liquid (surfaceless) depth.

The impossibility of the self's breaking through the surface of language and the recognition that "God" is an idealized self-projection upon that surface would require an alternative reading for that apparent linguistic penetration of the misty curtain that occurs when the "gigantic and pallidly white birds" fly "from beyond the veil" with their cry "the eternal Tekeli-li!" Within the Christian context of transfiguration and resurrection, the white birds might be an allusion to the iconography of the Holy Spirit as a white dove, or they might simply be a visual representation of the flight of the soul to God. (Just after seeing the white birds, Pym remarks that the black man Nu-Nu's "spirit departed.") But if one interprets the misty figure as an unrecognized self-projection, then the cry of the birds suggests not some mystic word from beyond the veil but the origin of human speech as phonetic doubling. According to the so-called bow-wow theory of linguistic origin, man's original words were onomatopoetic—phonetic imitations of the natural sounds of objects or actions. Near the end of the narrative, Poe lays the groundwork for such an interpretation of the birds' cry: Pym remarks that in the speech of the black islanders, "the commencement of the words *Tsalemon* and *Tsalal* was given with a prolonged hissing sound, which we found it impossible to imitate, even after repeated endeavours, and which was precisely the same with the note of the black bittern we had eaten up on the summit of the hill" (3:239).

As the cry of the black bird provides the phonic root (presumably *ṣl*, "shadow") for the name of the dark realm and, apparently, for the names of all dark-colored objects (for example, *Tsalemon*), so the cry of the white bird provides the sound associated with the white polar region, a word used by the black islanders upon sighting any white object. In each case, the natural sound of an object has, by association, been turned into the phonetic signifier of one of the object's most striking qualities— its color. In terms of the bow-wow theory of origin, the animal cry Tekeli-li cannot be a word from beyond the veil because it only becomes a *word* on this side of the veil, within the realm of self-projected doubling which the veil (back)grounds. It is only when the islanders phonetically double the birds' cry in their own speech that the sound becomes symbolic. Poe has, then, so constructed the final episode that the cry of the white birds exhibits the same indeterminacy as the misty figure: just as the figure can be interpreted as either a body or a shadow, the birds' cry can be interpreted as either a phonetic penetration of the veil's surface (an auditory experience of depth, equivalent to seeing a body emerge from behind the misty curtain) or a phonetic doubling that is the equivalent, on the sonic level, of hieroglyphic doubling on the visual level.

But this raises one further question concerning the precise meaning of the word Tekeli-li. In the philological note, Poe gives the meanings of the Ethiopic, Arabic, and Coptic words found in the caverns, and he provides a clue to the decipherment of the name Tsalal by suggesting that "philological scrutiny" of the word may reveal "some reference to the Ethiopian characters" inscribed in the caverns' shapes. Yet what seems curious about this procedure is that the same philological scrutiny is neither applied to nor suggested for the word Tekeli-li, even though its association with whiteness and the polar region is discussed at some length. According to one critical interpretation, the word Tekeli-li is an allusion to the Biblical "mene, mene, tekel, upharsin," the Chaldean words inscribed on the wall during Belshazaar's feast as a prophecy of God's vengeance (Daniel 5:25). This interpretation is usually part of a larger reading that sees in the ending of *Pym* a proslavery allegory of the permanent degradation of the black race as divine revenge for the sin of Ham. Yet the authentic philological data of the concluding note and the fact that the word Tekeli-li functions in the text as a polar opposite to the name Tsalal tempt us to apply to Tekeli-li the same philological analysis recommended for the name of the black island, indeed, tempt us without explicitly authorizing such an inquiry. This lure in a work by Poe should immediately make us suspicious. Is the author encouraging us to go too far, inviting us as decipherers of meaning to assume an interpretive stance that is the opposite of Pym's? In the inscription on the chasm wall Pym confronts authentic words having ascertainable meanings, yet dismisses them as the random traces of natural process; in carrying out a philological examination of the word Tekeli-li, we may find ourselves in the opposite situation of imposing a meaning upon a group of phonemes that have no more inherent significance than the sound of a bird's cry. Yet if this willed self-projection of significance, this making of meaning, is what Poe is luring us to, he must have, in order for the trick to work, a specific pitfall in mind, a particular resemblance that he is encouraging us to impose upon the word in the act of interpretation.

Taking our clue from the fact that Tsalal and Tekeli-li are both words in the language of the black islanders and that the name Tsalal has an Ethiopic root, we find in Hiob Ludolf's *Lexicon Aethiopico-Latinum* (1699), a work to which Poe would have had access, an Ethiopic root *tkl* whose general meaning is "that which is immovable, fixed, firmly established" and whose specific meanings include "post" or "pole" (*paxillus*), "pin" or "nail" (*clavus*), "innate, original" (*insitum, ingenitum*), and "unmoving" (*immobilis,* used of the fixed stars).[64] In its verbal form the root is used to translate the ending of Psalm 93:1 ("the world also is stablished, that it cannot be moved") in the Ethiopic version of the Bible. All of these meanings are obviously appropriate to the notion of a fixed geographic pole and thus to the name of the polar region in *Pym*.

If the ultimate root of Tsalal is *ṣl* (shadow) and that of its polar opposite Tekeli-li is *tkl* (original, fixed spot), then together the origins of the two words are a hieroglyph of the final scene in *Pym*—the shadow at the

pole—a pictograph of that shadowing or doubling that is the origin of
the bipolar oppositions of the linguistic world. Further, if Poe intended
that Tekeli-li suggest the Ethiopic root *tkl*, then he may well, in noticing
that one of its meanings is *clavus,* have savored the wordplay *clavus/clavis*
(nail/key), not simply because the key to a cipher is that fixed spot where
the external code and the encrypted meaning must be immovably linked
to one another (any slippage at this spot renders the message undecipherable), but also because nail and key, as objects meant to be inserted
in an opening, are hieroglyphs of that return to the womb awaiting Pym
and his phallic double Dirk Peters in the abyss.

We should note, however, that there exists no form of the Ethiopic
root *tkl* that corresponds exactly to the shape of the word Tekeli-li.
Since the substantive form of the Ethiopic root is *takel* and the adjectival
form is *tekul,* one must ignore not only the final syllable of Tekeli-li but
also one of the first two vowels. On the other hand, it should be noted
that in Ethiopic the vowels are written as slight modifications of the
shape of the preceding consonant, so that in using Ludolf's *Lexicon* Poe
could have been certain of the consonants in the word but could easily
have been in doubt about the vowels. Admittedly, Poe altered the
Ethiopic form *tsalala* to the name Tsalal. Moreover, the name of "the
region of the south," which Poe gives as **ⲡⲁⲩⲅⲣⲏⲥ** (Pathures), appears in the Rheims-Douay Version of the Bible as Phatures and in the
King James Version as Pathros. There are, then, in the philological note
other instances of transliterations that distort the exact shape of a word,
though the transformation of *tkl* to Tekeli-li would be the most extreme
case.

What the reader is left with is a series of hermeneutic problems: Is the
resemblance of the Ethiopic root *tkl* to the word Tekeli-li, along with
the appropriateness of the root's meaning to the narrative context, the
result of random coincidence or authorial intention? Of the five foreign
words cited in the concluding note, will Tekeli-li be the only one that
does not yield an authentic meaning to philological scrutiny? Is it intended, then, to be the joker in the deck? Or has Poe so constructed the
evidence that various interpretations are possible without any one of
them being certain? If we dismiss the word Tekeli-li as meaningless, we
may be doubling Pym's blindness in the chasm; but if we interpret it as
Poe's intentional alteration of the Ethiopic root *tkl,* we may be doubling
Pym's blindness before the misty curtain when he fails to recognize his

own self-projected image. Any decision that we make in this case will be more a matter of will than knowledge, of temperament than enlightenment. Such a decision may bear much the same arbitrary relationship to the philological science of the concluding note that the ending of *Eureka* bears to the astronomical science of its text. Yet if, in that ceaseless pursuit of meaning that characterizes human behavior, we interpret the resemblance between *tkl* and Tekeli-li as the author's intention and are left with the uneasy feeling that we have gone too far, that we have exceeded the limit of what can be known from the evidence, then perhaps we have been made to act out the deepest significance of *Pym*'s ending—the indeterminate status of any interpretation of nature's script, of any reading that discovers the world's meaning, the existence of its Author, or His intentions. Such an interpretation may simply be a self-projection that creates the illusion of depth, a shadow mistaken for a body.

It is precisely this uncertainty between body and shadow that the ending of *Pym* poses and refuses to resolve. For Pym the fixed pole of certainty turns out to be the inevitable fixity of his own death. But for those who remain on this side of the veil in the world between the poles, every recognition is constitutively doubled by a nonrecognition, every figure rests upon an indefinite ground. If the figure in the mist is Pym's shadow, then his failure to recognize himself as he approaches the abyss may be, for the reader, a hieroglyphic representation of death as personal annihilation. Certainly, Pym's nonrecognition of spatial doubling at the abyss is consistent with his earlier nonrecognition of temporal doubling in the repeated scenario of symbolic death and rebirth. What Pym fails to recognize is that in terms of both space and time the self is an essentially repetitive entity and thus incompatible with a nonrepetitive finality that dissolves symbolic (that is, doubled) re-presentation, or re-cognition. As we noted earlier, the contradictory senses of death's finality are particularly evident in Christianity, where the finality is denied through the doctrine of personal survival and simultaneously reaffirmed in the concept of a last judgment whose permanent arresting of the wicked is imaged as the "second death."

That blindness to repetition, to spatial and temporal doubling, which characterizes Pym as a writing self *within* the story, is a necessary blindness to the final meaning of the narrative act that constitutes his written self. For if the sense of an individual life's meaningfulness inheres precisely in its narratability, in its possessing the unified shape of a story, and if such a unified shape requires a narrative closure synonymous with death, then this precludes a person's being both the actor and the narrator of his own story, precludes at last the double role of image and mirror, so that the narrative of one's own life is always unfinished, a fragment in which meaningful closure is either a fictionalized foreshadowing or a postscript in another hand. As readers, as survivors of the textual journey to the *vor*-textual abyss, our standpoint is the uncertain ground of the closing note where, as necrology turns back into philology and the historical oscillations of interpretation, we see the quest for fixed certainty, that univocal sense which is the linguistic equivalent of *Eureka*'s primal Oneness, for what it is—a death wish.

PART THREE
Hawthorne and Melville

And wrecks passed without sound of bells,
The calyx of death's bounty giving back
A scattered chapter, livid hieroglyph,
The portent wound in corridors of shells. . . .

The fabulous shadow only the sea keeps.

Hart Crane, "At Melville's Tomb"

. . . suppose that in the desert you find a stone covered with hieroglyphics. You do not doubt for a moment that, behind them, there was a
subject who wrote them. But it is an error to believe that each signifier is
addressed to you—this is proved by the fact that you cannot understand
any of it. On the other hand you define them as signifiers, by the fact
that you are sure that each of these signifiers is related to each of the
others.

Jacques Lacan, *The Four Fundamental Concepts of Psycho-Analysis*

Section 15

Hawthorne: The Ambiguity of the Hieroglyphics; The Unstable Self and Its Roles; Mirror Image and Phonetic Veil; The Feminine Role of the Artist; Veil and Phallus; The Book as Partial Object

For Hawthorne and Melville, the ambiguous character of the hieroglyphics was their prime significance. The hieroglyphics were the linguistic analogue of an enigmatic external world whose shape was various enough to sustain almost any interpretation that man projected on it in the act of knowing. Both writers understood that questions of meaning were finally questions of value and that Champollion's scientific reading of the hieroglyphics had not rendered the nearly four centuries of metaphysical interpretations either worthless or meaningless. Ancient Egyptian hieroglyphics, seventeenth-century metaphysical interpretations, and nineteenth-century scientific readings are in a sense all of equal value, in that each is a representative product of the ordering power of the human imagination in a different historical period. The sense that value and meaning are a function of historical process and that at any given moment in history man finds the truth he needs to find are insights that, in the works of Hawthorne and Melville, frequently center upon the image of the hieroglyphs.

Certainly, it would be difficult to overestimate the importance of the symbol of the hieroglyphics to the structure of a novel like *The Scarlet Letter* (1850). Hester's insignia is a hieroglyphic emblem, and the manuscript that accompanies it is its apparent explication—"apparent" because the very point of the novel is to present us not with the one true meaning of the hieroglyph but rather with a host of possible meanings from which to choose. In his first description of the scarlet letter, Hawthorne notes that the insignia is the product of a lost skill in embroidery, thereby emphasizing its mysterious, hieroglyphic nature: "The stitch (as I am assured by ladies conversant with such mysteries) gives evidence of a now forgotten art, not to be recovered even by the process of picking out the threads" (1:31). Gazing at the letter, he adds, "Certainly, there was some deep meaning in it, most worthy of interpretation, and which, as it were, streamed forth from the mystic symbol, subtly communicating itself to my sensibilities, but evading the analysis of my mind" (1:31). That "deep meaning" remains ambiguous to the last. Significantly, Hawthorne never tells us that Hester's scarlet A stands for adultery. Rather, he reports that after some years had elapsed during

239

which Hester devoted herself to charitable actions, "many people refused to interpret the scarlet A by its original signification. They said
that it meant Able; so strong was Hester Prynne, with a woman's
strength" (1:161).

The scenario of multiple perspectives, in which an enigmatic object is
variously interpreted by one individual whose point of view changes or
by a series of individuals who each have a different point of view, is a
major structural element in *The Scarlet Letter*. At the start a dual
viewpoint is introduced into the very fabric of the narrative when
Hawthorne presents himself not as the author of the story but rather as
its revisor and elaborator. He tells us that when he discovered the embroidered letter in the Salem customhouse, he found with it an explanatory manuscript written by an eighteenth-century surveyor of the customs named Jonathan Pue and that it is this manuscript that he has made
the basis of his own work. *The Scarlet Letter* is, then, a story set in the
seventeenth century, ostensibly written by one man in the eighteenth
century, and redacted by another man in the nineteenth century.

The divergence in historical perspective that this fiction necessarily
entails becomes the subject of direct comment in the novel whenever Mr.
Pue's narrative includes events that appear to have a supernatural explanation. The most striking example of such a commentary occurs in Hawthorne's description of the night scene at the scaffold when Dimmesdale,
Hester, and Pearl are startled by the appearance of a meteor. The de-
scriptior contains Hawthorne's most explicit statements on both the
hieroglyphic nature of the scarlet letter and the essential ambiguity
of the hieroglyphic emblem. He says: "Nothing was more common, in
those days than to interpret all meteoric appearances, and other natural
phenomena, that occurred with less regularity than the rise and set of
sun and moon, as so many revelations from a supernatural source. Thus,
a blazing spear, a sword of flame, a bow, or a sheaf of arrows, seen in the
midnight sky, prefigured Indian warfare. Pestilence was known to have
been foreboded by a shower of crimson light" (1:154–55). He points out
that sometimes the phenomenon was seen by multitudes, but oftener

... its credibility rested on the faith of some lonely eyewitness, who
beheld the wonder through the colored, magnifying, and distorting
medium of his imagination, and shaped it more distinctly in his
after-thought. It was, indeed, a majestic idea, that the destiny of

nations should be revealed, in these awful hieroglyphics, on the cope of heaven.... But what shall we say, when an individual discovers a revelation, addressed to himself alone, on the same vast sheet of record! In such a case, it could only be the symptom of a highly disordered mental state, when a man, rendered morbidly self-contemplative by long, intense, and secret pain, had extended his egotism over the whole expanse of nature, until the firmament itself should appear no more than a fitting page for his soul's history and fate.

We impute it, therefore, solely to the disease in his own eye and heart, that the minister, looking upward to the zenith, beheld there the appearance of an immense letter,—the letter A,—marked out in lines of dull red light. Not but the meteor may have shown itself at that point, burning duskily through a veil of cloud; but with no such shape as his guilty imagination gave it; or, at least, with so little definiteness, that another's guilt might have seen another symbol in it. (1:155)

The tone of the voice in this passage is partly ironic, for when Hawthorne speaks of that disordered mental state, that morbid self-contemplation wherein man's egotism extends itself over the whole expanse of nature until even the firmament is "no more than a fitting page for his soul's history and fate," he is commenting on his own condition as much as on Dimmesdale's. The post-Kantian awareness that what a man knows is not an objective external world but simply the internal structure of his own mind projected upon an essentially indeterminate ground, the feeling of being trapped in the self, the sense of the shattering of all absolutes because of the loss of objective knowledge—these are what the concept of the hieroglyphic emblem evokes for Hawthorne. His remark that the meteor's shape as it passed through the cloud was of so little definiteness that another man might have seen it as an entirely different symbol receives its fulfillment on the morning after the scaffold scene. The old sexton, commenting on Governor Winthrop's death the previous night, says to Dimmesdale, "But did your reverence hear of the portent that was seen last night? A great red letter in the sky,—the letter A,—which we interpret to stand for Angel. For, as our good Governor Winthrop was made an angel this past night, it was doubtless held fit that there should be some notice thereof!" (1:158).

In essence, it is a repetition of the multiple perspectivism of the night scene at the scaffold that forms the novel's conclusion. On the day of the election sermon when Dimmesdale has reached the peak of his career, he once again mounts the scaffold, this time to acknowledge Hester and Pearl, to accept his guilt, and to reveal the letter imprinted on his chest. It is a scene that contains some of Hawthorne's best writing, a scene whose emotional power sweeps up spectators and reader alike in its climax of revelation, retribution, and eleventh-hour repentance. And yet the next chapter begins with the deflating remark: "After many days, when time sufficed for the people to arrange their thoughts in reference to the foregoing scene, there was more than one account of what had been witnessed on the scaffold" (1:258). Most of the spectators testified to having seen a scarlet letter imprinted on the minister's breast, but as to its origin there were various explanations, all of which were conjectural. Some believed that the letter was a self-inflicted penance, others that it was the result of Roger Chillingworth's magic and poisonous drugs, and still others that it was the mark "of the ever active tooth of remorse, gnawing from the inmost heart outwardly" (1:258). Hawthorne adds, "The reader may choose among these theories" (1:259). Indeed, there were even those who denied the existence of any mark at all on the minister's breast; nor, they said, had his dying words acknowledged the slightest connection "with the guilt for which Hester Prynne had so long worn the scarlet letter" (1:259). They explained that Dimmesdale, realizing that death was near, had decided to make the manner of his death a parable. "By yielding up his breath in the arms of that fallen woman," he meant "to impress on his admirers the mighty and mournful lesson, that, in the view of Infinite Purity, we are sinners all alike" (1:259).

Hawthorne observes that this version of the story is "an instance of that stubborn fidelity with which a man's friends—and especially a clergyman's—will sometimes uphold his character; when proofs, clear as the mid-day sunshine on the scarlet letter, establish him a false and sin-stained creature of the dust" (1:259). Hawthorne is again being ironic. Although he calls the proofs of Dimmesdale's guilt "clear as the mid-day sunshine on the scarlet letter," he knows that noon light is no absolute, that it is simply one in a series of constantly changing lights. Throughout the novel Hawthorne evokes the relativity of truth to one's perspective through images of objects whose significance radically alters with the changing light, and he characterizes his own viewpoint as novelist (and the imaginative alterations that it creates) in the famous image of everyday objects illuminated by firelight and moonlight and reflected in a mirror. Moreover, Hawthorne tells us what these clear proofs of Dimmesdale's guilt amount to: "a manuscript of old date, drawn up from the verbal testimony of individuals, some of whom had known Hester Prynne, while others had heard the tale from contemporary witnesses" (1:259-60). Not only is the authority of the manuscript based on hearsay, it is an authority that Hawthorne himself has called into question at various points in the novel and in exactly the same way that Dimmesdale's friends questioned the minister's final confession. As they claimed that his dying actions were intended to be parabolic, so Hawthorne, in dealing with the manuscript accounts of the reputed witch Mistress Hibbins, suggests that her reported activities may be not the literal truth but only a parable (1:117, 222).

The novel's central hieroglyph is the scarlet letter, but the letter has an equally important human counterpart—the child Pearl. Hawthorne calls Pearl "the scarlet letter in another form; the scarlet letter endowed with life" (1:102), and it is the effort to discover in the "character" of the child the identity of its maker that forms one of the principle sources of the novel's action. Roger Chillingworth explicitly poses the problem to the elders of Salem: "Would it be beyond a philosopher's research, think ye, gentlemen, to analyze that child's nature, and, from its make and mould, to give a shrewd guess at the father?" (1:116). But it is not only the wronged husband Chillingworth who is in search of Pearl's father, it is the child as well. When Pearl asks her mother where she came from and Hester replies, "Thy Heavenly Father sent thee," Pearl cries out, "He did not send me! . . . I have no Heavenly Father. . . . Tell me! Tell me! . . . It is thou that must tell me!" (1:98).

Pearl's rejection of a heavenly father in her search for a human father is a counterpoint to Hester's own situation, for while Hester knows Pearl's human father, the heavenly father remains hidden from her, and she searches for some trace of his existence in the hieroglyph of her daughter. Hawthorne tells us that Hester was a freethinker: "The world's law was no law for her mind. . . . She assumed a freedom of speculation, then common enough on the other side of the Atlantic, but which our forefathers, had they known of it, would have held to be a deadlier crime than that stigmatized by the scarlet letter" (1:164). Hester wants to believe in the existence of a God who created the hieroglyph of the world as an obscure image of himself and who stands credit for its ultimate decipherability, but when she looks at the hieroglyph that is Pearl, she sees not the lineaments of a heavenly father but the willfulness of a human mother. Hawthorne says that Pearl was "the living hieroglyphic in which was revealed the secret" that Hester and Dimmesdale "so darkly sought to hide,—all written in this symbol,—all plainly manifest,—had there been a prophet or magician skilled to read the character of flame!" (1:207). Looking at this hieroglyph, Hester sees her diminutive double: "a shadowy reflection of the evil that had existed in herself" (1:94). From "the small black mirror of Pearl's eye," from its "unsearchable abyss" (1:97), an "evil spirit" seems to gaze back at Hester. As both "living hieroglyphic" and Hester's "shadowy reflection," Pearl is an obvious instance of the hieroglyphic doubling that pervades not only *The Scarlet Letter* but all of Hawthorne's works in which the reading of character is the principal activity, an activity whose basic assumption is that human character is pictographically inscribed.

Hawthorne's most explicit presentation of the body's shadow outline as a hieroglyphic double occurs in *The Blithedale Romance* (1852) when the narrator, Miles Coverdale, who has been trying to decipher the mystery of Zenobia's character, is discovered watching Zenobia through the window of her drawing room. Zenobia lets down the curtain as if, Coverdale says, "such were the proper barrier to be interposed between a character like hers, and a perceptive faculty like mine" (3:160). Later, "the glow of an astral lamp was penetrating mistily through the white curtain of Zenobia's drawing-room. The shadow of a passing figure was now-and-then cast upon this medium, but with too vague an outline for even my adventurous conjectures to read the hieroglyphic that it presented" (3:161-62). Zenobia, by veiling herself behind the white curtain, unwittingly presents a hieroglyph of the secret that Coverdale will ultimately unveil—the hidden relationship between herself and the mysterious clairvoyant known as the Veiled Lady, her half-sister Priscilla. Coverdale is unable at that moment to understand the emblematic veiling of Zenobia, even though at the beginning of the narrative he had remarked, "Zenobia . . . is merely her public name; a sort of mask in which she comes before the world, retaining all the privileges of privacy—a contrivance, in short, like the white drapery of the Veiled Lady, only a little more transparent" (3:8). Part of the novel's action is the reversal of roles between Zenobia and her antithetical double, Priscilla. As Priscilla emerges from the mesmeric bondage of the white veil to assume her own identity, she supplants her half-sister in Hollingsworth's affections and finally deprives Zenobia of her inheritance. Feeling that she has somehow exchanged places with the forlorn creature who originally sought her protection, Zenobia tells Coverdale shortly before her suicide, "When you next hear of Zenobia, her face will be behind the black veil" (3:227-28).

The constitutive uncertainty between body and image basic to hieroglyphic doubling assumes in *The Scarlet Letter* a series of forms already familiar from *Pym*. Hester, Dimmesdale, Chillingworth, and Pearl are each, at some point in the narrative, either shown looking at their images in a mirror or described in a self-reflective moment as if they were contemplating themselves in a glass, and in each case what they confront is the unpredictable oscillation between the literal and the figurative, the substantial and the imaginary. When Pearl, who functions as Hester's mirror image, finds *herself* mirrored in a seaside pool, the problematic relationship between the "reality" of the self and the "illusion" of its roles is projected upon the scenario of Narcissus: "Forth peeped at her, out of the pool, with dark, glistening curls around her head, and an elf-smile in her eyes, the image of a little maid, whom Pearl, having no other playmate, invited to take her hand and run a race with her. But the visionary little maid, on her part, beckoned likewise, as if to say,—'This is a better place! Come thou into the pool!' And Pearl, stepping in, mid-leg deep, beheld her own white feet at the bottom; while, out of a still lower depth, came the gleam of a kind of fragmentary smile, floating to and fro in the agitated water" (1:168). At last Pearl decided that "either she or the image was unreal" (1:177).

While Pearl is occupied with this puzzling choice, Hester has sought out Roger Chillingworth and forced him to confront the reversal that has occurred between his real self and his demonic role as Dimmesdale's treacherous friend, a role that he had believed was only a temporary mask but that has now become his "true character," relegating his former self, the loving husband and honored scholar, to the status of mere illusion. Chillingworth says that Dimmesdale "with the superstition common to his brotherhood" had "fancied himself given over to a fiend": "But it was the constant shadow of my presence!—the closest propinquity of the man whom he had most vilely wronged!—and who had grown to exist only by this perpetual poison of the direst revenge!

Yea, indeed!—he did not err!—there was a fiend at his elbow!" (1:172). Hawthorne adds: "The unfortunate physician, while uttering these words, lifted his hands with a look of horror, as if he had beheld some frightful shape, which he could not recognize, usurping the place of his own image in a glass. It was one of those moments ... when a man's moral aspect is faithfully revealed to his mind's eye," a moment in which Chillingworth permitted "the whole evil within him to be written on his features" (1:172–73).

Besides functioning as Dimmesdale's demonic shadow, Chillingworth acts as the minister's double in another sense: like the physician, Dimmesdale himself experiences that reversal of character that occurs when one constantly plays a false role. During nightlong vigils the minister contemplates "his own face in a looking-glass, by the most powerful light which he could throw upon it," thus typifying "the constant introspection wherewith he tortured, but could not purify, himself. In these lengthened vigils, his brain often reeled, and visions seemed to flit before him ... ," but "none of these visions ever quite deluded him. At any moment, by an effort of his will, he could discern substances through their misty lack of substance" (1:145). Yet what Dimmesdale gradually comes to doubt is his own substance, since any man who constantly "shows himself in a false light, becomes a shadow, or, indeed, ceases to exist" (1:146). Concerning the oscillation between Dimmesdale's hypocritical public role and his anguished "inner" self, Hawthorne remarks, "No man, for any considerable period, can wear one face to himself, and another to the multitude, without finally getting bewildered as to which may be the true" (1:216). What Hawthorne questions is the very notion of an "inner" self that is independent of its external image, the tempting illusion of inner depth that leads Pearl to step into the mirroring pool only to find that the other little girl has vanished and that "out of a still lower depth" comes "the gleam of a kind of fragmentary smile." It is the image's lack of sub*stance,* its in*sta*bility, that constitutes the self's unreality. For Dimmesdale this sense of the self's instability puts the whole moral order in play, undermining both the notion of individual responsibility based on the continuity of personality and the concept of a moral sanction based on the survival of the self after death.

The metaphysical implications of the self's dependence upon its public role (upon a visible image) are exhibited in the confrontation between

Hester and Dimmesdale in the forest. Walking back to the village along a shadowy woodland path, Dimmesdale hears his name called: "Throwing his eyes anxiously in the direction of the voice, he indistinctly beheld a form under the trees, clad in garments so sombre, and so little relieved from the gray twilight into which the clouded sky and the heavy foliage had darkened the noontide, that he knew not whether it were a woman or a shadow. It may be, that his pathway through life was haunted thus, by a spectre that had stolen out from among his thoughts" (1:189). As with the misty figure in *Pym,* the first question is whether the shape is a body or an image ("a woman or a shadow"), and then, if an image, whether it is another's shadow or one's own projection ("a spectre that had stolen out from among his thoughts"). Hawthorne immediately places this uncertainty concerning the substantial and the imaginary within the context of personal survival:

> It was no wonder that they thus questioned one another's actual and bodily existence, and even doubted of their own. So strangely did they meet, in the dim wood, that it was like the first encounter, in the world beyond the grave, of two spirits who had been intimately connected in their former life, but now stood coldly shuddering, in mutual dread; as not yet familiar with their state, nor wonted to the companionship of disembodied beings. Each a ghost, and awe-stricken at the other ghost! They were awe-stricken likewise at themselves; because the crisis flung back to them their conscious-ness, and revealed to each heart its history and experience, as life never does, except at such breathless epochs. The soul beheld its features in the mirror of the passing moment. (1:189–90)

As equal partners in an event that has shaped their lives, Dimmesdale and Hester see themselves as both split and doubled in this "mirror of the passing moment," their personal survival somehow being dependent upon a recognition of the other that turns out to be a self-recognition, consciousness "flung back" upon itself. In Hester, Dimmesdale sees the publicly inscribed character that he has concealed, the letter that she wears upon her dress but that he keeps hidden beneath his garment where it eats into his flesh. And in Dimmesdale, Hester sees the visible image of what she has concealed, sees that by hiding the identity of Pearl's father from the community, she has helped to deprive Dimmesdale of his true character and that by hiding Chillingworth's identity from Dimmesdale, she has allowed the minister's bodily existence to be undermined as if by the action of a familiar demon.

By submitting themselves to an otherworldly morality, Hester and Dimmesdale have come to resemble the ghostly inhabitants of "the world beyond the grave," yet what they act out in their forest encounter is a parody of transfiguration and resurrection, a desperate attempt to reject the metaphysical sanction that has transformed them into shadows, and thereby retain the life of the body. When Hester tells Dimmesdale that Chillingworth is her husband, the minister undergoes "a dark transfiguration," frowning at Hester "with all that violence of passion, which— intermixed, in more shapes than one, with his higher, purer, softer qualities—was, in fact, the portion of him which the Devil claimed, and through which he sought to win the rest" (1:194). Suddenly, his strength exhausted, Dimmesdale sinks to the ground as if he is dying. But already a moral shift has begun that will restore Dimmesdale's bodily vitality, for with the revelation of Chillingworth's revenge, Dimmesdale begins to feel justified in comparison: "That old man's revenge has been blacker than my sin"(1:195). Insofar as he recognizes Chillingworth as his dark shadow, Dimmesdale seems to recover a kind of bodily presence; for however unreal his public self, it is more substantial than Chillingworth's; however sinful, it is not demonic.

In this mood, Hester proposes that Dimmesdale leave Salem and start a new life, that he preserve his bodily existence even if it means giving up his identity: "Do any thing, save to lie down and die! Give up this name of Arthur Dimmesdale, and make thyself another, and a high one, such as thou canst wear without fear or shame" (1:198). For Hester, Dimmesdale's name, like the letter on her dress, is a garment that he can "wear" or not as he chooses, a phonetic sign that, because it is only arbitrarily linked to its referent, can be changed for another by finding a new communal context, a new signifying convention. Hester tells Dimmesdale that if he decides to leave, she will go with him; they will recover the life of the body together. In words that are an ironic allusion to the resurrection, Dimmesdale responds to her energy: "'Do I feel joy again?' cried he, wondering at himself. 'Methought the germ of it was dead in me! O Hester, thou art my better angel! I seem to have flung myself— sick, sin-stained, and sorrow-blackened—down upon these forest-leaves, and to have risen up all made anew, and with new powers to glorify Him that hath been merciful! This is already the better life" (1:201–02). Hester now undergoes her own transfiguration and resurrection: she unfastens the scarlet letter and casts it away, and then, "by another impulse," takes off her cap, letting her hair fall upon her shoulders "with at once a shadow and a light in its abundance" (1:202). "Her sex, her youth, the whole richness of her beauty, came back from what men call the irrevocable past," and suddenly "the obscure forest" was flooded with sunshine so that "the objects that had made a shadow hitherto, embodied the brightness now" (1:202–03). Such, says Hawthorne, was the sympathy of "that wild, heathen Nature of the forest" with the lovers, for "love, whether newly born, or aroused from a deathlike slumber, must always create a sunshine" (1:203).

This play of light and dark reverses, of course, the Christian transfiguration of the bodily shadow of death into the radiant, immortal soul, for the shining new life that Hester and Dimmesdale seek is physical rather than metaphysical. The instability of this reversal is immediately foreshadowed by the return of Pearl who, during her parents' interview, has been playing in another part of the woods. Her reappearance, like the first moments of Hester and Dimmesdale's meeting, is described in terms of an uncertainty between body and image. Dimmesdale sees her "standing in a streak of sunshine, a good way off, on the other side of the brook" (1:203). She looks "like a bright-apparelled vision, in a sunbeam": "The ray quivered to and fro, making her figure dim or distinct,—now like a real child, now like a child's spirit,—as the splendor went and came again" (1:203–04).

With Pearl's return the value/meaning of light and dark reverts to a privileging of the spirit over the body. Where Hester and Dimmesdale's *ghostly* appearance was associated with the shadowy obscurity of the forest and their recovery of *bodily* energy (through an implicit rejection of the otherworldly) with the sudden burst of sunshine, Pearl's *bodily* reality is associated with the dimness of the forest and her *spiritual* appearance with the splendor of the light. Hester can cast aside the scarlet letter and Dimmesdale can contemplate changing his name because both letter and name are arbitrary phonetic signs; but Pearl is "the scarlet letter in another form; the scarlet letter endowed with life" and that other form is not phonetic but pictographic, not a sign that is arbitrarily linked to its referent by convention, but one that is necessarily linked by resemblance. And this necessary link cannot be broken unless the referents (Hester and Dimmesdale) alter so drastically that they no longer resemble themselves, change so completely that their former selves have been annihilated, for Pearl is "the oneness of their being" in the sense not just of their mutual union but of their individual sameness as well.

The danger of annihilating their former selves through the change that they contemplate is enacted for Hester and Dimmesdale in another image of an encounter beyond the grave and a nonrecognition of the self. Having reached the brook that separates her from her parents, Pearl refuses to cross:

> Just where she had paused the brook chanced to form a pool, so smooth and quiet that it reflected a perfect image of her little figure, with all the brilliant picturesqueness of her beauty, . . . but more refined and spiritualized than the reality. This image, so nearly identical with the living Pearl, seemed to communicate somewhat of its own shadowy and intangible quality to the child herself. It was strange, the way in which Pearl stood, looking so stedfastly at them through the forest-gloom; herself, meanwhile, all glorified with a ray of sunshine, that was attracted thitherward as by a certain sympathy. In the brook beneath stood another child,—another and the same,—with likewise its ray of golden light. Hester felt herself, in some indistinct and tantalizing manner, estranged from Pearl; as if the child, in her lonely ramble through the forest, had strayed out of the sphere in which she and her mother dwelt together, and was now vainly seeking to return to it.
>
> There was both truth and error in this impression; the child and mother were estranged, but through Hester's fault, not Pearl's. Since the latter rambled from her side, another inmate had been admitted within the circle of the mother's feelings, and so modified the aspect of them all, that Pearl, the returning wanderer, could not find her wonted place, and hardly knew where she was. (1:208)

Observing Pearl's reluctance to cross the stream, Dimmesdale tells Hester that he has "a strange fancy . . . [that] this brook is the boundary between two worlds, and that thou canst never meet thy Pearl again" (1:208). Depicted as antithetical mirror images, the opposing perspectives of Hester and Dimmesdale on one side of the brook and Pearl on the other evoke a problematic coincidence of origin and end. To Hester and Dimmesdale, Pearl, looking "like a bright-apparelled vision . . . all glorified with a ray of sunshine," seems to be a spirit that has reached its ultimate goal in eternal life, while to Pearl the sight of Hester and Dimmesdale together in the forest, each transfigured by the rebirth of physical love, is like a primal scene (consider the sexual overtones of the remark "another inmate had been admitted within the circle of the mother's feelings"), a child's glimpse of the ground from which it originated. (One assumes that this child of nature was conceived on the floor of the forest.) Yet what Pearl sees in this unwitting glimpse of her origin is her own absence; she sees the world prior to her birth and thus cannot "find her wonted place." Her absence from the scene is symbolically represented by the absence of the scarlet letter from her mother's breast. Hester without the letter on her breast is an image of Hester as she was before the adulterous act that gave Pearl life. Cast away by Hester, the embroidered letter lies on the edge of the brook opposite Pearl, "so close upon the margin of the stream, that the gold embroidery was reflected in it" (1:210). The simultaneous reflection in the brook of both Pearl and the letter not only emphasizes their equivalence as inscribed characters but also expresses the symbolist desire, everywhere present in Hawthorne and everywhere put in question, that phonetic script achieve a mimetic correspondence to its referent equivalent in force to the correspondence between a pictographic ideogram and the object whose shape it mirrors.

That the child's reflected image, "so nearly identical with the living Pearl," communicates "somewhat of its own shadowy and intangible quality to the child herself" reminds us that Pearl is Hester's "shadowy reflection," so that Pearl's inability to find herself in this primal scene, her refusal to recognize Hester until her mother puts on the scarlet letter again, mirrors that nonrecognition of herself which the changed Hester would experience in an otherworldly setting. Hester's living image "spiritualized" by the "ray of golden light" no longer reflects this woman newly transfigured by the life of the body. As a "living hieroglyphic," Pearl bears a necessary, pictographic relation to Hester's character and to the central event that has shaped it, and she enforces the continuity of Hester's character by preventing that erasure of the inscription of personal history that Hester seeks in casting aside the letter.

Pearl attempts to enforce this same continuity of identity in Dimmesdale by making the self that he reveals at night and in the shadows of the forest show itself in the daylight world of the village. In the night scene at the scaffold, Pearl asks the minister, "Wilt thou stand here with mother and me, to-morrow noontide?" (1:153). And after the meeting in the forest, she asks her mother, "Will he go back with us, hand in hand, we three together, into the town?" (1:212). Later, when Pearl sees Dimmesdale pass in procession on his way to deliver the Election Day Sermon, she asks, "Mother, . . . was that the same minister that kissed me by the brook?" (1:240), echoing Hester's own thoughts on seeing how different Dimmesdale seems from the man she met in the forest.

That discontinuity between Dimmesdale's public image and his private self, which threatens to dissolve the minister's identity, receives its own hieroglyphic representation in a passage that foreshadows the lengthy descriptions of painting and sculpture found in *The House of the Seven Gables* and *The Marble Faun*. Hawthorne tells us that the walls of Dimmesdale's room "were hung round with tapestry, said to be from the Gobelin looms, and, at all events, representing the Scriptural story of David and Bathsheba, and Nathan the Prophet, in colors still unfaded, but which made the fair woman of the scene almost as grimly picturesque as the woe-denouncing seer" (1:126). The tapestry depicts the moment described in 2 Samuel 12:1–15 when David, having committed adultery with Bathsheba and having arranged for her husband Uriah to be killed in battle, is confronted by the prophet Nathan. Nathan presents David with a veiled picture of himself in the parable of a rich man with many sheep who steals a poor man's only ewe in order to feed a stranger. Not recognizing his own image, David condemns the rich man to death, and Nathan replies, "Thou art the man." When Dimmesdale returns to the village after his meeting in the forest with Hester, he fancies that if he were to be greeted by any of his friends he would tell them that he is not the man they take him for, that the godly minister has been left behind in the forest, "flung down there like a cast-off garment," but that his friends would insist, "Thou art thyself the man!" (1:217).

Dimmesdale's tapestry is a hieroglyph of the novel's central action, evoking the moral doubleness involved in the same man's being both the adulterer and the servant of God who must denounce him. This doubleness is made even more complex by Dimmesdale's equating his true, inner self with the hypocritical adulterer and his false, public role with the godly minister. He thereby creates the morally bewildering opposition true-bad/false-good on which the novel's paradoxical climax is based; for it is Dimmesdale's "hypocritical" persistence in a false, visible role of goodness that allows him at last to redeem his true, "inner" self by

sacrificing, in a single act, both the role and his bodily life. In this interplay of self and image, there is a final ironic reversal: as Nathan de-
nounced the adulterous King David in a parable, so Dimmesdale's de-
nunciation of himself is interpreted by members of his congregation not
as a literal admission of adultery but as "a parable" of man's inherently
unjustified condition in relation to God. So convincing has Dimmesdale
been in the role of the godly minister that he has lost the credibility
needed to reveal his own sinfulness.

Dimmesdale's sense of the instability of a moral order that is based on
the mutually constitutive opposition of good and evil and on a belief in
the continuity of the self is presented most explicitly upon his return to
the village from his forest meeting with Hester. Suddenly, all the familiar objects of the village have a changed aspect: "The minister's deepest
sense seemed to inform him of their mutability. A similar impression
struck him most remarkably, as he passed under the walls of his own
church. The edifice had so very strange, and yet so familiar, an aspect,
that Mr. Dimmesdale's mind vibrated between two ideas; either that he
had seen it only in a dream hitherto, or that he was merely dreaming
about it now" (1:216–17). Hawthorne adds, "This phenomenon, in the
various shapes which it assumed, indicated no external change," but a
sudden and important "change in the spectator of the familiar scene, . . .
a revolution in the sphere of thought and feeling, . . . a total change of
dynasty and moral code, in that interior kingdom" (1:217). In this altered condition Dimmesdale feels like committing "some strange, wild,
wicked" act, "with a sense that it would be at once involuntary and
intentional; in spite of himself, yet growing out of a profounder self than
that which opposed the impulse" (1:217). Meeting an aged member of
his congregation, Dimmesdale feels a compulsion to whisper in her ear
"a brief, pithy, and, as it then appeared to him, unanswerable argument
against the immortality of the human soul" (1:219). This sudden change
in emotional perspective causing a doubt of both the reality of appearance and the continuity of the observing self (a continuity basic to the
notion of personal survival) is summed up by Whitman in one of the
Calamus poems:

> Of the terrible doubt of appearances,
> Of the uncertainty after all, that we may be deluded,
> That may-be reliance and hope are but speculations
>   after all,

That may-be identity beyond the grave is a beautiful
    fable only,
May-be the things I perceive, the animals, plants, men,
    hills, shining and flowing waters,
The skies of day and night, colors, densities, forms,
    may-be these are (as doubtless they are) only
    apparitions, and the real something has yet to be known,
(How often they dart out of themselves as if to confound
    me and mock me!
How often I think neither I know, nor any man knows,
    aught of them,)
May-be seeming to me what they are (as doubtless they
    indeed but seem) as from my present point of view,
    and might prove (as of course they would) nought of
    what they appear, or nought anyhow, from entirely
    changed points of view. . . .

                                                    (7:120)

That liminal condition in which "Dimmesdale's mind vibrated between
two ideas"—either that he had been "in a dream hitherto" or that he was
dreaming now—a condition induced by the oscillation of light and dark
in the lawless, natural world of the forest, recalls the situation of the
central figure in Hawthorne's short story "Young Goodman Brown"
(1835). At night in the woods outside Salem, Goodman Brown sees or
dreams he sees a witches' coven attended by many of the village's most
pious citizens. His belief in the reality of daytime appearances undermined, Goodman Brown steps forward to be initiated into the company
of devil worshipers and finds that his wife Faith is there for the same
purpose. A satanic figure addresses the husband and wife: "Depending
upon one another's hearts, ye had still hoped, that virtue were not all a
dream. Now are ye undeceived! Evil is the nature of mankind" (10:88).
At the last moment before their baptism, Brown repents and adjures his
wife: "Faith! Faith! . . . Look up to Heaven, and resist the Wicked One"
(10:88). Suddenly the gathering vanishes, and Brown is left alone in the
dark forest. The next morning "Goodman Brown came slowly into the
street of Salem village, staring around him like a bewildered man"
(10:88). What Brown has seen by firelight in the shadowy forest has
made him doubt the moral privileging of light over dark by putting in

question its epistemological basis—the privileging of the daylight world of waking consciousness as enduring, bodily reality over the night-time world of dreams and visions as illusory appearance. "Had Goodman Brown fallen asleep in the forest, and only dreamed a wild dream of a witch-meeting?" asks Hawthorne. "Be it so if you will. But, alas! it was a dream of evil omen for young Goodman Brown. A stern, a sad, a darkly meditative, a distrustful, if not a desperate man did he become, from the night of that fearful dream" (10:89).

Brown's fear that his wife Faith was lost to the powers of darkness at the witch meeting is itself the loss of faith it fears. What Brown's wife represents is a faith (like that of the doubting apostle Thomas) grounded on the sense of touch, that sense upon which man falls back when he begins to doubt the testimony of his other senses. At one point in his forest sojourn, Goodman Brown thinks he hears the voices of the minister and the deacon of his church passing through the woods on their way to the devil worship: "Young Goodman Brown caught hold of a tree, for support, being ready to sink down on the ground, faint and overburthened with the heavy sickness of his heart. He looked up to the sky, doubting whether there really was a Heaven above him. Yet, there was the blue arch, and the stars brightening in it. 'With Heaven above, and Faith below, I will yet stand firm against the devil!' cried Goodman Brown" (10:82). In the pairing "Heaven above and Faith below" (which may be an ironic allusion to Kant's "The starry heavens above and the moral law within"), Brown's wife represents the stable ground on which his belief in heavenly goodness stands. As the being with whom Brown is in the most intimate physical contact, Faith is associated in the first half of the story with the sense of touch and its power to verify the solid presence of bodily reality and dispel the illusory appearances of disturbing dreams. Having seen and heard things in the forest that make him wonder if he is dreaming, Brown thinks "what calm sleep would be his, that very night," if instead of leaving home he had spent it "purely and sweetly . . . in the arms of Faith!" (10:80–81). But after "seeing" Faith at the witch meeting, Brown realizes that even the sense of touch cannot provide him with any certainty about things that lie beyond his senses. However close the physical contact between Brown and Faith, her thoughts remain beyond Brown's observation unless she chooses to express them. Yet precisely because her thoughts *are* beyond his direct observation, he can never be certain that what she visibly expresses corresponds to her true inner life. Faith, as she appears in Salem village, may simply be acting a false role, while Faith, as she appears at night in the forest, may be showing her true character.

The uncertainty that Brown feels about Faith's invisible inner life applies as well to the invisible otherworld of religious belief. Brown's vision in the forest makes him suspect that the supreme power in the invisible world is not good but evil, or at least that evil is a coequal power, ruling in darkness as goodness rules in the light. Yet it is as impossible for Brown to verify the correspondence between the visible and invisible worlds as it is for him to verify the correspondence between Faith's inner and outer lives. Brown faces a dilemma. A religious faith based on the testimony of the senses is—as Jesus makes clear when the apostle Thomas refuses to believe unless he touches the resurrected body—no faith at all, for if faith in God means belief in a Being who is essentially imageless, belief in a supersensual world, then faith cannot be grounded on sense perception. Indeed, its ultimate test would be the ability to stand firm in one's belief even when it was contradicted by the testimony of the senses. True faith should have enabled Brown to believe in his wife's good character in spite of the appearances that he had seen by firelight in the forest, should have enabled him to classify those appearances as demonic hallucinations or dreams.

Yet if the real test of metaphysical faith is to believe in spite of physical appearances, it is just as true that faith, understood as an unwavering certainty of conviction, becomes a meaningless concept, a word emptied of significance, if separated from a belief in the reality of physical appearances. For if we doubt the testimony of our senses, what would convince us? What would the word "convince" mean? What more basic ground than sense experience could we fall back on to provide the referent for the word? All that one could appeal to would be an inner feeling or intuition, a purely subjective state, as when Descartes, unable to verify the real existence of external objects, falls back upon the thinking subject's certainty of its own existence. Yet the difficulty is that subject and object, as reciprocal opposites, cannot be wholly separated. There cannot be a purely subjective state. Moreover, without an implicit belief in the reality of physical appearances and in the kind of reality-testing (for example, touch) associated with waking consciousness, there exists no means of differentiating between subjective states, no way of distinguishing thinking from dreaming and thus of affirming anything certain about the subject's mode of being. That is, Descartes' "I think, therefore I am" as an example of certain knowledge already assumes that the subject is certain that he is thinking as opposed to dreaming or hallucinating, yet the differentiation of thinking from other subjective states depends upon an implicit privileging of waking consciousness (and its various modes of testing) as the norm, just as that notion of stable, certain being which Descartes affirms of the thinking subject derives its meaning from the being of waking consciousness. Consequently, if the real existence of the external world is uncertain, the existence of the thinking subject is equally uncertain.

This sudden unhinging of the stable world, the oscillation between faith and skepticism caused by a shadowy glimpse of the interdependence and reversibility of the moral-epistemological poles of light and dark, is evoked by Melville in a chapter from *Pierre* entitled "More Light, and the Gloom of That Light. More Gloom, and the Light of That Gloom":

> In those hyperborean regions, to which enthusiastic Truth, and Earnestness, and Independence, will invariably lead a mind fitted by nature for profound and fearless thought, all objects are seen in a dubious, uncertain, and refracting light. Viewed through that rarefied atmosphere the most immemorially admitted maxims of men begin to slide and fluctuate, and finally become wholly inverted; the very heavens themselves being not innocent of producing this confounding effect, since it is mostly in the heavens themselves that these wonderful mirages are exhibited.
>
> But the example of many minds forever lost, like undiscoverable Arctic explorers, amid those treacherous regions, warns us entirely away from them; and we learn that it is not for man to follow the trail of truth too far, since by so doing he entirely loses the directing compass of his mind; for arrived at the Pole, to whose barrenness only it points, the needle indifferently respects all points of the horizon alike. (P. 165)

Though the initial image is that of the northern lights, the passage as a whole suggests scenes as disparate as Pym's confrontation with the white shadow in the polar mist, the reversal of the compass near the end of

Moby-Dick, and the meteoric appearance during the midnight encounter at the scaffold in *The Scarlet Letter*—scenes in which the familiar suddenly becomes unfamiliar and thus uncertain in the profoundest sense.

When Dimmesdale returns to his "accustomed room" with "its books, its windows, its fireplace, and the tapestried comfort of the walls," he is affected by "the same perception of strangeness that had haunted him throughout his walk from the forest-dell into town" (1:222), though now this uncanny sense of the unfamiliarity of familiar objects is explicitly related to a division in the self manifested by a written text. Dimmesdale sees on the table "an unfinished sermon, with a sentence broken in the midst" and thinks that "it was himself, the thin and white-cheeked minister" who had "written thus far into the Election Sermon! But he seemed to stand apart, and eye this former self with scornful, pitying, but half-envious curiosity. That self was gone! Another man had returned out of the forest; a wiser one; with a knowledge of hidden mysteries which the simplicity of the former never could have reached" (1:223). As Dimmesdale looks at the "tapestried comfort of the walls" and then at his unfinished manuscript, Hawthorne encourages the reader to equate the pictograph embroidered on the veil and its revelation of Dimmesdale's double role with the phonetic script of Dimmesdale's text and its manifestation of his divided self. The internally split / externally doubled terms of this equation are Hawthorne's means of questioning the symbolist effort to make opaque phonetic script achieve a force of expression equivalent to the necessary transparency of a pictograph. For Hawthorne implies that a pictograph's transparency is simply the uncertain, illusory transparency of a mirror image.

Hawthorne's most concentrated examination of the mystery of a mirror image is found in the sketch "Monsieur du Miroir" (1837). Treating his reflection as if it were another person, Hawthorne communicates some of its pictographic doubleness to the phonetic script of his text in the form of endlessly proliferating double meanings. Thus he says of Monsieur du Miroir that "there is nobody, in the whole circle of my acquaintance, whom I have more attentively studied, yet of whom I have less real knowledge, beneath the surface which it pleases him to present" (10:159). Doubting "whether M. du Miroir have aught of humanity but the figure," Hawthorne complains of "his impenetrable mystery" (10:159–60). Although he acknowledges Miroir's pictographic sameness, noting that he "bears, indisputably, a strong personal resemblance to myself," Hawthorne points out Miroir's phonetic difference: "His name would indicate a French descent; in which case, infinitely preferring that my blood should flow from a bold British and pure Puritan source, I beg leave to disclaim all kindred with M. du Miroir. Some genealogists trace his origin to Spain, and dub him a knight of the order of the Caballeros de los Espejoz, one of whom was overthrown by Don Quixote" (10:160). Besides evoking the opaque arbitrariness of phonetic script—its concealment of the sameness of meaning (the mirror image) beneath a difference in translation (Monsieur du Miroir, Caballero de los Espejoz)—the passage also suggests, through its location of Miroir's genealogical origin in a fictive character, that the reflected image Hawthorne has in mind is less the visual twin in his mirror than the hieroglyphic double constituted by his own writings. He observes that the principal cause of the phonetic difference between himself and his pictographic double is that Miroir, like Narcissus's image in the pool, "lacks the faculty of speech": "His lips are sometimes seen to move; his eyes and countenance are alive with shifting expression, as if corresponding by visible hieroglyphics to his modulated breath; and anon, he will seem to pause, with as satisfied an air, as if he had been talking excellent sense" (10:160).

Beginning with the reference to his image's shifting expressions as "visible hieroglyphics," Hawthorne brings together, within the space of a few pages, virtually all the structural elements and imagery associated with hieroglyphic doubling by the writers of the American Renaissance. Said to be possessed by a "dumb devil," Miroir is depicted as Hawthorne's daemonic other, the bodily image of Hawthorne's fate: "The singular and minute coincidences that occur, both in the accidents of the passing day and the serious events of our lives, remind me of those doubtful legends of lovers, or twin-children, twins of fate, who have lived, enjoyed, suffered, and died, in unison, each faithfully repeating the last tremor of the other's breath, though separated by vast tracts of sea and land" (10:161). As one might expect from Monsieur du Miroir's narcissistic background, he exhibits an inordinate "fondness for water," an absolute determination to "souse himself over head and ears, wherever he may meet with it" (10:163). Speculating that Miroir may be "a merman, or born of a mermaid's marriage with a mortal, and thus amphibious by hereditary right," Hawthorne remarks: "Wandering along lonesome paths, or in pathless forests, when I have come to virgin-fountains, of which it would have been pleasant to deem myself the first discoverer, I have started to find M. du Miroir there before me. The solitude seemed lonelier for his presence. . . . Were I to reach the sources of the Nile, I should expect to meet him there" (10:163–64). As the image of originality metamorphoses from the preempted discovery of a virgin fountain into the quest for the fountains that are the origin of the Nile, one can predict, given the symbolic association of the Nile's source with the simultaneous origin of self and image, Hawthorne's comment that his fate and Miroir's "appear inseparably blended. It is my belief, as I find him mingling with my earliest recollections, that we came into existence together, as my shadow follows me into the sunshine, and that, hereafter, as heretofore, the brightness or gloom of my fortunes will shine upon, or darken, the face of M. du Miroir" (10:166). He concludes that "had not our union been a necessary condition of our life, we must have been estranged ere now" (10:168).

Yet this simultaneous origin confronts Hawthorne with a fundamental indeterminacy as to whether he originates Miroir's actions or Miroir his, confronts him with the reversibility of self and image: "Is it too wild a thought, that my fate may have assumed this image of myself, and therefore haunts me with such inevitable pertinacity, originating every act which it appears to imitate, while it deludes me by pretending to share the events, of which it is merely the emblem and prophecy? . . . So inimitably does he counterfeit, that I could almost doubt which of us is the visionary form, or whether each be not the other's mystery, and both twin brethren of one fate, in mutually reflected spheres" (10:168, 170–71). Hawthorne associates Miroir with a series of natural optical phenomena basic to the scenario of unrecognized self-projection and already familiar to us from Poe: "Shape of mystery, did the tremor of my heart-strings vibrate to thine own, and call thee from thy home, among the dancers of the Northern Lights, and shadows flung from departed sunshine, and giant spectres that appear on clouds at daybreak and affright the climber of the Alps?" (10:170).

As the reversal of self and image is one of the possibilities raised by Miroir's presence, so the substitution of images is another. Hawthorne observes: "Many former instances are recorded, in successive ages, of similar connections between ordinary mortals and beings possessing the attributes of M. du Miroir. Some now alive, perhaps, besides myself, have such attendants. Would that M. du Miroir could be persuaded to transfer his attachment to one of those, and allow some other of his race to assume the situation he now holds in regard to me! If I must needs have so intrusive an intimate, who stares me in the face in my closest privacy, and follows me even to my bed chamber, I should prefer— scandal apart—the laughing bloom of a young girl, to the dark and bearded gravity of my present companion" (10:166). That Miroir's role is equivalent to, is a substitute for, that of the female beloved sheds light on Hawthorne's earlier remark that he and Miroir were "twins of fate," like "lovers, or twin-children." Besides recalling the version of the Narcissus myth from Pausanias, in which Narcissus mistakes his image for that of his dead twin sister, this substitution of female for male explains Miroir's later reversal of roles, as the pursuing daemon becomes the guiding Psyche: "Reflecting upon his power of following me to the remotest regions and into the deepest privacy, I will compare the attempt to escape him to the hopeless race that men sometimes run with memory, or their own hearts, or their moral selves, which, though burdened with cares enough to crush an elephant, will never be one step behind. I will be self-contemplative, as nature bids me, and make him the picture or visible type of what I muse upon, that my mind may not wander so vaguely as heretofore, chasing its own shadow through a chaos, and catching only the monsters that abide there" (10:169-70).

As Hawthorne and Miroir "came into existence together," so Hawthorne says that his death will be Miroir's end as well. But the destiny of these "twins of fate" divides at this point in a curious and contradictory fashion. Hawthorne remarks, "When the ray of Heaven shall bless me no more, nor the thoughtful lamplight gleam upon my studies, nor the cheerful fireside gladden the meditative man, then, his task fulfilled, shall this mysterious being vanish from the earth forever. He will pass to the dark realm of Nothingness, but will not find me there" (10:167). Although the apparent meaning of the last sentence is that at death Miroir will be annihilated, while Hawthorne will survive in the bright realm of Being that is the opposite of "the dark realm of Nothingness," the metaphor of annihilation as nonrecognition of the self ("but will not find me there"), that is, the mirror image's inability to find (reflect) the self in darkness, implicitly raises the question of how Hawthorne could survive in the realm of pure light, how he could recognize himself, without an image.

What makes this apparent annihilation of Miroir at death especially

curious is that earlier Hawthorne had described Miroir's "power of gliding through all impediments" in terms reminiscent of the appearance of
Christ's resurrected body to the disciples in the locked room: "Brick
walls, and oaken doors, and iron bolts, are no impediment to his passage.
Here in my chamber, for instance, as the evening deepens into night, I
sit alone—the key turned and withdrawn from the lock—the keyhole
stuffed with paper, to keep out a peevish little blast of wind. Yet, lonely
as I seem, were I to lift one of the lamps and step five paces eastward, M.
du Miroir would be sure to meet me, with a lamp also in his hand"
(10:164–65). And later, Hawthorne proposes Miroir as "an illustration, if
not an argument" for the reality of the spiritual world:

> . . . as we have only the testimony of the eye to M. du Miroir's
> existence, while all the other senses would fail to inform us that such
> a figure stands within arm's length, wherefore should there not be
> beings innumerable, close beside us, and filling heaven and earth
> with their multitude, yet of whom no corporeal perception can take
> cognizance? A blind man might as reasonably deny that M. du
> Miroir exists, as we, because the Creator has hitherto withheld the
> spiritual perception, can therefore contend that there are no spirits.
> Oh, there are! And, at this moment, when the subject of which I
> write has grown strong within me, and surrounded itself with those
> solemn and awful associations which might have seemed most alien
> to it, I could fancy that M. du Miroir himself is a wanderer from the
> spiritual world, with nothing human, except his delusive garment of
> visibility. Methinks I should tremble now, were his wizard power, of
> gliding through all impediments in search of me, to place him sud-
> denly before my eyes. (10:170)

The contradiction between Miroir's being annihilated in "the dark
realm of Nothingness" and his serving as an "illustration" (Latin *illus-
trare,* "to light up, illuminate") of the spiritual world's reality accounts for
the oscillations in the argument as Hawthorne, shifting from one trope
to another, makes Miroir illustrative in a double sense. As a "being" who
cannot be perceived by four of the five senses, Miroir serves first to
illustrate the possible existence of beings who are entirely beyond sense
perception. Yet Hawthorne is aware that not only is this not an argument
for the real existence of spiritual beings, it is not even, strictly speaking,
an illustration, since the kind of existence that Miroir possesses is depen-

dent both on the material body of which it is a reflected image and on the mirror of consciousness in which the mirror image of the body is re-reflected; while the essence of that spiritual existence whose reality he affirms is precisely its independence, its transcendence, of both matter and human consciousness.

But there is another, indirect sense in which Miroir illustrates the "reality" of the spiritual world, and it is upon this sense that Hawthorne falls back in remarking that "when the subject of which I write has grown strong within me, and surrounded itself with those solemn and awful associations which might have seemed most alien to it, I could fancy that M. du Miroir himself is a wanderer from the spiritual world, with nothing human, except his delusive garment of visibility." There is, one would suspect, a double meaning in the phrase "the subject of which I write," for in the mirror-sketch "Monsieur du Miroir," Hawthorne's own subjectivity is the subject of his writing—his temporal, ceaselessly mobile writing self imaged and observed (that is, held in an illusorily enduring mental existence) as written self, Hawthorne as "Miroir" as *Hawthorne.* To treat the living, temporal subject as a dead, spatial image is to surround the self with "those solemn and awful associations which might have seemed most alien to it"—the writer's paradoxical attempt to survive through the undying (because nonliving, alien) image of his own death. It is, then, precisely as an image that Miroir obliquely "illustrates" the spiritual world's real mode of existence in this world, its wholly mental existence in our contradictory (that is, self-annihilating) *idea* of the self after death as an immaterial (which is to say, mental and thus physically invisible) image that is not only disembodied but wholly separated from that physically grounded mental life from which it sprang— an apotheosized image translated from the mirror of the mind to the realm of the Other.

In imagining Miroir as "a wanderer from the spiritual world, *with nothing human, except his delusive garment of visibility*" (italics mine), Hawthorne erases the point of his supposed illustration; for in making the visibility of an image the crucial difference between the human world and the invisible world beyond death, he implicitly characterizes the spiritual world as one to which the personal self could have no access. Whatever exists in the spiritual world, nothing that we could recognize as human, nothing possessing the means of self-recognition, could persist from our world into that realm. Since this "illustration" of the reality of the spiritual world is, in terms of personal survival, as unsatisfactory as the first, Hawthorne, in doubting Thomas fashion, asks Miroir for a sign of his substantial existence, the proof of touch:

> Oh, friend, canst thou not hear and answer me? Break down the barrier between us! Grasp my hand! Speak! Listen! A few words, perhaps, might satisfy the feverish yearning of my soul for some master-thought, that should guide me through this labyrinth of life, teaching wherefore I was born, and how to do my task on earth, and what is death. Alas! Even that unreal image should forget to ape me, and smile at these vain questions.—Thus do mortals deify, as it were, a mere shadow of themselves, a spectre of human reason, and ask of that to unveil the mysteries, which Divine Intelligence has revealed so far as needful to our guidance, and hid the rest.
>
> Farewell, Monsieur du Miroir! Of you, perhaps, as of many men, it may be doubted whether you are the wiser, though your whole business is Reflection (10:171)

Having dismissed Miroir as an apotheosized shadow of self-reflective thought, Hawthorne has in that same act voided our "image" of God, so that with the shadowy figure removed from the ground, the image from the mirror, we are left with the unfigured and unfigurable ground, the humanly unintelligible "Divine Intelligence," as pure light devoid of any delineating dark outline, an object not for reason's scrutiny but for faith's self-affirming affirmations as in Hawthorne's conclusion. Yet earlier in the sketch Hawthorne has twice raised the question of his own credibility regarding the events of the narrative. At the beginning he says, "However extraordinary, marvellous, preternatural, and utterly incredible, some of the meditative disclosures may appear, I pledge my honor to maintain as sacred a regard to fact, as if my testimony were given on oath, and involved the dearest interests of the person in question" (10:159–60). And midway in the piece he adds: "I have endeavored to pave the way for stranger things to come, which, had they been disclosed at once, M. du Miroir might have been deemed a shadow, and myself a person of no veracity, and this truthful history a fabulous legend. But, now that the reader knows me worthy of his confidence, I will begin to make him stare" (10:164). Hawthorne has so closely linked his own credibility, his own image, to the truth of Miroir's story that when he dismisses Miroir at the end as "that unreal image, . . . a spectre of human reason" in order to affirm his belief in the unintelligible Divine Intelligence, the reader can only wonder if Hawthorne has intentionally undermined the ground of credibility from which he makes his leap of faith. For if Hawthorne rejects Miroir (who was to have illustrated the reality of the spiritual world) as a fantastic being, a delusive image without a body, why should we then accept his testimony concerning the existence of an even more fantastic being who lacks both an image and a body? Should the ending of "Monsieur du Miroir" remind us, as do so many other moments in Hawthorne and Melville, indeed as does the whole of *The Confidence-Man,* of Nietzsche's remark that the subtlest way to argue against a position is to argue in its favor—but badly?

Keeping in mind Hawthorne's phonetic veiling of his mirror image as the fictive "Monsieur du Miroir," let us return to Dimmesdale, whom we left standing in his room between the pictographic tapestry revealing his double role and the phonetic script of his unfinished text manifesting his divided self. As we noted earlier, it is an uncanny moment for Dimmesdale, one filled with a "perception of strangeness," a sudden awareness of self-alienation and the unfamiliarity of familiar objects. But it is an uncanny moment for the reader as well, a moment whose imagery, at once familiar and strange, seems to be a veiled repetition of the book's opening moment—Hawthorne's explanation of the "autobiographical impulse" that moved him to write about the novel's origin in "The Custom-House." Hawthorne says that when an author "casts his leaves forth upon the wind" he addresses

> . . . not the many who will fling aside his volume, or never take it up, but the few who will understand him, better than most of his schoolmates and lifemates. Some authors, indeed, do far more than this, and indulge themselves in such confidential depths of revelation as could fittingly be addressed, only and exclusively, to the one heart and mind of perfect sympathy; as if the printed book, thrown at large on the wide world, were certain to find out the divided segment of the writer's own nature, and complete his circle of existence by bringing him into communion with it. It is scarcely decorous, however, to speak all, even when we speak impersonally. But—as thoughts are frozen and utterance benumbed, unless the speaker stand in some true relation with his audience—it may be

pardonable to imagine that a friend, a kind and apprehensive, though not the closest friend, is listening to our talk; and then, a native reserve being thawed by this genial consciousness, we may prate of the circumstances that lie around us, and even of ourself, but still keep the inmost Me behind its veil. (1:3-4)

The shifts in Hawthorne's imagery are enlightening. The Shelleyan trope of casting the leaves of the book to the wind turns into an image of sowing and winnowing (the separation of the chosen few who understand the author from the indifferent many), a process whose ideal goal would be to unite the writer with that "one heart and mind of perfect sympathy," the spouse of his inmost self. Yet to achieve this ideal match of writer and reader, the writer would have to reveal his inmost self, an act that would leave him dangerously vulnerable and that would embarrass all those who are not the one reader "of perfect sympathy." The image of winnowing leads into the image of the veil ("such confidential depths of revelation"), and this in turn leads to the image of the book as an unveiling of the writer's divided nature, a division that the book seeks to heal by discovering, in *symbolon* fashion, the divided half of the writer's self and reuniting the two so as to complete the author's "circle of existence."

The image of the self as half of a circle seeking communion with its divided half suggests the Platonic myth of primordial man's division by Zeus. In the *Symposium* (190ff.), Aristophanes relates that originally "each of these beings was globular in shape, with rounded back and sides, four arms and four legs, and two faces, both the same" (p. 542). Because they tried to "scale the heights of heaven" and overthrow the gods, Zeus split each of the spherical beings in two, leaving the halves with "a desperate yearning for each other" (p. 543). Zeus allowed the divided beings to mate, and Aristophanes comments, "Our innate love for one another . . . is always trying to redintegrate our former nature, to make two into one, and to bridge the gulf between one human being and another" (p. 544). Aristophanes then explicitly links this process of rematching the divided halves of human nature to the image of the *symbolon*, a divided coin or token whose broken edges are matched as a sign of recognition, the Greek root of the word "symbol": "We are all like pieces of the coins that children break in half for keepsakes—making two out of one, like the flatfish—and each of us is forever seeking the half that will tally with himself" (p. 544). In a book as concerned with the hiero-glyphics as *The Scarlet Letter,* it is only appropriate that Hawthorne's dis-cussion of the work's origin should invoke this myth of the divided being's search for reunion as an image for that "communion" which the book seeks to achieve between the writer's inmost self and the reader "of perfect sympathy," for it is a myth that figures both human origin and the origin of symbolization as a simultaneous act of splitting and doubl-ing.

One should be properly skeptical of Hawthorne's stated intention to "keep the inmost Me behind its veil," since if the remark is true, that process of veiling has been at work from the very first word of "The Custom-House" section and thus his expressed intention to conceal "the inmost Me" is part of that deceptive process. Indeed, Hawthorne tells us in a veiled manner what he really desires—that *The Scarlet Letter* seek out "the one heart and mind of perfect sympathy" and bring this "divided segment of the writer's own nature" into "communion" with itself. But he also tells us that this communion with the reader of perfect sympathy is not to be achieved by an overt act of self-revelation. What Hawthorne intends is a veiled unveiling of "the inmost Me," not a drawing back of the veil, but an imprinting on the veil's surface of a hieroglyph of what lies "behind" it, a pictographic cipher addressed to "the few who will understand him." Hawthorne's use of the veil image to characterize the concealment of his inmost self in the text should put us on our guard, since the various instances of writing on the veil's surface that occur later in the work—ranging from the enigmatic letter on Hester's dress, to the same letter repeated on the "veil of cloud" in the midnight scaffold scene, to the pictographic tapestry in Dimmesdale's room—point up the problematic nature of both veiling and revelation.

The image of the veil is, of course, one of the great recurring tropes in Hawthorne's work from "The Minister's Black Veil" (1836) onward. In its major occurrences the image of veiling a face or figure is usually accompanied by a phonetic veiling, the use of an assumed name to conceal a character's true identity. We noted earlier Hawthorne's refer-ence, in *The Blithedale Romance,* to Zenobia's pen name as "a sort of mask in which she comes before the world, retaining all the privileges of privacy—a contrivance, in short, like the white drapery of the Veiled Lady, only a little more transparent" and the way that this develops into the image of Zenobia's "hieroglyphic" shadow inscribed on the curtain.

In *The House of the Seven Gables* (1851), the image of a hieroglyphic character on the front of a veil is provided by the portrait of Colonel Pyncheon. Hawthorne describes the portrait's effect on Hepzibah Pyncheon in terms of a simultaneous veiling/unveiling:

> In one sense, this picture had almost faded into the canvas, and hidden itself behind the duskiness of age; in another, she could not but fancy that it had been growing more prominent, and strikingly expressive, ever since her earliest familiarity with it, as a child. For, while the physical substance and outline were darkening away from the beholder's eye, the bold, hard, and, at the same time, indirect character of the man seemed to be brought out in a kind of spiritual relief. Such an effect may occasionally be observed in pictures of antique date. They acquire a look which an artist (if he have anything like the complacency of artists, now-a-days) would never dream of presenting to a patron as his own characteristic expression, but which, nevertheless, we at once recognize as reflecting the unlovely truth of a human soul. In such cases, the painter's deep conception of his subject's inward traits has wrought itself into the essence of the picture, and is seen, after the superficial coloring has been rubbed off by time. (2:58–59)

Contrasting his own method of portraiture with that of an oil painter, the daguerreotypist Holgrave shows Phoebe Pyncheon a picture that he has made of her cousin Jaffrey and remarks: "There is a wonderful insight in Heaven's broad and simple sunshine. While we give it credit only for depicting the merest surface, it actually brings out the secret character with a truth that no painter would ever venture upon, even could he detect it" (2:91). The dual irony of Holgrave's remark is that Phoebe promptly mistakes the daguerreotype likeness for the portrait of Colonel Pyncheon, while Holgrave, vaunting the daguerreotype's ability to reveal "secret character," conceals his own character behind a phonetic veil, the name Holgrave masking his true identity as a descendant of the Maules. Further, because of his descent Holgrave knows the deepest and most problematic sense in which Colonel Pyncheon's portrait is a hieroglyphic veil concealing a secret character, knows that behind the canvas there is a compartment in which his ancestor, the son of Matthew Maule, hid the Indian deed granting a large Eastern territory to the Pyncheons, "a folded sheet of parchment . . . an ancient deed, signed with the hieroglyphics of several Indian sagamores" (2:316). For genera-

tions the descendants of Colonel Pyncheon have searched for the missing parchment with its hieroglyphic signatures, the written characters
of the original "deed" thus coming to symbolize a character trait in
Colonel Pyncheon (the greed that dispossessed both Maule and the Indians of their land) reinscribed from generation to generation in the
characters of his descendants. In the preface Hawthorne says that the
moral of his story is "the truth . . . that the wrong-doing of one generation lives into the successive ones, and, divesting itself of every temporary advantage, becomes a pure and uncontrollable mischief" (2:2).

In *The Scarlet Letter* Roger Chillingworth is the obvious example of that
phonetic veiling of character in an alias that usually accompanies the
image of the hieroglyph inscribed on the veil's surface. Yet there is in the
novel a less obvious instance of such phonetic concealment that directly
pertains to Hawthorne's veiled unveiling of his inmost self. I refer to the
masking of Hawthorne's authorship behind the name of the historical
figure Jonathan Pue. By presenting himself as the revisor of Jonathan
Pue's manuscript, Hawthorne surely does not intend to fool anyone.
Rather, the transparent fiction of Hawthorne's editorship obliquely
points to his own ambivalence about the role of an author, and in particular to his uneasiness about *his* authorship of the story of Hester
Prynne. For what the introductory section makes clear is that Hawthorne's
tenure as surveyor of customs represented a crisis in his career as a
writer not simply for economic reasons but for psychological reasons
deeply related to the resemblance that emerges between Hawthorne, as
he describes himself in the introduction, and the central character of his
novel.

Like his earlier job in the Boston Custom House (1839–41), Hawthorne's post in Salem (1846–49) grew out of his inability to support
himself as a writer. Though Hawthorne makes no explicit reference to
his financial difficulties in the introduction, he does draw a sharp contrast between himself as a writer and his two most illustrious and successful ancestors—William Hathorne, who had been speaker of the house of
deputies, and his son John, one of the judges at the Salem witch trials—a
contrast based in part on the Puritan opposition between art and business. Hawthorne imagines the judgment that these two substantial citizens would have passed on their impecunious descendant:

> . . . either of these stern and black-browed Puritans would have
> thought it quite a sufficient retribution for his sins, that, after so

long a lapse of years, the old trunk of the family tree, with so much
venerable moss on it, should have borne, as its topmost bough, an
idler like myself. No aim, that I have ever cherished, would they
recognize as laudable; no success of mine—if my life, beyond its
domestic scope, had ever been brightened by success—would they
deem otherwise than worthless, if not positively disgraceful. "What
is he?" murmurs one gray shadow of my forefathers to the other. "A
writer of story-books! What kind of a business in life,—what mode
of glorifying God, or being serviceable to mankind in his day and
generation,—may that be? Why, the degenerate fellow might as well
have been a fiddler!" Such are the compliments bandied between
my great-grandsires and myself, across the gulf of time! And yet, let
them scorn me as they will, strong traits of their nature have intertwined themselves with mine. (1:10)

Beneath such epithets as "idler," "worthless," "disgraceful," "degenerate," and the question "What is he?" lies the unspoken question, "What
kind of work is this for a *man,* to be an artist, a writer of story-books?" In
Hawthorne's day, as in that of his ancestors, financial dependence in
adulthood was a feminine characteristic, and in terms of the Puritan
work ethic the role of the artist—insofar as it involves sensitivity and
sympathy, the love of beauty, an observer's passivity, and long periods of
rumination outwardly indistinguishable from idleness—has always been
considered a feminine role, whatever the sex of the person who assumes
it. The stern Puritan fathers who would have disapproved of Hawthorne
the writer are the same people who condemn his written character Hester, marking her with a publicly inscribed character of their own. On
first examining the embroidered letter, Hawthorne is struck by the
"wonderful skill" of its handiwork, its "evidence of a now forgotten art,"
thus establishing Hester as a symbolic artist in letters long before we
meet her in any other capacity. Hawthorne's uncanny sympathy with
Hester is presented in the same passage, when he places the embroidered letter on his chest: "It seemed to me, then, that I experienced a
sensation not altogether physical, yet almost so, as of burning heat; and
as if the letter were not of red cloth, but red-hot iron. I shuddered, and
involuntarily let it fall upon the floor" (1:32). The art that Hester
lavishes on the embroidered letter is meant to express her defiance of
the townspeople of Salem—who interpret it precisely that way, one ma-
tron remarking that through her "good skill at her needle" Hester has

made "a pride out of what" was "meant for a punishment" (1:54). Hawthorne makes his own feelings about the people of Salem clear at the end of "The Custom-House." Bidding farewell to his native place, he says, "My good townspeople will not much regret me; for—though it has been as dear an object as any, in my literary efforts, to be of some importance in their eyes, and to win myself a pleasant memory in this abode and burial-place of so many of my forefathers—there has never been, for me, the genial atmosphere which a literary man requires, in order to ripen the best harvest of his mind. I shall do better amongst other faces; and these familiar ones, it need hardly be said, will do just as well without me" (1:44–45). As Hester's art transforms a punishment into a pride, so Hawthorne's art in the drawing of Hester's character transforms reproach into praise; for Hester, representing the feminine role of the artist in a Puritan, business-oriented society, turns out to be more energetic and able, to possess more strength of will and courage, than any of the men surrounding her. One can imagine Hawthorne saying to Hester what Freud once said to his daughter Anna, "Remember, you are my only son."

The figure of a bold, active, and often doomed woman as symbolic artist occurs again and again in Hawthorne's fiction, most notably in the characters of Zenobia and Miriam Schaefer. In *The Marble Faun* (1860), Hawthorne, commenting on Miriam's self-portrait, says that the artist, "like all self-painters, may have endowed herself with certain graces which other eyes might not discern. Artists are fond of painting their own portraits; and, in Florence, there is a gallery of hundreds of them, including the most illustrious; in all of which there are autobiographical characteristics, so to speak; traits, expressions, loftinesses, and amenities, which would have been invisible, had they not been painted from within" (4:49). That "artists are fond of painting their own portraits" is as true of writers as of painters. Thus, one of the "autobiographical characteristics" that Miriam expresses in her work has a personal significance for Hawthorne as well, and, by implication, for Hester:

> In all those sketches of common life, and the affections that spiritualize it, a figure was pourtrayed apart; now, it peeped between the branches of a shrubbery, amid which two lovers sat; now, it was looking through a frosted window, from the outside, while a young wedded pair sat at their new fireside, within; and, once, it leaned from a chariot, which six horses were whirling onward in

pomp and pride, and gazed at a scene of humble enjoyment by a
cottage door. Always, it was the same figure, and always depicted
with an expression of deep sadness; and in every instance, slightly as
they were brought out, the face and form had the traits of Miriam's
own. (4:46)

What Miriam portrays in each instance is the artist as passive observer, as
that attentive watcher whose part in any scene is always to be "apart,"
peeping through the branches, looking in a window, gazing from a passing vehicle at a drama in which the artist, who must record the action in
paint or words, can never directly participate. The sense of the artist as
outsider, as social outcast, characterizes the relationship between
Hawthorne and the townspeople of Salem in "The Custom-House," and
it underlies the relation between Hester as symbolic artist and the community of Salem in the rest of the book.

Hawthorne's description of Miriam Schaefer's self-portrait recalls at
moments his description of his own mirror image in "Monsieur du
Miroir." Upon seeing Miriam's portrait, Donatello tells her that "the
resemblance is as little to be mistaken as if you had bent over the smooth
surface of a fountain, and possessed the witchcraft to call forth the image
that you made there! It is yourself!" (4:48). Elsewhere, Hawthorne describes Miriam's estrangement from society as being like that of an illusory image that eludes the sense of touch: "By some subtile quality, she
kept people at a distance, without so much as letting them know that they
were excluded from her inner circle. She resembled one of those images
of light, which conjurers evoke and cause to shine before us, in apparent
tangibility, only an arm's length beyond our grasp; we make a step in
advance, expecting to seize the illusion, but find it still precisely so far
out of our reach. Finally, society began to recognize the impossibility of
getting nearer to Miriam, and gruffly acquiesced" (4:21). Hawthorne
suggests that the narcissism that lies at the core of any self-reflective
art—an art preoccupied with veiled self-portraiture, the artist forever
contemplating his own illusory image in a variety of masks—is as much
responsible for the artist's estrangement from society as any action of
society's. It is as if the artist's narcissistic bond with the illusory image of
himself is so complete that it precludes any merely social bond with
another living body or with the communal body.

It is significant that in the preface to *The Marble Faun* Hawthorne raises once again the question of an ideal reader, the "one heart and mind of perfect sympathy" as he calls him in "The Custom-House," but raises it in a curiously valedictory manner. He says that he never believed the ideal reader "to be merely a mythic character. I had always a sturdy faith in his actual existence, and wrote for him, year after year, during which the great Eye of the Public (as well it might) almost utterly overlooked my small productions" (4:1–2). He continues:

> Unquestionably, this Gentle, Kind, Benevolent, Indulgent, and most Beloved and Honoured Reader, did once exist for me, and (in spite of the infinite chances against a letter's reaching its destination, without a definite address) duly received the scrolls which I flung upon whatever wind was blowing, in the faith that they would find him out. But, is he extant now? . . . If I find him at all, it will probably be under some mossy grave-stone, inscribed with a half-obliterated name, which I shall never recognize.
>
> Therefore, I have little heart or confidence (especially, writing, as I do, in a foreign land, and after a long, long absence from my own) to presume upon the existence of that friend of friends, that unseen brother of the soul, whose apprehensive sympathy has so often encouraged me to be egotistical in my Prefaces, careless though unkindly eyes should skim over what was never meant for them. I stand upon ceremony, now, and, after stating a few particulars about the work which is here offered to the Public, must make my most reverential bow, and retire behind the curtain. (4:2)

The "apprehensive sympathy" of "that unseen brother of the soul" had encouraged Hawthorne's acts of self-revelation in his prefaces, encouraged him to be "egotistical," but the imagined death of the ideal reader (rhetorically figured as Hawthorne's inability to "recognize" the reader's "half-obliterated name" inscribed on a "mossy grave-stone") causes the author to veil himself again, to "retire behind the curtain." Whether or not Hawthorne ever really believed in the "actual existence" of this reader of perfect sympathy whose attentive gaze mitigates Hawthorne's solitary estrangement from a public that "overlooked" his works, a public whose "unkindly eyes" skimmed over "what was never meant for them"—such a reader, idealized by the author, can be nothing but the author's own projection of himself gazing back at the written self of the text, the illusion of an outsider whose sympathy allows him to see the work as if from the inside. Such a reader must necessarily be "the divided segment of the writer's own nature," since it is precisely this division in the self that constitutes artistic self-reflection. It is not surprising, then, that this reader's imagined death, the obliteration of the phonetic script of his name from the crypt stone, coincides with the author's disappearing behind the curtain/veil.

Keeping in mind this later occurrence of the image of the ideal reader and the veil in *The Marble Faun*, let us consider again Hawthorne's rhetorical strategy in "The Custom-House" section of *The Scarlet Letter*. The reversal of masculine and feminine traits (whereby the supposedly passive artist is shown to be more truly active than the men of customary business) underlies most of the other reversals in the autobiographical preface. Thus Hawthorne finds upon assuming his duties as surveyor of customs that most of the men in his department are "ancient sea-captains" (1:12) who exhibit both "lack of energy" (1:7) and general decay. He adds that no "public functionary of the United States . . . has ever had such a patriarchal body of veterans under his orders" (1:12), though his "position in reference to them" was "paternal and protective" (1:15). Coming soon after the passage in which Hawthorne's "great-grandsires," the patriarchal William and John Hathorne, pass their stern judgment on this "writer of story-books," the detail of Hawthorne's "patriarchal" subordinates being retired sea captains cannot help but remind anyone familiar with the author's biography that Hawthorne's father and grandfather were sea captains. Hawthorne's response to the imagined ancestral censure of his vocation takes the form of a reversal of generations: the "patriarchal body" of "ancient sea-captains" that represent Hawthorne's commercial, Puritan ancestors become Hawthorne's dependents, the objects of his "paternal and protective" care. Dependent on Hawthorne's good will for the continuance of their livelihood in the customhouse, the "aged men" under his charge fear that the new surveyor may, according to political custom, bring their "white heads under the axe of the guillotine" (1:14). Hawthorne says that he was both pained and amused "to behold the terrors" that attended his advent: "to see a furrowed cheek, weather-beaten by half a century of storm, turn ashy pale at the glance of so harmless an individual as myself; to detect, as one or another addressed me, the tremor of a voice, which, in long-past days, had been wont to bellow through a speaking-trumpet, hoarsely enough to frighten Boreas himself to silence" (1:14). In this fantasized reversal of generations, the patriarchal sea captains have been reduced to helpless, frightened children by the "paternal" (that is, authorial) "writer of story-books."

The only inmate of the customhouse with whom Hawthorne can at all identify is the collector of the port, a certain General Miller who had been a hero in the War of 1812 and was ultimately rewarded with a government sinecure. Hawthorne says that the General "was as much out of place as an old sword . . . would have been, among the inkstands, paper-folders, and mahogany rulers, on the Deputy Collector's desk" (1:23); or, he might have added, as a writer among customs inspectors, since he speculates that the General "lived a more real life within his thoughts, than amid the unappropriate environment of the Collector's office" (1:23). One of the qualities that separates the General from his companions, but that Hawthorne finds particularly sympathetic, is an almost feminine sensitivity to beauty: "A trait of native elegance, seldom seen in the masculine character after childhood or early youth, was shown in the General's fondness for the sight and fragrance of flowers. An old soldier might be supposed to prize only the bloody laurel on his brow; but here was one, who seemed to have a young girl's appreciation of the floral tribe" (1:23). Immediately preceding this revelation of a feminine trait in a masculine character, Hawthorne applies to the General the veil image that he had earlier applied to himself, thus linking the General to Hester and her symbolic representation of the masculine artist's feminine role. Observing that "in respect of grace and beauty, there were points well worth noting" in the General's appearance, Hawthorne continues, "A ray of humor, now and then, would make its way through the veil of dim obstruction" that surrounded the old soldier (1:22).

Granting the symbolic association of Hester and the General as projections of the same element in Hawthorne's inmost self, it is not surprising that Hawthorne ends his brief portrait of General Miller with the same image he uses to end his book-length portrait of Hester—that of a heraldic emblem. He says that "if, in our country, valor were rewarded by heraldic honor," then the words that the General spoke at his moment of greatest heroism in the War of 1812 "would be the best and fittest of all mottoes for the General's shield of arms" (1:23–24). On the stone that stands above Hester and Dimmesdale's graves "there appeared the semblance of an engraved escutcheon. It bore a device, a herald's wording of

which might serve for a motto and brief description of our now concluded legend... —'On a field, sable, the letter A, gules'" (1:264).
Hawthorne implies that Hester has transformed what was originally intended as a badge of dishonor into a heraldic escutcheon of nobility like
that awarded for bravery.

The customhouse figure to whom Hawthorne opposes the General is
"a certain permanent Inspector," the "father of the Custom-House—the
patriarch" (1:16). He says, "Looking at him merely as an animal,—and
there was very little else to look at," one observed "the rare perfection of
his animal nature, the moderate proportion of intellect, and the very
trifling admixture of moral and spiritual ingredients; these latter qualities, indeed, being in barely enough measure to keep the old gentleman
from walking on all-fours. He possessed... no higher moral respon-
sibilities than the beasts of the field" (1:17–18). Although the Inspector
seems physically to be a fine figure of a man, he is, in Hawthorne's
opinion, no man at all, lacking those qualities that confer humanity, that
distinguish man from animal; while the almost feminine sensitivity that
Hawthorne detects in the General's character is an expression of that
humane element that grounds true manliness.

Manliness is a recurring concern in "The Custom-House" precisely
because the imagined patriarchal censure of the author seems to raise
the question of whether masculinity is compatible with the role of the
artist. Hawthorne's response is an elaborate trope in which manliness is
shown to reside in the son's resistance to his father's will rather than in
his continued residence in the patriarchal "custom" house. Hawthorne
breaks with family custom by being the first male in six generations to
follow a sedentary occupation, and he signifies this break by rewriting
the patronymic Hathorne as Hawthorne. If A is the mark that distinguishes Hester from the Puritan community of Salem, the mark by
which she stands out in opposition to, in rebellion against, the customs of
the village, then W is the mark that distinguishes Hawthorne the writer
from his Puritan forebears and, by implication, from the commercial
Salem of his own day.

As a symbol of both patriarchal tradition and Puritan commercialism,
the customhouse is an image of exhausted energy—the impotence of
decay, the loss of manhood. Hawthorne doubts whether a man can remain in the customhouse receiving "Uncle Sam's gold" without his soul
losing "its sturdy force, its courage and constancy, its truth, its self-

reliance, and all that gives the emphasis to manly character" (1:39). In his own case, as he felt his powers of mind begin to deteriorate, he "endeavoured to calculate how much longer" he could "stay in the Custom-House, and yet go forth a man": "To confess the truth, it was my greatest apprehension ... that I was likely to grow gray and decrepit in the Surveyorship, and become much such another animal as the old Inspector" (1:39–40). Hawthorne feels that in entering the customhouse to provide for his physical existence, his merely animal nature, he has jeopardized himself as a writer, thereby endangering his essential humanity, his manhood: "Literature, its exertions and objects, were now of little moment in my regard. ... A gift, a faculty, if it had not departed, was suspended and inanimate in me" (1:25–26). It is in this context that the fiction of Jonathan Pue's manuscript becomes particularly significant; for Pue's manuscript confronts Hawthorne with the image of a previous surveyor who had also been an author, confronts him at precisely the moment when Hawthorne feels that he himself "had ceased to be a writer of tolerably poor tales and essays, and had become a tolerably good Surveyor of the Customs" (1:38). So moved is Hawthorne by the tale told in Pue's manuscript that he feels as if he had suddenly come face to face with "the ancient Surveyor" and that "with his own ghostly hand, the obscurely seen, but majestic, figure had imparted to me the scarlet symbol, and the little roll of explanatory manuscript" (1:33).

The illusory, that is, "ghostly," figure of the surveyor evoked in Hawthorne's mind by Pue's written text is Hawthorne's own reverse mirror-image—the figure of a surveyor who can write confronting a writer who has become a surveyor—a daemon who makes Hawthorne *see* what he was and what he has become. Yet, Hawthorne tells us, when he tried to exercise his art on Hester's story, he found that his "imagination was a tarnished mirror": "It would not reflect, or only with miserable dimness, the figures with which I did my best to people it. The characters of the narrative would not be warmed and rendered malleable, by any heat that I could kindle at my intellectual forge. They would take neither the glow of passion nor the tenderness of sentiment, but retained all the rigidity of dead corpses, and stared me in the face with a fixed and ghastly grin of contemptuous defiance. ... In short, the almost torpid creatures of my own fancy twitted me with imbecility, and not without fair occasion" (1:34–35). The daemonic function shifts from the figure of Pue to the characters of the narrative in an image that is to govern the final reversal by which Hawthorne leaves the customhouse. The written characters taunt Hawthorne with his loss of artistic vitality, his loss of the godlike creative energy to resurrect a corpse. The image of resurrection first occurs in relation to Pue's manuscript when Hawthorne, rummaging through some ancient documents of the town "with the saddened, weary, half-reluctant interest which we bestow on the corpse of dead activity," exerts his fancy, "sluggish with little use, to raise up from these dry bones an image of the old town's brighter aspect" (1:29). As if in response to the figure of raising up an image from dry bones, Hawthorne chances at that instant to lay his hand on a small package containing Pue's commission as surveyor and his manuscript. As Hawthorne examines the manuscript, the image of resurrection oscillates from figurative to literal and back to figurative again:

> I remembered to have read (probably in Felt's Annals) a notice of the decease of Mr. Surveyor Pue, about fourscore years ago; and likewise, in a newspaper of recent times, an account of the digging up of his remains in the little grave-yard of St. Peter's Church, during the renewal of that edifice. Nothing, if I rightly call to mind, was left of my respected predecessor, save an imperfect skeleton, and some fragments of apparel, and a wig of majestic frizzle; which, unlike the head that it once adorned, was in very satisfactory preservation. But, on examining the papers which the parchment commission served to envelop, I found more traces of Mr. Pue's mental part, and the internal operations of his head, than the frizzled wig had contained of the venerable skull itself. (1:30)

Pue's literal resurrection, the disinterment of his corpse, reveals that nothing has survived but dry bones; while the resurrection of his written self, the disinterment of the corpus of his work from its burial place among the corpses "of dead activity," reveals that the "traces of Mr. Pue's mental part," his writing self, live on. By entering public service Hawthorne has sacrificed the vitality of his writing self to the maintenance of his physical existence, an existence that must finally end in the death and corruption of his body. For Hawthorne to achieve the kind of survival associated with Pue's manuscript, his public self must die so that his writing self can be reborn. A change of political administrations provides the means for this symbolic death of the public man, and Hawthorne provides a particularly significant image for it—decapitation. He remarks: "If the guillotine, as applied to office-holders, were a literal fact, instead of one of the most apt of metaphors, it is my sincere belief, that the active members of the victorious party were sufficiently excited to have chopped off all our heads.... My own head was the first that fell! ... In view of my previous weariness of office, and vague thoughts of resignation, my fortune somewhat resembled that of a person who should entertain an idea of committing suicide, and, altogether beyond his hopes, meet with the good hap to be murdered" (1:41–42). And this symbolic death leads to the expected revitalization: "The press had taken up my affair, and kept me, for a week or two, careering through the public prints, in my decapitated state, like Irving's Headless Horseman; ghastly and grim, and longing to be buried, as a politically dead man ought. So much for my figurative self. The real human being, all this time, with his head safely on his shoulders, had brought himself to the comfortable conclusion, that everything was for the best; and, making an investment in ink, paper, and steel-pens, had opened his long-disused writing-desk, and was again a literary man" (1:42–43).

Earlier, Hawthorne had connected the image of the guillotine with the retribution that the patriarchal, aged (thus, helpless and childlike) customs officers expected from his "paternal" authority. This linking of decapitation to the father/son conflict suggests the guillotine as a symbol of castration. And since castration, the traditional patriarchal threat to the son's creative power and independence, produces a feminized male, such an interpretation of the guillotine image becomes even more significant when we recall that Hester, who personifies the feminine role of the artist, is first exhibited in conflict with the Puritan fathers of Salem upon the scaffold of the pillory, an instrument of punishment that "was held, in the old time, to be as effectual an agent in the promotion of good citizenship, as ever was the guillotine among the terrorists of France" (1:55). Like the guillotine, the pillory was "so fashioned as to confine the human head in its tight grasp, and thus hold it up to the public gaze.... There can be no outrage, methinks, against our common nature,— whatever be the delinquencies of the individual,—no outrage more fla- grant than to forbid the culprit to hide his face for shame; as it was the essence of this punishment to do" (1:55). What the pillory exhibits to public view is not simply the victim's shame but his powerlessness, his passivity. Hester, though made to stand upon the pillory scaffold, is not confined within the stocks, since this would conceal the scarlet letter from view; and Hester's punishment involves the victim's being unable to veil either her face or the public mark of her shame.

By figuring his expulsion from the customhouse as a symbolic decapitation/castration, Hawthorne carries out an ironic revenge upon his Puritan forefathers, for it is his public self (the customs official who represents his Puritan ancestors) that is the victim of this patriarchal punishment administered by the "inmost Me," the artistic self who provides the specific image of the guillotine for his loss of office. It is not surprising that Hawthorne should associate this self-inflicted (that is, self-imagined) decapitation with the "idea of committing suicide," nor surprising that if such a symbolic castration evokes the figure of the feminized male as representative of the artist's feminine role, this figure should, in a scenario of death and resurrection, give birth to the reborn literary man recovered from the creative impotence of the customhouse and wielding once more the phallic pen.

It is within the context of symbolic castration (that loss of the object which allows the presence of the symbol in its place) that the image of the veil achieves its full significance; for the veil (considered as a specifically feminine garment) masks the female genitalia (the absence of a penis, the missing object), just as the veil of mist in *Pym* masks the womblike abyss. And it is this loss that calls forth the artist's desire to fill the void (symbolically represented by the blankness of the veil) by projecting upon the veil the symbolic representation of the object. The shape inscribed on the veil can represent both a part of the body (phallus) and an image of the self (shadow). If the written character inscribed on Hester's garment represents the phallic linking power of the symbol, then Hawthorne's description of Pearl as a "living hieroglyphic," "the scarlet letter endowed with life," is an equation of phallus and child similar to the Freudian association of penis and child. (One recalls in this connection the phallic character of the figure in the mist at the end of *Pym*, the shadow self whose sudden erection in Pym's path, as he approaches the veiled abyss of origin with his dark double Dirk Peters, evokes the resurrection of the body—generation standing for regeneration.)

The tradition of the veil and phallus as related images includes among its most notable eighteenth-century examples Schiller's poem "The Veiled Image at Sais" (1795), where the reference to the statue of Isis in the Egyptian temple at Sais points to the literal veiling of the phallic mysteries. Plutarch in his treatise *De Iside et Osiride* says that the Egyptians' "philosophy... is veiled in myths and in words containing dim reflexions and adumbrations of the truth.... In Sais the statue of Athena, whom they believe to be Isis, bore the inscription: 'I am all that has been, and is, and shall be, and my robe no mortal has yet uncovered.'"[1] Of Isis's brother/spouse Osiris, whom the Egyptians called "the living phallus" and the "phallus of Ra wherewith he was united to himself,"[2] Plutarch adds:

> Not only the Nile, but every form of moisture they call simply the effusion of Osiris.... And by the picture of a rush they represent a king and the southern region of the world, and the rush is interpreted to mean the watering and fructifying of all things, and in its nature it seems to bear some resemblance to the generative member. Moreover, when they celebrate the festival of the Pamylia which, as has been said, is of a phallic nature, they expose and carry about a statue of which the male member is triple; for the god is the Source, and every source, by its fecundity, multiplies what proceeds from it.... In fact, the tale that is annexed to the legend to the effect that Typhon cast the male member of Osiris into the river, and Isis could not find it, but constructed and shaped a replica of it, and ordained that it should be honoured and borne in processions, plainly comes round to this doctrine, that the creative and germinal power of the god, at the very first, acquired moisture as its substance.... (5:88–89)

In the worship of Osiris, the phallus stood as a symbol of the god, part for whole, so that through the equation of phallus and body the rebirth of Osiris was ritually represented either by the ceremonial erection of the phallus or the erection of the *djed* (a tree trunk with the stumps of branches projecting on either side at the top), a symbol of the god's backbone—vitality thus being indicated, in either phallic or bodily form, by the ability to stand upright, to rise from the dead. There are numerous instances in antiquity of the phallus as a mortuary monument symbolizing rebirth.[3] Whitman, in an uncollected poetic fragment, describes the Egyptian pharaoh Sesostris as a builder of "phallic memorials" (7:687). John Gardner Wilkinson's *A Second Series of the Manners and Customs of the Ancient Egyptians* (1841), which Whitman had apparently read, devotes some ninety pages to the cult of Isis and Osiris, with lengthy quotations from Plutarch, Herodotus, and Diodorus Siculus. Wilkinson discusses "the Phallic ceremonies, said to have been performed in honour of Osiris,"[4] and after citing Plutarch's account of the statue of Osiris "with the triple phallus," he quotes from Herodotus's description of the same ceremonies: "'The Egyptians ... celebrate the rest of this festival nearly in the same manner as the Greeks ... ; but in lieu of phalli, they make little puppets about a cubit high, which women carry about the towns and villages, and set in motion by a string. ...' The historian then describes the appearance of these phallic figures, which he ascribes to a sacred reason; and it is a curious fact that similar puppets are made by the Egyptians on the occasions of public rejoicing at the present day" (1:343–44).

Wilkinson notes that the custom of applying "the name of Osiris to both men and women, who were supposed to partake sufficiently of the qualities of the good being to be worthy of that honour, appears to have some connection with the Greek notion of Dionysus or Bacchus (who was thought to answer to Osiris) being both male and female" (1:322). This observation tallies with Plutarch's remark that the Egyptians "make the power of Osiris to be fixed in the Moon, and say that Isis, since she is generation, is associated with him. For this reason they also call the Moon the mother of the world, and they think that she has a nature both male and female" (5:105). One of the mysteries that the cult of Isis and Osiris seems to have veiled from the uninitiated was the paradoxical reversibility of the divine nature whereby the god Osiris is the father without a phallus and the goddess Isis the mother with a phallus, a blurring of the male/female distinction not uncommon among deities of the vegetative cycle and consistent with a notion of divinity as undifferentiated. In Godfrey Higgins's *Anacalypsis, An Attempt to Draw Aside the Veil of the Saitic Isis; or, An Inquiry into the Origin of Languages, Nations, and Religions* (1836), the imagery of the veil, the phallic cult of Isis and Osiris, and the concealed origin of language are woven into a single network. (The word "anacalypsis," from the Greek *ana,* "back or up," plus *kalyptra,* "veil, covering for the head," may be meant to suggest the botanical use of the word "calyptra," meaning "the remains of the female sex organ, or archegonium, of a moss or fern, forming the caplike covering of the spore case.") Concerning the Egyptian worship of Osiris, Higgins notes: "In their caves or the adyta of their temples they annually, during the mysteries of Isis, celebrated the mysteries and tragical death of Osiris, in a species of drama, in which all the particulars were exhibited;

accompanied with loud lamentations and every mark of sorrow. At this time his images were carried in procession covered, as were those in the temples, with black veils. On the 25th of March, exactly three months from his birth, his resurrection from the dead was celebrated ... with great festivities and rejoicings."[5]

The network of images by which Hawthorne represents his expulsion from the womb/tomb of the customhouse can be seen as a series of rewritings of a single underlying equation: the Puritan self subjected to a symbolic death/castration generates (and therefore equals) the feminized male plus the separated phallus, or the artistic self plus the book called *The Scarlet Letter,* or the mother plus the child (Hester and Pearl), or the veiled, womblike abyss plus the phallic (linguistic) shadow of the self. In this context Dimmesdale represents the Puritan self that conceals within it the artistic self ("the inmost Me"), just as Dimmesdale's ministerial gown conceals the letter inscribed on his skin. Dimmesdale's unveiling of that hidden self on the scaffold of the pillory occurs at the moment of his death, the death of the Puritan self. And what he reveals is his hidden relationship to Hester, the correspondence between the letter on his flesh and the letter on Hester's garment—A equals A. In his final confession Dimmesdale says that the letter that Hester wears "is but the shadow of what he bears on his own breast" (1:255), recalling the moment when the author placed the scarlet letter on *his* breast and felt a sensation as "of burning heat, ... as if the letter were not of red cloth, but red-hot iron." In declaring that he is the father of Pearl, Dimmesdale reveals his authorship of "the living hieroglyphic," "the scarlet letter in another form." Thus, beyond the words "adultery," "able," and "angel," the enigmatic letter A may also signify "author" and "Arthur." In the Oedipal economy of these relations, it is appropriate that Dimmesdale's authorship involves a liaison with an older man's wife and that this adulterous act is represented as a sin against the ultimate Puritan patriarch, God the Father, an act for which Dimmesdale's death is the punishment.

Near the end of "The Custom-House," Hawthorne says that he had originally intended to publish the tale of the scarlet letter as part of a larger work. Having thus characterized the book as a partial object, he immediately links it to the motif of symbolic decapitation/castration: "Keeping up the metaphor of the political guillotine, the whole may be considered as the Posthumous Papers of a Decapitated Surveyor; and the sketch which I am now bringing to a close, if too autobiographical for a modest person to publish in his lifetime, will readily be excused in a gentleman who writes from beyond the grave. Peace be with all the world! My blessing on my friends! My forgiveness to my enemies! For I am in the realm of quiet!" (1:43–44). What was only the author's figurative death at the time Hawthorne wrote became within fifteen years of the book's publication a real death, so that present readers experience this passage as literally addressed from "beyond the grave," as the cryptic figure on the stone. Yet it is precisely by this prefiguration that Hawthorne subtly points to the written survival of his own consciousness in that very passage, in that act of imagining and inscribing his own death in advance *as if* it were written from beyond the grave.

Aware that his survival in the memories of his fellow townspeople seems doubtful, Hawthorne counters their rejection in advance and threatens to forget them first, implying that a community has a long-term memory only because of the mnemic inscriptions of its writers: "The life of the Custom-House lies like a dream behind me. The old Inspector, . . . and all those other venerable personages . . . are but shadows in my view; white-headed and wrinkled images, which my fancy used to sport with, and has now flung aside for ever. . . . Soon, likewise, my old native town will loom upon me through the haze of memory, a mist brooding over and around it. . . . Henceforth, it ceases to be a reality of my life. I am a citizen of somewhere else" (1:44). This reduction of the townspeople to the status of mnemically inscribed images—"shadows in my view; . . . images, which my fancy used to sport with"—is in effect an apotheosis of the author's imagination, for it makes the townspeople's survival dependent upon their persistence in the author's godlike memory, in his book of life. Referring to his sketch "A Rill from the Town Pump," Hawthorne concludes, "The great-grandchildren of the present race may sometimes think kindly of the scribbler of bygone days, when the antiquary of days to come, among the sites memorable in the town's history, shall point out the locality of The Town Pump!" (1:45). Humorously imagining himself as an original, as a living source in their midst (the town pump), Hawthorne obliquely expresses his desire that the book— the phallic shadow/child, the partial object of the imagination—will perpetuate him from generation to generation, will be a "living hieroglyphic," its meaning and destiny as vitally indeterminate as his own.

Section 16

Melville: The Indeterminate Ground; A
Conjunction of Fountain and Vortex;
The Myth of Isis and Osiris; Master
Oppositions; The Doubleness of the Self
and the Illusion of Consistent
Character; Dionysus and Apollo; Mask
and Phallus; The Chain of Partial
Objects

Hawthorne's reference to Pearl as a "living hieroglyphic" may well be an ironic allusion to Emerson's famous dictum that every man's condition "is a solution in hieroglyphic to those inquiries he would put." Hawthorne was skeptical of the ease with which the opaque emblem of the world became transparent for Emerson, and though Hawthorne says that both he and Mr. Pue believed Pearl's future was happy, he refrains from giving us any definite knowledge of this. The ultimate fate of his living hieroglyphic remains, like almost everything else in the novel, a matter of conjecture at last. Whether Hawthorne is making a thrust at Emerson is itself a matter of conjecture, but we can be fairly sure that Hawthorne's friend Melville had Emerson's remark in mind when he introduced into *Moby-Dick* a character whose condition is literally hieroglyphic. Melville says that Queequeg's "tattooing . . . had been the work of a departed prophet and seer of his island, who, by those hieroglyphic marks, had written out on his body a complete theory of the heavens and the earth, and a mystical treatise on the art of attaining truth; so that Queequeg in his own proper person was a riddle to unfold; a wondrous work in one volume; but whose mysteries not even himself could read, though his own live heart beat against them; and these mysteries were therefore destined in the end to moulder away with the living parchment whereon they were inscribed, and so be unsolved to the last" (p. 300).

As in *The Scarlet Letter,* the inherently undecipherable character of the hieroglyph is a continuing motif in *Moby-Dick.* Melville describes the markings on the sides of the sperm whale as "hieroglyphical; that is, if you call those mysterious cyphers on the walls of pyramids hieroglyphics, then that is the proper word to use in the present connexion. By my retentive memory of the hieroglyphics upon one Sperm Whale in particular, I was much struck with a plate representing the old Indian characters chiselled on the famous hieroglyphic palisades on the banks of the Upper Mississippi. Like those mystic rocks, too, the mystic-marked whale remains undecipherable" (p. 260). If, as Melville says, "you call those mysterious cyphers on the walls of pyramids hieroglyphics," then Moby Dick with his "pyramidical white hump" (p. 159) and his mystic-

marked brow is the central hieroglyph in the novel. But as the hieroglyphic letter in Hawthorne's novel has its human counterpart, so the
white whale has in the person of Ahab its hieroglyphic human equivalent. Ahab is described as being like a "pyramid" (p. 115), as having an
"Egyptian chest" (p. 160), and the marks on his brow are like the hieroglyphic markings on the forehead of the sperm whale.

That indeterminacy is the essential characteristic of the hieroglyph for
Melville is made clear in Ishmael's discussion of the whiteness of the
whale. Moby Dick's whiteness strikes Ishmael with a "vague, nameless
horror" (p. 163), but Ishmael's feeling is not so much a horror that is
vague and nameless as a horror *of* the vague and nameless, a revulsion at
the ultimately indefinite and uncertain nature of the world symbolized
by the color white. He says: "Is it that by its indefiniteness it shadows
forth the heartless voids and immensities of the universe, and thus stabs
us from behind with the thought of annihilation, when beholding the
white depths of the milky way? Or is it, that as in essence whiteness is not
so much a color as the visible absence of color, and at the same time the
concrete of all colors; is it for these reasons that there is such a dumb
blankness, full of meaning, in a wide landscape of snows—a colorless,
all-color of atheism from which we shrink?" (p. 169).

Melville's focusing on the essential "indefiniteness" of this color that
he takes to represent the truth about the external world reminds us of
Hawthorne's remark that the shape of the meteor's track, which Dimmesdale saw as a scarlet letter, was of "so little definiteness, that another's
guilt might have seen another symbol in it." With the loss of belief in an
external absolute, the self expands to fill the void, but at the moment
when the self becomes the absolute, at the moment when it sees that
everything is a projection of itself, then the self realizes that it has become nothing, that it is indistinguishable, "a colorless all-color." Hawthorne speaks of that "disordered mental state, when a man, rendered
morbidly self-contemplative" extends "his egotism over the whole expanse of nature." And in the same vein, Melville says:

> ... when we consider that other theory of the natural
> philosophers, that all other earthly hues ... are but subtile deceits,
> not actually inherent in substances, but only laid on from without; so
> that all deified Nature absolutely paints like the harlot, whose al-
> lurements cover nothing but the charnel-house within; and when we

proceed further, and consider that the mystical cosmetic which produces every one of her hues, the great principle of light, for ever
remains white or colorless in itself, and if operating without medium
upon matter, would touch all objects, even tulips and roses, with its
own blank tinge—pondering all this, the palsied universe lies before
us a leper; and like wilful travellers in Lapland, who refuse to wear
colored and coloring glasses upon their eyes, so the wretched infidel
gazes himself blind at the monumental white shroud that wraps all
the prospect around him. And of all these things the Albino whale
was the symbol. Wonder ye then at the fiery hunt? (Pp. 169–70)

Melville knows that there is a self-destructive irony at work here. The
external world appears to be a void, but if all the various appearances of
that world are only projections of the self, then the real void is within the
self. And if, for Ishmael, Moby Dick has come to symbolize this predica-
ment, then the attempt to hunt down the whale and kill it is a quest that
must ultimately be suicidal. Thus the ironic significance of what Ishmael
tells us of himself at the beginning of the novel: He says that when he
grows "grim about the mouth," when it is "a damp, drizzly November" in
his soul, when the "hypos" get the upper hand, he goes to sea: "This is
my substitute for pistol and ball. With a philosophical flourish Cato
throws himself upon his sword; I quietly take to the ship" (p. 12).
Ishmael's voyage, then, is intended to be an alternative to self-
destruction. In a sense, it is because Ahab acts out so completely the
self-destructive potential in Ishmael that Ishmael is freed of having to act
it out for himself and thus escapes to tell the story.

The qualities attributed to Moby Dick in the novel are simply the
projected attributes of his pursuers, and in particular, the chief of his
pursuers, Ahab: "The White Whale swam before him as the monomaniac
incarnation of all those malicious agencies which some deep men feel
eating in them, till they are left living on with half a heart and half a lung"
(p. 160). The whale's intelligent malignity is Ahab's own, the whale's
ubiquity is but the self's own sense that, look where it will, it sees only
some aspect of itself.

Ahab's sense of the self's inescapable presence is apparent in the chapter called "The Doubloon" where, examining the coin nailed to the mast,
he interprets its hieroglyphic markings—three mountains, one bearing a
flame, one a tower, and one a crowing cock—as personal emblems: "The

firm tower, that is Ahab; the volcano, that is Ahab; the courageous, the undaunted, and victorious fowl, that, too, is Ahab; all are Ahab; and this round gold is but the image of the rounder globe, which, like a magician's glass, to each and every man in turn but mirrors back his own mysterious self" (p. 359). As an illustration of this remark the rest of the chapter is a study in multiple perspectivism. Starbuck, Stubb, Flask, the Manxman, Queequeg, Fedallah, and Pip successively approach the coin and find in its design an embodiment of their own subjective states. Having interpreted the zodiac around the coin's edge as a symbol of the stages in man's life, Stubb steps aside to observe the other interpreters. After overhearing the comments of the Manxman, Stubb says: "There's another rendering now; but still one text. All sorts of men in one kind of world, you see" (p. 362). And when Queequeg approaches, Stubb remarks that his tattooing makes him look "like the signs of the Zodiac himself" (p. 362). The process of interpretation has come full circle, for when the tattooed Queequeg stands before the emblematic coin, a "doubloon" appropriately enough, the hieroglyphic subject confronts the hieroglyphic object. And we understand that the hieroglyph of the world is doubly undecipherable. It is indefinite in itself, and in its indefiniteness it allows the individual subject to project onto it the structure of a self as undecipherable as the world.

In *Pierre,* Melville represents this double ambiguity of physical nature and the self as that of reciprocal texts. He says, "Nature is not so much her own ever-sweet interpreter, as the mere supplier of that cunning alphabet, whereby selecting and combining as he pleases, each man reads his own peculiar lesson according to his own peculiar mind and mood" (p. 342). Yet later, Pierre, in jail awaiting his "untimely, timely end," speaks of "life's last chapter well stitched into the middle! Nor book, nor author of the book, hath any sequel, though each hath its last lettering!—It is ambiguous still" (p. 360).

Trapped in this circular, reciprocal ambiguity, Ahab says that the round coin is an image of the round globe that like a mirror reflects each man's mysterious self. Earlier, Ishmael, in one of his water-gazing watches at the foremasthead, had sighted "a gigantic Sperm Whale . . . glistening in the sun's rays like a mirror" (p. 242). From the very beginning of the novel the suicidal potential of introspection is identified with Narcissus. Noting that "meditation and water are wedded for ever" (p. 13), Ishmael points out the "still deeper" meaning of "that story of

Narcissus, who because he could not grasp the tormenting, mild image he saw in the fountain, plunged into it and was drowned. But that same image, we ourselves see in all rivers and oceans. It is the image of the ungraspable phantom of life; and this is the key to it all" (p. 14). And near the end of the book the figure recurs when Ahab, leaning over the side of the ship, observes "how his shadow in the water sank and sank to his gaze, the more and the more that he strove to pierce the profundity" (p. 443). Seeking to know the ultimate reality, Ahab means "to strike through the mask," but this sinking of his shadow as he tries "to pierce the profundity" foreshadows the inability of self-consciousness (which requires a surface as background for the self's image) to penetrate the ultimate surface without annihilating itself.

In a work as dominated by the concept of hieroglyphic doubling as *Moby-Dick*, it is less a matter of finding inscribed shadow selves than of trying to stop finding them. Beyond Ahab's shadowing forth of his dark self on the indefinite whiteness of the whale and his doubling of Ishmael's self-destructive introspection, Ahab and Ishmael both have dark doubles in the persons of Fedallah and Queequeg; and thus captain and crewman double each other again. True to Ahab's remark that the round globe is like a mirror, this doubling of doubles creates the giddy sensation of a house of mirrors; one not only finds an image of the self everywhere but an infinite multiplication of images as the mirrors re-double the contents of opposing mirrors. Ahab and Fedallah are presented as polar twins of fate in a reversible master/slave relationship: "Though such a potent spell seemed secretly to join the twain; openly, and to the awe-struck crew, they seemed pole-like asunder. . . . Ahab in his scuttle, the Parsee by the mainmast; but still fixedly gazing upon each other; as if in the Parsee Ahab saw his forethrown shadow, in Ahab the Parsee his abandoned substance. . . . Ahab seemed an independent lord; the Parsee but his slave. Still again both seemed yoked together, and an unseen tyrant driving them" (p. 439). Exasperated at the reversibility of opposites, Ahab admonishes Starbuck and Stubb on the first day of the chase: "Ye two are the opposite poles of one thing; Starbuck is Stubb reversed, and Stubb is Starbuck; and ye two are all mankind" (p. 452).

The relationship between Ishmael and his hieroglyphic double is from the first described as a marriage after they share a bed at the Spouter Inn. Trying to free himself from the sleeping Queequeg's "bridegroom clasp," Ishmael finds that "he still hugged me tightly, as though naught

but death should part us twain" (p. 33). Later Queequeg tells Ishmael
that henceforth they are "married; meaning, in his country's phrase, that
we were bosom friends" (p. 53). As a token of this, he entrusts his fate to
his friend by giving him the choice of the whale ship on which they will
embark. Immediately after Ishmael's selection of the *Pequod,* Queequeg
begins to function as a visible representation of his shipmate's inner life.
Thus the suicidal bent of Ishmael's introspective temperament—those
"hypos" from which he had sought to escape by going to sea, only to
embark on Ahab's self-destructive quest for the ultimate reality—is
hieroglyphically foreshadowed when Queequeg's trancelike meditation
at the Spouter Inn is mistaken for suicide (p. 79). On board ship, the
linking of their fates is emblemized by the monkey rope that binds them
together while Queequeg works over the side, so that, as Ishmael says,
"for better or for worse, we two, for the time, were wedded; and should
poor Queequeg sink to rise no more, then both usage and honor demanded, that instead of cutting the cord, it should drag me down in his
wake. . . . Queequeg was my own inseparable twin brother" (pp. 270–71).
But unlike Fedallah who foreshadows and shares Ahab's death in the
whale hunt, Queequeg acts as a kind of sacrificial substitute for his "twin
brother"—Queequeg's *prefigured* death (symbolized by his hieroglyphically inscribed coffin that surfaces in the vortex to be a lifebuoy for
Ishmael) saves his twin's life.

The blank background on which the novel's hieroglyphic shadow
selves are projected is either the sea or the whiteness of the whale hidden
beneath the sea's surface, or a conjunction of these two in the white mist
of sea water jetted from the whale's spout. And to each of these the
image of the veil is applied. Ishmael begins the "Cetology" chapter by
quoting contemporary zoologists on the impossibility of pursuing their
research "in the unfathomable waters" where the whale lives, so that
there is an "impenetrable veil covering our knowledge of the cetacea"
(p. 117). And Ishmael adds that "far above all other hunted whales," the
sperm whale's "is an unwritten life" (p. 118). Discussing the whiteness of
the whale, Ishmael says that white "is at once the most meaning symbol
of spiritual things, nay, the very veil of the Christian's deity; and yet . . .
the intensifying agent in things the most appalling to mankind" (p. 169).
Because of the pallor of death and the hue of the shroud, "in our super-
stitions" we "throw the same snowy mantle round our phantoms; all
ghosts rising in a milk-white fog" (p. 166). Reminiscent of the "shrouded

human figure" at the end of *Pym*, the image of a phantom in a milk-white fog prefigures the moment when Ahab, on the first day of the chase, draws close enough to Moby Dick to see "the glistening white shadow from his broad, milky forehead, a musical rippling playfully accompanying the shade" (p. 447). (Ishmael's reference to "the glorified White Whale" [p. 447] soon after suggests that Moby Dick's white shadow is a form of the halo phenomenon discussed earlier.) Throughout the novel Moby Dick is described as a phantom and is thus associated with the "ungraspable phantom of life" that Narcissus "saw in the fountain" and that "we ourselves see in all rivers and oceans." As Ahab's mirror, Moby Dick reflects in his white monotone that monomania which at moments transforms Ahab into "a ray of living light, . . . but without an object to color, and therefore a blankness in itself" (p. 175)—the old man's will to obliterate the dark shadow of evil. The "musical rippling" that accompanies Moby Dick's "white shadow" recalls Poe's strategy in *Pym* of describing the veil of mist in the same terms he uses to depict the sublimity of the musical element in poetry—music's nonvisual presence functioning as an "image" of the fictive transcendence of language in the sublime, that is, of language understood as pictographically inscribed.

In the chapter called "The Fountain," Ishmael makes the veil of mist jetted from the whale's spiracle an image of indeterminacy, noting that "the mystery of the spout—whether it be water or whether it be vapor" prevents "absolute certainty" about various aspects of the whale's existence (p. 312). The danger of trying to determine "the precise nature of the whale spout" is that "if the jet is fairly spouted into your eyes, it will blind you" (p. 313). Ishmael's hypothesis is "that the spout is nothing but mist. And besides other reasons, to this conclusion I am impelled, by considerations touching the great inherent dignity and sublimity of the Sperm Whale. . . . He is both ponderous and profound. And I am convinced that from the heads of all ponderous profound beings, such as Plato, Pyrrho, the Devil, Jupiter, Dante, and so on, there always goes up a certain semi-visible steam, while in the act of thinking deep thoughts. While composing a little treatise on Eternity, I had the curiosity to place a mirror before me; and ere long saw reflected there, a curious involved worming and undulation in the atmosphere over my head" (pp. 313–14). One senses the influence of both *Pym* and *Eureka* in Melville's linking of the uncertainty of human verification and the indefiniteness of the veil of mist to the indeterminacy of self-reflective thought as it attempts to deal with the notion of eternity, with the survival of the self as a linguistic (that is, repetitive) entity in a condition of atemporality.

On the last day of the chase Moby Dick suddenly surfaces "shrouded in a thin drooping veil of mist" and hovers "for a moment in the rainbowed air" (p. 464). As Ahab approaches Moby Dick for the final confrontation, he enters "the smoky mountain mist . . . thrown off from the whale's spout" (p. 466). Earlier, in "The Town-Ho's Story," the description of Radney's fatal encounter with the whale combines the penetration of the veil with the descent into the maelstrom: After his boat is swamped, Radney "for an instant, was dimly seen through that veil, wildly seeking to remove himself from the eye of Moby Dick. But the whale rushed round in a sudden maelstrom; seized the swimmer between his jaws; and rearing high up with him, plunged headlong again, and went down" (p. 222).

Besides being the ultimate cause of the vortex that consumes the *Pequod* and its crew, Moby Dick, because of his habit of swimming in circles when attacked, is described on several occasions as creating a maelstrom or whirlpool. This connection is made at the very beginning, in the "Extracts," when Melville quotes Pliny on the subject of "the biggest fishes," among which are "the Whales and Whirlpooles called Balaene" (p. 3). Moreover, since the whale's spout is usually described as a fountain (p. 310ff.), Moby Dick represents a conjunction of fountain and whirlpool images similar to that in Shelley's *Alastor*. Imaging the coincidence of origin and end, of source and abyss, the union of fountain and whirlpool alogically symbolizes a supralinguistic (nonsymbolic) reality as the fusing of opposites, as a primal conjunction/undifferentiation of the phallic spout and the womblike vortex. As in *Alastor*, the fountain and the whirlpool are each images of self-conscious thought's inability to conceive of its origin or end. Thus the first appearance of the fountain image is in the "story of Narcissus, who because he could not grasp the tormenting, mild image he saw in the fountain, plunged into it and was drowned." And the most memorable use of the vortex image prior to the sinking of the *Pequod* is in Ishmael's description of the dangerous belief that the end of individual self-consciousness is its return to origin in a universal consciousness. Standing watches at the masthead, an "absent-minded youth" can be lulled into such an opium-like listlessness of vacant, unconscious reverie ... by the blending cadence of waves with thoughts, that at last he loses his identity; [and] takes the mystic ocean at his feet for the visible image of that deep, blue, bottomless soul, pervading mankind and nature. . . .

There is no life in thee, now, except that rocking life imparted by a gently rolling ship; by her, borrowed from the sea; by the sea, from the inscrutable tides of God. But while this sleep, this dream is on ye, move your foot or hand an inch; slip your hold at all; and your identity comes back in horror. Over Descartian vortices you hover. And perhaps, at mid-day, in the fairest weather, with one half-throttled shriek you drop through that transparent air into the summer sea, no more to rise for ever. Heed it well, ye Pantheists! (P. 140)

If Moby Dick represents the ultimate reality beyond death as a fusing of opposites, the merging of masculine and feminine in a condition "indefinite as God" (p. 97), then it is not surprising that Melville associates the "mistic" veiling of the white whale with the veiling of the phallic rites of Isis and Osiris at Sais: Ishmael says that unless you take the whale into account, "you are but a provincial and sentimentalist in Truth. But clear Truth is a thing for salamander giants only to encounter; how small the chances for the provincials then? What befel the weakling youth lifting the dread goddess's veil at Sais?" (pp. 285–86). H. Bruce Franklin has convincingly demonstrated the influence of the myth of Osiris (as recorded in Plutarch and Herodotus) on the conception and plot of *Moby-Dick*.[6] In Melville's long poem *Clarel* (1876), Rolfe, Clarel, and Vine discuss the similarities between the myth of Osiris and the story of Christ and raise the possibility that the latter is a rewriting of the former:

> Rolfe, in tone
> Half elegiac, thus went on:
> "Phylae, upon thy sacred ground
> Osiris' broken tomb is found:
> A god how good, whose good proved vain—
> In strife with bullying Python slain.
> For long the ritual chant or moan

> Of pilgrims by that mystic stone
> Went up, even much as now ascend
> The liturgies of yearning prayer
> To one who met a kindred end—
> Christ, tombed in turn, and worshipped *there*,"
> And pointed.—"Hint you," here asked Vine,
> "In Christ Osiris met decline
> Anew?"—"Nay, nay; and yet, past doubt
> Strange is that text St. Matthew won
> From gray Hosea in sentence: *Out*
> *Of Egypt have I called my son.*"
>   Here Clarel spake, and with a stir
> Not all assured in eager plight:
> "But does not Matthew there refer
> Only to the return from flight,
> Flight into Egypt?"—"May be so,"
> Said Rolfe; "but then Hosea?—Nay,
> We'll let it pass."—And fell delay
> Of talk; they mused.[7]

In light of Melville's association of Christ with Osiris and Plutarch's suggestion that the phallic myths blur the sexual differentiation of Isis and Osiris in the notion of a double (indeterminate) divine nature, we can glimpse part of the background to Ishmael's curious remark about Christ in the chapter called "The Tail": "Whatever they may reveal of the divine love in the Son, the soft, curled, hermaphroditical Italian pictures, in which his idea has been most successfully embodied; these pictures, so destitute as they are of all brawniness, hint nothing of any power, but the mere negative, feminine one of submission and endurance, which on all hands it is conceded, form the peculiar practical virtues of his teachings" (p. 315).

In a novel heavily influenced by the myth of Osiris, about a sperm whale named Moby Dick, it is no surprise to find phallic imagery. What is remarkable is the explicitness with which Melville, in the chapter called "The Cassock," associates the phallus of the whale with ancient cult worship and points out the symbolic part/whole equivalence of phallus and body in such cults, without ever using the word "phallus" or mentioning Osiris. Ishmael says that during the "post-mortemizing of the

whale" one could see on the deck of the *Pequod* "a very strange, enigmatical object," an "unaccountable cone,—longer than a Kentuckian is tall,
nigh a foot in diameter at the base, and jet-black as Yojo, the ebony idol
of Queequeg. And an idol, indeed, it is; or, rather, in old times, its
likeness was. Such an idol as that found in the secret groves of Queen
Maachah in Judea; and for worshipping which, King Asa, her son, did
depose her, and destroyed the idol, and burnt it for an abomination at
the brook Kedron, as darkly set forth in the 15th chapter of the first
book of Kings" (pp. 350–51). This "enigmatical object," which the sailors
call "the grandissimus," is skinned, and the "dark pelt" becomes the
protective garment worn by the mincer while he cuts the "horse-pieces of
blubber" into thin sheets called "bible leaves"—a name that allows Melville a final obscene pun: "Arrayed in decent black; occupying a con-
spicuous pulpit; intent on bible leaves; what a candidate for an arch-
bishoprick . . . were this mincer" (p. 351).

Perhaps Melville's wittiest and most single-minded use of phallic symbolism is the short story "I and My Chimney" (1856), in which the association of the phallus with the cult worship of Osiris is directly alluded to.
The narrator says that his chimney is less "a pile of masonry" than "a
personage. It is the king of the house,"[8] "a huge, corpulent old Harry
VIII of a chimney," and he adds that he uses the phrase "*I and my
chimney,* as Cardinal Wolsey used to say, I and my King" (p. 159). As
"king of the house," the chimney is the symbol of the narrator's domestic
authority, but the narrator's wife, who "would have been just the wife for
Peter the Great, or Peter the Piper" (p. 169), wants to tear down the
chimney because "it stands midway in the place where a fine entrance-
hall ought to be" (p. 167). The narrator says his wife "is desirous that,
domestically, I should abdicate; that, renouncing further rule, like the
venerable Charles V, I should retire into some sort of monastery. But
indeed, the chimney excepted, I have little authority to lay down"
(p. 172). If there remains any doubt as to what the chimney symbolizes,
the narrator dispels it with his remark that "the chimney's gentle heat"
causes his "wife's geraniums" to bud—"Bud in December. Her eggs,
too—can't keep them near the chimney, on account of hatching. Ah, a
warm heart has my chimney" (p. 168). The problem, says the narrator, is
that although he and his wife are both growing old, "in spirit she is
young as my little sorrel mare, Trigger, that threw me last fall," and she
believes that she is still young in body: "My wife never thinks of her end.

Her youthful incredulity, as to the plain theory, and still plainer fact of death, hardly seems Christian. Advanced in years, as she knows she must be, my wife seems to think that she is to teem on, and be inexhaustible forever.... At that strange promise in the plain of Mamre, my old wife, unlike old Abraham's, would not have jeeringly laughed within herself" (pp. 169–70)—the promise is, of course, that Sara will bear a child.

The narrator characterizes his wife's attempt to fell the chimney as a symbolic decapitation/castration, remarking that "whenever, against her most ambitious innovations, those which saw me quite across the grain, I, as in the present instance, stand with however little steadfastness on defence, she is sure to call me Holofernes.... Holofernes ... is with her a pet name for any fell domestic despot" (p. 178). It is also the name of the Assyrian general who is decapitated by Judith in the Apocrypha. Earlier, the narrator, pursuing the metaphor of the chimney as "king of the house," compares the previous owner's removal of part of the chimney's top to the decapitation of Charles I: the "beheading" of the "royal old chimney" is "a regicidal act which ... should send that former proprietor down to posterity in the same cart with Cromwell" (p. 163).

Melville's explicit linking of the phallic chimney to the cult worship of Osiris occurs when the narrator takes a master mason named Hiram Scribe down to the cellar to show him the base of the chimney: "We seemed in the pyramids; and I, with one hand holding my lamp overhead, and with the other pointing out, in the obscurity, the hoar mass of the chimney, seemed some Arab guide, showing the cob-webbed mausoleum of the great god Apis" (p. 175). Wilkinson, in *A Second Series of the Manners and Customs of the Ancient Egyptians,* points out that Osiris "was also worshipped under the form of Apis, the Sacred Bull of Memphis, or as a human figure with a bull's head, accompanied by the name 'Apis-Osiris'" (1:347). And Plutarch, noting the connection between Apis and Osiris, adds, "Most of the priests say that Osiris and Apis are conjoined into one, thus ... informing us that we must regard Apis as the bodily image of the soul of Osiris" (5:71). The narrator says that his wife regards the chimney as "the bully of the house" (p. 173). Moreover, the common representation of Apis-Osiris as "a human figure with a bull's head," resembling the minotaur, sheds light on the narrator's remark that, because of the central position of the bully of the house and the many passageways around it, "never was there so labyrinthine an abode" (p. 173).

If the base of the chimney reminds the narrator of the mausoleum of Apis, it is not surprising that "the huge bricks in the chimney walls" evoke another Egyptian image: "The architect of the chimney must have had the pyramid of Cheops before him; for after that famous structure it seems modeled, only its rate of decrease towards the summit is considerably less, and it is truncated. From the exact middle of the mansion it soars from the cellar, right up through each successive floor, till, four feet square, it breaks water from the ridge pole of the roof, like an anvil-headed whale, through the crest of a billow" (p. 163). And so the phallic chimney modeled on a pyramid is related to the sperm whale Moby Dick with the "pyramidical white hump."

In *Anacalypsis* Godfrey Higgins refers to "the great Pyramid where the bones of the Beeve were found" (2:104), and he speculates that the Beeve (Apis) "is both *cow* and *bull*," just as "Abba was both *parent* and *father*" (2:181). In accordance with the double nature of the dying and reviving god Osiris, the chimney is associated with both the dismembered/life-giving phallus and the pyramid as tomb/womb. At the instigation of the narrator's wife the master mason Hiram Scribe warns the narrator, "There is architectural cause to conjecture that somewhere concealed in your chimney is a reserved space, hermetically closed, in short, a secret chamber, or rather closet" (p. 179), and hinting that the chimney should be dismantled, Scribe wonders "whether it is Christian-like knowingly to reside in a house, hidden in which is a secret closet" (p. 180). When his wife begins to speculate on the possible contents of such a closet, the narrator suggests "dry bones," emphasizing the sepulchral aspect of the chimney.

The detail of the secret closet may well be based on the significance of the coffin in the Osiris myth. Plutarch recounts the "treacherous plot" against Osiris by his evil half-brother Typhon:

Typhon, having secretly measured Osiris's body and having made ready a beautiful chest of corresponding size artistically ornamented, caused it to be brought into the room where the festivity was in progress. The company was much pleased at the sight of it and admired it greatly, whereupon Typhon jestingly promised to present it to the man who should find the chest to be exactly his length when he lay down in it. They all tried it in turn, but no one fitted it; then Osiris got into it and lay down, and those who were in

the plot ran to it and slammed down the lid, which they fastened by
nails from the outside. . . . Then they carried the chest to the river
and sent it on its way to the sea through the Tanitic Mouth. (5:35–37)

After a lengthy search, Isis discovers that "the chest had been cast up
by the sea near the land of Byblus and that the waves had gently set it
down in the midst of a clump of heather. The heather in a short time ran
up into a very beautiful and massive stock, and enfolded and embraced
the chest with its growth and concealed it within its trunk. The king of
the country admired the great size of the plant, and cut off the portion
that enfolded the chest (which was now hidden from sight), and used it
as a pillar to support the roof of his house" (5:39–41). Isis discloses
herself to the king and asks for the pillar "which served to support the
roof. She removed it with the greatest ease and cut away the wood of the
heather which surrounded the chest; then, when she had wrapped up
the wood in a linen cloth . . . , she entrusted it to the care of the kings;
and even to this day the people of Byblus venerate this wood which is
preserved in the shrine of Isis. . . . Having placed the coffin on board a
boat, she put out from land" (5:41–43). In the cult worship of Osiris the
erection of the *djed* pillar (the tree trunk representing the backbone of
the god) commemorated his entombment in the tree, his rebirth from
the trunk with his sister as midwife, and the continued veneration of the
pillar in the shrine of Isis at Byblus. The narrator of "I and My Chimney" compares the chimney to "a hollow beech tree," and when his
wife proposes to abolish it, he replies, "Abolish the chimney? To take
out the backbone of anything, wife, is a hazardous affair. Spines out
of backs, and chimneys out of houses, are not to be taken like frosted
lead-pipes from the ground. . . . No, no, wife, I can't abolish my backbone" (p. 175).

According to Plutarch, Isis brought the chest containing Osiris to Buto
and hid it, "but Typhon, who was hunting by night in the light of the
moon, happened upon it. Recognizing the body he divided it into fourteen parts and scattered them, each in a different place" (5:45). After a
search, Isis regathered all the parts of the body except "the male
member," which could not be found, so "Isis made a replica of the
member to take its place, and consecrated the phallus, in honour of
which the Egyptians even at the present day celebrate a festival" (5:47).
Plutarch concludes his summary of the myth of Isis and Osiris by men-

tioning that he has omitted "the most infamous of the tales, such as that about the dismemberment of Horus and the decapitation of Isis" (5:49)—an indication of the symbolic linking of castration and decapitation in the myth.

The "chest" of Osiris that Isis brings back by ship to Buto as part of the scenario of rebirth is transformed by Melville into Queequeg's hieroglyphically inscribed coffin/lifebuoy on board the *Pequod*. Watching the ship's carpenter altering the coffin to a new purpose, Ahab muses, "Here now's the very dreaded symbol of grim death, by a mere hap, made the expressive sign of the help and hope of most endangered life. A lifebuoy of a coffin! Does it go further? Can it be that in some spiritual sense the coffin is, after all, but an immortality-preserver! I'll think of that. But no. So far gone am I in the dark side of earth, that its other side, the theoretic bright one, seems but uncertain twilight to me" (p. 433). Bruce Franklin has shown how the battle between Ahab and Moby Dick is, in many respects, modeled on the battle between Osiris and Typhon. But what needs to be emphasized is that in the earliest forms of the myth Osiris and his half-brother Typhon are reciprocal deities. They have the same mother (Rhea); but Osiris's father is the sun, while Typhon's is Cronus. As a reviving god, Osiris is identified with his father and the vivifying power of sunlight. Plutarch notes: "Everywhere they point out statues of Osiris in human form of the ithyphallic type, on account of his creative and fostering power; and they clothe his statues in a flame-colored garment, since they regard the body of the Sun as a visible manifestation of all the perceptible substance of the power for good.... In the sacred hymns of Osiris they call upon him who is hidden in the arms of the Sun.... There are some who without reservation assert that Osiris is the Sun and is called the Dog-star (Sirius) by the Greeks even if among the Egyptians the addition of the article has created some ambiguity in regard to the name" (5:125–29).

As Osiris is identified with the life-giving power of light and moisture, so Typhon is identified with their opposites. Plutarch says that there "are some who give the name of Typhon to the Earth's shadow, into which they believe the moon slips when it suffers eclipse" (5:109). Likewise, "the insidious scheming and usurpation of Typhon ... is the power of drought, which gains control and dissipates the moisture which is the source of the Nile and its rising" (5:95). Thus there attaches to Typhon "nothing bright or of a conserving nature, no order nor generation nor movement possessed of moderation or reason, but everything the reverse" (5:125). Yet what Plutarch repeatedly points out is that Osiris and Typhon are mutually constitutive deities: "The great majority and wisest of men hold this opinion: they believe that there are two gods, rivals as it were, the one the Artificer of good and the other of evil. There are also those who call the better one a god and the other a daimon, as, for example, Zoroaster the sage" (5:111–13). And again: "The fact is that the creation and constitution of this world is complex, resulting, as it does, from opposing influences, which, however, are not of equal strength, but the predominance rests with the better. Yet it is impossible for the bad to be completely eradicated, since it is innate, in large amount, in the body and likewise in the soul of the Universe, and is always fighting a hard fight against the better" (5:121).

Plutarch's singling out Zoroaster as the obvious example of a sage who taught the mutually constitutive opposition of light and dark as good and evil reminds us that Ahab's dark double, Fedallah, is a Zoroastrian (a "Parsee") and that in the chapter called "The Candles" Ahab says, "Oh! thou clear spirit of clear fire, whom on these seas I as Persian once did worship, till in the sacramental act so burned by thee, that to this hour I bear the scar; I now know thee, thou clear spirit, and I now know that thy right worship is defiance" (p. 416). Earlier, in discussing the whiteness of the whale, Ishmael had remarked that "the Persian fire worshippers" considered "the white forked flame" to be "the holiest on the altar" (p. 164). The white forked flame that scars the fire-worshiping Ahab is, of course, Moby Dick.

Wilkinson quotes Plutarch at length regarding the mutually constitutive nature of Osiris and Typhon and observes that the Egyptians, "looking . . . upon the bad as a necessary part of the universal system, and inherent in all things equally with the good, treated the Evil Being with divine honours, and propitiated him with sacrifices and prayers" (1:423). Wilkinson then takes the change that occurred in Typhon's status during a later period of Egyptian religion as an example of the way that an original insight into the complex relationship of man and the universe was lost when one half of a bipolar opposition was wholly separated from, and privileged over, the other half. He speculates:

> . . . good and bad, which were viewed abstractedly at one period, were afterwards treated literally; nothing then remaining but the mere opposition of Osiris and Typho, the positively good and the

positively bad Being,—the one all that was beneficial, the other all that was noxious to mankind. If one was the Nile, which fertilised the country; the other was the desert, which destroyed all vegetable life: and they no longer entertained the opinions of those earlier philosophers, who contended that good and bad formed part of one great principle; that evil proceeded from good, as good from evil; and that both were intended for the benefit of mankind.

It was not until men considered the bad distinctly separate from the good, in a positive and literal sense, that Typho was treated as the enemy of man. Such was the idea entertained by the Roman votaries of Osiris. There is even reason to believe that a similar change in the sentiments of the Egyptians towards this Deity is hinted at by Plutarch.... (1:425–26)

In *Moby-Dick* Melville's use of the Osiris myth pits its original sense of the reciprocal nature of good and evil, of light and dark, against Ahab's desire for an absolute separation of opposites and the destruction of one by the other. In reworking the battle between Osiris and Typhon, Melville indicates their mutually constitutive character by giving elements of each deity to both Ahab and Moby Dick, so that hunter and hunted periodically reverse roles within the mythic scenario. Thus Ahab's dismemberment by Moby Dick is described in terms that seem to identify Ahab with the dying and reviving Osiris. Melville says that "though unlimbed of a leg ... vital strength yet lurked" in Ahab's "Egyptian chest" (p. 160). And Moby Dick, in his role as "dismemberer" (p. 147), corresponds to the common representation of Typhon as some form of water monster. (Typhon is frequently depicted in Egyptian mythology as a crocodile, and in the chapter called "The Prairie," Ishmael, discussing the whale's "pyramidical silence," compares the whale to the crocodile which, according to Plutarch, was deified by the Egyptians because it was tongueless and thus silent like God [p. 292].) But where Typhon is associated with darkness and drought, the sperm whale Moby Dick is associated with whiteness and with the life-giving power of water—even to the extent of bearing a "fountain" on his back. Further, though Ahab addresses the "clear spirit of clear fire" as his "father" (p. 417), reminiscent of Osiris's descent from the Sun, Melville refers at one point to "Ahab's larger, darker, deeper part" (p. 161). And though Moby Dick dismembers Ahab, the only castration mentioned in the novel is that which the *Pequod*'s crew performs upon the sperm whales during the slaughtering process. Indeed, one of the most important characteristics of Osiris as a dying and reviving god is assigned to the sperm whales rather than to Ahab—the transformation into the light.

The myth of Osiris presents the conjugate mysteries of death and rebirth in the vegetative cycle and of waning and waxing in the solar cycle. Osiris's annual *sparagmos,* by which the land is fertilized and life born out of death, is part of a seasonal vegetative cycle linked to the waning of daylight and vital warmth in fall and winter as the god of light is losing his battle with the god of darkness and to the waxing of the light after the winter solstice as the year moves toward summer. Linking the vegetative and solar cycles, Osiris represents that characteristic religious moment in which the notion of "life" is translated from the material to the spiritual, from earth to sky, visible to invisible—a moment whose annual celebration in the ancient world occurred, either at the winter solstice or the vernal equinox, as an epiphany of light. This epiphany, in which the vivifying power of light frees itself from the cold, dark shadow of earth, took various archetypal forms such as the light in the cave, the light in the tree, and the light rising above the hill. Thus the birth of Christ at the winter solstice combines the iconography of both the light in the cave (manger) and the light in the tree, while his resurrection (rebirth) at the vernal equinox combines that of the light in the cave (tomb) and the light rising above the hill.

In *Moby-Dick* the Osiris-like transformation of the dying physical body into the incorruptible light is assigned to the sperm whales. Through their death and dismemberment the whales are changed into pure oil for lamps and into spermaceti candles. Ishmael says that the sperm whale "must die the death and be murdered, in order to light the gay bridals and other merry-makings of men, and also to illuminate the solemn churches that preach unconditional inoffensiveness by all to all" (p. 301). And in *Mardi* Melville speaks of the "whale, whose brain enlightens the world" (p. 3). As the figure of Osiris links the generative power of light to the life-giving power of the phallus, so the *sperm*aceti candle made from the dismembered whale emits light from a phallic shape. When, in the chapter called "The Candles," the epiphany of the "clear spirit of clear fire" in the form of atmospheric electricity leaves the masts of the *Pequod* "silently burning ... like three gigantic wax tapers before an altar" (p. 415), Stubb takes it for a sign of good luck, explaining that the "masts are rooted in a hold that is going to be chock a' block with sperm-oil, d'ye see; and so, all that sperm will work up into the masts, like sap in a tree. Yes, our three masts will yet be as three spermaceti candles" (p. 416). The comparison of the mast to both a tree and a candle suggests that epiphany of the light in the tree that is celebrated annually at Christmas as the candle on the tree. Earlier, Melville explicitly associates phallus, tree, and sun in the image of the hieroglyphic doubloon nailed to the mast. The coin shows "the likeness of three Andes' summits; from one a flame; a tower on another; on the third a crowing cock; while arching over all was a segment of the partitioned zodiac, the signs all marked with their usual cabalistics, and the keystone sun entering the equinoctial point at Libra" (p. 359). When the hieroglyphically inscribed Queequeg examines the coin, Stubb remarks, "He's comparing notes; looking at his thigh bone; thinks the sun is in the thigh.... And by Jove, he's found something there in the vicinity of his thigh—I guess it's Sagittarius, or the Archer" (p. 362).

Paralleling the transformation of a physical body into incorruptible light within the Osiris myth is the translation of the god's body into an inscribed memory. Associating the body of Osiris with the corpus of sacred writings in his cult, Plutarch notes that just as Typhon dismembers and scatters the pieces of Osiris's body, which Isis regathers, so Typhon also "tears to pieces and scatters to the winds the sacred writings, which the goddess collects and puts together and gives into the keeping of those that are initiated into the holy rites" (5:9). The initiated are those "who within their own soul, as though within a casket, bear the sacred writings about the gods clear of all superstition and pedantry; and they cloak them with secrecy, thus giving intimations, some dark and shadowy, some clear and bright, of their concepts about the gods, intimations of the same sort as are clearly evidenced in the wearing of the sacred garb" (5:11). Typhon's scattering of the sacred writings and their regathering in the minds of the initiated, as an analogue of the inseminating *sparagmos* of Osiris, is an ancestor of the trope of the leaves in Shelley's "Ode to the West Wind" ("Drive my dead thoughts over the universe / Like withered leaves to quicken a new birth! / And, by the incantation of this verse, / Scatter, as from an unextinguished hearth / Ashes and sparks, my words among mankind!" [p. 642]), and thus of Hawthorne's image, in the preface to *The Scarlet Letter,* of the author casting "his leaves forth upon the wind" in order to regather the divided self. Further, the veiling, in a cloak of secrecy, of the sacred writings contained in the Osirian "casket" of the votary's soul, along with the "shadowy" intimations of the mysteries given by "the wearing of the sacred garb," is the same type of veiled unveiling associated with the garment images in Hawthorne's novel.

The transformation of the god's body into a written corpus is the governing trope for Ishmael's translation of Moby Dick into *Moby-Dick* and the basis for his continuing image of the whale's body as a book. *Moby-Dick* begins with an etymological section in which Melville traces the origin of the English word "whale" and then gives the word's equivalent in thirteen other languages, two of which he invents. He also presents a collection of seventy-nine extracts from world literature ranging from the Book of Genesis to Nantucket folk songs, evoking the history of the whale as a written entity. In the chapter called "Cetology," where he attempts a "systematized exhibition of the whale in his broad genera" (p. 116), nothing less than "the classification of the constituents of a chaos" (p. 117), Ishmael orders this chaos by arranging the whales according to size, and the ordering metaphor for this arrangement is the sizes of books. Thus there are three major divisions of whales—folio, octavo, and duodecimo—and the subdivisions range from chapter 1 of the folio (the sperm whale) to chapter 3 of the duodecimo (the mealy-mouthed porpoise). Beyond the fact that the thin sheets of whale blubber are called "bible leaves," the bookish character of the whale's body is emphasized by Ishmael's remark that the outer covering of the whale's skin, which resembles isinglass, makes a perfect bookmark: "It is transparent . . . and being laid upon the printed page, I have sometimes pleased myself with fancying it exerted a magnifying influence" (p. 259). Ishmael adds that the whale's skin itself is "obliquely crossed and re-crossed with numberless straight marks in thick array, something like those in the finest Italian line engravings" (p. 260); and these marks form "hieroglyphical" shapes resembling "those mysterious cyphers on the walls of pyramids."

Since the shape of the whale's body as well as the markings on its surface are hieroglyphs, Ishmael employs the pictographic analyses of physiognomy and phrenology in attempting to decipher the whale's meaning:

> To scan the lines of his face, or feel the bumps on the head of this Leviathan; this is a thing which no Physiognomist or Phrenologist has as yet undertaken. . . . Still, in that famous work of his, Lavater

not only treats of the various faces of men, but also attentively studies the faces of horses, birds, serpents, and fish; and dwells in detail upon the modifications of expression discernible therein. Nor have Gall and his disciple Spurzheim failed to throw out some hints touching the phrenological characteristics of other beings than man. (P. 291)

But the difficulty that the sperm whale poses to physiognomic analysis is the "god-like" indeterminacy of his head. He seems to be all brow and no features, a ground without a figure: looking at the whale's brow "you see no one point precisely; not one distinct feature is revealed . . . nothing but that one broad firmament of a forehead, pleated with riddles; dumbly lowering with the doom of boats, and ships, and men" (p. 292). And, says Ishmael, "If the Sperm Whale be physiognomically a Sphinx, to the phrenologist his brain seems that geometrical circle which it is impossible to square" (p. 293). But where physiognomy was thwarted by the whale's divine indeterminacy, its lack of any distinct surface feature, phrenology is defeated by the illusory structure of the whale's head.

Ishmael says that "phrenologically the head of this Leviathan, in the creature's living intact state, is an entire delusion. As for his true brain, you can see no indications of it, nor feel any. The whale, like all things that are mighty, wears a false brow to the common world" (p. 293). The structure of the whale's head does not exhibit a necessary correspondence between outer shape and inner meaning, between the configuration of the skull and the functions of the brain, so that "indeterminacy" as modified by this example seems to be another name for the illusion of meaning itself, the illusion that there exists a determinate, objective meaning (beyond the surface of self-projected, self-interpreted significance) in opposition to which the word "indeterminate" signifies. In a passage that anticipates the description of the world in *Pierre* as "nothing but surface stratified on surface," Ishmael says of his attempt to anatomize the whale that "dissect him how I may, . . . I but go skin deep; I know him not, and never will" (p. 318). And he adds, parodying God's words in Jeremiah 18:17: "Thou shalt see my back parts, my tail, he seems to say, but my face shall not be seen. But I cannot completely make out his back parts; and hint what he will about his face, I say again he has no face" (p. 318).

In the midst of his unsuccessful physiognomic and phrenological analyses, Ishmael contrasts his attempt to decipher the whale's "pyramid-ical silence" with the work of Champollion: "Champollion deciphered the wrinkled granite hieroglyphics. But there is no Champollion to de-cipher the Egypt of every man's and every being's face. Physiognomy, like every other human science, is but a passing fable. If then, Sir William Jones, who read in thirty languages, could not read the simplest peasant's face in its profounder and more subtle meanings, how may unlettered Ishmael hope to read the awful Chaldee of the Sperm Whale's brow? I but put that brow before you. Read it if you can" (pp. 292–93). Melville had used this image of Champollion and the undecipher-able hieroglyphics of the human face in *Mardi* two years earlier: The narrator says that the priest Aleema looked "like a scroll of old parchment, covered all over with hieroglyphical devices, harder to in-terpret . . . than any old Sanscrit manuscript. And upon his broad brow, deep-graven in wrinkles, were characters still more mysterious, which no Champollion nor gipsy could have deciphered. He looked old as the elderly hills; eyes sunken, though bright; and head white as the summit of Mont Blanc" (p. 130). In this earlier version, the ground on which the hieroglyphic marks are engraved is compared to the Shelleyan Mont Blanc rather than to an Egyptian pyramid. Yet the allusion to Shelley's poem may be intended to evoke both the veiled figure at Sais and the unanswering silence of the pyramids.

In "Mont Blanc" Shelley's opening image of the river of Being metamorphoses into a description of the "Ravine of Arve," where "earthly rainbows" arch "across the sweep / Of the aethereal waterfall, whose veil / Robes some unsculptured image" (pp. 583–84). The source of the Arve is the mountain glaciers moving

> Like snakes that watch their prey, from their
>   far fountains,
> Slow rolling on; there, many a precipice,
> Frost and the Sun in scorn of mortal power
> Have piled: dome, pyramid, and pinnacle,
> A city of death, distinct with many a tower
> And wall impregnable of beaming ice.
> Yet not a city, but a flood of ruin
> Is there, that from the boundaries of the sky

Rolls its perpetual stream;
 . . . the rocks, drawn down
From yon remotest waste, have overthrown
The limits of the dead and living world,
Never to be reclaimed.

(P. 585)

Above the glaciers stands Mont Blanc, its distant, blank whiteness silent to all questioning. In a final apostrophe to the mountain, the poet says,

The secret Strength of things
Which governs thought, and to the infinite dome
Of Heaven is as a law, inhabits thee!
And what were thou, and earth, and stars, and sea,
If to the human mind's imaginings
Silence and solitude were vacancy?

(P. 586)

As solidified water, the glaciers occupy the shifting boundary between stasis and motion, between mountain and river—"the limits of the dead and living world." Just as the deathlike frost can turn flowing water into rocky ice, so the sun can reverse the process and restore it to life-giving moisture. The glacier image thus phrases the question of death and rebirth as the epistemological problem of accepting such oppositions as animate/inanimate or motion/stasis as the criteria of the opposition living/dead. (Are the "mobile" atoms and molecules that constitute water and rock "alive" or "dead"?) Just as "the secret Strength of things" inhabits the rock of the mountain even though Mont Blanc seems static and inanimate to human perception, so the mountain's silence to human inquiry may not mean the absence of intelligence. For that very "silence" and "solitude" (in the sense of monotonal whiteness), that godlike reticence of nature, provides the aural and visual space for the projection of human intelligence whereby, perhaps, a pantheistic Power contemplates itself through the mode of human thought.

That death is an internal rather than an external limit of life, that annihilation is an illusion born of a limited human perspective, is a central theme of the myth of Isis and Osiris. Yet the problem posed by the notion of a vital persistence through radical changes of form is clearly exhibited in the paradoxical mode of survival associated with hieroglyphic writing. As we noted earlier, the Egyptian hieroglyphs are the preeminent form of monumental (that is, funerary) writing, the product of a civilization obsessed with death and survival, with carving figures in stone to outlast time, or turning corruptible bodies into per-durable, mummified images of themselves. The paradox of the hiero-glyphs is that the persistence of the engraved pictographic forms, the survival of intelligible morphology, depends on the "secret Strength" of stone, its hard, inanimate, "nonliving" quality, depends on an impervi-ousness to change far surpassing that of any living organism. One can recognize the persistence of the same chemical substance in steam, water, and ice, or the persistence of the human form from infancy to old age, but when that human form is lost as the chemical compounds in the dead body are dispersed into earth and water, then one is faced with the task of imagining the persistence of human intelligence in the survival of the body's material ground, a ground devoid of any symbolic shape. And in fact we associate the amorphous fluidity of water with the non-survival of the self, with the obliteration of a signifying inscription, as when Ishmael refers to "the proverbial evanescence of a thing writ in water" (p. 453), echoing Keats's despairing epitaph, "Here lieth one whose name was writ on water."

In the trope of the hieroglyphics, the writers of the American Renais-sance frequently associate the hardness of the stone that preserves the inscription with the "hardness" of breaking the crypt to decipher an ultimate meaning. In *A Week on the Concord and Merrimack Rivers* (1849), Thoreau remarks that the "monument of death will outlast the memory of the dead."[9] The "pyramids do not tell us the tale that was confided to them" (1:161), because the inhuman perdurability of stone preserves signs beyond the limits of human comprehension, beyond the bounds of living memory. In a passage that works a variation on the ending of *Pym*, Thoreau maintains: "Strictly speaking, the historical societies have not recovered one fact from oblivion, but are themselves instead of the fact that is lost. The researcher is more memorable than the researched. The crowd stood admiring the mist and the dim outlines of the trees seen through it, when one of their number advanced to explore the phenom-enon, and with fresh admiration all eyes were turned on his dimly re-treating figure. . . . Critical acumen is exerted in vain to uncover the past; the *past* cannot be *presented;* we cannot know what we are not. But one veil hangs over past, present, and future, and it is the province of the historian to find out, not what was, but what is" (1:161–62). Perhaps the most famous statement of this theme in classical antiquity is Plutarch's treatise "The E at Delphi," in which the various possible meanings of the enigmatic letter E (Greek EI) inscribed on Apollo's temple at Delphi are debated. Arguments are advanced for each of the three major possibilities ("five," "if," "thou art"), but as the analysis of "thou art" (considered as a salutation of Apollo) turns into a discussion of eternal Being, it becomes clear that the basic point of the treatise is the unrecoverability of the inscription's original meaning. Within the interpretive flux of history, the one, true meaning of the E is as unknowable as the eternal nature of the god. The letter carved in stone remains, the interpretations change.

Melville alludes to Plutarch's essay in *Pierre*, first, by matching the enigmatic E at Delphi with his own equally enigmatic "S. ye W." (p. 133) carved on the Memnon Stone near Pierre's home, and then by giving the title "EI" (p. 210) to Plotinus Plinlimmon's philosophical treatise on the incommensurability of an unchanging, eternal God and a fleeting, temporal world. Throughout *Pierre* the image of petrifaction is associated with a glimpse of the eternal, as in the book's dedication to "the majestic mountain, Greylock . . . eternally challenging our homage" or in the transformation that occurs in Pierre as he works at his book in stony silence: "In the midst of the merriments of the mutations of Time, Pierre hath ringed himself in with the grief of Eternity. Pierre is a peak inflexible in the heart of Time, as the isle-peak, Piko, stands unassaultable in the midst of waves" (p. 304).

Pierre's quest for fixed certainty, for an unmoving origin, is symbolically represented by his incestuous attachment to his half-sister Isabel—brother/sister incest serving as a substitutive reenactment of the primal scene of generation. (Pierre and his mother characteristically address each other as "brother" and "sister.") And Pierre's fate is foreshadowed in his dream of being transformed into the stone figure of the mutilated Titan Enceladus, who was "both the son and grandson of an incest" (p. 347): " 'Enceladus! It is Enceladus!'—Pierre cried out in his sleep. That moment the phantom faced him; and Pierre saw Enceladus no more; but on the Titan's armless trunk, his own duplicate face and features magnifiedly gleamed upon him with prophetic discomfiture and woe" (p. 346). Certainly, one of the allusive backgrounds to Pierre's quest for an unchanging absolute within the flux of time is the founding of an "eternal" church with the words "Thou art Peter, and upon this rock I will build my church" (Matthew 16:18)—Pierre, Peter, *petra*. Melville may also have been influenced in the conception of the novel by a passage in Novalis's *The Novices of Sais* (1800) in which one of the novices discusses the petrifying effect of the sublime:

> Whether anyone has ever understood the stones and the stars, I do not know, but if so, he must surely have been a noble creature. Only those statues that have come down to us from a lost age of mankind's glory, are illumined by so deep a spirit, so rare an understanding of the stone world; they cover the sensitive beholder with a rind of stone that seems to grow inward. The sublime has the power to petrify, hence we should not be surprised at the sublime in nature or its influence, or fail to know where to seek it. Might nature not have turned to stone at the sight of God? Or from fear at the advent of man?[10]

It is worth noting that in *Pierre* the veil image is most often associated with Isabel's dark, luxuriant hair, which cloaks her face and figure when she plays her mother's guitar (guitar→female torso→womb→indefiniteness of music). And what the veil of hair conceals from her half-brother is the sight of the father's phallus/child. When Pierre reads the letter in which Isabel reveals her identity, he is shocked by the truth—his "sacred father is no more a saint" (p. 65)—and exclaims: "Thou Black Knight, that with visor down, thus confrontest me, and mockest at me; Lo! I strike through the helm, and will see thy face, be it Gorgon!—Let me go, ye fond affections; all piety leave me;—I will be impious, for piety hath juggled me, and taught me to revere, where I should spurn. From all idols, I tear all veils; henceforth I will see the hidden things; and live right out in my own hidden life" (pp. 65–66). Later, when Pierre has broken with his mother because of Isabel, his half-sister asks him, "Do I blast where I look? is my face Gorgon's?" (p. 189). Medusa, the sight of whose face turned men to stone, is a petrifying image of the primal scene, of the "original" merging of opposites represented by the conjunction of the Gorgon's phallic, snaky hair and *vagina dentata* mouth (one recalls the painting by Caravaggio); and the Gorgon's fate—its decapitation by Perseus—as clearly links petrifaction and castration as does the tale of Enceladus, where the two are associated as punishments for incest (the substitutive reenactment of the primal scene). (In *Moby-Dick* Ishmael says that Perseus was "the first whale-man" [p. 304] by reason of his slaying the sea monster that threatened the virgin Andromeda.)

The mysterious quality of Isabel's face is a recurring theme in *Pierre* precisely because Isabel's facial resemblance to the so-called chair-portrait of Pierre's father is the main evidence that convinces Pierre that she is his half-sister and that he must give her their father's name, even if that means pretending that she is his wife and thereby sacrificing his own future. (Isabel had originally learned her father's name when the strange gentleman who came to see her as a child left behind, on his last visit, a handkerchief with his name inscribed on it. Isabel hid the handkerchief until she "mastered the alphabet, and went on to spelling, and by-and-by to reading, and at last to the complete deciphering of the talismanic word—Glendinning" [p. 147]. The writing on the handkerchief/veil at once conceals and reveals: the patronymic [the phonetically veiled phallus] replaces in part/whole fashion the father whom she is never to see again.) Near the end of the novel, Pierre, Isabel, and Lucy visit a picture gallery where Pierre and his half-sister are astonished by a painting entitled *A stranger's head, by an unknown hand.* The painting shows "a dark, comely, youthful man's head, portentously looking out of a dark, shaded ground, and ambiguously smiling. There was no discoverable drapery; the dark head, with its crisp, curly, jetty hair, seemed just disentangling itself out of curtains and clouds. But to Isabel, in the eye and on the brow, were certain shadowy traces of her own unmistakable likeness; while to Pierre, this face was in part as the resurrection of the one he had burnt at the Inn" (p. 351), that is, the chair-portrait of his father. On the gallery wall directly opposite the portrait of the stranger is a copy of the "Cenci of Guido," the unfortunate Beatrice being a figure "double-hooded, as it were, by the black crape of the two most horrible crimes (of one of which she is the object, and of the other the agent) possible to civilized humanity—incest and parricide" (p. 351). Isabel's resemblance to the portrait of the stranger makes Pierre realize how uncertain is the evidence of his own relationship to her—her mere resemblance to a portrait of his father. Judging simply on the grounds of resemblance, one might conclude that "the original of this second portrait was as much the father of Isabel as the original of the chair-portrait" (p. 353). What Pierre must finally assent to is the essential ambiguity, that is, undecipherability, of the hieroglyphics of the human face. But the portrait of Beatrice Cenci on the opposite wall is a reminder that this ambiguity cuts in two directions, for if Pierre cannot be certain that Isabel is his half-sister, he also cannot be certain that she is not, in which case his feelings for her are incestuous and represent a kind of parricidal displacement of the father's authority— both of which offenses are punishable by castration, by being turned to stone.

In *Moby-Dick* the undecipherability of the marks on the whale's "pyramidical white hump" is associated with the inability to break through a stone wall. Ahab tells Starbuck that man must strike through "the unreasoning mask" of "visible objects" to reach what lies beyond it: "How can the prisoner reach outside except by thrusting through the wall? To me, the white whale is that wall, shoved near to me. Sometimes I think there's naught beyond. But 'tis enough" (p. 144). Yet later, Ahab admits, "The dead, blind wall butts all inquiring heads at last" (p. 427). In "Bartleby the Scrivener" (1853), the main character spends long periods "looking out, at his pale window behind the screen, upon the dead brick wall."[11] The narrator has some inkling of the subject of Bartleby's "dead-wall reveries" (p. 111) when he observes that the scrivener "seemed alone, absolutely alone in the universe. A bit of wreck in the mid Atlantic" (p. 116). After Bartleby is imprisoned within the "Egyptian ... masonry" of New York City's "Tombs," the narrator finds him "standing all alone in the quietest of yards, his face towards a high wall" (p. 128). And when the narrator again discovers him in the same place some days later, lying dead against the wall, he says that the spot seemed like "the heart of the eternal pyramids" (p. 130).

In *Mardi* Melville links the undecipherable hieroglyphics of the human face to the image of the hard, silent, indeterminate Mont Blanc within the context of the ancient mystery cults. When the narrator Taji first sees the hieroglyphic brow of Aleema, the old priest and his sons are embarked on a native sailing vessel that bears a mysterious tent upon its stern:

They pointed toward the tent, as if it contained their Eleusinian mysteries. And the old priest gave us to know, that it would be profanation to enter it.

But all this only roused my curiosity to unravel the wonder.

At last I succeeded.

In that mysterious tent was concealed a beautiful maiden. And, in pursuance of a barbarous custom, by Aleema, the priest, she was being borne an offering from the island of Amma to the gods of Tedaidee. (P. 131)

Taji decides to rescue the maiden, and after a skirmish in which he kills Aleema, he draws back the veil of the tent as the frightened natives "covered their faces." Within the tent he finds a maiden with "snow-white skin," "fair hair," and "blue, firmament eyes" who trembles "like a sound" and speaks an unknown language of "musical words" (pp. 136–37). The maiden says that her name is Yillah and that Aleema, who raised her, claimed that she was "more than mortal, a maiden of Oroolia, the Island of Delights, somewhere in the paradisiacal archipelago of the Polynesians" (p. 137). Before their sea journey Aleema had told Yillah "that the spirits in Oroolia had recalled her home by the way of Tedaidee, on whose coast gurgled up in the sea an enchanted spring; which streaming over upon the brine, flowed on between blue watery banks; and, plunging into a vortex, went round and round, descending into depths unknown. Into this whirlpool Yillah was to descend in a canoe, at last to well up in an inland fountain of Oroolia" (p. 138).

The manner of the maiden's proposed return to her mysterious origin via the whirlpool/fountain conjunction, along with her subsequent disappearance and the narrator's fruitless search throughout the rest of the novel, recall the quest for the dream-maiden by the poet in Shelley's *Alastor*. Further, the reference to the Eleusinian mysteries in connection with the veiling of Yillah evokes the worship of the mysterious goddess (Demeter/Persephone, Isis) and recalls the story of Hyacinth and Rose Petal in Novalis's *The Novices of Sais*. One of the novices at the temple of Isis tells the story of the youth Hyacinth who left his childhood sweetheart Rose Petal to seek the dwelling of "the mother of things, the veiled maiden": "Everywhere he asked for the sacred goddess Isis" (p. 63), and after much wandering "he fell asleep, for only a dream could take him to the holy of holies. And the strange dream led him through endless halls full of curious things, amid melodious sounds and changing harmonies. It seemed to him all so familiar and yet of a radiance such as he had never beheld; the last trace of earth vanished as though dissolved in air, and he stood before the heavenly maiden. He raised the light, shimmering veil, and Rose Petal sank into his arms. A distant music surrounded the mysteries of the lovers' meeting" (p. 67).

The story called "The Silvery Veil" that Zenobia tells in Hawthorne's *The Blithedale Romance* is a variation on this theme. The youth Theodore makes a wager with some friends that he will "find out the mystery of the Veiled Lady," even though rumor has it that the veil conceals "the face of a corpse," or "the head of a skeleton," or "a monstrous visage, with snaky locks, like Medusa's, and one great red eye in the centre of the forehead," or "the features of that person, in all the world, who was destined to be his fate" (3:110). Theodore steals into the Veiled Lady's dressing room and confronts her, asking to know who and what she is. She says that in order to learn her identity he must lift the veil, but she adds, "Before raising it, I entreat thee, in all maiden modesty, to bend forward, and impress a kiss, where my breath stirs the veil; and my virgin lips shall come forward to meet thy lips; and from that instant, Theodore, thou shalt be mine, and I thine, with never more a veil between us! And all the felicity of earth and of the future world shall be thine and mine together" (3:113). But Theodore, "whose natural tendency" is "towards scepticism," refuses, and "grasping at the veil," he flings it back, catching "a glimpse of a pale, lovely face, beneath; just one momentary glimpse; and then the apparition vanished, and the silvery veil fluttered slowly down, and lay upon the floor. Theodore was alone. Our legend leaves him there. His retribution was, to pine, forever and ever, for another sight of that dim, mournful face—which might have been his life-long household fireside joy—to desire, and waste life in a feverish quest, and never meet it more!" (3:113–14). Where the story of Hyacinth and Rose Petal represents the return to origin, to the womb, as an entry into a dreamlike state whose uncanny halls (at once "familiar" and strange) reveal that the "mother of things" is Hyacinth's childhood sweetheart, the story of Theodore and the Veiled Lady represents the necessary requirement for successfully penetrating the veil of maidenhead and avoiding the taboo of virginity (the woman's castratory animus against the first man) as a prior surrender of the phallic self to what lies behind the veil.

Pierre, "The Silvery Veil," and *The Novices of Sais* present an interesting anatomy of the image of petrifaction: in *Pierre* the petrifying gaze of Medusa is associated with the punishment for violating the authority of the father in the incest taboo; while in "The Silvery Veil" a Medusa-like figure with "one great red eye" is associated with the related taboo of virginity (correlatively, the desire to be the first to enter the beloved represents a form of the son's desire to supplant the father in the mother's affections by a return to origin so absolute that the son becomes the original man); and in *The Novices of Sais* the quest for "the mother of things, the veiled maiden" is associated with the search for the ultimate knowledge, for "the sublime" with its "power to petrify," the "sight of God"—imageless undifferentiated Being imaged as the conjunction father/mother, Osiris/Isis.

It is particularly appropriate that the transformation of the godlike whale into the book, of Moby Dick into *Moby-Dick,* is superimposed upon the myth of Isis and Osiris; for the figure of Osiris, besides combining the notion of personal survival with the image of the god's corpse transformed into the corpus of the sacred writings, is associated with the origin of writing and thus with the effort to penetrate the inscribed surface of the veil. In his *Travels to Discover the Source of the Nile* James Bruce, amplifying upon a passage from Diodorus Siculus (1:16.1), remarks, "If Osiris is a real personage, if he was king of Egypt, and Tot his secretary, they surely travelled to very good purpose, as all the people of Europe and Asia seem to be agreed, that in person they first communicated letters and the art of writing to them, but at very different, and very distant periods."[12] Bruce's description of "the secretary of Osiris" (*secretarius,* one entrusted with secrets) suggests Tot's phallic character, his function as a partial object in relation to his principal Osiris, his role as scribe, writing instrument, pen(is), abbreviated name:

> The word *Tot* is Ethiopic, and there can be little doubt it means the dog-star. It was the name given to the first month of the Egyptian year. The meaning of the name, in the language of the province of Sirè, is an *idol,* composed of different heterogeneous pieces; it is found having this signification in many of their books. Thus a naked man is not a *Tot,* but the body of a naked man, with a dog's head, an ass's head, or a serpent instead of a head, is a *Tot.* According to the import of the word, it is I suppose, an almanack, or section of the phaenomena in the heavens which are to happen in the limited time it is made to comprehend, when exposed for the information of the public. . . .
>
> Besides many other emblems or figures, the common Tot, I think, has in his hand a cross with a handle, as it is called *Crux Ansata,* which has occasioned great speculation among the decypherers.

This cross, fixed to a circle, is supposed to denote the *four elements,* and to be the symbol of the influence of the sun over them. Jamblichus records, that this cross, in the hand of Tot, is the name of the *divine Being* that travels through the world. Sozomen thinks it means the *life* to come, the same with the ineffable image of eternity. Others, strange difference! say it is the *phallus,* or human genitals, while a later writer maintains it to be the mariner's compass. My opinion, on the contrary is, that, as this figure was exposed to the public for the reason I have mentioned, the Crux Ansata in his hand was nothing else but a monogram of his own name TO, and ♀T signifying TOT, or as we write Almanack upon a collection published for the same purpose.

The changing of these emblems, and the multitude of them, produced the necessity of contracting their size, and this again a consequential alteration in the original forms; and a stile, or small portable instrument, became all that was necessary for finishing these small *Tots,* instead of a large graver or carving tool, employed in making the larger ones. But men, at last, were so much used to the alteration, as to know it better than under its primitive form, and the engraving became what we may call the first elements, or root, in preference to the original. (2:53–54).

(Melville mentions Bruce in *Mardi* [p. 298] and cites information found in the *Travels,* though Melville's usual image for the inaccessible origin of a river is that of the Niger rather than the Nile. In *Mardi* the narrator says, "Oh! where's the endless Niger's source? Search ye here, or search ye there; on, on, through ravine, vega, vale—no head waters will ye find" [p. 256], and in *Moby-Dick* Ahab speaks of "the Niger's unknown source" [p. 629].)

The variety of possible interpretations of Tot's *crux ansata* (the four elements, the name of the divine being, the ineffable image of eternity, the phallus, the mariner's compass, the cryptic abbreviation) and the fact that Tot's name signifies an idol of a composite character point to his role as the inscribed/inscribing symbol of Osiris's infinite meanings—to Tot as a symbol of symbolization. Through a network of bipolar oppositions (Osiris/Isis, Osiris/Typhon, Osiris/Horus, Osiris/Tot) in which one term remains the same while the opposing terms vary, the myth of Osiris attempts to explain the complex interrelationship of such dual concepts as life/death, light/dark, good/evil, true/false, masculine/ feminine, father/son, self/image, visible/invisible, presence/absence, symbol/meaning, and so on. The difficulty is that though the pairs of opposites are often of radically different logical orders, the process of differentiation by opposition is the same in each case and thus tends to encourage an equation of first terms from pair to pair and an equation of second terms. Thus, for example, the oppositions life/death, light/dark, good/ evil, true/false, up/down are rewritten as two equations (life equals light equals good equals true equals up and death equals dark equals evil equals false equals down) in Plato's allegory of the cave. In *De Iside et Osiride* Plutarch, discussing the idea that the universe "has come about, as the result of two opposed principles," "two antagonistic forces, . . . two gods, rivals as it were, the one the Artificer of the good and the other of evil" (5:111), says: "The adherents of Pythagoras include a variety of terms under these categories: under the good they set Unity, the Determinate, the Permanent, the Straight, the Odd, the Square, the Equal, the Right-handed, the Bright; under the bad they set Duality, the Indeterminate, the Moving, the Curved, the Even, the Oblong, the Unequal, the Left-handed, the Dark, on the supposition that these are the underlying principles of creation. For these, however, Anaxagoras postulates Mind and Infinitude, Aristotle Form and Privation, and Plato, in many passages, as though obscuring and veiling his opinion, names the one of the opposing principles 'Identity' and the other 'Difference'" (5:119). In the case of the Pythagoreans, Plutarch records the way in which a master opposition (good/bad) is made to govern the alignment of all other oppositions and thus the equation of all good first terms and all bad second terms. And in the cases of Anaxagoras, Aristotle, and Plato, he notes three different versions of the master opposition. Plutarch's late, comparatist perspective allows him to see Anaxagoras, Aristotle, Plato, and the Pythagoreans as moments in a continuing historical process—the effort, in Heidegger's words, to say the same about the Same—much the way that Melville's reading in comparative religion and mythology allowed him to view Osiris, Dionysus, and Christ as three successive versions of the same archetype.

As the master opposition of the Pythagoreans represents the privileging of a normative or valuative criterion, so those of Anaxagoras, Aristotle, and Plato represent, in Plutarch's account, the privileging of an epistemological criterion. One might broadly describe the intellectual

tradition in which Melville found himself at the middle of the nineteenth
century as the modern movement from the first of these criteria to the
second, a movement in which questions that had once been defined as
metaphysical and that had been reinterpreted as epistemological questions in the seventeenth and eighteenth centuries were just beginning to
be reinterpreted once more as linguistic questions in the nineteenth
century—the movement from an interest in an otherworld of absolute
values to an interest in how the mind knows the physical world to an
interest in how symbolization in a sense creates our "world." Since in this
historical process the oppositions that have to do with the very nature of
symbolization (identity/difference, self/other, figure/ground, and so on)
seem more basic than those that have to do with valuation, one can
understand how someone operating in this tradition might look at the
myth of Isis and Osiris, for example, and see the opposition between
Osiris and Tot (between the unseen self and its inscribed/inscribing phallic image) as more important than those oppositions (Osiris/Isis, Osiris/
Typhon, Osiris/Horus) with which the myth is mainly concerned. Indeed, when Nietzsche in *The Birth of Tragedy* reimagines the Greek
version of Osiris—"Osiris is identical with Dionysus" (5:85), Plutarch
repeatedly points out in *De Iside et Osiride*—he makes the primary significance of the opposition between Dionysus and Apollo the process of
symbolization itself: the tragic myth is an attempt to represent musical
(that is, indefinite) Dionysian wisdom in Apollonian dream images, to
express indeterminate (because overdetermined) meaning in determinate symbols. By making the very fact of human consciousness the primary object of that consciousness, by making the critique of symbolization the most important human study, one necessarily moves "beyond
good and evil," beyond any single differential opposition that is given to
us by/within the continuous system of differences that is language.

This movement can be clearly observed in a passage from *Pierre* in
which Isabel, feeling the growing attraction between herself and her
half-brother, asks him to explain why such an attraction is forbidden, to
explain virtue and vice:

> "What are they, in their real selves, Pierre? Tell me first what is
> Virtue:—begin!"
> "If on that point the gods are dumb, shall a pigmy speak? Ask the
> air!"

"Then Virtue is nothing."

"Not that!"

"Then Vice?"

"Look: a nothing is the substance, it casts one shadow one way, and another the other way; and these two shadows cast from one nothing; these, seems to me, are Virtue and Vice."

"Then why torment thyself so, dearest Pierre?"

"It is the law."

"What?"

"That a nothing should torment a nothing; for I am a nothing. It is all a dream—we dream that we dreamed we dream."

"Pierre, when thou just hovered on the verge, thou wert a riddle to me; but now, that thou art deep down in the gulf of the soul,—now, when thou wouldst be lunatic to wise men, perhaps—now doth poor ignorant Isabel begin to comprehend thee. Thy feeling hath long been mine, Pierre. Long loneliness and anguish have opened miracles to me. Yes, it is all a dream!"

Swiftly he caught her in his arms: "From nothing proceeds nothing, Isabel! How can one sin in a dream?"

"First what is sin, Pierre?"

"Another name for the other name, Isabel." (P. 274)

A moral question (the incest prohibition) becomes a question of the ontological status of the moral norm ("What are they, in their real selves"), but Pierre's sense of the bipolar norm virtue/vice is precisely that the poles have no separate, external existence in themselves, that they are a mutually constitutive opposition, a function of the bipolar structure of self-consciousness and thus that it is not a question of their ontological but of their epistemological or linguistic status ("Another name for the other name"). Having bracketed the moral question by making it secondary to the more "basic" epistemological question, Pierre then permanently defers it by invoking the idealist critique of the "reality" of waking consciousness—the fact that the equation of first terms in the oppositions waking/dream, reality/phantasy is based on an act of faith in the "real" existence of the external world, on an implicit privileging of physical nature as the test of reality.

Though Pierre expresses Melville's own doubts, Melville, by his ironic treatment of Pierre, tries to distance himself from those doubts, tries to remain, like Ishmael, outside the vortex, to avoid the self-destructive descent into "the gulf of the soul" that Pierre succumbs to as an author. Yet it is precisely Melville's concern with the mystery of the split and doubled nature of human consciousness that keeps drawing him back toward the abyss, toward an inescapable notion of the self as "a nothing" that "casts one shadow one way, and another the other way" and toward the question of why "a nothing should torment a nothing." It is an almost inevitable movement: from recognizing the mutually constitutive nature of bipolar opposites and thus the illusory character of any privileging of one pole over the other (for example, good over evil); to recognizing that the notion of a single master opposition such as good/evil is equally illusory in a network of symbolic relationships where meaning always involves translation and thus where the master opposition's meaning would be wholly dependent on all the other oppositions into which it is translated (whose polarities it aligns); to feeling that the self with its mysterious bipolar structure is not in itself a thing, not an enduring substance, but rather a changing function of symbolic relationships and thus subject not only to radical fluctuations within any given opposition (reversal into the opposite) but also to the ceaseless circulation of meaning, to the continual wandering from one opposition to another, so that the meaning of any object, for example, the "doubloon" nailed to the mast, is indeterminate because indefinitely overdetermined. This sense of the self's inherent instability, of its ability to adopt any role or mask, to become anything, precisely because in itself it is nothing, comes more and more to dominate Melville's thought. From *Mardi* to *The Confidence-Man* there is a growing sense that the privileging of the "self," the belief in its stable, independent existence, its godlikeness (God being the name for the personified absoluteness of the self), is the ultimate illusion, and that the clearest indication of the self's nonpersistence after death is its nonpersistence in life, its radical inconsistency.

One of the recurring themes of *The Confidence-Man* (1857) is the inconsistency of the self in real life versus that fictive consistency of character expected of figures in novels. Devoting the whole of chapter 14 to the discussion of an apparently inconsistent action by one of his characters, Melville notes the generally accepted principle that "in the depiction of any character, its consistency should be preserved," but then counters with the rule that "fiction based on fact should never be contradictory to it; and is it not a fact, that, in real life, a consistent character is a *rara avis*?"[13] Melville concludes that the unpopularity of books containing inconsistent characters is due not to their "untrueness" to fact but to the difficulty that readers find in understanding them: "But if the acutest sage be often at his wits' ends to understand living character, shall those who are not sages expect to run and read character in those mere phantoms which flit along a page, like shadows along a wall?" (p. 94).

In comparing human character inscribed on a page to a shadow outline projected on a wall, Melville makes explicit the image of hieroglyphic doubling present in his work from *Mardi* on, an image personified in the hieroglyphically inscribed double, Queequeg. Yet just as Queequeg could not decipher the hieroglyphics on his skin and just as Ishmael dismissed the attempts of physiognomy and phrenology to decipher the hieroglyphics of the human face and figure, so in chapter 14 Melville notes, "All those sallies of ingenuity, having for their end the revelation of human nature on fixed principles, have, by the best judges, been excluded with contempt from the ranks of the sciences—palmistry, physiognomy, phrenology, psychology" (p. 97). In place of the rule specifying that novelists "should represent human nature not in obscurity, but transparency,... it might rather be thought, that he, who, in view of its inconsistencies, says of human nature the same that, in view of its contrasts, is said of the divine nature, that it is past finding out, thereby evinces a better appreciation of it than he who, by always representing it in a clear light, leaves it to be inferred that he clearly knows all about it" (p. 96).

The main problem in deciphering the human "characters" inscribed by hieroglyphic doubling is precisely their doubleness—that doubleness which is at once the theme and method of *The Confidence-Man* and its masquerade. At the very beginning of chapter 14 Melville presents us with a hieroglyph of the inherently "two-faced" quality of self-consciousness: "As the last chapter was begun with a reminder looking forwards, so the present must consist of one glancing backwards" (p. 94). Since the word "chapter" ultimately derives from the Latin *caput* ("head"), the image of two chapters, one looking forward, the other backward, suggests two heads facing one another as if one contemplated a mirror image (the inconsistency of the character presented in chapter 13 is reflected upon in chapter 14), or a single, Janus-like head with two faces looking in opposite directions (the confrontation between Frank Goodman and Charlie Noble later in the novel contains a series of subtle references to the opposition of Dionysus and Apollo, and as Godfrey Higgins notes in *Anacalypsis*, "Precisely the same actions are attributed to Janus, which are attributed by the Greeks to Dionysus, and by the Egyptians to Osiris" [1:351]).

By raising the question of the ideal consistency of a fictional character versus the real inconsistency of the self, Melville obliquely draws attention to the central problem posed in the first half of the novel—whether the series of confidence men who precede the appearance of the Cosmopolitan are different individuals or simply one or two individuals going through a series of impersonations. Melville suggests the latter possibility at the novel's start when the mute stranger confronts the "placard . . . offering a reward for the capture of a mysterious impostor" (p. 4), yet the subsequent appearances of the confidence men are constructed with such purposeful ambiguity that we cannot decide for certain on one possibility or the other. Moreover, by placing this problem within the context of comparative religion, as Melville does through a series of allusions, he raises the question of whether the countless gods worshiped by mankind throughout its history, those idealized objects of human confidence, are individual deities or simply the masks (Janus, Osiris, Dionysus, Christ) of a single deity; indeed, he raises the question so that he can raise at the same time the possibility that the multiplication of these gods with their contradictory natures reveals their true origin as idealized projections of the inconsistent human self. The gods would thus be the historical track left by man's attempt to produce an image of the self so absolutely stable and independent that the process eventually reversed itself and God became imageless. One could, then, "in view of its inconsistencies," say "of human nature the same that, in view of its contrasts, is said of the divine nature, that it is past finding out"— precisely because the divine "contrasts" are the absolute projections of the human "inconsistencies."

In discussing the way that the consistency of fictional characters is achieved, Melville suggests the cause of the self's inconsistency, of its inherent doubleness: "That fiction, where every character can, by reason of its consistency, be comprehended at a glance, either exhibits but sections of character, making them appear for wholes, or else is very untrue to reality; while, on the other hand, that author who draws a character, even though to common view incongruous in its parts, as the flying-squirrel, and, at different periods, as much at variance with itself as the butterfly is with the caterpillar from which it changes, may yet, in so doing, be not false but faithful to facts" (p. 95). If the self is a composite made up of incongruous parts (like the Tot idols that Bruce describes as having human bodies and animal heads), then the illusion of consistency can only be achieved by making one part of the self stand for the whole, by the kind of illusory equation of part and whole that, within the scenario of hieroglyphic doubling, is understood to constitute the original symbolic act, the visible outline of the body being made to stand for the whole self (a composite of both the seen and the unseen). As we noted earlier, this mythic original act of symbolization provides an image of unity for the self by providing the self with the unity of a visible image, that unity which inheres in being "comprehended at a glance," in being present in a single look. Indeed, since any object of sight only presents one aspect of itself at a time to our glance, part always being hidden from view, the very concept of a visual object necessarily involves an illusory part/whole equation.

Yet there is an even more complex illusion involved in the image of the self as an object; for the self is not just the image in the mirror of self-reflective thought, it is the mirror as well. Melville's description in *Mardi* of the Polynesian native Samoa (a prototype of Queequeg as hieroglyphic double) suggests, through the style of Samoa's tattooing, the dual status of the self as image and mirror: "an obelisk in stature," Samoa has markings that cover "but a vertical half of his person, from crown to sole; the other side being free from the slightest stain. Thus clapped together, as it were, he looked like a union of unmatched moieties of two distinct beings; and your fancy was lost in conjecturing, where roamed the absent ones. When he turned round upon you suddenly, you thought you saw some one else, not him whom you had been regarding before" (pp. 98–99). A composite of mirror and image, ground and figure, the character of Samoa is split in two in *Moby-Dick* to produce Ishmael and Queequeg—the writing self and the written self.

In keeping with his role as a visible representation of the split and doubled nature of the self, Samoa is used by Melville to put in question the religious notion of personal survival based on the belief in man's composite nature as mortal body and immortal soul. The amputation of Samoa's infected arm provides the opportunity for challenging the equation of first terms in the oppositions whole/part, life/death, self/other:

. . . superstitiously averse to burying in the sea the dead limb of a body yet living; since in that case Samoa held, that he must very soon drown and follow it ... [and] equally dreading to keep the thing near him, he at last hung it aloft from the topmast-stay; where yet it was suspended, bandaged over and over in cerements. The hand that must have locked many others in friendly clasp, or smote a foe, was no food, thought Samoa, for fowls of the air nor fishes of the sea.

Now, which was Samoa? The dead arm swinging high as Haman? Or the living trunk below? Was the arm severed from the body, or the body from the arm? The residual part of Samoa was alive, and therefore we say it was he. But which of the writhing sections of a ten times severed worm, is the worm proper?

For myself, I ever regarded Samoa as but a large fragment of a man, not a man complete. (P. 78)

In the same vein Melville remarks that Samoa's "style of tattooing ... seemed rather incomplete" (p. 98).

The assumption that life resides in the whole rather than in the dismembered part and that personal identity belongs to life and thus to the whole begins to break down in dealing with relatively simple living forms like the worm, forms whose articulation is so slight or so barely perceptible that the part/whole distinction becomes uncertain. The association of life and identity with the whole runs into still further difficulties in the subsequent discussion of life after death by Media and his companions, for in this context the whole is understood to be the totality of living matter and the part the individual being. Denying that he would be guilty of any discourtesy to "the anonymous memory of the illustrious dead," Babbalanja reasons:

"... if death be a deaf-and-dumb death, a triumphal procession over their graves would concern them not. If a birth into brightness, then Mardi must seem to them the most trivial of reminiscences. Or, perhaps, theirs may be an utter lapse of memory concerning sublunary things; and they themselves be not themselves, as the butterfly is not the larva."

Said Yoomy, "Then, Babbalanja, you account that a fit illustration of the miraculous change to be wrought in man after death?"

"No; for the analogy has an unsatisfactory end. From its chrysalis state, the silkworm but becomes a moth, that very quickly expires. Its longest existence is as a worm. All vanity, vanity, Yoomy, to seek in nature for positive warranty to these aspirations of ours. Through all her provinces, nature seems to promise immortality to life, but destruction to beings." (Pp. 209–10)

Directly or indirectly Melville evokes most of the perplexing questions about the relationship of such concepts as life, self-consciousness, unity, and identity to the notion of a signifying form. Is there a basic chemical or biological form identified with life, a unit whose presence is an unfailing indicator of the difference between living and dead matter? And is there also a basic chemical or biological or physiological form identified with self-consciousness, a form whose persistence beyond the death of the body is a sure sign of the self's survival? How are self-consciousness and physical life joined in a human body, and how do they separate at death? If by "form" we understand a stable, identifiable unit or an identifiable recurrence in a dynamic system, and if our notion of living things is that they have organic forms in which parts are organized into a whole for the performance of specific functions, then what kinds of part/whole divisions are possible within living units? If an amoeba splits in two, it produces two living amoebas. If a man's body is split in two, we have two halves of a dead body. In the former case, where splitting is doubling, the part equals the original whole, and life inheres in both. In the latter case the part does not equal the whole, and neither life nor consciousness inheres in the parts. In the myth of the origin of self-consciousness as an act of hieroglyphic doubling, a part (the shadow outline of the body) is symbolically divided (differentiated) from the whole and at the same time considered as symbolically equal to the whole, is split and doubled. Does the very illusion that constitutes symbolization (the illusory equation of part and whole) imprint on the symbolic entity the illusion that life and consciousness can inhere in the symbolic part, in the image, just as they do in the body? Is the notion of the self's persistence after death simply a projection of that illusory consistency of the self in life achieved, as Melville says of consistent characters in fiction, by exhibiting "sections of character, making them appear for wholes"? In the case of Samoa's severed arm, though physical life and self-identity are understood to remain with the body rather than the detached limb, Samoa still feels that there is a symbolic equation of arm and body such that if the arm is cast into the sea he will soon "drown and follow it." In the myth of Osiris, the phallus is the part that is symbolically equal to the whole, the idol that stands for the god; but it is also the part in which life inheres, for it represents the power to generate life out of death, to create new life by cutting off a part from the living whole (a symbolic death) and having that part become a living whole of its own, as the seed becomes the child.

The original point of myths like those of Osiris and Dionysus was to explain the persistence of vegetative life through changes in form, to explain that immortality which nature, in Babbalanja's words, promises to life as a whole at the expense of its parts, individual beings. The dismemberment and scattering of the god's body represented the burial of the seed that would rise from the ground in the spring, the fertilizing of the land with the "effusion of Osiris." But as we noted earlier, from being explanations of the persistence of physical life in the whole, these myths developed into explanations of the persistence of spiritual life in the parts, explanations of personal survival. In 1 Corinthians 15, Paul reveals by his choice of imagery the vegetative origins of the resurrection of the body at the same time that he reveals his own uneasy sense of the alogic of imaging the transformation from physical life to spiritual life by the transformation from one state of physical life to another:

35 But some man will say, How are the dead raised up? and with what body do they come? 36 Thou fool, that which thou sowest is not quickened, except it die: 37 And that which thou sowest, thou sowest not that body that shall be, but bare grain, it may chance of wheat, or of some other grain: 38 But God giveth it a body as it hath pleased him, and to every seed his own body. 39 All flesh is not the same flesh: but there is one kind of flesh of men, another flesh of beasts, another of fishes, and another of birds. 40 There are also celestial bodies, and bodies terrestrial: but the glory of the celestial is one, and the glory of the terrestrial is another. 41 There is one glory of the sun, and another glory of the moon, and another glory of the stars: for one star differeth from another star in glory. 42 So also is the resurrection of the dead. It is sown in corruption; it is raised in incorruption: 43 It is sown in dishonour; it is raised in glory: it is sown in weakness; it is raised in power: 44 It is sown a natural body; it is raised a spiritual body. There is a natural body, and there is a spiritual body. 45 And so it is written, The first man Adam was made a living soul; the last Adam was made a quickening spirit. 46 Howbeit that was not first which is spiritual, but that which is

natural; and afterward that which is spiritual. 47 The first man is of
the earth, earthy: the second man is the Lord from heaven. . . . 49
And as we have borne the image of the earthy, we shall also bear the
image of the heavenly. 50 Now this I say, brethren, that flesh and
blood cannot inherit the kingdom of God; neither doth corruption
inherit incorruption. 51 Behold, I shew you a mystery; We shall not
all sleep, but we shall all be changed. . . .

The rhetorical maneuvers of the passage show the problems involved
in trying to image the invisible life of the spirit. To the question of how
the complex form of the body will be restored from the formless decay
of death, Paul replies by pointing out the difference in form between the
"bare grain" of wheat and the stalk that grows from it and noting that the
transformation from one to the other requires that the seed "die," that it
decay in the ground. He then observes that just as there are different
forms of living bodies on earth, so there are different forms of celestial
bodies in the heavens, whose light varies "in glory" as much as the flesh
of different living species varies in composition. Using the analogy between living bodies and astronomical "bodies" to associate the flesh that
composes the former with the light that composes the latter, Paul evokes
the change from earth to heaven, from corruption to incorruption, as
the transformation of the mortal body into the light, that transformation
which the apostles glimpsed in a veiled manner when Christ's body
shone like the sun at the transfiguration. Now if we grant that what
"light" stands for in this scenario is spirit (pure mind as illumination),
then the transformation of the corruptible body into the incorruptible
light, the "birth into brightness" as Babbalanja calls it, is simply the
parturitive separation of the mind from the body—the notion of the self
as a wholly independent intellectual substance, a pure mind without a
body. Since our physical bodies are identified with corruption and since
"flesh and blood cannot inherit the kingdom of God" nor "corruption
inherit incorruption," that "spiritual body" which is raised at the resurrection will no more be a literal human body than are those celestial
"bodies" that are composed of light. All that the word "body" signifies in
the phrase "spiritual body" is the abstract notion of a whole, a unit, an
identity, without any visible image attached to it, in the same way that the
words of transubstantiation ("This is my body") by dissolving the necessary connection between substance and appearance reduce the word

"body" to the abstract notion of a whole composed of parts, as in the concept of "the mystical body of Christ," which one becomes part of by eating the consecrated bread.

Acknowledging that his task is the impossible one of providing images for a life that is essentially imageless, Paul says, "I shew you a mystery." The ultimate root of the word "mystery" is the Greek verb *myein*, "to shut the eyes," for what the mystic "sees" is invisible to the eye—Paul's "the image of the heavenly" no more referring to a visible image than his "spiritual body" refers to a real body. Yet the transformation from one visible form to another radically different but still visible form—for example, from a grain of wheat to a stalk of wheat or a larva to a butterfly—is not, in Yoomy's words, "a fit illustration of the miraculous change to be wrought in man after death," for though the transformation process in the case of both the grain and the larva is hidden from view and is thus in a sense mysterious, the mystery of the hidden does not illustrate the mystery of the imageless, the absence of illustration.

In chapter 14 of *The Confidence-Man,* Melville uses the butterfly image to evoke the metamorphic inconsistency of human character, "at different periods, as much at variance with itself as the butterfly is with the caterpillar from which it changes" (p. 95). The butterfly is, of course, a frequent symbol of the soul in late antiquity, yet in *Mardi* Babbalanja uses this image to depict death as a radical break in the mnemic continuity of the self, speculating that the dead may suffer "an utter lapse of memory concerning sublunary things; and they themselves be not themselves, as the butterfly is not the larva." The image occurs again in *The Confidence-Man* when Pitch and the man from the Philosophical Intelligence Office discuss the character of boys. Pitch contends that "all boys are rascals" and since " 'the child is father of the man,' . . . so are all men" (p. 165). To refute this, the PIO man says that he must "proceed by analogy from the physical to the moral" (p. 167)—a method that turns out to be a parody of Emerson's. In his first analogy the PIO man compares a boy to a simplified, miniature image, a rough sketch of the human form—"a little preliminary rag-paper study, or careless cartoon, so to speak, of a man" (p. 167). Advancing "one step further," he says, "We must now drop the figure of the rag-paper cartoon, and borrow one . . . from the horticultural kingdom. Some bud, lily-bud, if you please," for "like the bud of the lily," the boy "contains concealed rudiments . . . , points at present invisible, with beauties at present dor-

mant" (p. 168). The PIO man then proceeds to the moral application of
the physical image, remarking that if a boy has evinced "no noble quality" in childhood, yet just as that boy, though at present beardless, will
have a beard when mature, so he may have hidden within him, like the
incipient beard, some noble quality ready to bud when he is a man.
Wearying of the PIO man's analogical reasoning, Pitch exclaims, "But is
analogy argument? You are a punster. . . . you pun with ideas as another
man may with words" (p. 171).

Pitch asserts that just as a punster takes advantage of an accidental
resemblance in the sounds of words, a phonic doubleness, to link unrelated ideas, so the PIO man takes advantage of an accidental or insignificant resemblance in ideas, a conceptual doubleness, to equate things or
processes whose differences are more important than their similarities.
The PIO man replies that if Pitch despises the processes of human
reason, then it is vain to reason with him, and immediately proceeds to
give him another analogy. The PIO man says that if someone alleged of
a man that he was untrustworthy because he had a bad character as a
boy, he would reply, "Madam, or sir, would you visit upon the butterfly
the sins of the caterpillar? In the natural advance of all creatures, do they
not bury themselves over and over again in the endless resurrection of
better and better? Madam, or sir, take back this adult; he may have been
a caterpillar, but is now a butterfly" (p. 172). And Pitch rejoins, "Pun
away; but even accepting your analogical pun, what does it amount to?
Was the caterpillar one creature, and is the butterfly another? The butterfly is the caterpillar in a gaudy cloak; stripped of which, there lies the
impostor's long spindle of a body, pretty much worm-shaped as before"
(p. 172). The PIO man's analogy seems to deny the continuity of the self
from childhood to maturity (as well as the personal responsibility for
one's previous conduct which that continuity entails), it seems to strike at
Pitch's Wordsworthian notion that "the child is father of the man";
whereas Pitch's rejection of the analogy denies, according to the PIO
man, "that a youth of one character can be transformed into a man of an
opposite character" (p. 172).

The argument between Pitch and the PIO man is skillfully constructed
to lay the philosophical groundwork for the Cosmopolitan, whose first
appearance in the novel occurs at the argument's end. What begins as a
discussion of the character of boys soon turns into a discussion of the
persistence or nonpersistence of "character" from one stage of life to

another. We noted earlier that rites of passage from adolescence to maturity usually depict this transformation as a symbolic death and re-birth and that the deepest significance of the ritual lies in its acting out by a kind of sympathetic magic the communal hope that the transformation from life to death is a passage from one stage of life to another. In the butterfly analogy the PIO man explicitly associates the passage from adolescence to maturity with the image of burial and resurrection as well as with the question of personal accountability for sin. What the argument does, then, in effect, is to associate three different meta-morphoses—one from vegetative life (bud/lily), one from animal life (caterpillar/butterfly), and one from human life (boy/man)—by pre-senting the first two as analogies of the third. But these three metamorphoses also represent three standard types of analogy for the transformation from life to death in man, as in St. Paul's use of the grain image for the resurrection, Babbalanja's use of the butterfly image for the "miraculous change" at death, and the PIO man's association of the passage from adolescence to maturity with burial and resurrection. Thus when the argument calls into question the reliability of reasoning by analogy, when it asks whether these metaphors drawn from changes of state within vegetative and animal life can provide the certainty of a proof about a change of state within human life, it also implicitly calls into question the still more tenuous analogy between a change of state within life and the change from life to death.

Further, the argument, by juxtaposing two different types of trans-formation (metamorphosis and analogy, a change of physical form and a change of symbolic form, of bodily shape and of "character"), raises the question of whether there is ever a *necessary* correspondence between a physical form and a symbolic form, between one's bodily image and one's self. If the self is the indeterminate sum of its symbolic relation-ships (a virtual whole that images itself to itself by making a part stand for, be symbolically equal to, the whole), if the self is only metaphorically an entity, a unity, then could one ever reason about it in any other way than by analogy? And if reasoning by analogy is unreliable, could there ever be any certain knowledge of the self? Could there ever be a literal image of a metaphoric entity, a necessary, that is, pictographic, repre-sentation of the self? Although one's visible image is necessarily *linked* to one's self, the physical form of the one does not necessarily *correspond* to the symbolic form of the other. Is every symbol of the self, then, whether visible image, name, book, or whatever, an illusory part / whole equation that elicits our confidence by concealing parts of the self, by concealing its own arbitrariness?

Clad in a "parti-hued" costume whose composite style unites "a Highland plaid, Emir's robe, and French blouse" (p. 184), Frank Goodman, the Cosmopolitan, appears at the end of the argument between Pitch and the PIO man as if he were the butterfly into which the drably attired confidence men of the first half of the book had metamorphosed, the butterfly that Pitch described as an impostor "in a gaudy cloak." And for the rest of the novel the Cosmopolitan's presence dissolves any certainty of meaning in a constant undermining of the stability of signifying forms, whether pictographic or phonetic. Yet perhaps we are being too quick in judging Frank Goodman simply from his physical appearance. And if we prejudge him, won't that determine our interpretation of the subsequent ambiguous evidence? Near the end of the novel Goodman cautions the ship's barber, a trafficker in physical appearances, "Don't be too sure what I am. You call me *man,* just as the townsfolk called the angels who, in man's form, came to Lot's house; just as the Jew rustics called the devils who, in man's form, haunted the tombs. You can conclude nothing absolute from the human form, barber" (p. 313). And indeed, examples of the uncertain significance of the human form abound within the novel, ranging from Goneril in chapter 12 ("one of those natures, anomalously vicious, which would almost tempt a metaphysical lover of our species to doubt whether the human form be, in all cases, conclusive evidence of humanity, whether, sometimes, it may be not a kind of unpledged and indifferent tabernacle" [p. 83]); to the Indian-hater John Moredock in chapter 27 (who is "an example of something apparently self-contradicting, certainly curious, but, at the same time, undeniable: namely, that nearly all Indian-haters have at bottom loving hearts" [p. 218], a man who is an affectionate husband and father, a good friend and neighbor, a pillar of the community, and yet who, upon entering the forest, becomes a ruthless slaughterer of Indians, undergoing a change of character like that of Jekyll to Hyde but without the corresponding change in physical appearance); to the Indians who are slaughtered because, although they have human forms, they are not really human, being either savage animals or devils (the title of chapter 26 is "Containing the metaphysics of Indian-hating, according to the views of one evidently not so prepossessed as Rousseau in favor of savages"); to the Christian God who concealed himself in human form and in whose name confidence is preached throughout the novel.

Yet if the human form is ambiguous or opaque, perhaps a cryptic signature can provide the necessary transparency, can afford a key to human character. In order to warn the Cosmopolitan against further association with Charlie Noble, Mark Winsome enunciates a favorite Emersonian doctrine that holds that "when any creature is by its make inimical to other creatures, nature in effect labels that creature, much as an apothecary does a poison" (p. 268). And he continues:

> "... yet something in you bids me think now, that whatever latent design your impostor friend might have had upon you, it as yet remains unaccomplished. You read his label."
>
> "And what did it say? 'This is a genial soul.' So you see you must either give up your doctrine of labels, or else your prejudice against my friend. But tell me," with renewed earnestness, "what do you take him for? What is he?"
>
> "What are you? What am I? Nobody knows who anybody is. The data which life furnishes, towards forming a true estimate of any being, are as insufficient to that end as in geometry one side given would be to determine the triangle."
>
> "But is not this doctrine of triangles someway inconsistent with your doctrine of labels?"
>
> "Yes, but what of that? I seldom care to be consistent...." (P. 271)

A natural signature is no more reliable as an indicator of the self than the human form; for each is a part in relation to the whole, one side of a triangle, and if the whole is inconsistent with itself, then no part can faithfully represent it. Uncertainty is, then, a function not of any particular type of symbol, but of the symbol itself—a function of the partial nature of a sign, of the indeterminate "wholeness" of the self (the fullness of meaning) that must always exceed any sign, and of the consequent indefinite excess of signs. As the old man at the end of the novel remarks when he tries to use the counterfeit bank note detector, "I don't know, I don't know.... there's so many marks of all sorts to go by, it makes it kind of uncertain" (p. 345). And if pictographic signs are uncertain, how much more so are phonetic signs.

Earlier in the novel the herb-doctor produces his own phonetic version of a natural signature or "label" when he tells the miser how to distinguish the authentic herb medicine that nature has provided, the Omni-Balsamic Reinvigorator, from its imitators: "Take the wrapper from any of my vials and hold it to the light, you will see water-marked in capitals the word '*confidence*,' which is the countersign of the medicine, as I wish it was of the world. The wrapper bears that mark or else the medicine is counterfeit" (p. 114). The miser says that the herb-doctor had previously told him that confidence was necessary in order for the medicine to work, to reveal itself as authentic, but that now he tells him that skepticism is required in order to discover the authentic medicine: "But to doubt, to suspect, to prove—to have all this wearing work to be doing continually—how opposed to confidence. It is evil!" (p. 115). To which the herb-doctor replies, "From evil comes good. Distrust is a stage to confidence" (p. 115).

In the novel, uncertainty of meaning often involves simply an unexpected reversal in the alignment of oppositions, as when the equation of first terms in the oppositions confidence/skepticism, good/evil starts to wobble. But these sudden reversals are compounded, either accidentally or intentionally, by the phonetic doubleness of words, by the sudden shifts in meaning that occur when one word has two opposed or unrelated significances or when two different words have the same sound. The old man at the end of the novel finds that, according to his counterfeit bank note detector, if a certain bill is good "it must have in one corner, mixed in with the vignette, the figure of a goose, very small, indeed, all but microscopic; and, for added precaution, like the figure of Napoleon outlined by the tree, not observable, even if magnified, unless the attention is directed to it," but try as he may, he "can't see the goose" (p. 346). To which the Cosmopolitan replies:

"Can't see the goose? why, I can; and a famous goose it is. There" (reaching over and pointing to a spot in the vignette).

"I don't see it—dear me—I don't see the goose. Is it a real goose?"

"A perfect goose; beautiful goose."

"Dear, dear, I don't see it."

"Then throw that Detector away, I say again; it only makes you purblind; don't you see what a wild-goose chase it has led you?"
(P. 346)

The "perfect goose" that the Cosmopolitan sees but the old man doesn't is clearly the old man himself—a goose because he relies on the counterfeit detector without ever thinking that someone skillful enough to counterfeit a bank note would be skillful enough to counterfeit its authenticating marks as well (bank note and countersign being of the same order of inscription), especially if those authenticating marks were publicized in a counterfeit detector.

But the old man may not be the only goose involved in a wild-goose chase, for as he sits reading a description in phonetic writing of a pictograph ("the figure of a goose"), a description that he tries to match with an image hidden on a piece of paper, he may well remind the reader of someone else who is engaged in the problematic activity of visualizing a pictographic shape from its presentation in phonetic script, a shape that is somehow concealed on a sheet of paper but that must be recognized and distinguished from similar shapes around it. This activity is thematized at the very start of the novel when the mysterious stranger confronts the placard offering a reward for the capture of "a mysterious impostor." The placard contains "what purported to be a careful description of his person," but that description is pointedly not given, and the reader, alerted to the presence of an impostor but lacking his description, is soon provided with a list of individuals who, he is encouraged to believe, are either confidence men or the disguises of a single confidence man. When the beggar, Black Guinea, is accused of being "some white operator, betwisted and painted up for a decoy," he names a series of individuals on board who he claims will vouch for him: a "ge'mman wid a weed, and a ge'mman in a gray coat and white tie . . . ; and a ge'mman wid a big book, too; and a yarb-doctor; and a ge'mman in a yaller west; and a ge'mman wid a brass plate; and a ge'mman in a wiolet robe; and a ge'mman as is a sodjer" (pp. 19–20). As a bystander goes off in search of Guinea's character references, Guinea's accuser exclaims, "Wild goose chase!"

The problem with Guinea's list is that all the individuals are described in terms of an accidental quality—a garment, an object they carry, their ostensible profession—something that can be assumed or discarded at will. Some of Guinea's descriptions correspond to a single character who appears later in the novel, while others correspond to no character in the book, and still others correspond to several characters. Thus the "ge'mman wid a big book" may be the president of the Black Rapids Coal Company with his ledger, or the old man reading the Bible, or perhaps the author of *The Confidence-Man* who has sent the reader on a wild-goose chase. (One recalls that the mysterious stranger who starts the novel and against whom our suspicions are first aroused, presents himself as a writer whose cryptic inscriptions on a slate first puzzle and then anger his readers.) The point is that even if Black Guinea had given a minute description of each individual's physical appearance, any description, in phonetic writing, of a visual shape would by its very nature be ambiguous enough to fit many people, just as any individual's physical appearance could be translated into phonetic writing in a variety of ways, ways that need not be consistent with one another.

At the very least Melville is out to sharp those unselfconscious readers who, like the old man with the counterfeit detector, are so intent on *seeing* through the words that they never see *through* the words— readers who never become aware of their own reflection in the book, their own shadow cast on the page. For any description, no matter how detailed, must always be visualized, be translated into images, by the person reading the description, so that any character in a book, considered as a pictographic shape, always bears the imprint of the reader's imagination. A sense of this is evoked by the mirroring that occurs between the phonetic description of "the figure of a goose" and the figurative goose who reads the description; for the old man, as a character in a book, is himself a description, in phonetic script, of a pictographic shape. Further, it is precisely the movement from the pictographic to the phonetic level that turns the figure of a goose into a figurative (metaphoric) goose, that introduces the phonetic doubleness that allows the metaphoric mirroring of reader and text. One of Melville's favorite tricks from *Moby-Dick* onward is to construct sentences of such ambiguous complexity that they function as syntactic mirrors in which an unselfconscious reader can always find his own prejudices reflected without ever being aware that he has projected them there in the process of interpretation and that the sentence could, with the same certainty, be interpreted to precisely the opposite effect by a reader of opposite mind.

If the very least that Melville intended in *The Confidence-Man* was to ridicule the simple-minded readers who had reacted first with puzzlement and then with outrage to the growing subtlety and profundity of his work, to exhibit both his superiority and his scorn in a veiled manner meant to be penetrated only by those of equal superiority, then perhaps the most that he intended was to call into question the basic conventions by which character is depicted in fiction to such an extent that the "book," as an image of mnemic continuity and persistence after death,

would be wholly undermined. The notion that the self's unity, its enduring stability, is like that of a pictographic inscription would then dissolve
as the text itself demonstrated that though the phonetic inscription that
depicts a character (attributes to it the unity of a pictographic shape) may
be stable, its meaning (the shape) is not. One could then say of books
what Thoreau had said of the pyramids: they "do not tell us the tale that
was confided to them."

There are three principal ways in which a written character exists on
the page: as a proper name or title, as a description of physical appearance, mannerism, or action, and as the transcription of speech or
thought. And in the confrontation between Frank Goodman and Charlie
Noble, these three modes of written existence are made to oscillate before our eyes. Frank Goodman's name, for example, would seem to be
like one of Mark Winsome's natural "labels," attesting to the character's
frankness, goodness, and manliness, just as the name of his acquaintance
Charlie Noble would seem to stand credit for that character's nobility of
spirit. But as Bruce Franklin has pointed out, "Charley Noble" was the
sailors' slang name for the galley smoke pipe, and a favorite shipboard
joke was to send landsmen in search of the fictitious Charley Noble
(p. 228); while "Goodman," though it was the Puritan title of address, was
also "a cant term for a thief . . . and a Scottish title for the Devil" (p. 227).
The nautical significance of Charlie Noble's name may be an allusion to
the literal and figurative smoke screen that he lays down during his
conversation with Frank Goodman, just as Charlie's middle name, Arnold, may be an allusion to the doubleness of the most famous Arnold in
American history.

In terms of personal appearance, mannerisms, and actions there is an
uncanny resemblance between Goodman and Noble, and the reader can
only wonder whether that resemblance is something created or masked
by the translation from the pictographic to the phonetic level. The most
striking color in each man's apparel is a kind of reddish violet: Charlie
Noble wears a "violet vest" (p. 196), while Frank Goodman sports "a
vesture barred with various hues, that of the cochineal predominating"
and topped off with a "smoking cap of regal purple" (pp. 184-85). (Are
we to associate the predominant color of Charlie's and Frank's apparel
with the "ge'mman in a wiolet robe" mentioned by Black Guinea?) Further, the composite style of Frank's clothing shows him to be "a cosmopolitan, a catholic man; who, being such, ties himself to no narrow

tailor or teacher, but federates, in heart as in costume, something of the various gallantries of men under various suns" (p. 186). This same quality of being everything and nothing characterizes the appearance of Charlie Noble: "A man neither tall nor stout, neither short nor gaunt; but with a body fitted, as by measure, to the service of his mind. . . . upon the whole, it could not be fairly said that his appearance was unprepossessing; indeed, to the congenial, it would have been doubtless not uncongenial" (p. 196–97).

As to their opinions, Frank and Charlie are virtually indistinguishable, a circumstance that leads Frank to remark, "Indeed, . . . our sentiments agree so, that were they written in a book, whose was whose, few but the nicest critics might determine" (p. 224). A remark that is soon put to the test when Melville, either by accident or design, has the Cosmopolitan in the course of the conversation address Charlie as "Frank" (p. 249), momentarily reversing the poles of the dialogue. Significantly, this reversal occurs during a conversation in which Frank had previously pretended to be duped by the double meaning of a word, a double meaning that turns out to be an allusion to the opposition of Dionysus and Apollo and to two opposing images of survival. To pledge their friendship, Frank and Charlie order port wine, and when the waiter brings a bottle with "a handsome red label . . . bearing the capital letters, P. W.," Charlie asks, "Now what does P. W. mean?" When Frank suggests that it stands for port wine, Charlie agrees, and Frank ironically remarks, "I find some little mysteries not very hard to clear up" (p. 228). Indeed, it is only logical to assume that in this context "P. W." stands for port wine; but a logical assumption is not a certain proof, and everyone has had at one time or another the experience of having the logical answer to a mystery turn out to be simply wrong. In its phonetic indeterminacy "P. W." could stand for any number of two-word combinations with these initials. And since Charlie immediately raises the question of whether "now-a-days *pure wine* is unpurchasable" (p. 229, italics mine), whether it is all adulterated or poisoned wine as the "gloomy skeptics" claim, the significance of "P. W." in this context becomes less certain. Remarking that skeptics believe the human heart to be a bottle of poisoned wine, Frank adds, "Not medicines, not the wine in sacraments, has escaped them. The doctor with his phial, and the priest with his chalice, they deem equally the unconscious dispensers of bogus cordials to the dying" (p. 230).

The comparison of physical life and spiritual life, of wine as medicine and wine as sacrament, sets the stage for the opposition of Dionysus and Apollo (of vegetative god and solar god) that occurs when Charlie offers to repeat for Frank's benefit "a panegyric on the press" that he had recently read. Frank, interpreting the word "press" to mean journalism, launches into his own panegyric in advance of Charlie. Disdaining for the press "the poor name of diffuser of news," Frank claims for it "the independent apostleship of Advancer of Knowledge:—the iron Paul! . . . for not only does the press advance knowledge, but righteousness. In the press, as in the sun, resides, my dear Charlie, a dedicated principle of beneficent force and light. For the Satanic press, by its coappearance with the apostolic, it is no more an aspersion to that, than to the true sun is the coappearance of the mock one. For all the baleful-looking parhelion, god Apollo dispenses the day" (p. 237). Frank says that he holds the press to be the "defender of the faith in the final triumph of truth over error, metaphysics over superstition, theory over falsehood, machinery over nature, and the good man over the bad" (p. 237)—as curious an alignment of oppositions as one could wish, since the privileging of the first terms in each pair leads to the problematic equation of the press, truth, metaphysics, theory, machinery, and the good man.

Having let Frank speak his piece, Charlie replies with his own poetical eulogy, not to the printing press, but to the wine press "from which breaketh the true morning . . . , the red press of Noah, from which cometh inspiration. . . . Praise be unto the press, the free press of Noah, which will not lie for tyrants, but make tyrants speak the truth . . . , the press . . . from which flow streams of knowledge which give man a bliss no more unreal than his pain" (p. 239). Earlier, Charlie had introduced the topic of wine with a quotation from Leigh Hunt's "Bacchus in Tuscany: A Dithyrambic Poem, Translated from the Italian of Francesco Redi" (1825), a poem in which the wine god says:

> "Oh how widely wandereth he,
> Who in the search for verity
> Keeps aloof from glorious wine!
> Lo the knowledge it bringeth to me!"
>   (P. 225)

Bacchus is, of course, one of the names of Dionysus, the name generally given to his ecstatic aspect; for Dionysus as a dying and reviving god

has a double face—tragic and joyful. But Apollo also has a double
aspect—he is the god who shines in the sky for half the day and who
descends into darkness for the other half. For the Greeks, Dionysus and
Apollo were not two separate gods, but rather two opposing aspects of
the same god—a god at once dark and bright, tragic and joyful. Dionysus
and Apollo are thus reciprocal halves, each possessing a dual nature.
The name for the Apollonian aspect of Dionysus is Bacchus, and the
name for the Dionysian aspect of Apollo is Pythios. In *Anacalypsis* Higgins says, "Virgil gives the conduct of the year to Liber or Bacchus,
though it was generally thought to be in the care of Apollo. It also
appears from the Scholia in Horace, that Apollo and Dionysus were the
same. In fact, they were all three the same, the Sun" (1:45). In his study
of Dionysus, Kerényi remarks, "In the prophetic realm Apollo and
Dionysos are scarcely distinguishable" (p. 219). Noting that this "connection between Apollo and Dionysos . . . was stated by the tragic poets of
Athens," he adds: "In the Lykourgos tetralogy of Aischylos, the cry
'Ivy-Apollo, Bakchios, the soothsayer,' rings out, probably when the
Thracian bacchantes, the Bassarai, attack Orpheus, the worshipper of
Apollo and the sun. The cry suggests a higher knowledge of the connection between Apollo and Dionysos, the dark god, whom Orpheus
seemed to deny in favor of the luminous god—Apollo and the sun as one
person. In the *Lykymnios* of Euripides the same connection is attested by
the cry, 'Lord, laurel-loving Bakchios, Paean Apollo, player of the lyre'"
(p. 233). At the oracle of Apollo in Delphi the Pythia (priestess) sat upon
a symbolic "tomb of Dionysos," since it was "the sphere of the subterranean Dionysos, from which Apollo derived his revelations" (p. 232).

  Frank says that Charlie's panegyric on the wine press "was quite in the
lyric style—a style I always admire on account of that spirit of Sibyllic
confidence and assurance which is, perhaps, its prime ingredient"
(p. 239). To which Charlie replies, "The lyre and the vine forever! . . . the
vine, the vine! is it not the most graceful and bounteous of all growths?
And, by its being such, is not something meant—divinely meant? As I
live, a vine, a Catawba vine, shall be planted on my grave!" (p. 239).
According to Frank and Charlie, the popular press and the grape press
each have to do with enlightenment or illumination, with the revelation
of truth, one by printed words, the other by wine. And since the
panegyric that Charlie repeats is, as he says, something that he had
recently read in print, its "lyric style" and "spirit of Sibyllic confidence"

in praise of the truth-inspiring power of wine suggest the prophetic interaction whereby Apollo, the god of the lyre, translates into verbal images revelations from the subterranean (unconscious) realm of the wine god Dionysus, from the world beneath the grave. And the central truth that Dionysus and Apollo reveal is the survival of life. One can see in the structure of Dionysian/Apollonian revelation the basic structure of the translation of a body into the light, of matter into mind, the same structure that we find in the ascension from the dark, subterranean cavern into the bright realm of Ideas in Plato's allegory of the cave and from the grave into the pure light of the Logos in Christianity.

From a single word ("press") with two different meanings emerges the image of a single deity with a double aspect, and we are faced with the question of how the image of Apollo and Dionysus is to be applied to Frank and Charlie, one of whom praises the power of words, the other the power of wine, yet whose sentiments so agree that "were they written in a book, whose was whose, few but the nicest critics might determine." Perhaps the answer lies in two different senses of doubleness. As poles of a mutually constitutive opposition, Dionysus and Apollo are halves (the dark god and the bright god) and doubles (the dark god has a bright aspect named Bacchus and the bright god has a dark aspect named Pythios). Their opposition of light and dark, life and death, joyful and tragic, does not represent a privileging of one opposite over the other. One god is not considered good, the other evil; one true, the other false; one real, the other illusory. But in the case of the two presses, each has a doubleness that involves just such a privileging within the context of logical discourse, within the Socratic dialectic and its master opposition of logical truth and error as good and evil. Frank says that there is a true and a false, an "apostolic" and a "Satanic press," and that they are related as the "true sun" is to the "mock one" (the "baleful-looking parhelion"), that is, as reality is to an illusory image, as truth to perceptual error. Similarly, Frank and Charlie had, earlier in their conversation, distinguished between true wine and adulterated substitutes that are wine in name only. Yet because this privileging rests on the notion of logic, of reasoning in words, as the basic ground of certainty in knowledge, it is subject to the masking effect of phonetic signs and to the slippages that take place behind these arbitrary masks.

As a single word with a double meaning evoked the Dionysian/ Apollonian opposition, so the relationship of that opposition to Frank and Charlie is indicated by two words with the same sound. Composing the reciprocal forms of enlightenment involved in the two different senses of "press," Charlie proposes a toast, "The lyre and the vine forever!"—Apollo and Dionysus. But if we attend simply to the sounds of the words, his toast could equally be "The liar and the vine forever!" Indeed, throughout their conversation regarding the inherent trustworthiness and benevolence of man, each speaker keeps urging wine on the other, as if trying through intoxication to mask his own intentions or unmask those of his companion.

The fact that the gods of lyre and vine are also the presiding deities of Greek drama and its masked revelations of the truth accounts for the theatrical conclusion of Charlie's and Frank's conversation. After Charlie's toast, the discussion turns to the subject of those characters in Shakespeare's plays, such as Polonius and Autolycus, who preach distrust of human nature or the foolishness of honesty and trust. When Frank admits that he doesn't "exactly see how Shakespeare meant the words he puts in Polonius' mouth," Charlie remarks, "Some say that he meant them to open people's eyes; . . . others say he meant to corrupt people's morals; and still others, that he had no express intention at all, but in effect opens their eyes and corrupts their morals in one operation" (pp. 245–46). Rejecting "so crude an hypothesis," Frank admits that in reading Shakespeare he has noticed a certain doubleness in the man, which he characterizes in a true Apollonian/Dionysian image: "There appears to be a certain—what shall I call it?—hidden sun, say, about him, at once enlightening and mystifying. Now, I should be afraid to say what I have thought that hidden sun might be" (p. 246). And when Charlie asks him if he thinks it is "the true light," Frank replies, "Shakespeare has got to be a kind of deity. Prudent minds, having certain latent thoughts concerning him, will reserve them in a condition of lasting probation" (p. 246).

The discussion of dramatic characters leads Frank to attempt a dramatic performance of his own. Telling Charlie that wine "opens the heart," Frank proposes to reveal one of his "little secrets," trusting in that "nobleness" that Charlie's "whole character" bespeaks. Charlie concurs, and Frank tells him that he is in "urgent want" of money and that Charlie must lend him fifty dollars. In a half-page chapter entitled "A metamorphosis more surprising than any in Ovid," Charlie drops his mask of benevolence and, calling Frank a "beggar" and an "impostor," tells him to "go to the devil" (p. 256). While "speaking or rather hissing those words," Charlie "underwent much such a change as one reads of in fairy-books. Out of old material sprang a new creature" (p. 257). When Frank takes fifty dollars in gold from his pocket and entreats Charlie to return to his accustomed self, Charlie says that he had suspected Frank was simply playing a joke and that he had played along with it. To which Frank replies, "You played your part better than I did mine; you played it, Charlie, to the life," and Charlie rejoins, "You see, I once belonged to an amateur play company" (p. 258).

Frank's dramatic performance reveals the truth about Charlie—that he is wearing a mask and playing a role. But to reveal that truth, Frank himself had to play a false role, to lie about needing money. Can truth come from falsehood, or good from evil? The moral in its simplest form is that the differential opposition true/false provides only relative values. Consequently, to distinguish a true god from false gods is no guarantee that the nature of the true god is absolute truth. Or rather, there is only such a guarantee in a tradition like the Platonic-Christian one of God as the Logos, a tradition in which God is logically incapable of falsehood. But is it a falsehood to wear a mask and play a role? When the Maker of the universe masked himself as the son of a Jewish carpenter, was that a falsehood? If Frank's remark that Shakespeare has become "a kind of deity" is meant to evoke the image of the author as god of his fictive world and of God as author of the universe, are we to assume that the way the author of *The Confidence-Man: His Masquerade* behaves with his fictive world represents Melville's idea of the way God behaves with His world?

Pitch says that "the entire ship is a riddle" (p. 165), and Melville likens the compartments in the steamer *Fidele* to the "secret drawers in an escritoire" (p. 12), thus alerting the reader to that written masquerade upon which he has embarked, a masquerade whose intentions he will be hard pressed to define as true or false, as the desire "to open people's eyes," or "to corrupt their morals," or to open their eyes and corrupt their morals "in one operation." When Frank and Charlie discuss the relationship of Shakespeare's own character to the characters in his plays—whether a certain character is a true or false representation of the author's thoughts, and in what sense an author is responsible for his characters (Frank says of Shakespeare, "At times seeming irresponsible, he does not always seem reliable" [p. 246])—it is surely intended that the reader apply the terms of that discussion to both the author of *The Confidence-Man* and the presumed Author of the world. Indeed, Melville's satirizing of Emerson and Thoreau in the characters of Mark Winsome and Egbert is based on his perception of them as authors who, in dramatizing themselves in their writings, have presented false characters to the world. Their so-called "philosophy" masks Yankee shrewdness and cold-blooded selfishness under the names of plain dealing and self-reliance. When Egbert offers to explain Mark Winsome's philosophy, Frank proposes instead that he give Egbert "some common case in real life" to which Egbert can make a practical application of that philosophy. Frank presents the case of two bosom friends, "one of whom . . . seeks a loan from the other. . . . And the persons are to be you and I: you, the friend from whom the loan is sought—I, the friend who seeks it; you, the disciple of the philosophy in question—I, a common man. . . . For brevity, you shall call me Frank, and I will call you Charlie" (p. 282). Frank and Charlie (Egbert) then play out the scenario, with Frank seeking a loan and Egbert successfully fending him off by means of Winsome's philosophy. At one point in their dramatic dialogue, Frank, seemingly exasperated with Egbert's parroting of Winsome's opinions, says, "Oh, this, all along, is not you, Charlie, but some ventriloquist who usurps your larynx. It is Mark Winsome that speaks, not Charlie" (p. 289)—the remark being directed, under the mask of a dramatic performance, at the role that Egbert plays in real life.

To illustrate a point, Charlie (Egbert) tells Frank the story of China Aster, a man who is ruined by accepting a loan from a friend. The moral, says Egbert, is that "however indulgent and right-minded I may seem to you now, that is no guarantee for the future. And into the power of that uncertain personality which, through the mutability of my humanity, I may hereafter become, should not common sense dissuade you, my dear Frank, from putting yourself? . . . the difference between this man and that man is not so great as the difference between what the same man may be to-day and what he may be in days to come. For there is no bent of heart or turn of thought which any man holds by virtue of an unalterable nature or will" (p. 309). To which Frank replies, "But Charlie, dear Charlie, what new notions are these? I thought that man was no poor drifting weed of the universe, as you phrased it; that, if so minded, he could have a will, a way, a thought, and a heart of his own? But now you have turned everything upside down again, with an inconsistency that amazes and shocks me" (p. 285).

Beyond the irony of Frank's taking Egbert to task for the inconsistency of character that he reveals in arguing for the inconsistency of character, and the further irony that only a few chapters earlier Melville had apologized for the apparent inconsistency of Frank Goodman's character, the main point of the episode lies in the distinction that it makes between the logical truth or falsehood of a statement, on the one hand, and the truth or falsehood of one's intentions in making the statement, on the other. When Egbert finishes the story of China Aster, Frank's first words are, "With what heart have you told me this story?" (p. 308); for Winsome's philosophy seems based on the principle of speaking the truth for a false purpose, and his doctrine of the self's inconsistency merely a rhetorical mask for self-indulgence. Yet as with so many of the Cosmopolitan's remarks, the question he asks Egbert reverberates on various levels throughout the novel: With what heart has the Cosmopolitan unmasked people's false roles by assuming different masks himself? With what heart has Melville told us this story? With what heart has Shakespeare created characters that seem at once to open our eyes and corrupt our morals? Frank Goodman ends the interview by rejecting Winsome's philosophy with "grand scorn," yet he leaves Egbert "at a loss to determine where exactly the fictitious character had been dropped, and the real one, if any, resumed. If any, because, with pointed meaning, there occurred to him, as he gazed after the cosmopolitan, these familiar lines:

> 'All the world's a stage,
> And all the men and women merely players,
> Who have their exits and their entrances,
> And one man in his time plays many parts.'"
>
> (P. 311)

As with all of the novel's references to drama and the theater—references that compare self-representation to role playing, as in this passage, or reading a novel to seeing a play, as in chapter 33, or the confidence man's masquerade to the masquerade of *The Confidence-Man*—we are not only reminded of the necessary uncertainty involved in moving from a medium employing both a phonetic language of words and a pictographic language of actors and scenes to a medium employing only a phonetic language through which the pictographic must be conveyed; we are also reminded that no matter how skillful one is in interpreting the meaning of phonetic or pictographic signs, there is no certain way of establishing whether a person really means what he says or does, precisely because all the modes of verifying intention, all the means of access to the self, are linguistic (either phonetic or pictographic). And if one chooses to tamper with those modes, to counterfeit them, there exists no extralinguistic means by which they can be checked. Unlike an omniscient god, a man can never know directly another man's heart, can never know if he is speaking the truth for a false reason. Satan can quote Scripture, as the proverb says. Or as the barber tells the Cosmopolitan, "I recalled what the son of Sirach says in the True Book: 'An enemy speaketh sweetly with his lips;' and so I did what the son of Sirach advises in such cases: 'I believed not his many words'" (p. 326).

It is to verify whether words "so calculated to destroy man's confidence in man" (p. 337) really appear in the Bible that Frank Goodman approaches the old man reading the Bible in the ship's cabin. The old man tells the Cosmopolitan that the Book of Sirach is not part of the Bible but the Apocrypha and then demonstrates the difference with the book in front of him, which has the Apocrypha bound between the Old and New Testaments:

> "Look," turning the leaves forward and back, till all the Old Testament lay flat on one side, and all the New Testament flat on the other, while in his fingers he supported vertically the portion between, "look, sir, all this to the right is certain truth, and all this to the left is certain truth, but all I hold in my hand here is apocrypha."
>
> "Apocrypha?"
>
> "Yes; and there's the word in black and white," pointing to it. "And what says the word? It says as much as 'not warranted'. . . . The word itself, I've heard from the pulpit, implies something of uncertain credit." (P. 337)

At the end of the old man's explanation of the word "apocrypha," a voice calls out from one of the darkened berths in the cabin, "What's that about the Apocalypse?" (p. 337). The novel's apocalypse (*apo,* "from," plus *kalyptein,* "to veil"), its concluding revelation, concerns the original indeterminacy of self-consciousness, the apocryphal (*apo,* "away," plus *kryptein,* "to hide") nature of symbolization and the knowledge it provides. The old man's demonstration with the Bible is a hieroglyph. In the bipolar structure of self-consciousness, "certain truth" seems to reside at the poles (to right and left in this case), but in between the poles—where the human vertical (ideal) intersects the world's horizontal (real), and the human horizontal (real) intersects the divine vertical (ideal)—lies the realm of uncertainty, the apocryphal. And we know all too well the fate of those who seek "certain truth" at the Pole. As Melville says in *Pierre,* "It is not for man to follow the trail of truth too far, since by so doing he entirely loses the directing compass of his mind; for arrived at the Pole, to whose barrenness only it points, there, the needle indifferently respects all points of the horizon alike." As the *Pequod* descends into the vortex, Ahab salutes the "death-glorious ship" and its "Pole-pointed prow" (p. 468).

Because the poles in a differential opposition are relational entities, the truth that waits at the pole is that all truth is relative, that in life there is no absolute except death: "In those hyperborean regions . . . , the most immemorially admitted maxims of men begin to slide and fluctuate, and finally become wholly inverted" (*Pierre,* p. 165). It is precisely in the relational character of linguistic oppositions (for example, black/white, the traditional image of differential certainty as well as of written stability) that uncertainty resides: "Apocrypha?" "Yes; and there's the word in black and white." The Cosmopolitan objects that binding the Apocrypha in with the Bible is confusing: "The uncanonical part should be bound distinct" (p. 337). But the episode of the counterfeit bank note detector that follows suggests that the distinction between certainty and uncertainty as represented by two physically separated documents (the detector and the bank note) cannot be verified, for since the bank note and the counterfeit detector belong to the same order of inscription, the latter can be counterfeited as easily as the former. Because there is no self-authenticating sign, no unequivocal, wholly transparent sign, nothing linguistic can serve as a standard of certainty.

It is not the least melancholy aspect of a generally melancholy book—Melville's last as a professional novelist—that the ending of *The Confidence-Man* seems to be a bitter parody of the conclusion of *Moby-Dick* and the notion of the writing self's survival in the written self of the work. Each book ends with the image of a life preserver. In *Moby-Dick*

the hieroglyphically inscribed coffin-lifebuoy saves Ishmael's life, allowing him to write the narrative in which he will survive beyond his own
death. An image of rebirth, the Osirian coffin that emerges from the
womblike vortex supports Ishmael until the *Rachel*, cruising in search of
"her missing children," finds "another orphan" (p. 470). The associative
chain of partial objects by which the self symbolically survives runs: life
preserver equals phallus equals seed equals child equals book. But in *The
Confidence-Man* the image of the life preserver evokes another kind of
partial object. The old man reading the Bible says that his son had told
him to make sure that he had a life preserver in his stateroom, but he
doesn't know what one looks like. The Cosmopolitan replies:

> "They are something like this, sir, I believe," lifting a brown stool
> with a curved tin compartment underneath; "yes, this, I think, is a
> life-preserver, sir; and a very good one, I should say, though I don't
> pretend to know much about such things, never using them myself."
>
> "Why, indeed, now! Who would have thought it? *that* a life-
> preserver? That's the very stool I was sitting on, ain't it?"
>
> " . . . Still, I think that in case of a wreck, barring sharp-pointed
> timbers, you could have confidence in that stool for a special provi-
> dence."
>
> "Then, good-night, good-night; and Providence have both of us
> in its good keeping."
>
> "Be sure it will," eying the old man with sympathy, as for the
> moment he stood, money-belt in hand, and life-preserver under
> arm, "be sure it will, sir, since in Providence, as in man, you and I
> equally put trust. But, bless me, we are being left in the dark here.
> Pah! what a smell, too." (P. 349)

The chamber pot life preserver ("a brown stool") suggests that the symbolic partial object by which the self seeks to survive the body's death is
not seminal but fecal, not the seed of a new birth but poisonous waste.

The god of the world of *The Confidence-Man: His Masquerade* is a
masked god, at once "an original genius" (p. 4) and an "original character," of which there can be but "one to a book" (p. 331). Yet this origin of
which the book goes in search cannot be "born in the author's imagination" (p. 331) precisely because it *is* that imagination (the original genius)
and its inscribed image (the original character) as mutually constitutive,
as that simultaneous ground of symbolic relationships that masks itself in

the idea of a beginning. One could apply to the masked god of *The Confidence-Man* Kerényi's observations regarding the masked god of the Greeks. He notes that in the Archaic period there were "two characteristic Dionysian idols" that "complemented one another" (p. 281). One was the phallus, the other was the mask. Of the "unphallic" idol, he says: "Over a column in the sanctuary a mask was hung and below the mask a long garment... which also embraced the column. A column with a capital is a recurrent component of this rigid composition" (p. 281) which symbolizes "an emasculated Dionysos," the "god during his absence beneath the earth" (p. 282). Kerényi associates this idol with the tree that enclosed the coffin of Osiris and became the pillar of the king's palace at Byblos. When Isis reclaimed the coffin, she "wrapped the heath column in a garment, ... and left it with the kings of Byblos to be worshipped in her own temple" (p. 282). Thus, among the Greeks the mask and garment on a column with a capital "could be regarded as the tomb of a dead god" (p. 282). Kerényi adds that "if among his idols in the Attic countryside there were double masks, ... these meant... that in both his aspects Dionysos was ruler over the whole year. *One* mask was never the *whole god,* for only in half his being was Dionysos the 'mask god'" (p. 283). And as the mask god is only half of the original deity, so the bitter mask of *The Confidence-Man: His Masquerade* is only half the truth of its author's mind. We should, in closing, balance his last novel's devastating critique of the self's mnemic survival in a book against the shortest chapter in *Moby-Dick,* "The Lee Shore," and its attempt to memorialize the sailor Bulkington.

On his first night at the Spouter Inn, Ishmael had noticed, among a group of seamen newly returned from a four-year voyage aboard the *Grampus,* a man named Bulkington as remarkable for "his fine stature" as for the fact that "in the deep shadows of his eyes floated some reminiscences that did not seem to give him much joy" (p. 23). And when the *Pequod* sails, Bulkington is at the helm, having reembarked "for still another tempestuous term" (p. 97). Ishmael says, "Wonderfullest things are ever the unmentionable; deep memories yield no epitaphs; this six-inch chapter is the stoneless grave of Bulkington" (p. 97). We know little more of Bulkington than his name and that he has vanished at sea— without even a stone tablet to his memory in the Whaleman's Chapel at New Bedford. Yet Ishmael remembers him as a man "full six feet in height, with noble shoulders, and a chest like a coffer-dam," indeed he had "seldom seen such brawn in a man" (p. 23). The very name "Bulkington" suggests physical size and substance, and that this brawny six-footer has disappeared without a trace, "a six-inch chapter" his grave, evokes the deepest mystery of the human condition—that what is, and knows that it is, should ever cease to be, that what is so substantial, so rich and full, should at last turn to nothing.

The "six-inch chapter" is a column with a capital, like the column on which the mask and garment of the god were hung during his absence. (The word "chapter" derives from the Middle English *chapiter;* Old French *chapitre, chapitle;* Latin *capitulum,* "head, chapter of a book," diminutive of *caput,* "the head"—the same derivation as the English word "chapiter," the architectural term meaning "the capital of a column.") And as the column with the mask and garment was "regarded as the tomb of a dead god," so the six-inch chapter turns out to be the tomb of a demigod:

> Know ye, now, Bulkington? Glimpses do ye seem to see of that mortally intolerable truth; that all deep, earnest thinking is but the intrepid effort of the soul to keep the open independence of her sea; while the wildest winds of heaven and earth conspire to cast her on the treacherous, slavish shore?
>
> But as in landlessness alone resides the highest truth, shoreless, indefinite as God—so, better is it to perish in that howling infinite, than be ingloriously dashed upon the lee, even if that were safety! For worm-like, then, oh! who would craven crawl to land! Terrors of the terrible! is all this agony so vain? Take heart, take heart, O Bulkington! Bear thee grimly, demigod! Up from the spray of thy ocean-perishing—straight up, leaps thy apotheosis! (Pp. 97–98)

What leaps up from the spray of his ocean perishing is the phallic coffin/ life preserver/book—the part/whole relation of the phallic six-inch chapter to the body of the text prefiguring the symbolic relationship of the book to the self. And what Bulkington represents for Ishmael is that godlike impulse of the self to be immortal, to leave a lasting trace of itself. Even if *The Confidence-Man*'s meditation on the death of God shows that the self's impulse to be immortal is meaningless, the impulse does not die—it remains the poignant fate of people who vanish.

EPILOGUE

We have come to the end of a long and often circuitous journey that began with Champollion's decipherment of the Rosetta stone and that has led us to the cabin of a Mississippi riverboat late at night, where two men, one of whom may be an impostor using a false name, discuss the difference between the Bible and the Apocrypha, between a divine book of "certain truth" and a human book of "uncertain credit." For a synoptic glimpse of our track, let us turn in closing to the text of another habitué of Mississippi riverboats who wrote under a false name, a name that bespeaks the doubleness of inscriptions. Here is the beginning of Mark Twain's sketch "As Concerns Interpreting the Deity," written in 1905:

> This line of hieroglyphs was for fourteen years the despair of all the scholars who labored over the mysteries of the Rosetta stone:

> After five years of study Champollion translated it thus:
>
> *Therefore let the worship of Epiphanes be maintained in all the temples; this upon pain of death.*
>
> That was the twenty-fourth translation that had been furnished by scholars. For a time it stood. But only for a time. Then doubts began to assail it and undermine it, and the scholars resumed their labors. Three years of patient work produced eleven new translations; among them, this, by Grünfeldt, was received with considerable favor:
>
> *The horse of Epiphanes shall be maintained at the public expense; this upon pain of death.*

But the following rendering, by Gospodin, was received by the learned world with yet greater favor:

The priest shall explain the wisdom of Epiphanes to all these people, and these shall listen with reverence, upon pain of death.

Seven years followed, in which twenty-one fresh and widely varying renderings were scored—none of them quite convincing. But now, at last, came Rawlinson, the youngest of all the scholars, with a translation which was immediately and universally recognized as being the correct version, and his name became famous in a day. So famous, indeed, that even the children were familiar with it; and such a noise did the achievement itself make that not even the noise of the monumental political event of that same year—the flight from Elba—was able to smother it to silence. Rawlinson's version reads as follows:

Therefore, walk not away from the wisdom of Epiphanes, but turn and follow it; so shall it conduct thee to the temple's peace, and soften for thee the sorrows of life and the pains of death. . . .

Our red Indians have left many records, in the form of pictures, upon our crags and boulders. It has taken our most gifted and painstaking students two centuries to get at the meanings hidden in these pictures; yet there are still two little lines of hieroglyphs among the figures grouped upon the Dighton Rocks which they have not succeeded in interpreting to their satisfaction. These:

The suggested solutions of this riddle are practically innumerable; they would fill a book.

Thus we have infinite trouble in solving man-made mysteries; it is only when we set out to discover the secret of God that our difficulties disappear. It was always so.[1]

However much one agrees with Twain's conclusion, the evidence by which he arrives at it should give us pause. No doubt but that the scholars who labored over the text of the Rosetta stone would have found the line of hieroglyphs that Twain cites difficult to decipher—if they could have found it at all. It does not occur in the Rosetta text, nor, one would surmise, in any other inscription, being a meaningless collection of hieroglyphic signs. Further, if Henry Rawlinson translated the line of hieroglyphs in the year of Napoleon's flight from Elba (1815), he would indeed have been "the youngest of all the scholars." Rawlinson was born in 1810. Of the translators Grünfeldt and Gospodin one may remark that at the time Twain wrote, only God and Twain knew who they were, and now only Twain knows. Finally, since Rawlinson's translation was done in 1815, it preceded the decipherment of the Egyptian hieroglyphics by seven years. That man characteristically creates the meaning he seeks is a truth Twain not only expresses but embodies in that pensive Masquerade from which something always follows.[2]

NOTES

Part One: Emerson, Thoreau, and Whitman

1 Erik Iversen, *The Myth of Egypt and Its Hieroglyphics in European Tradition* (Copenhagen: Gec Gad, 1961), pp. 124–25.
2 Edward Everett, "The Zodiac of Denderah," *The North American Review* 17 (1823), 233.
3 John A. Wilson, *Signs and Wonders upon Pharaoh* (Chicago: University of Chicago Press, 1964), p. 37.
4 Ibid.
5 Ibid., p. 38.
6 Ibid., pp. 37–38.
7 Ibid., pp. 36–37.
8 Herman Melville, "Bartleby the Scrivener," in *Selected Tales and Poems by Herman Melville,* ed. Richard Chase (New York: Holt, Rinehart and Winston, 1950), p. 130.
9 Wilson, *Signs and Wonders,* pp. 41–42.
10 Henry Wheaton, "Egyptian Antiquities," *The North American Review* 29 (1829), 361–88.
11 Edward Everett, "Hieroglyphics," *The North American Review* 32 (1831), 109. Subsequent quotations from this article are cited in the text by volume and page number.
12 *Edinburgh Review* 45 (1826–27), 106. Subsequent quotations from this article are cited in the text by volume and page number.
13 See Don Cameron Allen, *Mysteriously Meant* (Baltimore, Md.: Johns Hopkins University Press, 1970), pp. 107–33; and Liselotte Dieckmann, *Hieroglyphics* (St. Louis, Mo.: Washington University Press, 1970).
14 J. G. H. Greppo, *Essay on the Hieroglyphic System of M. Champollion,* trans. with notes and illus. Isaac Stuart (Boston: Perkins and Marvin, 1830), p. 46.
15 Kenneth Walter Cameron, *Emerson the Essayist,* 2 vols. (Raleigh, N.C.: Thistle Press, 1945), 1:292.
16 Sampson Reed, *New Jerusalem Magazine* 4 (1830–31), 69. Subsequent quotations from Reed's article are cited in the text by volume and page number.
17 Dieckmann, *Hieroglyphics,* p. 156.
18 J. D., Letter to the Editor, *New Jerusalem Magazine* 4 (1830–31), 233.
19 Greppo, *Essay on the Hieroglyphic System,* p. 201.
20 Ralph Waldo Emerson, *The Complete Works of Ralph Waldo Emerson,* ed. E. W. Emerson, 12 vols. (Boston: Houghton Mifflin, 1903–04), 2:10. Unless otherwise noted, all subsequent quotations from Emerson are taken from this edition.
21 Ralph Waldo Emerson, *Journals and Miscellaneous Notebooks of Ralph Waldo Emerson,* ed. W. H. Gilman et al., 14 vols. to date (Cambridge, Mass.: Harvard University Press, 1960–), 6:346.
22 Percy Bysshe Shelley, *Shelley's Prose,* ed. David Lee Clark (Albuquerque:

University of New Mexico Press, 1954), p. 280. All subsequent quotations from "A Defence of Poetry" are taken from this edition.

23 Cameron, *Emerson the Essayist*, 2:83n.

24 Ibid., p. 84.

25 Ibid., p. 92.

26 John Locke, *An Essay Concerning Human Understanding*, collated and annotated by Alexander Campbell Fraser, 2 vols. (New York: Dover Publications, 1959), 2:5.

27 Jacob Bryant, *A New System or, An Analysis of Antient Mythology*, 2 vols. (London: Payne, Elmsly, White, Walter, 1774–76), 1:1–128.

28 Cameron, *Emerson the Essayist*, 2:88.

29 Henry David Thoreau, *Walden*, ed. J. Lyndon Shanley (Princeton, N.J.: Princeton University Press, 1971), p. 305. All subsequent quotations from *Walden* are taken from this edition.

30 Plato, *The Collected Dialogues of Plato*, ed. Edith Hamilton and Huntington Cairns, Bollingen Series 71 (Princeton, N.J.: Princeton University Press, 1961), p. 460. All subsequent quotations from Plato are taken from this edition.

31 Walt Whitman. *Leaves of Grass, The Collected Writings of Walt Whitman,* ed. Gay Wilson Allen, Scully Bradley et al., 13 vols. to date (New York: New York University Press, 1961–), 7:34. Unless otherwise noted, all subsequent quotations from Whitman are taken from this edition.

32 Iversen, *The Myth of Egypt*, pp. 142–43.

33 Ibid., p. 142.

34 Floyd Stovall, *The Foreground of the Leaves of Grass* (Charlottesville: University of Virginia Press, 1974), p. 162.

35 Ibid., p. 163.

36 Walt Whitman, *New York Dissected,* intro. and notes by Emory Holloway and Ralph Adimari (New York: Rufus Rockwell Wilson, 1936), pp. 36–37.

37 Ibid., p. 206, n. 19.

38 Michel Foucault, *The Order of Things* (New York: Random House, Vintage Books, 1973), pp. 26–27. All subsequent quotations from Foucault are taken from this edition.

39 Cameron, *Emerson the Essayist,* 2:95–96. All subsequent quotations from Oegger are taken from this edition.

40 W. A. Clouston, *Hieroglyphic Bibles, Their Origin and History* (Glasgow: David Bryce and Son, 1894), p. 124. Unless otherwise noted, all subsequent quotations from hieroglyphic Bibles are taken from Clouston's book, which will be cited by page number in the text.

41 Stovall, *The Foreground of the Leaves of Grass,* p. 156, n. 17.

42 Ibid.

43 *Mother Goose in Hieroglyphics* (1849; reprinted, New York: Dover Publications, 1973), p. 62.

44 *A New Hieroglyphical Bible* (New York: J. C. Riker, 1852).

45 Walt Whitman, *Notes and Fragments,* ed. Richard Maurice Bucke, (Folcroft, Pa.: Folcroft Library Editions, 1972), p. 57.

46 See Mircea Eliade, *Patterns in Comparative Religion,* trans. Rosemary Sheed (London and New York: Sheed and Ward, 1958), pp. 273ff., 327ff. for elements and bibliography of the Cosmic Tree.

47 Johann Gottfried Herder, "*Essay on the Origin of Language,*" in *On the Origin of Language,* trans. John H. Moran and Alexander Gode (New York: Frederick Ungar, 1966), p. 127. For a discussion of Herder's shifting position on the question of the priority of writing to speech, see James H. Stam, *Inquiries into the Origin of Language* (New York: Harper and Row, 1976), pp. 169–174.

48 Walt Whitman, *Walt Whitman's Leaves of Grass, The First (1855) Edition,* ed. Malcolm Cowley (New York: The Viking Press, 1959), pp. 138–39.

49 Walter Pater, *The Renaissance* (London: Macmillan, 1910), p. 139.

Part Two: Poe

1 Edgar Allan Poe, *The Complete Works of Edgar Allan Poe,* ed. James A. Harrison, 17 vols. (New York: Thomas Y. Crowell, 1902), 15:81. Unless otherwise noted, all subsequent quotations from Poe are taken from this edition.

2 *The Humboldt Library, A Catalogue of the Library of Alexander von Humboldt* (London, 1863; reprint ed., Leipzig: Zentral-Antiquariat Der Deutschen Demokratischen Republik, 1967), p. 563, item no. 7832.

3 Thomas Young, *An Account of Some Recent Discoveries in Hieroglyphical Literature, and Egyptian Antiquities* (London: John Murray, 1823), p. v.

4 *Dictionary of Scientific Biography,* ed. Charles C. Gillispie, 14 vols. (New York: Scribner's, 1970–76), 6:550–51.

5 Alexander von Humboldt, *Researches, Concerning the Institutions and Monuments of the Ancient Inhabitants of America, with Descriptions and Views of Some of the Most Striking Scenes in the Cordilleras,* trans. Helen Maria Williams, 2 vols. (London: Longman et al., 1814), 1:148–50.

6 Alexander von Humboldt, *Cosmos: A Sketch of a Physical Description of the Universe,* trans. E. C. Otté, 4 vols. (New York: Harper and Brothers, 1858), 2:120. All subsequent quotations from *Cosmos* are taken from this edition.

7 Jean-Jacques Rousseau and Johann Gottfried Herder, *On the Origin of Language,* trans. John H. Moran and Alexander Gode (New York: Frederick Ungar, 1966), p. vi.

8 Ferdinand de Saussure, *Course in General Linguistics,* ed. Charles Bally and Albert Sechehaye, trans. Wade Baskin, (New York: McGraw-Hill, 1966), pp. 71–72.

9 Humboldt, *Cosmos,* 1:355.

10 Ibid., pp. 353–54.

11 Reginald Horsman, "Scientific Racism and the American Indian in Mid-Nineteenth Century America," *American Quarterly* 27, no. 2 (May 1975), 152–68. See also William Stanton, *The Leopard's Spots* (Chicago: University of Chicago Press, 1960).

12 Pliny, *Natural History,* trans. H. Rackham, 10 vols., Loeb Classical Library (Cambridge, Mass.: Harvard University Press, 1952), 9:271.

13 Robert Rosenblum, "The Origin of Painting: A Problem in the Iconography of Romantic Classicism," *Art Bulletin* 39, no. 4 (Dec. 1957), 287. All subsequent quotations from Rosenblum are taken from this article.

14 George Levitine, "Addenda to Robert Rosenblum's 'The Origin of Painting: A Problem in the Iconography of Romantic Classicism,'" *Art Bulletin* 40, no. 4 (Dec. 1958), 331.

15 Ibid., p. 331n.
16 *History of the Expedition Under the Command of Captains Lewis and Clark, to the Sources of the Missouri, Thence Across the Rocky Mountains and Down the Columbia River to the Pacific Ocean,* ed. Paul Allen, 2 vols. (Philadelphia: Bradford and Inskeep, 1814), 1:xiv–xviii. All subsequent quotations from Thomas Jefferson's instructions to Lewis are taken from this edition.
17 Nathaniel Hawthorne, *The Centenary Edition of the Works of Nathaniel Hawthorne,* ed. William Charvat et al., 13 vols. to date (Columbus: Ohio State University Press, 1962–), 3:140. All subsequent quotations from Hawthorne are taken from this edition.
18 William Wordsworth, *The Prelude,* ed. Ernest De Selincourt, rev. Helen Darbishire (Oxford: Oxford University Press, 1959), pp. 209, 211. All subsequent quotations from *The Prelude* are taken from this edition.
19 Lucan, *The Civil War,* trans. J. D. Duff, Loeb Classical Library (Cambridge, Mass.: Harvard University Press, 1951), p. 605. All subsequent quotations from Lucan are taken from this edition.
20 John Livingston Lowes, *The Road to Xanadu* (Boston and New York: Houghton Mifflin, 1927), pp. 133–34.
21 Samuel Taylor Coleridge, *The Notebooks of Samuel Taylor Coleridge,* ed. Kathleen Coburn 3 vols., Bollingen Series 50 (vol. 1, New York: Pantheon Books, 1957; vols. 2, 3, Princeton, N.J.: Princeton University Press, 1961, 1973), 1:n. 1056.
22 Leslie Brisman, "Coleridge and the Ancestral Voices," *The Georgia Review* 29, no. 2 (Summer 1975), 474.
23 Samuel Taylor Coleridge, *The Complete Poetical Works of Samuel Taylor Coleridge,* ed. E. H. Coleridge, 2 vols. (Oxford: The Clarendon Press, 1912), 1:297. All subsequent quotations from Coleridge's poetry are taken from this edition.
24 James Bruce, *Travels to Discover the Source of the Nile, In the Years 1768, 1769, 1770, 1771, 1772, and 1773,* 5 vols. (Edinburgh: J. Ruthven, 1790), 3:654–58. Unless otherwise noted, all subsequent quotations from Bruce are taken from this edition.
25 Percy Bysshe Shelley, *The Complete Poetical Works of Shelley,* ed. Thomas Hutchinson (Oxford: The Clarendon Press, 1904), p. 487. All subsequent quotations from Shelley's poetry are taken from this edition.
26 Herman Melville, *Mardi: and A Voyage Thither,* ed. Harrison Hayford, Hershel Parker, and G. Thomas Tanselle (Evanston and Chicago: Northwestern University Press and the Newberry Library, 1970), p. 296. All subsequent quotations from *Mardi* are taken from this edition.
27 Steven Weinberg, *The First Three Minutes* (New York: Basic Books, 1977), p. 149.
28 Ludwig Wittgenstein, *Tractatus Logico-Philosophicus,* trans. D. F. Pears and B. F. McGuinness (London: Routledge and Kegan Paul, 1961), p. 51. All subsequent quotations from the *Tractatus* are from this edition.
29 This translation of the Schopenhauer passage is quoted from Friedrich Nietzsche, *The Birth of Tragedy,* trans. Walter Kaufmann (New York: Random House, Vintage Books, 1967), pp. 101–02. All subsequent quotations from *The Birth of Tragedy* are taken from this edition, and all subsequent quotations from Schopenhauer's *The World as Will and Representation,* with the exception

of the quotation referenced in footnote 30, are taken from the passage in *The Birth of Tragedy* cited here.

30 Arthur Schopenhauer, *The World as Will and Representation*, trans. E. F. J. Payne, 2 vols. (New York: Dover Publications, 1969), 1:257.

31 Nietzsche, *The Birth of Tragedy*, p. 101.

32 Friedrich Nietzsche, *Philosophy in the Tragic Age of the Greeks*, trans. Marianne Cowan (Chicago: Henry Regnery, 1962), p. 62.

33 Edgar Allan Poe, *The Works of Edgar Allan Poe*, ed. E. C. Stedman and G. E. Woodbury, 10 vols. (Chicago: Stone and Kimball, 1894–1901), 9:138.

34 Nietzsche, *The Birth of Tragedy*, p. 37.

35 Wallace Stevens, *The Collected Poems of Wallace Stevens* (New York: Alfred A. Knopf, 1954), pp. 129–30.

36 F. Scott Fitzgerald, *The Great Gatsby* (New York: Charles Scribner's Sons, 1925), p. 182.

37 Edgar Allan Poe, *The Portable Edgar Allan Poe* (New York: The Viking Press, 1945), p. 23.

38 Edmund Burke, *A Philosophical Enquiry into the Origin of our Ideas of the Sublime and the Beautiful*, ed. J. T. Boulton (London: Routledge and Kegan Paul, 1958), p. 60. All subsequent quotations from Burke are taken from this edition.

39 Edgar Allan Poe, *The Short Fiction of Edgar Allan Poe*, ed. Stuart and Susan Levine (Indianapolis, Ind.: Bobbs-Merrill, 1976), p. 69. See also Locke, *An Essay Concerning Human Understanding*, 1:449, for Locke's definition of "personal identity" as "the sameness of a rational being."

40 Shelley, *Complete Poetical Works*, p. 15.

41 Friedrich Nietzsche, *The Will to Power*, trans. Walter Kaufmann and R. J. Hollingsdale (New York: Random House, Vintage Books, 1968), p. 233. All subsequent quotations from *The Will to Power* are taken from this edition.

42 Alan Gardiner, *Egyptian Grammar*, 3rd ed. rev., (London: Oxford University Press, 1957), pp. 172–73.

43 *Encyclopaedia Britannica*, 11th ed. (Cambridge: Cambridge University Press, 1910), s.v. "Egypt," 9:55.

44 Sigmund Freud, *The Standard Edition of the Complete Psychological Works of Sigmund Freud*, trans. James Strachey, 24 vols. (London: The Hogarth Press, 1953–74), 23:8. All subsequent quotations from Freud are taken from this edition.

45 Ibid., p. 24.

46 Herman Melville, *Pierre; or, The Ambiguities*, ed. Harrison Hayford, Hershel Parker, and G. Thomas Tanselle (Evanston and Chicago: Northwestern University Press and The Newberry Library, 1971), pp. 304–05. All subsequent quotations from *Pierre* are taken from this edition.

47 Ovid, *Metamorphoses*, trans. Frank Justus Miller, 3rd ed., rev. G. P. Goold, 2 vols., Loeb Classical Library (Cambridge: Harvard University Press, 1977), 1:155, 157. All subsequent quotations from the *Metamorphoses* are taken from this edition.

48 Herman Melville, *Moby-Dick; or, The Whale*, ed. Harrison Hayford and Hershel Parker (New York: W. W. Norton, 1967), p. 376. All subsequent quotations from *Moby-Dick* are taken from this edition.

49 Jorge Luis Borges, *Labyrinths*, ed. Donald A. Yates and James E. Irby (New

York: New Directions, 1964), pp. 65–66. All subsequent quotations from Borges are taken from this edition.

50 Lewis Carroll, *The Complete Works of Lewis Carroll* (New York: Random House, Vintage Books, 1976), p. 617.

51 Walt Whitman, *Notes and Fragments,* pp. 76–77.

52 Mircea Eliade, *Rites and Symbols of Initiation* (New York: Harper and Row, 1958), pp. 13–14, 30–35, 131–32.

53 Ibid., pp. 131–32.

54 Edmund Fry, *Pantographia* (London: Arch, White, Edwards, and Debrett, 1799), p. ii.

55 Sidney Kaplan, "An Introduction to *Pym,*" in *Poe: A Collection of Critical Essays,* ed. Robert Regan (Englewood Cliffs, N.J.: Prentice-Hall, 1967), p. 159.

56 William Gesenius, *Hebrew and English Lexicon of the Old Testament,* trans. Edward Robinson (Boston: Crocker and Brewster, 1836), pp. 868–69. All subsequent citations from Robinson's translation of Gesenius are taken from this edition.

57 H. Wehr, *A Dictionary of Modern Written Arabic,* ed. G. Cowan (Wiesbaden: Harrassowitz, 1961), p. 504.

58 William Gesenius, *Thesaurus Philologicus Criticus Linguae Hebrae et Chaldaeae Veteris Testamenti* (Leipzig: F. C. G. Vogel, 1829–35), pp. 1168–70.

59 James Hogg, *The Private Memoirs and Confessions of a Justified Sinner* (New York: W. W. Norton, 1970), p. 35. All subsequent quotations from Hogg are taken from this edition.

60 Thomas DeQuincey, *The Collected Writings of Thomas DeQuincey,* ed. David Masson, 14 vols. (London: A. and C. Black, 1896–97), 1:51, 52 n. 1.

61 David Brewster, *Letters on Natural Magic* (New York: J. and J. Harper, 1832), p. 145. All subsequent quotations from Brewster are taken from this edition.

62 William Warburton, *The Divine Legation of Moses Demonstrated,* 2 vols. (London: Thomas Tegg and Son, 1837), 2:67–68.

63 Henry David Thoreau, *The Writings of Henry David Thoreau,* 20 vols. (1906; reprint ed., New York: AMS Press, 1968), 1:61. All subsequent quotations from *A Week on the Concord and Merrimack Rivers* are taken from this edition.

64 Hiob Ludolf, *Lexicon Aethiopico-Latinum* (Frankfurt: J. D. Zunnerum, 1699), cols. 265–66. See also F. A. Dillmann, *Lexicon Linguae Aethiopicae* (Leipzig: Weigel, 1865), cols. 564–65.

Part Three: Hawthorne and Melville

1 Plutarch, *Moralia,* trans. Frank Cole Babbitt, 15 vols., Loeb Classical Library (Cambridge, Mass.: Harvard University Press, 1936), 5:23–25. All subsequent quotations from Plutarch are taken from this edition.

2 *The Book of the Dead,* trans. E. A. Wallis Budge, 2nd ed., (London: Routledge and Kegan Paul, 1951), p. 95.

3 C. Kerényi, *Dionysos,* trans. Ralph Manheim, Archetypal Images in Greek Religion, vol. 2, Bollingen Series 65 (Princeton, N.J.: Princeton University Press, 1976), p. 311. All subsequent quotations from Kerényi are taken from this edition of *Dionysos.*

4 J. Gardner Wilkinson, *A Second Series of the Manners and Customs of the Ancient*

Egyptians, 3 vols. (London: John Murray, 1841), 1:342. All subsequent quotations from Wilkinson are taken from this edition.

5 Godfrey Higgins, *Anacalypsis, An Attempt to Draw Aside the Veil of the Saitic Isis; or, An Inquiry into the Origin of Languages, Nations, and Religions*, 2 vols. (London: Longman, 1836), 2:102. All subsequent quotations from Higgins are taken from this edition.

6 H. Bruce Franklin, *The Wake of the Gods* (Stanford, Calif.: Stanford University Press, 1963), pp. 53–98. See also Dorothee Metlitsky Finkelstein, *Melville's Orienda* (New Haven, Conn.: Yale University Press, 1961).

7 Herman Melville, *The Works of Herman Melville*, 16 vols. (London: Constable, 1922–24), 14:127–28.

8 Herman Melville, *Selected Tales and Poems*, ed. Richard Chase (New York: Holt, Rinehart and Winston, 1950), p. 166. All subsequent quotations from "I and My Chimney" are taken from this edition.

9 Thoreau, *Writings*, 1:161. All subsequent quotations from *A Week on the Concord and Merrimack Rivers* are taken from this edition.

10 Friedrich Leopold Hardenberg (Novalis), *The Novices of Sais*, trans. Ralph Manheim (New York: Curt Valentin, 1949), p. 91. All subsequent quotations from *The Novices of Sais* are taken from this edition.

11 Melville, *Selected Tales and Poems*, p. 111. All subsequent quotations from "Bartleby the Scrivener" are taken from this edition.

12 James Bruce, *Travels to Discover the Source of the Nile*, 6 vols. (Dublin: P. Wogan et al., 1790–91), 2:49. All subsequent quotations from Bruce are taken from this edition.

13 Herman Melville, *The Confidence-Man: His Masquerade*, ed. H. Bruce Franklin (Indianapolis, Ind.: Bobbs-Merrill, 1967), p. 94. All subsequent quotations from *The Confidence-Man* are taken from this edition.

Epilogue

1 Mark Twain, *The Writings of Mark Twain*, ed. A. B. Paine, 37 vols. (New York: Gabriel Wells, 1922–25), 26:265–67.

2 For a discussion of Twain's own form of hieroglyphical decipherment—fingerprint analysis—and its relation to doubling and black/white reversal, see the treatment of *Pudd'nhead Wilson* in my *Doubling and Incest / Repetition and Revenge* (Baltimore, Md.: Johns Hopkins University Press, 1975), pp. 11–14.

INDEX

D5